D1084703

BLACK'S NEW TESTAMENT COMMENTARIES

General Editor: Henry Chadwick, DD, FBA

THE EPISTLE TO THE ROMANS

BLACK'S NEW TESTAMENT COMMENTARY

THE
EPISTLE TO THE
ROMANS

Revised Edition

C. K. BARRETT

 HENDRICKSON PUBLISHERS

Second edition 1991
First published 1957

A & C Black (Publishers) Limited, London

Copyright © 1991, 1962, 1971 Charles Kingsley Barrett

Hendrickson Publishers, Inc. Edition

ISBN 1-56563-055-6

Reprinted by arrangement with A & C Black (Publishers) Limited.

The mosaic fretwork on the cover comes from the Galla Placidia
Mausoleum in Ravenna and is used courtesy of ITALCARDS, Bologna, Italy.

CONTENTS

PREFACE TO THE FIRST EDITION

The translation upon which this commentary is based is my own, and is intended to serve as part of the commentary; that is, I have used it in order to make clear what I think Paul meant. I have deliberately refrained from consulting other translations, though I do not doubt that my happier phrases will prove to be subconscious recollections; and I have never varied traditional renderings merely for the sake of novelty. The reader will find that in the commentary occasional Greek words appear. If he knows Greek, he will, I hope, be glad to see them; if he does not, he may pass over them without losing the thread of a single sentence. The occasional notes on variants in the Greek text may also be omitted without disturbance of the book as a whole.

There are few commentators (and I am not one of them) who do not build on the work of their predecessors. The commentator on Romans in particular enters into a goodly heritage, and cannot fail to feel regret when space forbids him to fill his pages with grateful – and controversial – footnotes.

For very much learned information I am indebted especially to Hans Lietzmann (see p. xii) and to Otto Michel (see p. xii). Also to be mentioned in this category is the work of W. Sanday and A. C. Headlam (*The Epistle to the Romans*, in the International Critical Commentary, Edinburgh; first edition, 1895; fifth edition, 1902; many subsequent reprints), which, old as it is, is by no means out of date.

Other writers to whom I am indebted are, among commentators, P. Althaus (in *Das Neue Testament Deutsch*, Göttingen, fifth edition, 1946), J. Denney (see p. xi), C. H. Dodd (see p. xi), E. Gaugler (see p. xi), K. E. Kirk (see p. 12), A. Nygren (*Commentary on Romans*, English translation, London, 1952), and A. Schlatter (*Gottes Gerechtigkeit*, Stuttgart, 1935; second edition, 1952); among others, R. Bultmann (especially *Theologie des Neuen Testaments*, Tübingen, 1948–1953), W. D. Davies (*Paul and Rabbinic Judaism*, London, 1948), W. L. Knox (*St Paul and the Church of Jerusalem*, Cambridge, 1925; *St Paul and the Church of the Gentiles*, Cambridge, 1939), and A. Schweitzer (*Paul and his Interpreters*, English translation, London, 1912; *The Mysticism of Paul the Apostle*, English translation, London, 1931).

Not a few others could be named, but I must reserve a paragraph for special mention of three; Martin Luther, John Calvin, and Karl Barth. Barth's commentary (see p. 160) I read as an undergraduate. If in those days, and since, I remained and have continued to be a Christian, I owe the fact in large measure to that book, and to those in

Cambridge who introduced it to me.[1] Calvin has long been a companion whose patient exegesis is a model of critical and theological thoroughness. In the summer of 1953, in the University Library at Göttingen, I read through Luther's Scholia on Romans (Weimar Edition, vol. 56, by J. Ficker, 1938) with a sustained enthusiasm and even excitement which I never thought 400 large pages of medieval Latin could evoke. Less sound in detail than Calvin, Luther wrestles at perhaps even greater depth with sin and righteousness, grace and predestination, and rarely fails to reach the heart of the matter, and to take his reader with him. To have sat at the feet of these three interpreters of Paul is one of the greatest of privileges. This book is by no means a transcript of their opinions; but I hope that it too may be used *in verbi divini ministerium*.

Durham   C. K. BARRETT

1 See also Barth's *Kurze Erklärung des Römerbriefs* (Munich, 1956; English translation, *A Shorter Commentary on Romans* (London, 1959).

PREFACE TO THE SECOND EDITION

There is nothing in the preface to the first edition of this Commentary that I wish to retract. My gratitude to the writers and teachers mentioned there is undiminished, but it is expanded now to include many more whose work on Romans and Pauline theology has greatly enhanced my own understanding. I must mention first the colleague and friend of over fifty years, Charles Cranfield, whose work is a splendid example to all who would write commentaries. Readers who are capable of handling more detail, and more profound thought, than they will find in the narrower limits of my book should consult his at every point – especially at those points where I have been obliged, with equal regret and trepidation, to disagree. Of equal (but different) value, and by translation available to those who read only English, is the work of another old and good friend, Ernst Käsemann. Another commentary on the grand scale, unfortunately so far untranslated, is the work of another friend, Ulrich Wilckens. Yet another large and detailed commentary is the two-volume work (in *Word Biblical Commentary*, 1988, but not available, I think, in England till 1989) of my successor in Durham, James Dunn. My revision was practically done before this book appeared, but it will undoubtedly be widely used in the future. Other commentaries are on a smaller scale, but are often of great value, and again in many cases they have been written by good friends of mine; such are the commentaries of Ernest Best, Matthew Black, F. F. Bruce, Rudolf Pesch.

It is not only commentaries that illuminate Paul's thought. In addition there must be mentioned the books of E. P. Sanders and J. C. Beker. Too late for use but not for mention is A. J. M. Wedderburn's *The Reasons for Romans* (Edinburgh, 1989).

Faced by such a wealth of learning the proper course would have been to scrap the first edition of my commentary and start again. This was impossible; it was almost equally impossible to go through each of the books I have mentioned (and there are more), noting at every point my agreements and disagreements. I have had to be content to correct where I felt it necessary to correct, and to expand where it seemed useful to do so, and possible to do so without producing a book on a different scale from that of the first edition.

One more word of gratitude. I am grateful to the publishers, not only for their help through more than thirty years but for giving me the occasion to work once more through 'das aller lauterst Euangelion'.

Durham
November 1989

C. K. BARRETT

ABBREVIATIONS

Alford	H. Alford, *The Greek Testament*, four volumes, London, 1894.
Bauer-Aland, *Wörterbuch*	W. Bauer, *Griechisch-deutsches Wörterbuch*, 6th edition, by K. and B. Aland, Berlin, 1988.
BDR	F. Blass and A. Debrunner, *Grammatik des neutestamentlichen Griechisch*, 15th edition, by F. Rehkopf.
Bengel	J. A. Bengel, *Gnomon Novi Testamenti*, London, 1862.
Black	M. Black, *Romans* (New Century Bible), London, 1973.
Calvin	J. Calvin, *The Epistles of Paul the Apostle to the Romans and to the Thessalonians*, translated by Ross Mackenzie, Edinburgh, 1961.
1 Corinthians	C. K. Barrett, *The First Epistle to the Corinthians* (Black's New Testament Commentaries), London, 1968.
2 Corinthians	C. K. Barrett, *The Second Epistle to the Corinthians* (Black's New Testament Commentaries), London, 1973.
Cranfield	C. E. B. Cranfield, *A Critical and Exegetical Commentary on the Epistle to the Romans* (International Critical Commentary), Edinburgh; vol. I, 1975, vol. II, 1979.
Denney	J. Denney, Commentary on Romans in *The Expositor's Greek Testament*, vol. II, London, 1900.
Dodd	C. H. Dodd, *The Epistle of Paul to the Romans* (Moffatt New Testament Commentary), London, 1932.
Donfried	K. P. Donfried (ed.), *The Romans Debate*, Minneapolis, 1977.
Freedom and Obligation	C. K. Barrett, *Freedom and Obligation, A Study of the Epistle to the Galatians*, London, 1985.
From First Adam to Last	C. K. Barrett, *From First Adam to Last*, London, 1962.
Gaugler	E. Gaugler, *Der Brief an die Römer*, Zürich; vol. I, 1945, vol. II, 1952.

JTS	*The Journal of Theological Studies.*
Käsemann	E. Käsemann, *An die Römer* (Handbuch zum Neuen Testament), Tübingen, 1973; English translation, London, 1980.
Lagrange	M. J. Lagrange, *Épître aux Romains*, Paris, 1950.
Lietzmann	H. Lietzmann, *An die Römer* (Handbuch zum Neuen Testament); 4th edition, Tübingen, 1933.
Michel	O. Michel, *Der Brief an die Römer* (Kritisch-exegetischer Kommentar über das Neue Testament); 10th edition, Göttingen, 1955.
Moule, *Idiom Book*	C. F. D. Moule, *An Idiom Book of New Testament Greek*, Cambridge, 1953.
Moulton, *Prolegomena*	J. H. Moulton, *A Grammar of New Testament Greek*, vol. I, Prolegomena; 3rd edition, Edinburgh, 1908.
Nestle-Aland	*Novum Testamentum Graece*; E. and E. Nestle, K. and B. Aland, 26th edition, Stuttgart, 1979/80.
New Testament Essays	C. K. Barrett, *New Testament Essays*, London, 1972.
Pastoral Epistles	C. K. Barrett, *The Pastoral Epistles* (New Clarendon Bible), Oxford, 1963.
SB	H. L. Strack and P. Billerbeck, *Kommentar zum Neuen Testament aus Talmud und Midrasch*, Munich, 1922–1928.
Signs	C. K. Barrett, *The Signs of an Apostle*, London, 1970.
TWNT	*Theologisches Wörterbuch zum Neuen Testament*, edited by G. Kittel and G. Friedrich, Stuttgart, 1933–1979.
Wilckens	U. Wilckens, *Der Brief an die Römer* (Evangelisch-Katholischer Kommentar zum Neuen Testament), Zürich and Neukirchen-Vluyn; vol. I, 1978, vol. II, 1980, vol. III, 1982.
Zahn	Th. Zahn, *Der Brief des Paulus an die Römer*, Leipzig, 1910.

TEXTUAL SIGLA

Greek Manuscripts

P^{46}	The Chester Beatty Papyrus of the Epistles. Third century.
P^{61}	A papyrus of about AD 700.
ℵ	Codex Sinaiticus. Fourth century.
A	Codex Alexandrinus. Fifth century.
B	Codex Vaticanus. Fourth century.
C	Codex Ephraemi Rescriptus. Fifth century.
D	Codex Claromontanus (Graeco-Latin). Sixth century.
G	Codex Boernerianus (Graeco-Latin). Ninth century.
L	Codex Angelicus. Ninth century.
P	Codex Porphirianus. Ninth century.
33	Minuscule. Ninth–tenth century.
1739	Minuscule. Tenth century.
ω	*Codices plerique* – as in A. Souter's *Novum Testamentum Graece*.

Versions

lat	Consensus of the Latin versions.
it	The Old Latin version.
vg	The Latin Vulgate
pesh	The Peshitto Syriac version.
hcl	The Harclean Syriac version.
sah	The Sahidic Coptic version.

INTRODUCTION

I Romans in the framework of Paul's career

That the Epistle to the Romans was written by the apostle Paul is a proposition which it is unnecessary to discuss because it is not in dispute. That this epistle is the apostle's greatest piece of sustained theological writing is self-evident. That its influence upon the life and thought of the Christian Church has been radical and far-reaching needs no demonstration; it suffices to mention the names of Augustine, Luther, Wesley, and Barth. The document before us can indeed be read simply as a work of apostolic theology, through which the unchanging Gospel of the grace and righteousness of God is proclaimed to each generation; but this proclamation may reach men of the twentieth century with greater clarity and power if they are prepared first to consider and understand the man of the first century who wrote it.

According to Acts (xxi. 39), Saul, or Paul, was born in Tarsus. There is nothing in Romans, or in any other of his epistles, to contradict (or to confirm) this statement. From his early years we can infer with certainty nothing that throws a clear light upon the background of his thought. Tarsus was a Hellenistic city in which many faiths and philosophies were taught. Of these, Paul as a youth may have heard something; but it is equally possible that, born into a strict Jewish home (Phil. iii. 5), he regarded all such doctrines as of the devil, and paid them no attention at all. His education took place not in Tarsus but in Jerusalem. He was 'brought up¹ at the feet of Gamaliel' (Acts xxii. 3). This was Rabban Gamaliel I, one of the most distinguished Rabbinic teachers before the fall of Jerusalem in AD 70. Acts v. 34–9 records his intervention on behalf of the apostles, but this narrative does not prove that Gamaliel adopted a favourable attitude to the Church. Paul's own statements indicate clearly enough that he had been brought up as an orthodox Jew. They show, moreover, that he was not content with a merely formal acceptance of the ancestral faith; he outstripped his contemporaries in zeal and in achievement (Gal. i. 14).

His zeal for Judaism led him to persecute the Church, which he no doubt quickly recognized as the one serious danger to Judaism, so like the parent faith, and so unlike. His activity as a persecutor is colourfully described in Acts (vii. 58; viii. 1; ix. 1 f.), and attested in his own epistles

---

1 The Greek word ἀνατεθραμμένος is admirably discussed by W. C. van Unnik, in *Tarsus of Jeruzalem, De Stad van Paulus' Jeugd* (Amsterdam, 1952), English translation, *Tarsus or Jerusalem* (London, 1962). The excellent philological discussion establishes the meaning but not of course the correctness of what is said in Acts.

(1 Cor. xv. 9; Gal. i. 13; Phil. iii. 6). He was in mid-career as a Jewish persecutor when he became a Christian, arrested (Phil. iii. 12) by the glorified Christ himself, who granted him an exceptional 'resurrection appearance' (1 Cor. xv. 8; Gal. i. 16). From this time onward it was impossible for Paul to doubt that Jesus was alive; Jesus was his Lord, and he was Jesus' slave. The theological consequences of this conviction will be discussed below. The immediate sequel was a visit to Arabia (Gal. i. 17). Three years later Paul visited Jerusalem, where he saw Cephas (Peter), and James the Lord's brother (Gal. i. 18 f.). He was in Jerusalem again fourteen (or seventeen)[1] years later, having spent some at least of the interval in Syria and Cilicia, without making direct contact with Judaea.

Paul's second visit to Jerusalem was the occasion of serious conflict, which touched the substance of his Gospel. The discord was for a time resolved, but broke out again later in Antioch, when agreement between Paul, Peter, and Barnabas was disturbed by 'certain' that 'came from James' (Gal. ii. 12). Of the outcome of this dispute we are not informed.

So far the record of Paul's Christian life has been given on the basis of his own words. There is a parallel narrative in Acts, but it is safer to follow Paul's own account. This continues to be true of Paul's later years, but it may be claimed that with Acts xvi we reach a narrative which, though by no means complete, furnishes us with a reasonably trustworthy outline of the middle period of Paul's work as an apostle. In broad outline, though not in detail, it agrees with the biographical data provided by the epistles. It is in this middle period that the writing of Romans must fall.

The narrative in Acts runs in outline as follows. After traversing Asia Minor Paul crossed the Aegean from Troas to Neapolis and passed through Macedonia to the neighbouring province of Achaea. Here Acts gives a long account (xviii. 1–18) of the founding of a church in Corinth. From Corinth Paul returned to Syria, touching at Ephesus on his way (Acts xviii. 19 ff.). On his next journey he settled for between two and three years in Ephesus (Acts xix. 8, 10, 23; xx. 31). During this period he maintained close relations with the church at Corinth, as his epistles show. Finally, he himself again travelled through Macedonia (2 Cor. ii. 13; Acts xx. 1), and spent three months in 'Greece' (Acts xx. 2 f.) – no doubt for the most part in and near Corinth. Throughout this 'Ephesian' period Paul was busy with the collection he had undertaken for the relief of the Jerusalem, or Judaean, church (1 Cor. xvi. 1–4; 2 Cor. viii,

1 The interval depends on whether the period mentioned in Gal. ii. 1 is counted from the conversion or the first visit to Jerusalem. The numbers 'fourteen' and 'seventeen' must be understood inclusively and as counting parts of years at the beginning and the end, so that we must think of 12–13 years and 15–16 years respectively.

ix; Acts xxiv. 17). When his arrangements were (as may be supposed) complete, he left Greece, travelling to Syria by way of Macedonia (Acts xx. 3), Troas (xx. 6), Miletus (xx. 15), Tyre (xxi. 3), Ptolemais (xxi. 7), and Caesarea (xxi. 8).

It is hardly open to question that Romans was written during this period. When Paul wrote, he had engaged in missionary work between Jerusalem and Illyricum (Rom. xv. 19). He was on the way to, or was about to set out for, Jerusalem (xv. 25). He hoped to visit Rome (i. 13, 15; xv. 22 ff., 28 f.), but before he could realize this hope had to complete the ministry he had undertaken to the poor at Jerusalem, in which the churches of Macedonia and Achaea were taking part (xv. 25 f.). He foresaw the possibility of danger in Judaea (xv. 31). These circumstances taken together can mean only that Paul was writing towards the close of his so-called 'Third Missionary Journey', at the end of his Ephesian period. It is further to be noted that the epistle contains a commendation of Phoebe, a minister of the church at Cenchreae (xvi. 1 – Cenchreae was the eastern port of Corinth, about seven miles distant; on the question whether ch. xvi is an original part of Romans see pp. 10–13, 257 f., 262 f.), and conveys greetings from (among others) Timothy, Sosipater, Gaius 'my host', and Erastus the city treasurer (xvi. 21 ff.). These are not unfamiliar names. Paul baptized a Gaius at Corinth (1 Cor. i. 14). He sent 'Timothy and Erastus' into Macedonia while he stayed in Asia (Acts xix. 22; cf. 2 Tim. iv. 20); a visit of Timothy to Corinth was planned in 1 Corinthians (iv. 17; xvi. 10), and Timothy and Sopater (possibly a variant form of the name Sosipater) appear among Paul's travelling companions on his last journey from Ephesus through Macedonia and Greece to Jerusalem (Acts xx. 4). It is thus overwhelmingly probable that Romans was written from Corinth (conceivably from Cenchreae) during the three months before Paul left Greece for Jerusalem. This view finds slight support, which it scarcely needs, in the manifest fact that Romans is the work of a theologian and preacher at the height of his powers, is akin to but represents an advance upon Galatians,[1] and lacks some of the themes developed in the 'Captivity Epistles'.[2]

So far we have endeavoured to place the writing of Romans within the framework of events that can be reconstructed with reasonable certainty out of Acts and the Epistles, but not to assign it to an absolute date. This is a much more difficult matter.

1 Written probably during the Ephesian period.
2 Of the 'Captivity Epistles' only Philippians can be claimed with confidence as written by the apostle; Colossians and Ephesians stand at increasing degrees of remoteness. Some think that Philippians was written from Ephesus. This is not probable, but it is certainly nearer in contents and tone to the letters of the Ephesian period than Colossians. Yet the probability is that it was written from Rome.

Fortunately it is possible to bring Paul's ministry in Corinth into relation with external history. According to Acts xviii. 12, when Gallio was proconsul of Achaea the Jews made an attack upon Paul, and brought him before the judgement seat. It appears, from a dated inscription set up in Delphi,[1] that Gallio was in office in his province in AD 52. Proconsuls in senatorial provinces were appointed for one or two years, and, since it is unlikely that Gallio had taken up his post immediately before the inscription was made, he must have held office for one of the following periods: 50–52; 51–52; 51–53. An overall period of 50–53 is a safe estimate. There is, further, much probability (though not certainty) in the view that the Jews made their attempt early in Gallio's proconsulship – they hoped to be able to win the new magistrate to their side. If this may be assumed, Paul was brought before Gallio in or about July (proconsuls entered upon office in early summer) in AD 51, or, a little less probably, in AD 50. How long had Paul then been in Corinth? According to Acts xviii. 11, Paul stayed in Corinth a year and six months; according to Acts xviii. 18, he remained, after Gallio had washed his hands of the case, 'a number of days' (ἡμέρας ἱκανάς). It is implied that the bulk of Paul's stay fell before his appearance in Gallio's court; this is not certain, but may be tentatively assumed. It seems probable then that Paul reached Corinth in March 50, and left in September 51 (each date being very approximate). This would enable him to sail, by one of the last boats of the summer, to Syria (Acts xviii. 21 f.). How long he spent in Antioch (Acts xviii. 23) we do not know; probably he renewed his travels with the return of favourable weather in the spring of the next year – 52. His journey through 'the region of Galatia and Phrygia' (Acts xviii. 23) and through the 'upper country' (Acts xix. 1) might well last most of the following summer; he would reach Ephesus (Acts xix. 1) in the autumn. The length of his stay there is given by Acts xix. 8 (three months) and xix. 10 (two years), confirmed by xx. 31; the Pentecost therefore that he was anxious to keep in Jerusalem will have been that of 55, and his three months in Greece (Acts xx. 3) must have come to an end a few weeks earlier.

This chronological scheme could be verified, (a) if Acts xxiv. 27 were unambiguous, (b) if the date when Porcius Festus succeeded Felix could be certainly established. There are good reasons for thinking that Felix was recalled very early in the principate of Nero – perhaps in AD 55.[2] On the usual view of Acts xxiv. 27 this will mean that Paul had been

1 See F. J. F. Jackson and K. Lake, *Beginnings of Christianity*, v (1933), pp. 460–4; C. K. Barrett, *The New Testament Background: Selected Documents* (revised edition, London, 1987), pp. 51 f.
2 For details, see Jackson and Lake, *op. cit.* v, pp. 466 f. This date has been attacked by various writers; a good example is R. Jewett, *Dating Paul's Life* (London, 1979), pp. 41–4, who places the event in 59 or 60. See also E. Schürer, *The History of the Jewish People in the Age of Jesus Christ*, revised and edited by
(for continuation of footnote see facing page)

arrested in Jerusalem in 53, which is sadly inconsistent with the date arrived at above. It is, however, possible that 'when two years were fulfilled', a clause which has no certain point of reference in the sentence, means not 'when Paul had been under arrest for two years' but 'when Felix had been procurator for two years'. If this view can be accepted, the data fall into place: Paul reached Jerusalem in the year in which Felix was recalled and Festus succeeded him. If not, an earlier alternative must be accepted for the date of Gallio; and it may be possible to place the date of Festus's accession a year or two later.

The chronology of Paul's movements cannot be settled beyond dispute, but on the whole no view meets with fewer difficulties than that which places the 'three months' of Acts xx. 3 in or about January–March 55. We have seen reason to think (pp. 3 f.) that the AD 55 Epistle to the Romans was written in this interval.

When Paul wrote the Epistle to the Romans he had reached in Corinth the most westerly point of his missionary travels;[1] but he was looking a further 600 miles north-west. The Roman church fell outside the scope of his own apostolic labour. Its origin is completely obscure. No early authority claims that it was founded by Peter (though the evidence that he visited Rome is early and seems sound), and it is probable that, if Paul had known that Peter had already, when he wrote, worked in Rome, he would have mentioned the fact in some way.

There was a considerable Jewish colony in first-century Rome.[2] It originated in the large number of Jewish slaves brought to the city by Pompey after his capture of Jerusalem in 63 BC and from that time appears steadily to have increased, notwithstanding occasional repressive measures. Of these we may note the expulsion of the Jews under Claudius. This is referred to in Acts xviii. 2 as the reason for the presence in Corinth of Aquila and Priscilla. According to Suetonius (*Claudius*, 25) the emperor acted against the Jews because they were *impulsore Chresto assidue tumultuantes*. The meaning of this clause is much disputed, but it seems quite probable that *Chresto* is an error for

1 On the map, Beroea lies half a degree further west, but marks an earlier stage in the journey.
2 See G. La Piana, 'Foreign groups in Rome during the first centuries of the Empire', in *Harvard Theological Review*, xx. (1927), pp. 183–403; now also R. Penna, 'Les Juifs à Rome au temps de l'Apôtre Paul', *New Testament Studies* 28 (1982), pp. 321–47, with further literature, especially in note 5.

G. Vermes and F. Millar, vol. I, Edinburgh, 1973, pp. 465 f. If 55 is judged too early, there is nevertheless no need to go as far as 60. Acts xxiv. 27 may be taken to refer after all to Paul's imprisonment; he may have taken a year longer over his travels than is suggested above, so that he could reach Jerusalem in 56 and remain a prisoner till 58. This is a not impossible date (if the earlier one is abandoned) for the succession of Festus to Felix.

Christo, and that riots had taken place when Jesus the Messiah had first been proclaimed in the Roman synagogues. Against this view is the profession of the Roman Jews in Acts xxviii. 21 f. that they had no first-hand knowledge of Paul or of the Church. This profession, however, must be treated with some reserve, since Romans itself is evidence that there was a sizeable Christian community in Rome some years before Paul reached the city.

The Jewish colony was organized in synagogues, but these did not form wholly distinct units; for example, there were common cemeteries.[1] It is not impossible that the first Christians in Rome, won to the faith by travellers unknown to us by name and perhaps of no official standing, formed a synagogue community within the general framework of the Jewish groups in the city; but if this was so at the beginning changes had happened before Romans was written, for the epistle presupposes the existence of a community which, though probably not exclusively Gentile, contained at least a strong Gentile element; see i. 6, 13; xi. 13, 25; xv. 16, and the notes. It is important to remember that there were a Gentile mission and Gentile churches independent of Paul's; the Gentile church of Antioch was not of his founding, and 1 and 2 Corinthians attest the independent activity of other missionaries in the Gentile world.[2]

Paul's letter, then, represents not merely his approach to the capital of the Empire, and not merely the first preparatory step to the mission in Spain: it is also Paul's exposition of 'his' Gospel to the Gentile churches which had come into existence independently of his efforts.

Paul's reason for writing the Epistle has been much discussed,[3] but there is perhaps a greater measure of agreement than some of the disputants allow. The occasion is clearly Paul's forthcoming visit to Rome (i. 10–13; xv. 22–4, 28, 29), which is a step preliminary to his mission to Spain. It was natural, almost inevitable, that he should write to introduce himself to those to whom he hoped to minister and from whom he hoped to receive help – spiritual and probably also material help. At present he was unknown to them, but it may have been known that it was contrary to his usual practice to visit a church he had not founded. It may be taken to go without saying that Paul's introduction of himself would be a theological introduction. He could define himself only in theological terms. He was a slave of Christ, an apostle called by God, a preacher of the Gospel; and the Gospel meant God's manifesta-

1 La Piana, *op. cit.* pp. 363–7.

2 'It is not an eviscerated Paulinism but a Hellenistic proselyte Christianity that we meet here in a pure form, an independent growth from a root in the early church, of importance for the future. The Roman church could trace its descent back to the Hellenistic circle of Stephen.' H. Lietzmann, *The Beginnings of the Christian Church* (London, 1937), p. 267.

3 See especially Donfried; also, too recently published to be discussed here, A. J. M. Wedderburn, *The Reasons for Romans*, Edinburgh, 1989.

tion of his righteousness (i. 17) and love (v. 8) in the crucifixion and resurrection of Jesus. It is the Gospel that validates Paul's apostleship; nothing else. But Paul could have stated the content of the Gospel in half-a-dozen lines; indeed he does state it in fewer, in i. 16, 17. Why should he go on to write at such length? Many recent writers have spoken of Romans as a summary, a manifesto, a last will and testament. There is truth in all these terms. Parallels to Romans can be collected from the other letters; in this sense it summarizes their content. The same observation shows that Paul is presenting here, and presents in vigorous terms, the essence of his message; it is his manifesto. 'Last will and testament' is perhaps a less suitable term because it is clear that Paul believed, or at least hoped, that he had many years of work before him; but it may be called a testament in the sense that it would answer the question, Paul, if you knew you would die tomorrow, what would you say to us today? But why this manifesto *now*? There may well be more answers than one. J. Jervell[1] thinks that Paul wrote to deal with the problem of the co-existence in the Church of Jew and Gentile, a problem which his own mission to Jerusalem (xv. 30–2) was likely to bring to a head. But there is more in the epistle than this theme. Rome was a great city, the centre of a great empire; if Paul was ever to put on paper a full account of his Gospel, of his theology, this was surely the occasion. But Rome had Christian as well as political significance. It was already a centre of Gentile Christianity, of Western Christianity, which he had not founded, a church that owed no personal allegiance to him. When he reached Rome, as he hoped he would, two lines of Christian development would meet. The representatives of these two lines did not see in all respects eye to eye; for example, the Roman Christians seem to have seen the future of the Jews differently from Paul. It would be well that Paul's person should be preceded by a full and careful statement of his basic theological position, of his understanding of God's purpose for his people, of the practical problems that may arise in any religious community. There is no good reason to think that Paul's views immediately carried the day; but it may well be that, but for this circumstance, we should not have had so full and vigorous an exposition of his theology.

II Romans in the framework of Paul's thought

On the road to Damascus, Paul met with Jesus Christ (above, p. 2). This is the plain meaning of the three narratives in Acts (ix. 4 ff.; xxii. 7–10; xxvi. 14–18), and it is confirmed by Paul's own references to the occasion (especially Gal. i. 15, 16). Jesus therefore was alive, and had appeared in the character of a supernatural Lord (κύριος). He had not

1 Donfried, pp. 61–74.

merely survived death as a man, or as a disembodied human spirit; he was a glorious, heavenly being, before whom the beholder could only prostrate himself in adoration and obedience. All this was certain; but it was equally certain that Jesus had lived a human life, and that he had been as truly dead as he was now truly alive. The past of frailty and corruption could be linked with the present of heavenly glory only by an act of divine power. Only God (as Paul the Rabbi well knew) could raise the dead. God therefore must have approved of Jesus; resurrection and exaltation could be understood only as the manifest seal of his approval. It followed that Jesus had all the time been right; he had been the Messiah, and Paul, the persecutor of the Church, had been wrong.

A man with a smaller mind than Paul's might have been content simply to accept this reversal of his opinions on the crucial issue; Paul could not. The basic assumptions of his thought had been proved wrong, and his theology had to be built up again from the foundations. He continued to be a Rabbi[1] in that a man who for thirty years or more has been brought up to a pattern of intellectual activity can scarcely be expected to free, or to desire to free, his thinking from that pattern; he ceased to be a Rabbi in the presuppositions of his thinking. In two fundamental points in particular his thought was revolutionized by the new conviction that the crucified Jesus had been raised from the dead and become Lord: eschatology, and the law.[2]

(1) It is very unlikely that it was as a Christian that Paul learned the eschatological language which appears in his espistles. It is much more probable that before his conversion he shared the widespread beliefs of Judaism, and looked to the coming of a Messiah (he may have used the term Son of man[3] also), and the establishment of the kingdom of the Messiah, the kingdom of God, and the Age to Come. It is not necessary for us to attempt to distinguish between these terms in Jewish usage. The essential point is that the Messiah and the Age to Come belonged to the future. For Paul the Christian, this was no longer true; or rather, it was not the whole truth. It remained true that Jesus would come in

1 This is emphasized, very convincingly, by W. D. Davies in *Paul and Rabbinic Judaism* (1948); but the discontinuity in Paul's thought is perhaps greater than Dr Davies suggests. Of many more recent books on Paul and Judaism it must suffice to mention E. P. Sanders, *Paul and Palestinian Judaism* (London, 1977).
2 In this new edition of the Commentary I have been strongly inclined to include a much fuller and more systematic account of the theology that Paul unfolds in Romans. I have decided not to do this, partly because of the conviction expressed in the last sentence of this part of the Introduction (on p. 9) – a commentary is a commentary, not a monograph, and it must allow an author to develop his points in his own way; and partly because I hope to have an opportunity elsewhere of expounding Paul's theology in a systematic way.
3 See especially the 'man from heaven', the 'heavenly man' in 1 Cor. xv. 47, 49; I have discussed these verses in *1 Corinthians* and also in *Résurrection du Christ et des Chrétiens*, ed. L. De Lorenzi, Rome, 1985, pp. 116–19.

glory to judge the secrets of men (Rom. ii. 16), and that the Age to Come was still to come; but it was also true that Jesus had come, and that at least the first-fruits of the future were available to faith (Rom. viii. 23).

The fact that God's ultimate dealings with mankind had thus been manifested in a person gave an objective content to the new faith, and the invasion of the present by the future made possible an immediate awareness of God's power which Judaism could not accept without blurring the distinction between divine and human. It was a proper reaction to the danger of such a blurring that prevented Judaism from using the sacramental and mystical language of the Hellenistic and oriental cults; in Paul this language enters decisively. It enters, however, not as an element in an eclectic religious philosophy, but as a means of expressing the re-orientation of eschatology caused by the coming of the Messiah.

(2) Jesus had been condemned by the law. He had been tried and found guilty of blasphemy (Mark xiv. 64) by the supreme court of his people; moreover, he had died a death which exposed him to the curse declared in the law (Deut. xxi. 23; Gal. iii. 13). Yet God had not cursed him; on the contrary, he had ratified his claims and declared his approval of him by raising him from the dead. On this crucial issue, therefore, the law – or, at least, Israel's understanding of the law – had been wrong. This did not mean that the law was to be rejected out of hand. Jesus himself had reaffirmed its validity as the word of God, and, rightly understood, it bore witness to him. But it must be rightly understood, and not understood in the old way. It could no longer be regarded as the mediator between God and man; this function had been assumed by Jesus Christ.[1]

Paul's theological development consists in the adjustment of old convictions based upon the Old Testament and formulated within Judaism to the new Christian conviction that Jesus is Lord. Many of the decisive steps in this development are represented in the Epistle to the Romans, and will therefore be traced in this commentary. It is better, however, to allow them to arise naturally out of the text, than to attempt to systematize them in an introduction.

III Literary Problems

In its familiar form the document before us appears as an epistle

---

1 This paragraph on Paul's new, Christian, understanding of law has at least one point in common with the very important exposition of Torah and of Paul's treatment of it by E. P. Sanders (op. cit.). Paul did not react against the law because he disliked it, or failed to see in it a good gift of the gracious God; rather he discovered positively that salvation was to be had, and had by all, in Jesus Christ.

directed to Rome (i. 7, 15), and ending, after much theological and practical instruction, with greetings from Paul himself, and from his companions, to the Roman church, and in particular to many named persons in that church. But certain facts cast doubt upon both the original form and the original destination of the letter. These are as follows.

(1) There is MS authority for the omission of the references to Rome in i. 7, 15. See pp. 17, 24. If in these verses the shorter text is accepted there is nothing in the epistle which necessarily connects it with Rome or with any other specific destination; though it may be noted that passages such as i. 6, 8–13; xv. 14, 22 ff., 28 f., as well as ch. xvi, suggest that the epistle was written to a clearly defined group of readers, whose circumstances cannot be shown to be inconsistent with their having been the Roman church.

(2) There are important textual variations in the last three chapters. These concern (a) the Grace, and (b) the Doxology.

(a) In AV the words 'The grace of our Lord Jesus Christ be with you [all]. Amen' occur twice, as xvi. 20 b, and as xvi. 24. This is the reading of the mass of late MSS – the so-called Byzantine text. But the formula is omitted in xvi. 20 by the Western text (D G it), and at xvi. 24 by the earliest non-Western authorities (P⁴⁶ B ℵ, et al.). There is some slight authority for placing the Grace after the Doxology (i.e. after xvi. 27). It will be noted that it is broadly true that only those MSS have the Grace at xvi. 24 that omit the Doxology (xvi. 25 ff.) or put it in another place (see (b)).

(b) In AV the epistle ends with a Doxology, 'Now unto him that is of power . . . To God only wise, be glory through Jesus Christ for ever. Amen', which occurs as xvi. 25 ff. In this reading AV follows the Latin Vulgate. A variety of different readings exists, which may be summarized in the following list (for Marcion's text see p. 11).

The Doxology appears

   (i) at the end of the epistle (after xvi. 23 (24)) in some of the oldest and best MSS, including B ℵ D vg it pesh, and in Origen;[1]
  (ii) after xiv. 23 in ω hcl, and in MSS known to Origen;
 (iii) after xiv. 23 *and* at the end of the epistle in A P 33;
 (iv) after xv. 33 in P⁴⁶;
  (v) not at all in G (but in this MS, a space is left after xiv. 23).

(3) Several other facts bearing on the transmission of the last three chapters must now be set out.

---

1 P⁶¹ places the Doxology at the end of chapter xvi, but since this papyrus preserves of Romans only xvi. 23, 25–7 it is possible that it may have had the Doxology also after xiv. 23 (or for that matter anywhere else).

(a) The vulgate MS Codex Amiatinus, which contains the text of the epistle in the usual vulgate form, contains also a set of *breves*, or chapter summaries, fifty-one in number. Of these the fiftieth runs:

> On the danger of grieving one's brother by one's food; and that the kingdom of God is not eating and drinking, but righteousness and peace and joy in the Holy Spirit.

Evidently this corresponds to xiv. 13–23. The fifty-first chapter summary runs:

> On the mystery of the Lord, kept in silence before his passion, but revealed after his passion.

This must correspond to xvi. 25 ff. It is clear therefore that the *breves* (though not the text) of Codex Amiatinus bear witness to the existence of a copy of Romans which consisted of only fourteen chapters followed immediately by the Doxology.

(b) Chs. xv, xvi are never quoted by Irenaeus, Tertullian, or Cyprian. Arguments based on silence are always precarious, but it is worth noting (i) that the works of these authors are considerable in extent; (ii) that Tertullian and Cyprian in particular could several times have used material from these chapters with effect; and (iii) that Clement of Alexandria uses the chapters.

(c) Tertullian not merely does not quote chs. xv, xvi; in *adv. Marcionem*, v. 14, he refers to Rom. xiv. 10 in these terms, '*in clausula tribunal Christi comminatur*'. In classical Latin, *in clausula* should mean 'at the end (of a document)'; this would be an odd (though not quite impossible) expression if the verse in question were followed by two and a half more chapters. But in later Latin *clausula* was used for any division of a document (commonly of a legal document), and little can be built on Tertullian's use of the word.

(d) The evidence of Tertullian (in *adv. Marcionem*) suggests that Marcion himself did not use chs. xv, xvi; this receives probable (though not quite certain) confirmation from a passage in Origen's commentary on Romans (on xvi. 25 ff.; unfortunately extant only in Rufinus's Latin translation).

(4) Finally, the contents of ch. xvi call for examination.

(a) Several scholars have maintained that the long list of salutations contained in xvi. 1–23 is a very unlikely constituent of a letter written by Paul to Rome, where he had never been. It is impossible, they think, that he should have known so many Christians in Rome; moreover, some of the names (especially Aquila and Priscilla) would be more appropriate in a letter directed to Ephesus. See pp. 257 f.

(b) xvi. 25 ff. has in part a Marcionite sound. The reference to the 'scriptures of the prophets' is indeed not Marcionite, but it is awkwardly attached to the sentence as a whole, and the conception of a mystery kept secret through the ages but at length made manifest at the command of the eternal God is consistent with Marcionite teaching, and the language in which it is expressed is not characteristically Pauline. It is accordingly possible to regard the Doxology, whose place in the epistle is so variable, as in essence a Marcionite production; at all events, not Pauline. See pp. 262 f.

To deal with the facts which have now been set forth in outline, several hypotheses have been constructed. They may be summarized under three heads.

(1) Some take seriously the readings of G in i. 7, 15, and suppose that the epistle existed in two or more different forms, of which not more than one was directed to Rome. A clear statement of a view of this kind is given by Dr G. Zuntz who writes:[1] 'The doxology [xvi. 25 ff., which Dr Zuntz believes to be Marcionite in origin] commended itself to orthodox believers, was adapted for their requirements, and variously added, in the copies used by the orthodox, at one or other of the points at which the Epistle in its varying forms ended; namely at the end of the Roman form, i.e. after ch. xv, or of the (?) Ephesian form, i.e. after xvi, or finally of the Marcionite form, i.e. after xiv'. It will be seen that it is here suggested that ch. xvi was directed not to Rome but to Ephesus, and that the shortest form of the epistle (i–xiv) was made by Marcion, presumably on account of objections he felt to chs. xv, xvi.

(2) The publication of P[46] (in 1934) naturally led to attempts to give full weight to its unique reading. One such attempt was made by K. E. Kirk.[2] It is most simply set out in the form of a diagram, in which (the

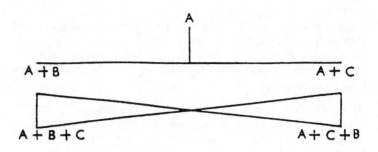

---

1 *The Text of the Epistles* (1953; Schweich Lectures for 1946), p. 227. See a fuller statement of a similar view (and a full discussion of the evidence) by T. W. Manson, in the *Bulletin of the Rylands Library*, xxxi (1948), pp. 224–40.
2 *The Epistle to the Romans* (Clarendon Bible; 1937), pp. 12–22.

bulk of the epistle, i–xiv, being taken for granted) A stands for xv, B for xvi. 1–23, C for xvi. 25 ff. A (that is, i–xiv+xv) represents the lost Pauline original. In one copy, B was added, either as a separate note, or as a message to Ephesus added by Paul himself to the original letter. In another copy the spurious ending C was added to A. Out of the forms A+B and A+C arose the forms A+B+C and A+C+B. A+B is contained in G; A+B+C in ℵ B C D lat pesh; and A+C+B in P⁴⁶.

(3) It may well be felt, however, that these two suggestions pay too great deference to the reading of P⁴⁶. In the epistle as a whole this MS contains a number of very curious readings which it is impossible to take very seriously. It is easy to understand how the text of P⁴⁶ could have arisen. 'If any copy of Romans was sent by Paul to another church because of the general interest and importance of its contents, it would not be at all surprising if the last chapter were omitted as not of general interest; and at a later date someone making a copy of Romans for the use of his own church might easily have omitted it for the same reason' (Cranfield, p. 10). It is wise to adopt this explanation of the text of P⁴⁶ and to explain the other readings on the lines set out by Lietzmann (pp. 130 f.). They are now adopted, with minor variations, by many students of Romans, and may be summarized as follows:

(a) The original text of the epistle was i. 1–xvi. 23.

(b) This was early shortened (perhaps by Marcion) to i. 1–xiv. 23. A conclusion was now wanting, so a liturgical formula (possibly of Marcionite origin) was appended, so giving rise to

(c) the form i. 1–xiv. 23; xvi. 25 ff. Once in circulation the Doxology became popular and was appended to the original text, thus producing

(d) the form i. 1–xvi. 23; xvi. 25 ff. At the same time, form (b) was expanded by the addition of chs. xv, xvi, together with the usual Pauline 'grace'. Thus arose

(e) the form i. 1–xvi. 23; xvi. 24. A similar expansion based on form (c) led to

(f) the form i. 1–xiv. 23; xvi. 25 ff.; xv. 1–xvi. 23; xvi. 24, or even in rare instances to

(g) the form i. 1–xiv. 23; xvi. 25 ff.; xv. 1–xvi. 23; xvi. 25 ff.

It is unlikely that this problem – which in no way affects the substance of the Epistle to the Romans – will ever be cleared up in a way that will satisfy every reader, but it is probable that this solution is not far from the truth.

ANALYSIS OF THE EPISTLE

THE EPISTLE TO THE ROMANS

1 THE ADDRESS

CHAPTER i. 1–7

(1) Paul, slave of Christ Jesus, by divine call an apostle, set apart for the Good News God is now setting forth (2) (Good News which in the past he promised through his prophets, whose word still stands in Holy Writ; (3) Good News about his Son, who in the sphere of the flesh was born of the family of David, (4) in the sphere of the Holy Spirit was appointed Son of God in power after his resurrection from the dead – Jesus Christ our Lord; (5) through whom we received grace and our apostolic commission to win believing obedience on his behalf among all the Gentiles – (6) among whom are you, Jesus Christ's, by divine call): (7) to all who in Rome[1] are God's beloved, by divine call, saints. I wish you grace and peace from God our Father and the Lord Jesus Christ.

Greek letters commonly opened with the formula, A to B, greeting. Paul, and other New Testament writers, follow this custom, but habitually expand the titles of writer and recipients, and give a Christian sense to the greeting. This expansion and modification are rarely carried out at greater length, and never more significantly, than in Romans.

Paul describes himself in the first instance as a **slave of Christ** 1 **Jesus**. This is a common term with him (cf. especially Gal. i. 10; Phil. i. 1), imitated also by other New Testament writers (James i. 1; 2 Pet. i. 1; Jude 1). It is particularly appropriate to an apostle, but can be used of any Christian (cf. vi. 22); that is, Paul begins by describing himself as a Christian before he goes on to mention his special status and vocation. The description is more striking in a Greek work, such as this epistle, than in Semitic literature. A Greek did not think of himself as the slave (δοῦλος) of his ruler or king, nor did he think of himself as the slave of his divine king, or god, or speak of his service to the god as slavery. The Semitic king, however, was a slave-owner, and the highest of his

---

1 The words 'in Rome' (ἐν 'Ρώμῃ) are omitted by G and a few other Greek MSS; there is some evidence that they were omitted by Origen. G, accompanied by some Latin MSS, which do not omit 'in Rome', continues 'in the love of God' (ἐν ἀγάπη θεοῦ, instead of ἀγαπητοῖς θεοῦ). Cf. the variant at i. 15; and for Paul's usage see 1 Cor. i. 2; 2 Cor. i. 1; Phil. i. 1. It is probable that the variant (here and at i. 15) reflects a desire to show that the epistle is of universal, and not merely local, application. See also Introduction, p. 10.

ministers could be regarded as his slave (e.g. 1 Sam. viii. 17; 2 Sam. xiv. 22). The king in turn is God's slave (e.g. 2 Sam. vii. 19). Other distinguished members of the theocracy are described in the same terms (e.g. Ps. cv. 26, 42; Amos iii. 7 – the prophets are outstanding as God's slaves). Thus Paul, as the slave of Christ Jesus, appears as a member – as the context will show, an outstanding and privileged member – of a people of God analogous with the people of God in the Old Testament.

Paul is also, **by divine call** (cf. *v.* 6), **an apostle.** Compare *v.* 5, where Paul refers to his 'apostolic commission', again emphasizing its divine origin. The pre-Christian history of the Greek word 'apostle' (ἀπόστολος) does little or nothing to illustrate its Christian usage; see K. H. Rengstorf, in *TWNT*, 1, pp. 406–44; *Signs*, especially pp. 23–81. The Cynic-Stoic use of *spy* (κατάσκοπος and similar words), for which see, for example, W. Schmithals, *Das kirchliche Apostelamt* (Göttingen, 1961), does not greatly illuminate the New Testament word, which calls to mind, however, the Hebrew *shaliaḥ*, *shaluaḥ* (from the verb *sh-l-ḥ*, 'to send'), which are commonly used in post-biblical Hebrew of an authorized representative or delegate, legally empowered to act (within prescribed limits) on behalf of his principal. It cannot be regarded as certain that Greek-speaking Jews already in the first century AD used the word *apostolos* to represent this technical term, but it is probable that they did so, and that this usage is reflected in Paul's own. At Phil. ii. 25 and 2 Cor. viii. 23 he uses it to describe men acting on behalf of Christian communities. Paul himself, however, is not an apostle 'of a church' (cf. Gal. i. 1), but an apostle of Jesus Christ (1 Cor. i. 1; 2 Cor. i. 1; Col. i. 1; cf. Gal. i. 1) from whom alone his mission and authority are derived. As such an apostle he appeals to men 'on behalf of Christ', 'as though God were entreating by us' (2 Cor. v. 20). The word of God has been entrusted to him, and through his proclamation faith is born (*v.* 5). His privileged status as a special representative of Christ gives him authority (2 Cor. x. 8) but none of the ordinary human accompaniments of authority; his privilege is suffering (1 Cor. iv. 9–13; Col. i. 24), a participation in, and manifestation of, the sufferings of Christ himself. Beyond the suffering lies resurrection (2 Cor. xiii. 4), but this is not the visible aspect of the apostle's ministry. Weakness and humiliation Paul shared with Christ himself (e.g. 2 Cor. xiii. 4) and with the Gospel (e.g. 1 Cor. i. 18, 23); they were the mark of his apostleship, but to many of his contemporaries they suggested that he was no apostle at all (1 Cor. ix. 2; 2 Cor. xi. 5; xii. 11 f.). This may be reflected also in the striking disuse of *apostle* as a designation of Paul in Acts (except at xiv. 4, 14).

The apostle is **set apart** for the Gospel. Again the background of Paul's thought is to be found in the Old Testament. The prophets were set apart by God for their work; for example, 'Before thou camest forth out of the womb I sanctified thee; I have appointed thee a prophet unto the nations' (Jer. i. 5). This passage is alluded to in Gal. i. 15, and may be in mind here also, as 'unto the nations' (cf. *v.* 5) suggests. 'Set apart' means much the same as 'sanctified', but may perhaps have further significance. The Greek word (ἀφωρισμένος) is not only similar in meaning to, but also has the same consonants as the Hebrew root *p-r-sh*, which underlies the word Pharisee. Paul had been a Pharisee (Phil. iii. 5), supposing himself to be set apart[1] from other men for the service of God; he now truly was what he had supposed himself to be – separated, not, however, by human exclusiveness but by God's grace and election.

He was set apart **for the Good News**; that is, in order to proclaim it. Here Paul's word (εὐαγγέλιον) has been translated Good News, in order to bring out its meaning. Elsewhere the familiar term Gospel is used; an English technical term is a suitable equivalent for the Greek word, which, in Paul's usage, has also a technical sense. It is the message of salvation he is commissioned to preach, the announcement of the manifestation of God's righteousness (see *vv.* 16 f.). Behind this usage, lies not only the common Greek meaning of the word but also its use in the Old Testament, especially in Isaiah where it (and particularly the cognate verb) points to the coming of God whose saving righteousness will bring deliverance to his people (e.g. Isa. xl. 9; lii. 7). Paul's Gospel is more than this. It is not merely an account of God's saving acts in Christ; the active righteousness of God is revealed in it; it is itself part of the eschatological event through which God brings salvation to men. See below on *vv.* 16 f.

Paul's words here could be literally rendered, 'Gospel of God'. The genitive can scarcely be objective in view of *v.* 3 ('about his Son'), and it is best to take it as a genitive of the author: the Gospel is the Good News **God is now setting forth.** What he had promised in the past (*v.* 2) he now causes to be proclaimed. Paul's theology is theocentric in that God is the source of salvation and thus of the Gospel, and of the theology that rests upon the Gospel; christocentric in that the historical manifestation of the truth of God lies in the deeds of Jesus Christ.

The Good News God is now setting forth through his apostles is **Good News which in the past he promised through his prophets, 2 whose word still stands in Holy Writ.** The relation between the Old Testament and the New (or rather, the apostolic proclamation upon which the New Testament rests) is one of the major themes of the epistle and will be discussed from time to time as it arises. Here Paul echoes the common conviction of the primitive Church that the saving acts of Christ were foretold by the prophets. The more difficult problem, of the relation between Law and Gospel, is not raised.

1 The origin of the word Pharisee is not certain, but this meaning was probably attached to it.

3   The Good News is **about his Son**, in whom all the Old Testament
promises were fulfilled (2. Cor. i. 20), and the saving acts were
wrought. A brief (perhaps credal) formula expounds the nature of the
Son of God in this verse and the next. It has often and plausibly been
suggested that behind Paul's words there lies a primitive Christological
statement which Paul was willing to use (in edited form), perhaps
because he had learned it in his early years as a Christian, perhaps
because he hoped that his readers (personally unknown to him) would
recognize it and by it be helped to recognize him as a fellow Christian. If
we may tentatively accept the hypothesis that Paul was both quoting
and editing, we may conjecture that the basis on which he was working
was a pair of lines in antithetical parallelism. Jesus Christ was

in the sphere of the flesh, born of the family of David;
4   **in the sphere of the Holy Spirit, appointed Son of God.**

The preposition (κατά) here rendered 'in the sphere of' could also
be rendered 'according to', and 'according to the flesh'[1] is a common
Pauline phrase; in this verse, however, Paul does not mean that on a
fleshly (human) judgement Jesus was a descendant of David, but that
in the realm denoted by the word flesh (humanity) he was truly a
descendant of David. Similarly, 'in the sphere of the Holy Spirit' does
not introduce a truer evaluation of Jesus' person, but a second
evaluation also true in another (divine) sphere. (For the translation
'Holy Spirit' see below.)
    That Jesus was of Davidic descent is attested in various parts of the
New Testament (e.g. Matt. i. 1; Acts ii. 30; Rev. v. 5), but nowhere else
by Paul (but cf. xv. 12, where, however, Paul is quoting the Old
Testament without specific concern for the expression 'the root of
Jesse'). It is a probable view that he mentions the matter here because
he is quoting a formula which he did not himself compose. Evidently he
saw no reason to question the fact; it was part of the conviction that
Christ had fulfilled the prophecies of the Old Testament (e.g. 2 Sam. vii.
12; Isa. xi. 1); but for him a more significant statement of the Old
Testament background out of which the Christ emerged was that he
was 'born under the law' (Gal. iv. 4; cf. Rom. xv. 8, with the note).
    Jesus, then, as a man was a descendant of David; but 'in the sphere of
the Holy Spirit he was appointed Son of God'. This translation is not
universally accepted. For 'in the sphere of' see above. 'The Holy Spirit'
is literally 'spirit of holiness', and this has been taken to refer not to the
Holy Spirit, but to Jesus' own (human) spirit, marked as it was by the
attribute of holiness. It is true that, though Paul frequently refers to the
Holy Spirit, he nowhere else uses this descriptive genitive, which is

1 For Paul's use of the word *flesh* (σάρξ) see p. 129.

probably of Semitic origin; but this fact is explained if we accept the view that the Christological formula is pre-Pauline. Conversely, the use of a Greek phrase that is reminiscent of an expression common in rabbinic use strengthens the case for regarding the statement in its original form as pre-Pauline. Further, the word here translated 'appointed' is sometimes translated 'defined', or 'declared' (to be). This rendering has the evident advantage that it avoids the charge of adoptionism which can be brought against 'appointed' (see below), but there is little else to be said for it. Hellenistic evidence and New Testament usage both favour 'appointed' (e.g. Acts x. 42; xvii. 31).

We now have before us an antithetical Christological couplet, which we have some reason for regarding as pre-Pauline. It is important to note what it contains.

The very fact of the antithesis is significant. It is implied that there are two things to be said about Christ, not indeed contradictory but complementary to and different from each other. Christ belongs to two spheres or orders of existence, denoted respectively by flesh and Spirit; in these he can be described as Son of David and as Son of God. He was *born* as Son of David, *appointed* Son of God. We have no grounds for taking any other than the most natural view, namely, that the birth preceded the appointment. When the appointment took place is not stated. The Baptism (Mark i. 9 ff. and parallels) may be suggested; or perhaps the further words **after his resurrection from the dead** belonged to the original formula, or, if added by Paul, were a true interpretation. The preposition (ἐξ) is consistent with this, since even if (as is possible) it means not 'after' but 'on the ground of', the resurrection of Christ must still have preceded his appointment. Jesus then was born Son of David and appointed Son of God, most probably, perhaps, at the resurrection (cf. Acts ii. 36). His descent from David means that he was the Messiah, in whom Judaism found its fulfilment (*v.* 2). When he was born, the Age to Come of Jewish expectation began to dawn; that is, the Gospel consists in the fulfilment of eschatology in Jesus. The fulfilment, however, was not yet complete, for the Messiah who had been exalted to the right hand of the Father was to return in power and glory when all his foes were subjected to him.

If the view suggested above is correct, Paul adds two supplements to the primitive formula. One, 'after his resurrection from the dead', has already been discussed. The other, **in power**, is ambiguous. It may be taken either adverbially (modifying 'appointed'), or adjectivally (qual-ifying 'Son of God'). If the sentence is taken as it stands, it seems impossible to decide between these alternatives. If, however, 'in power' is a Pauline addition, it is most plausibly understood as adjectival, and as intended to soften the adoptionism of the words quoted. If the passage is taken in this way, Paul means that Christ was, after the resurrection, appointed Son of God *in power*; this would not exclude his having previously been Son of God, though without the manifestation of power which took place in the resurrection. This would be consistent with what Paul says elsewhere of the weakness of Christ in his earthly life and death. God, in the person of his Son, disclosed himself in weakness and humility that men might know him and live by faith only, without the confirmation of sight.

Undoubtedly, the earliest Christology has superficially an adoptionist tinge; but this is not to say that it was 'Adoptionist' in the technical sense. The first attempts at Christological thought were made not in essential but in functional terms.[1] Pre-existence was a possibility that had not been explored (Paul himself was perhaps the first explorer); there was a manifest difference between the obscure private life of Jesus and the public ministry that was inaugurated at his baptism, and an even greater difference between the earthly life and the heavenly glory of **Jesus Christ our Lord** (on the term Lord see further on x. 9). The Son of man had come in weakness and humility; he was to come in glory and power. This was the primitive Christian conviction about Jesus; behind the Chalcedonian orthodoxy of 'two natures' united in Christ's person lies an earlier belief in the two tenses of his activity.[2]

5   It was Jesus the heavenly Lord who bestowed upon Paul **grace and our apostolic commission.** Here, as in *v.* 1, Paul speaks both as Christian and as apostle; hence, probably, the plural **we received,** since all Christians have received grace (xii. 6). Grace is the undeserved favour of God for sinful men, operative in the eschatological event of Jesus Christ (see further on iii. 24); for the 'apostolic commission' see above on the word apostle. It may be, however, that the two words are to be taken together and that 'we' is Paul's epistolary 'we' and refers to himself: 'we (that is, I) received the grace of apostleship'. He is at present concerned with his own vocation rather than with that of Christians in general.

The aim of Paul's apostleship is here defined as **to win believing obedience.** A literal translation is, 'unto obedience of faith'. It has been suggested that this means 'with a view to securing obedience to the faith', 'the faith' being 'the Christian religion'; but a better explanation is that Paul is using a shorthand expression and means that the object of his apostolic work is that men should (a) become obedient to Christ, and (b) put their faith in him. For the meaning of faith see on *vv.* 16 f., and many other passages; for the close relation of obedience and faith see, for example, vi. 15 ff. Cranfield (66) prefers to express this close relation as 'the faith which consists in obedience'. This seems to treat obedience and faith as actually synonymous, which overestimates the

---

1 See O. Cullman, *Die Christologie des Neuen Testaments* (Tübingen, 1957, English translation, London, 1959).
2 It is not denied that the doctrine of the two natures is a proper metaphysical interpretation of the primitive eschatological faith.

closeness of the relation. It is perhaps better to recognize that there are different kinds of obedience; there is what may be called a 'works obedience', concerned to produce works that may win favour from God, and a 'faith obedience', arising out of the faith that gratefully accepts the favour that God has already spontaneously shown. It is the latter that Paul seeks.

As an apostle, Paul acts **on his** (Christ's) **behalf** (literally, on behalf of his name). The scope of his activity also is laid down; it is **among all the Gentiles.** This was settled in consultation with the Jerusalem apostles; see Gal. ii. 9. The intention, interpretation, and execution of the agreement here described give rise to difficult problems; Paul certainly felt free to preach to Jews, and there was a Gentile mission independent of his – he was at this moment writing to a Gentile church which he had not founded. But the present verse emphasizes the fact that a real division of apostolic work was agreed upon (cf. xi. 13; xv. 16, 18).

The next words, **among whom are you,** show that a majority of the 6 Roman Christians were Gentiles. See Introduction, pp. 6 f. Apart from their racial origin, the Roman Christians were **Jesus Christ's, by divine call**; literally, 'called ones of Jesus Christ'. This genitive is not subjective – 'called *by* Jesus Christ' – for in Paul's usage it is God the Father who calls (iv. 17; viii. 30; *et al.*). Contrast 'God's beloved' (*v.* 7). Christians are the property of Jesus Christ. Like Paul himself (*v.* 1), they are his slaves; he is their Lord (*v.* 4). And he and they stand in this relationship not because they have chosen it but because they have been called to it by God himself, just as Paul, against his own inclination and will, was called to be an apostle.

The next verse adds to the description of the recipients of the letter. It is addressed to **all who in Rome are God's beloved, by divine call, 7 saints.** The readers of the letter are in the world – indeed, they are in the very heart of it. At the same time they are not of the world, for they are saints, that is to say, holy persons (ἅγιοι). The word is one of Paul's most common designations of Christians; in Romans see also viii. 27; xii. 13; xv. 25 f., 31; xvi. 2, 15. That the word is regularly plural (Phil. iv. 21 is only an apparent exception) confirms the fact that the usage looks back to the Old Testament (the holy people, e.g. Ex. xix. 6), as developed in later Judaism (e.g. Dan. vii. 18; Ps. Sol. xvii. 28; 1 Enoch xliii. 4). Christians are the elect, messianic people. Nothing is implied about their moral behaviour, though their separation from the world and for Christ is bound to have moral consequences. They are singled out as the people of God because of the love God has for them. This is the root out of which Christian doctrine and action grow (cf. v. 8).

Paul's **grace** (χάρις) may be a Christianizing of a common Greek salutation (χαίρειν). He adds, **peace** – which was, and is, a common greeting among Semitic peoples.[1] It is unthinkable, however, that he

---

1 In letters as well as in speech; e.g. *Sanhedrin* 11 *b*: 'To our brothers of upper Galilee . . . : May your peace multiply'.

did not enrich the word with its specific Christian content (see on v. 1).

The greeting may owe something to other sources. It recalls the priestly blessing of Num. vi. 24 ff. (The Lord ... be gracious unto thee ... and give thee peace), and there is a similar combination in 2 Baruch lxxviii. 2 (Thus saith Baruch the son of Neriah to the brethren carried into captivity: Mercy and peace). The Pauline formula may perhaps reflect an early Christian liturgical usage.

Paul has now introduced his letter, and, at the same time, in general terms, himself and his Gospel. He will say a little more about himself (i. 8–15) and then turn to expound the Gospel at length. So far he has said nothing to explain why he should be writing a letter to the church in Rome, which he had done nothing to found. The next section will supply at least a hint.

2 PAUL AND ROME

CHAPTER i. 8–15

(8) First of all, I give thanks to my God through Jesus Christ for you all, because your faith is spoken of in the whole world. (9) For God (to whom I render spiritual service in proclaiming the Gospel of his Son) is my witness that I make mention of you unceasingly, (10) always in my prayers making the petition that I really may in the end succeed (if that be God's will) in coming to you. (11) For I long to see you, that I may impart to you some gift of the Spirit, for your strengthening, (12) – or rather, what I wish is that we may be mutually encouraged when I am among you by our common faith, yours and mine. (13) Indeed, I should not like you, brethren, to be unaware that I have often intended to come to you that I might get some fruit among you too, as I have among the other Gentiles; only up to the present I have been prevented from doing this. (14) To Greeks and barbarians alike, to wise and foolish equally, I am under obligation; (15) that is why I desire to preach the Gospel to you in Rome[1] as well as to the rest.

In the first seven verses of the epistle Paul followed, though he also modified, the conventional form of a Greek letter. In the thanksgiving, intercession, and personal news of the present paragraph he continues, as he does elsewhere, to follow the same model.[2]

8   Paul's **First of all** is never followed by a 'secondly'; he is carried

---

1 The words 'in Rome' are omitted by G. See on i. 7, and Introduction, p. 10.
2 See P. Schubert, *Form and Function of the Pauline Thanksgivings* (Berlin, 1939); P. T. O'Brien, *Introductory Thanksgivings in the Letters of Paul* (Leiden, 1977).

away by his train of thought (cf. iii. 2). He can **give thanks** for the Roman Christians, **because your faith is spoken of,** publicly reported, **in the whole world.** 'Your faith' does not mean 'the Christian faith *which* you, in common with all other Christians, hold', for this would be pointless in a thanksgiving; but 'the faith *as* you hold it', that is, the understanding, constancy, and charity with which you hold it. There is doubtless a natural exaggeration in these words (cf. 1 Thess. i. 8), but they cannot be meaningless. The Roman church was not a foundation of yesterday; already it had made its presence felt. This harmonizes readily with the view (see Introduction, pp. 5 f.) that the riots *impulsore Chresto* (Suetonius, *Claudius*, 25) were provoked by the proclamation of Jesus as Messiah; less well with Acts xxviii. 21 f., where the Roman Jews appear to have no direct acquaintance with Christianity, though there are Christians in Rome (Acts xxviii. 15).

Paul not only gives thanks but makes intercession. **God . . . is my 9 witness** (an Old Testament form of asseveration: Gen. xxxi. 50; 1 Sam. xii. 5; Micah i. 2) **that I make mention of you unceasingly, always in 10 my prayers making the petition. . . .** This sentence may be punctuated differently. It is possible to place the comma after 'prayers'; the sentence might then be rendered, ' . . . that I always in my prayers unceasingly make mention of you, making the petition . . . '. But it seems better to separate 'unceasingly' and 'always' which are so nearly synonymous that in one clause they are tautologous. The God whom Paul calls to witness is he **to whom I render spiritual service in proclaiming the Gospel of his Son.** 'Spiritual' would be more literally rendered, 'in' or 'by my spirit'; it is by using his spirit, in the field of activities proper to the spiritual side of his nature, that Paul renders God service. Paul's word ($\pi\nu\epsilon\hat{\upsilon}\mu\alpha$) most frequently refers to the Spirit of God, but *my* makes this impossible here. The service is 'in the Gospel', that is, it consists in preaching the Gospel. For 'the Gospel', see on *v.* 1.

In particular, Paul prays **that I really may in the end succeed (if that be God's will) in coming to you.** Paul, though submitting himself to God's will, wishes to visit Rome, even though it was not a church of his own founding and it was his custom not to build on foundations laid by others (xv. 20). Reasons of a sort for this unusual proceeding are given in *vv.* 11 ff., 15. These could apply to any place; the basic and only specific reason does not appear till xv. 24: Paul is (or hopes to be) on his way to Spain, and for this new field of missionary activity Rome will prove an indispensable base.

The reason is sound enough; but Paul's plans are sufficiently anomalous to make him embarrassed, and his embarrassment appears in the loose and inaccurate construction of the next verses. He begins straightforwardly enough: **I long to see you, that I may impart to you 11 some gift of the Spirit.** 'Gifts' are dealt with at some length in xii. 6 ff.;

see also 1 Cor. xii. Whether it is explicitly stated (as here) or not, they are the result of the activity of the Spirit, and thus a sign of the Church's supernatural life. Since elsewhere Paul lays stress on the variety of such gifts it is hardly profitable here to inquire what precise gift he may have had in mind.

After this straightforward beginning the construction changes and it becomes difficult to establish Paul's meaning with certainty. The obscurity and confusion are probably due to Paul's recognition that, though a visit intended **for your strengthening** might have been mentioned appropriately in a letter to Corinth, where he was both apostle (1 Cor. ix. 2) and father (1 Cor. iv. 15), it came less suitably when he was writing as a stranger to an old-established and well-known (v. 8) church in the capital of the Empire. 'For your strengthening' needs

12 correction: **or rather, what I wish is** (these last four words are not expressed in the Greek, but if they are not supplied, 'that we may be mutually encouraged' must be made to depend on 'I long', which is very awkward) **that we may be mutually encouraged when I am among you by our common faith.** The stress falls on the mutuality of what will take place when Paul visits Rome. He trusts that he will be able to impart a spiritual gift, but he is equally sure that the Romans will have something to bestow on him. The translation 'encouraged' is not certain. Paul's word is συμπαρακαλεῖν, σύν (*together with*) compounded with παρακαλεῖν, which means sometimes 'comfort', sometimes 'exhort'. The latter sense would be difficult here (though doubtless exhortation or preaching is involved); on the other hand more than consolation seems to be intended, and in modern English 'comfort' is scarcely a strong enough word.

Paul may be a stranger in Rome, and the church there another man's

13 foundation; yet as an apostle he can write that **I have often intended to come to you that I might get some fruit among you.** 'Fruit' is the result of apostolic labour – the winning of new converts, and the building up of the Church; and Paul might expect to find it in Rome, **as I have among the other Gentiles** (cf. v. 6). Notwithstanding xv. 20, there was no question of his freedom, or of his desire, to preach in Rome. So far as that verse expresses a limitation, it was self-imposed and a matter of policy rather than principle. In general Paul chose, doubtless with good reason, to break fresh ground. Rome was an exceptional place and called for exceptional treatment. See v. 10.

I should not like you to be unaware is a common Pauline expression (xi. 25; *et al.*); and **brethren** is a word commonly used of fellow-members of both Jewish and heathen religious communities. It was common in early Christian usage too; cf. Mark iii. 35, as well as many passages in the epistles.

The sentence **only up to the present I have been prevented from doing this** has for clarity been taken out of the awkward parenthetical position it occupies in the Greek (between 'to you' and 'that I might get'). Paul does not here (as at 1 Thess. ii. 18) speak of a hindering by Satan; indeed, the use of the passive may (in Semitic fashion) conceal a reference to God – it had not been God's will that Paul should come (cf. Acts xvi. 6 f., and perhaps 1 Cor. xvi. 12). This should probably be understood to mean that urgent tasks (only recently completed – xv. 18 f., 22 f.) had kept him in the East.

Thus both Paul's desire to visit Rome (for its own sake, and as a stage on the journey to Spain), and the fact that he had so far failed to do so, were due to the obligation under which he stood as an apostle. **To 14 Greeks and barbarians alike** (the word Greeks is not to be taken in a strict racial sense; Paul means, Both those who inhabit the city states of the inner Mediterranean world, and those outside that cultivated circle), **to wise and foolish equally, I am under obligation.** The notion of debt is not emphasized (cf. viii. 12; xv. 27; Gal. v. 3); it is a duty Paul owes, and it is this duty which leads him to Rome: The construction of the concluding sentence is awkward and ambiguous. It is possible to take the opening words (τὸ κατ' ἐμέ) on their own and the next word as an independent substantive: 'so far as I am concerned, there is a readiness (or eagerness) to . . .' Alternatively, and perhaps better, the four words may be taken together, 'My readiness (or eagerness) is to . . .'. Fortunately there is little or no difference in sense and the construction may be smoothed out as in the translation: **That is 15 why I desire to preach the Gospel to you in Rome** (see n. 1 on p. 24) **as well as to the rest** (bringing out the force of καί).

But what does preaching the Gospel mean? What is the Gospel (cf. *v.* 1)? Paul begins at once to answer these questions, and is not done with them until the epistle is at an end.

3 THE GOSPEL

CHAPTER i. 16, 17

(16) For I am not ashamed of the Gospel, since it is the operation of God's power working towards salvation, effective for everyone who has faith – Jew first, and then the Gentile too. (17) For in it God's righteousness is revealed on the basis of nothing but faith – as it is written, He that is righteous by faith shall live.

These two verses are at once the continuation of *vv.* 8–15, and the beginning of *vv.* 18–32; it seems best to take them as a separate paragraph. Most commentators recognize in them the 'text' of the epistle; it is not wrong to see in them a summary of Paul's theology as a whole.

An obscure provincial, Paul plans to visit the centre of the world; a self-styled apostle, lacking the self-evident authorization of the Twelve, he approaches a church where his authority and even his credentials
16 may well be questioned; yet – **I am not ashamed** (cf. Mark viii. 38; 2 Tim. i. 8) **of the Gospel.** This is simply because the Gospel is what it is. The point however is not simply the psychological one that in intimidating circumstances Paul has the courage to maintain his position. The Gospel itself is the shameful story of one who was crucified in weakness (2 Cor. xiii. 4), one from whom even his followers, without regard to their own situation, might have turned away, ashamed to acknowledge him. If, as Paul goes on to say, the Gospel has to do with power and salvation, these are power that is made perfect in weakness (2 Cor. xii. 9) and salvation that lies in the future, power and salvation that are manifest only to faith.[1]

Paul's argument turns upon **salvation.** The word itself, even when the cognate verb 'to save' is included in the reckoning, is not one of the commonest in Paul, but it is certainly central in his thought. Salvation itself lies in the future (e.g. xiii. 11), and means man's eventual safe passage through human trials and divine judgement to eternal bliss. In particular, salvation means being saved from the wrath of God (v. 9); it is thus a term which belongs within the framework of eschatological thinking. Like all such terms, it suffered a change when it was taken over from the vocabulary of Judaism into that of primitive Christianity. The salvation ready to be revealed at the last time, though it could be complete only at the return of the Messiah in glory, was already, in virtue of his death and resurrection, anticipated in the present. Thus the Gospel itself is **the operation of God's power working towards** salvation; not merely an announcement of the fact that salvation will at some future time take place, but a divine activity or power leading to salvation. Like the word of God in the prophets, the Gospel itself is a power which leads either to life or to death (cf. 1 Cor. i. 23 f.; 2 Cor. ii. 15 f.). It is one element in the eschatological situation in which Paul believed that he and his fellow Christians stood.

The work of salvation was begun, though not completed, in the ministry, death, and resurrection of Jesus, and from the beginning it was marked by power: in the miracles, in the resurrection, and subsequently in the work of the Holy Spirit. It was in virtue of this power that the Gospel preached by Paul and his apostolic colleagues had its effect among those who heard it and experienced the 'powers of the age to come' (Heb. vi. 5). This proleptic enjoyment of salvation in the power of the Gospel, which at once announces and anticipates it, is a most important key to Paul's thought, for many of his central

---

1 See my paper, 'I am not ashamed of the Gospel', in *Foi et Salut selon S. Paul (Épître aux Romains, 1, 16)*; Analecta Biblica 42 (1970), pp. 19–50.

theological ideas (for example, the doctrines of justification, and of the Holy Spirit) are built upon it.

It is *God's* power which is at work in the Gospel, not man's; it is at work not because man has chosen that it should be, but because God has acted through Jesus. It follows that the divine power operative in the Gospel is not dependent upon any human activity or condition. It is never without its effect (see above); and that which determines what the effect shall be is not human virtue or wisdom, not works done in obedience to any law, however sacred, but nothing more or less than faith: the Gospel is the operation of God's power acting toward salvation, **effective for everyone who has faith.** What faith is will become gradually clearer as the epistle proceeds; but its primary meaning is already apparent. It is the 'believing obedience' of *v.* 5. He believes who accepts the power of God which is at work in the life, death, and resurrection of Jesus as – the power of God, and therefore submits himself to it, claiming no rights over against his Creator but ready to trust himself wholly to his grace and wisdom. It is the positive counterpart of what is negatively expressed in i. 21: it is to glorify God and give thanks to him, recognizing him as the God that he is. Only when man is prepared to stand still and see the glory of God can he apprehend God's action as salvation.

The Gospel means salvation for *everyone* who has faith, but it was delivered to the **Jew first, and then the Gentile too.** (The word here translated 'Gentile' was in *v.* 14 translated 'Greek'; the meaning is determined by the context, and especially by the contrasting partner, in each case). That the Jews were the first to hear the Gospel is to Paul more than a fact of history; it was due to God's election (see especially chs. ix–xi). It was inconceivable that God's Anointed should appear outside the context of messianic prophecy, where alone there existed a vocabulary suitable for describing him. Further, it was impossible that he should be understood except against the background of law. Only where human achievement in religion had reached its highest point could its absolute negation in the universality of human guilt (iii. 19 f.) and the freedom of God be proclaimed. Grace could be fully grace only where sin abounded (*v.* 20), and the exceeding sinfulness of sin could be demonstrated only through the law (vii. 13). Acts (xiii. 46; xviii. 6; xxviii. 28) represents Paul as applying this principle in a simple sequential sense: when the Jews reject the Gospel his next move is to address Gentiles. There is no reason to doubt that Paul did act in this way, but his own proposition is essentially theological.

No one insisted more strongly than Paul that the Gospel was for the 'Gentile too'; but it is important to see that for him the extension of the Gospel to the Gentiles was the result not of easy-going charity but of theological conviction; nor did it contradict the election of the Jews (see on chs. ix–xi). There is only one God (iii. 29), and therefore only one Gospel.

This short paragraph carries Paul's argument yet further in a second decisive step. Paul is not ashamed of the Gospel, because it is the divinely appointed means to salvation. It is this means because **in it God's righteousness is revealed.** Here for the first time we touch upon the dominating theme of the epistle. As a Jew, instructed in the Old Testament, Paul knows that salvation presupposes righteousness. On God's side, salvation means the operation of his righteousness, which is not simply his property or attribute of being right, or righteous, but also his activity in doing right, and (as we say) seeing right done; thus his righteousness issues in his vindicating – those whom it is proper that he should vindicate. This view of God's righteousness is brought out with special clarity in a number of passages in Isaiah and the Psalms (e.g. Isa. xlv. 21; li. 5; Ps. xxiv. 5; xxxi. 1; xcviii. 2; cxliii. 11), where righteousness appears to be almost a synonym of salvation; God manifests his righteousness by delivering his people.[1]

On man's side, salvation requires that he be found righteous before God; that, when the great assize is held, he secure a favourable verdict. If the verdict is Guilty, punishment, not salvation, must be his fate.

Thus, before salvation can be completed, righteousness must be manifested. God, the righteous judge, must do righteous judgement in his court; and, in this court, man must secure the verdict, Righteous. When defined in this way, salvation seems remote – remote in time, for the last judgement has not yet taken place, and remote as possibility, for there seems no likelihood that man will ever attain any verdict other than Guilty. Paul, however, asserts that the righteousness of God (not salvation, for that remains future) is now being revealed (ἀποκαλύπτε-ται). The very word he uses (in the present tense) confirms that he is thinking of a preliminary manifestation of that divine righteousness which, in orthodox Jewish thought, could be vindicated only at the last judgement. Paul, the Christian, is convinced that this judgement (and in some measure its consequences) has been anticipated through Jesus Christ, and that in the paradox of grace God has manifested his righteousness by establishing man's. As a Jew, Paul had believed that man's status of righteousness before God was to be achieved by himself, through obedience to the law. As a Christian, he had come to believe that God, gracious as Jesus had shown him to be, justified men freely on the basis not of works done in obedience to the law but of faith. This revision of fundamental conceptions was not the result of the academic

1 The importance of these passages should not be exaggerated. In them, God vindicates those who deserve to be vindicated; in Paul, he justifies – the ungodly.

manipulation of theological counters; it took place because God had sent his Messiah to suffer humiliation and death and thereby to manifest his righteousness in a way accessible to faith, the only human attitude corresponding to grace on God's part.

This discussion of righteousness has so far proceeded without explicit reference to the traditional and more recent analyses of the meaning of the word. There is no better account of these than that of Professor Cranfield (pp. 92–9, with bibliography; cf. pp. 824–6). Here it must suffice to point out the main divisions. (1) The righteousness of God refers to an activity of God analogous to that expressed in his deliverance of his people from bondage or exile and described by the same word (δικαιοσύνη; *tz^edaqah* or *tzedeq*; e.g. Isa. xlvi. 13; Ps. xcviii. 2).[1] (2) The righteousness of God refers to 'a status of man resulting from God's action, righteousness as a gift from God' (Cranfield, p. 96). (3) The righteousness of God refers to his faithfulness to the covenant implied in creation and is an apocalyptic term describing God's promised activity in setting his rebellious creation to rights.[2] If the discussion in this commentary is correct it will appear that it is impossible to keep (1) and (2) separate from each other: God's saving action consists precisely in conferring on man a state of righteousness (that is, in justifying him).[3] Even (3) is also included by the paradoxical use of the present tense *is being revealed* (ἀποκαλύπτεται). It is of course important to be as precise as possible in one's understanding of this word – as of all others – but the divisions and subdivisions are ours, not Paul's, and for him many thoughts were comprehended under the word δικαιοσύνη, righteousness, and the reader must be cautious before dismissing any of them from the consideration of any passage.[4]

God's righteousness, then, is revealed **on the basis of nothing but faith**; literally, from faith unto faith. Several formal parallels to this obscure expression can be adduced; for example, Ps. lxxxiv. 7 (They go from strength to strength); 2 Cor. iii. 18 (From glory to glory). These suggest the meaning, 'from one level of faith to a higher', 'to ever greater faith'. This does not, however, suit the present context; in all probability the phrase is rhetorical and means (as the translation suggests), 'faith from start to finish'. It is not impossible but also not likely that Paul is playing on the ambiguity of the Greek word πίστις

1 It is unfortunate that many recent translations of the Bible conceal this fact by translating the word not as *righteousness* but as *deliverance*, or some such word.
2 For this see E. Käsemann, *Exegetische Versuche und Besinnungen II* (1964), 181–93; P. Stuhlmacher, *Gerechtigkeit Gottes bei Paulus* (1965).
3 The noun *righteousness* and the verb *to justify* are etymologically close (δικαιοσύνη – δικαιοῦν). For justification see pp. 71 f.
4 That Paul uses *righteousness* in various ways is recognized by E. P. Sanders; see *Paul and Palestinian Judaism* (1977), especially pp. 502–8.

and means 'from (God's) faithfulness to (man's) faith'. The change of meaning would be very harsh.

Paul clinches his argument with a reference to the Old Testament: **He that is righteous by faith shall live** (Hab. ii. 4). The Greek contains here an ambiguity which has been retained in the translation. Does 'by faith' modify the adjective 'righteous' or the verb 'shall live'? The position of the phrase is indecisive. It is to be noted that both the Hebrew text and the LXX of Habakkuk supply possessive pronouns with 'faith'. The Hebrew has, 'He that is righteous shall live by his faithfulness', the Greek, '... by my faithfulness'. The fact that Paul drops both pronouns may lend some force to the view that he wishes to bring out his own characteristic phrase, 'righteous by faith'. More probably, however, he is again emphasizing the principle of 'faith all the time': man (if righteous at all) is righteous by faith; he also lives by faith.

These two verses contain a rich selection of Paul's characteristic vocabulary: Gospel, power, salvation, faith, Jew and Gentile, righteousness. Something has now been done to bring out the meaning of these basic terms, but the present exposition is not complete, and it will be necessary to return to them again and again, as Paul himself does. See especially on iii. 21–31.

4 JUDGEMENT AND THE GENTILE

CHAPTER i. 18–32

(18) A clear signal of the revealing of God's righteousness is the fact that his wrath is being revealed from heaven against all the ungodliness and unrighteousness of men who, by their unrighteousness, hold the truth imprisoned. (19) Justly so, for that which can be known of God is manifest among them, since God himself made it manifest to them. (20) From the creation of the world onwards, the invisible attributes of God are plainly seen, since the mind can grasp them in the things that he has made. By his 'invisible attributes' I mean his eternal power, his very Godhead. (21) These were manifested that men might be without excuse, because, though they knew God, they did not glorify him as God or give thanks to him; instead, they grew vain in their thinking, and their senseless heart was darkened. (22) Even as they made themselves out to be wise they were turned into fools, (23) and exchanged the glory of the incorruptible God for the mere shadowy image of corruptible man – or indeed of birds, animals, and snakes. (24) So God handed them over, as punishment, in the lusts of their own hearts, to an unclean life, that among them their bodies might be dishonoured. (25) This was the fate of men who

exchanged the truth of God for a lie, and worshipped and served the creation rather than the Creator – Blessed be he for ever. Amen.

(26) So God handed them over to dishonourable passions. For example, the women among them exchanged the natural kind of intercourse for an unnatural. (27) In the same way, the men forsook natural intercourse with a female partner and were consumed in their lust for one another. Men wrought obscenity with men, and received the due reward of their error in their own persons.

(28) And as they did not see fit to take cognizance of God, God handed them over to an unfit mind, to do unseemly things, (29) to be replete with every kind of unrighteousness, wickedness, covetousness, malice; full of envy, murder, strife, deceit, evil constructions. They became gossiping whisperers, (30) God-hated slanderers, insolent, proud, boastful persons, good at inventing new forms of evil, disobedient to parents, (31) senseless, faithless, loveless, pitiless. (32) They all are men who knew God's righteous ordinance, that those who practise such things as these are worthy of death; yet they do them, or (for I would include these also) they approve of those who practise them.

The first and most difficult problem to be solved in this paragraph is the question of its place in the argument of the epistle. It is often said that, after stating briefly, in *vv.* 16 f., the substance of the Gospel, Paul begins at this point a long digression which he continues until he resumes, in iii. 21, the theme of the saving righteousness of God. The digression deals (it is said) with the state of mankind apart from the Gospel; it is therefore by no means irrelevant to a presentation of the Gospel, but it is not directly connected with *v.* 17. This popular exegesis cannot be maintained.

Two points determine the exegesis of the opening verses of the paragraph. The first is the particle (γάρ, generally translated *for*, *because*) with which it is introduced. It is true that this particle is sometimes weakened so as to become no more than a note of transition, but it is well, if at all possible, to give it its proper force (as in the present translation). The second point is the fact that with the new subject (wrath) Paul uses the same verb, in the same tense, as with the subject (righteousness) in *v.* 17. Paul does not say that the wrath of God *was* revealed in the old time before the promulgation of the Gospel, or that it will be revealed at the last day. He says that God's **wrath is being** **revealed from heaven** now; and this is exactly what he has said of God's righteousness. We are therefore encouraged to see a close positive relation between *vv.* 17 and 18; and this is confirmed by detailed exegesis.

18

It has been noted that in only one other place does Paul add to the word 'wrath' the genitive 'of God' (Col. iii. 6; cf. Eph. v. 6), and that he never uses the verb 'to be wrathful' with God as subject; and deduced that Paul thought of the divine wrath in impersonal terms, as an almost automatic force which resists evil. It is doubtful whether this view can stand. When Paul speaks of wrath, it is in general quite clear from the context that the wrath is God's; so, for example, iii. 5; ix. 22. Wrath is God's personal (though never malicious or, in a bad sense, emotional) reaction against sin.

Properly, wrath belongs to the last day (ii. 5), but the idea of its anticipation in divine judgements is common. Here, however, it is a unique anticipation which is in mind. If the *for* (γάρ) which introduces *v.* 18 is a real *for*, the assertion of *v.* 17 must be understood to be demonstrated or supported by the manifestation of wrath which is described in the following verses. This is quite suitable to the context, for the latter part of the paragraph depicts an observable situation capable of forming the basis of an argument. Wrath, like salvation and righteousness, is an eschatological term. Righteousness (so Paul as a Jew would undoubtedly believe) would be manifested at the last judgement in terms of salvation and wrath. But (as Paul the Christian now believed) righteousness had been manifested *to faith* in the event of Jesus Christ, and in consequence salvation and wrath also were being anticipated in history (though each was still to be consummated in the future). It follows logically (assuming Paul's premises) that, if the revelation of wrath can be demonstrated (as Paul believes), the revelation of righteousness is demonstrated too.

Paul's argument is developed in a clear and consistent way. The Gospel rests upon a manifestation of righteousness; to those who believe, it proves to be the power of God unto salvation (cf. 1 Cor. i. 18) and is visible in the moral experience of conversion and in the gathering of churches, in which the Holy Spirit is at work; to those who do not believe, but are disobedient and rebellious, it means God's wrath (cf. 2 Cor. ii. 16) and is visible in the terrible process of mental and moral perversion that Paul observes in the world about him. The revelation of wrath therefore is **a clear signal of the revealing of God's righteousness.**

Wrath is revealed **from heaven** (that is, from God himself) **against all the ungodliness and unrighteousness of men who, by their unrighteousness, hold the truth imprisoned**; that is, the truth about God as Creator, Judge, and Redeemer, is concealed by the fact that they are what they are. The words 'hold imprisoned' translate the same word (κατέχειν) as is used in vii. 6 ('held fast'). The word has, however, another meaning, that of holding firmly doctrines or traditions (as at 1 Cor. xi. 2). If this meaning of the word is adopted, the ungodly and unrighteous men are blamed for their hypocrisy; they hold the truth in a state of ungodliness, their orthodox belief is accompanied by unrighteous life. But hypocrisy is not a sin attacked by Paul in this paragraph, and the other translation is to be preferred.

At this point a serious objection might be made. 'This manifestation of divine wrath would be credible, and just, if the abandoned Gentile world consisted of men who had wilfully rejected the Gospel. But this is not so. The vast majority have never heard of the Gospel.' The fact that Paul proceeds to meet precisely this objection confirms that our interpretation of his thought is on the right lines. The words **justly so** 19 are inserted in the translation as a necessary connecting link since it is evident that Paul intends in *v.* 19 to justify what he has said.

Men are without excuse, **for that which can be known of God is manifest among them, since God himself made it manifest to them.** It is not Paul's intention in this and the following verses to establish a natural theology; nor does he create one unintentionally. He is concerned with the moral principles of God's judgement, and in order to vindicate these he makes use of terminology which he draws mainly from the field of Hellenistic Judaism. His intention is the opposite of Greek natural theology, which sought to make man feel at home in a threatening universe; his argument is an accusation. What it is that can be 'known of God' will appear in the next verse. It is manifest 'among them'; an equally possible translation would be 'in them' – that is, in their minds and consciences. But the context shows that the men in question did not in fact possess this knowledge in themselves; it was available in their midst, in creation, where God himself had made it manifest, but it was not *in them.*

The next verse justifies the statement that God had manifested in creation what could be known about him.

From the creation of the world is here taken in a temporal sense, 20 partly because the word for creation (κτίσις) refers properly to the act or process of creation and partly because instrumentality is sufficiently suggested in the words **in** (or, by) **the things that he has made.** In creation, man is confronted by not-man; that is, he finds himself surrounded by objects which he knows he did not make. If he did not make them, some Other did. As long as there has been a created universe, **the invisible attributes of God are plainly seen.** These invisible attributes are not God's love and saving purpose; they are those that are mentioned in this verse; **his eternal power, his very Godhead.** That is, what is clearly seen is that God is God and not man. Observation of created life is sufficient to show that creation does not provide the key to its own existence. Paul does not teach that there exist rational means of proving from creation that God exists. A mechanistic or fortuitous account of the universe never occurs to him. Of course, men set in God's world should have perceived that they were his creatures and that their Creator stood infinitely above them. In fact, those with whom Paul is here concerned, and whose sins he castigates in this chapter, did not (for the most part) deny the existence of deity; but they did fail (*v.* 21) to give God due honour and praise.

These truths – where they are perceived at all – are perceived by the mind, **since the mind can grasp them** in the things that God has made. The contrast between perception by the eye and perception by the mind was common (e.g. Plato, *Republic*, VI, 507 b); Paul means simply that the being of God is inwardly perceived. His line of argument so far can be paralleled without difficulty; it appears in the Stoic literature, and, more significantly perhaps, in that of Hellenistic Judaism (e.g. Wisdom xiii. 5).

21 God manifested his power, and the fact that he was God, man's Creator and Lord, **that men might be without excuse.** 'That' (εἰς τὸ εἶναι) indicates not result merely but purpose. This (as was pointed out above) is the important result Paul seeks to establish in these verses. God may rightly visit men with wrath because, though they have not had the advantage of hearing the Gospel, they have rejected that rudimentary knowledge of God that was open to them. The inexcusability of man is similarly emphasized in Wisdom xiii. 8 f., but Paul's accusation is far more searching, because it penetrates further into the meaning of idolatry.

The root of the matter is that **though they knew God, they did not glorify him as God or give thanks to him.** Paul assumes that the raw materials of the knowledge of God exist among men. An awareness of this kind is in itself no great matter – it is God's knowledge of man that is really significant (1 Cor. viii. 1–3; Gal. iv. 9; cf. 1 Cor. xiii. 9, 12). As God's creature, man was bound to render glory and thanksgiving to his Creator; this means not merely to acknowledge his existence, and to employ the words and rites of religion, but to recognize his lordship and live in grateful obedience – in fact (in the Pauline sense) to believe, to have faith. This men failed to do; instead they rebelled against God, and their fault lay not in lack of knowledge but in their rebellion. Man was unwilling to recognize a Lord; he chose to be Lord himself, and to glorify himself.[1] This is the universal state of mankind, and it follows that God's wrath is justly visited upon men because the race as a whole is in revolt against him. In all this Paul probably has in mind the Old Testament story of Adam, the prototype of mankind. When Adam put himself in the place of God he was driven from Eden and became subject to death; equally terrible consequences were to befall his family.

In contemporary pagan society this revolt is manifested in idolatry. A vicious circle operates: denying the knowledge of God they have, men

---

1 This account of the root of sin is fundamentally the same as that given in ch. v; see p. 104.

plunge further and further into unbelief. The result is that they are
ignorant of God, and of themselves cannot know him; yet their
ignorance is culpable ignorance, for it is rooted in rebellion. Their
idolatrous minds and practices are themselves a punishment from
God. When they failed to honour God, **they grew vain in their
thinking, and their senseless heart was darkened** (for the language, cf. Ps. xciv. 11; Wisdom xi. 15). This, with all that follows in the
chapter, constitutes the visible manifestation (i. 18, ἀποκαλύπτεται)
of the wrath of God. Once man had fallen from his true relation
with God, he was no longer capable of truly rational thought about
him.

'Heart' is one of Paul's most important psychological terms, and has
a wide range of use. It is not necessarily good (i. 24; ii. 5), nor is it
necessarily evil (ii. 15; v. 5; vi. 17); it is the organ of thought (x. 6),
but also of feeling (ix. 2). It is essentially inward, hidden (ii. 29;
viii. 27).

At this point Paul resumes the main thread of his argument. The
manifest decadence of the pagan world is an indication to him that in
this last age of history God's wrath is already at work. He has shown
that this is no more than a just punishment of what is, ultimately, not
unfortunate ignorance but culpable rebellion, in which man has sought
to dethrone his Creator, and to render to himself the glory and praise
which were due to God. The immediate result of this rebellion was a
state of corruption in which men were no longer capable of distinguishing between themselves and God, and accordingly fell into idolatry,
behind which, in all its forms, lies in the last resort the idolization of the
self. All this was, in a sense, a natural process; but it was accelerated
and illuminated in the last age.

Even as they made themselves out to be wise they were turned 22
into fools; in their 'wisdom' they thought it possible to escape their
obligations to God. But God is not mocked. Men thought to attain a
higher place than that appointed them by God, by constructing new
gods of which they, the manufacturers, were undoubtedly the masters;
but instead of rising above their place they fell below it, for they were
now worshippers not of God but of idols. They **exchanged the glory of** 23
**the incorruptible God for the mere shadowy image of corruptible
man – or indeed of birds, animals, and snakes.** Paul's language owes
something to Ps. cvi. 20, but he has adapted his quotation to a
Hellenistic setting. The allusion probably accounts for the obscure
expression 'the mere shadowy image of . . . ', which is literally 'the
likeness of the image of . . . '. 'Likeness' (ὁμοίωμα) is the word of the
Psalm in Greek; 'image' (εἰκών) suggests the idolatrous object Paul
has in mind. Perhaps he uses the two words but means no more than
either would have signified separately; perhaps (as the translation
suggests) the reduplication emphasizes the inferior, shadowy char-

acter of that which is substituted for God.[1] Again, the Old Testament account of Adam is in mind.

Idolatry is not the end of the story. It was a commonplace of Jewish propaganda that false worship led to moral depravity (e.g. Wisdom xiv. 12), and that idolatry was punished by God with a punishment made to fit the crime (e.g. Wisdom xi. 15 f.). Paul uses these beliefs, but deepens them in the using. On the one hand, he understands idolatry acutely enough to perceive that the idol-hating Jew himself is not free from it (ch. ii); on the other, he has a far more terrible sense of the punishment of idolatry – the man who worships beasts is not (as in Wisdom xi) devoured by them, but becomes like them.

The process by which idolatry becomes moral evil is neither
24 automatic nor impersonal: **God handed them over, as punishment, in the lusts of their own hearts, to an unclean life.** For *in the lusts* it would be possible to translate *by the lusts*. The preposition (ἐν) is here taken to denote the area in which punishment takes place; it could be instrumental. The words 'God handed them over' stand three times in this paragraph (*vv.* 24, 26, 28), repeated with horrifying emphasis. God's judgement has already broken forth; only he has consigned sinners not to hell but to sin – if indeed these be alternatives. 'Lusts', though in non-Biblical Greek the word (ἐπιθυμίαι) is neutral, must here refer to sexual (or homosexual) passions (for the word see further on vii. 7), and the clause which follows – **that among them their bodies might be dishonoured** – is epexegetic. Again the translation of the preposition ἐν is doubtful, but it is harder here to take it as instrumental. By dishonouring God, men in the end dishonour their own bodies. Without reverence for God respect for creation suffers.

25 Paul sums up. **This was the fate of men who exchanged the truth of God for a lie** (some understand this to mean 'substituted a lie – that is, an idol – for the true God'), **and worshipped and served the creation rather than the Creator – Blessed be he for ever. Amen.** He adds a brief doxology in Jewish form; compare the very common 'The Holy One (blessed be he!) . . . ' of the Rabbinic writings.

Paul has now conducted his argument to its close, and made his point. In what follows, he adds nothing strictly new till *v.* 32, but contributes a number of practical illustrations of the ways in which idolators fall into sin.

26 **So God handed them over to dishonourable passions. For example, the women among them exchanged the natural kind of**
27 **intercourse for an unnatural. In the same way, the men forsook natural intercourse with a female partner and were consumed in their lust for one another. Men wrought obscenity** (the word

1 I have treated Paul's argument here more fully in *From First Adam to Last: A Study in Pauline Theology* (1962), pp. 17 ff.

(ἀσχημοσύνη) does not have this meaning elsewhere in Paul; but it is normal, and required by the context) **with men, and received the due reward of their error in their own persons.** No feature of pagan society filled the Jew with greater loathing than the toleration, or rather admiration, of homosexual practices. Paul is entirely at one here with his compatriots; but his disgust is more than instinctive. In the obscene pleasures to which he refers is to be seen precisely that perversion of the created order which may be expected when men put the creation in place of the Creator. That idolatry has such consequences is to Paul a plain mark of God's wrath.

And as they did not see fit to take cognizance of God, God 28
handed them over to an unfit mind. 'See fit . . . unfit' is an attempt to represent a word-play in the original (ἐδοκίμασαν-ἀδόκιμον). By rejecting God men show that their own mind (νοῦς) is, or is meet to be, rejected. The substance of the thought has already been noted above; here, however, it may be observed that for Paul (and here he differs from his Hellenistic contemporaries) the mind is not a higher, divine, element in man, or even necessarily good. It is capable of, but it is thereby implied that it needs, renewal (xii. 2). In Romans, the mind appears sometimes to be related to the conscience; see on vii. 23, 25; xiv. 5; and, for conscience, on ii. 15.

As in *v.* 24, an epexegetical clause follows. To have an unfit mind means in practice **to do unseemly things** (τὰ μὴ καθήκοντα). Paul here borrows – and negatives – a Stoic term for *duty, that which befits* a man. Thus Epictetus (II, xvii. 31) describes an inquirer who wishes to know 'what is my duty (καθῆκον) to the gods, what to my parents, what to my brothers, what to my country, what to strangers'. Paul, however, was not a Stoic, and does not think of the duty arising out of a man's place in society, but of that imposed by his place in creation. He and the Stoics agree, on the whole, in their account of unseemly things, but for Paul they are unseemly not because they are anti-social but because they are indicative of rebellion against God.

He proceeds with a list of vices, which has parallels in, and may be based upon, Hellenistic and Hellenistic-Jewish lists. Similar lists appear in the New Testament at xiii. 13; 1 Cor. v. 10 f.; vi. 9 f.; 2 Cor. xii. 20 f.; Gal. v. 19 ff.; Eph. iv. 31; v. 3 ff.; Col. iii. 5, 8; 1 Tim. i. 9 f.; 2 Tim. iii. 2–5; see also 1 Clem. xxxv. 5. Only a few of the details call for consideration here.

Covetousness (and cognate words) is fairly common in Paul; see 29
especially Col. iii. 5, where the word is given an important theological development which does not appear in Romans.

Full of . . . evil constructions. Paul's word (κακοήθεια) is defined by Aristotle (*Rhetoric*, II. xiii. 3) as 'taking everything for the worse'.

God-hated slanderers. The word (θεοστυγεῖς) translated 'God- 30
hated' is ambiguous, and might also be taken as active ('God-hating').

The Vulgate takes it as passive (*Deo odibilis*), and there is much to be said for this rendering; on the other hand, the passage as a whole deals with specific human activities. In 1 Clem. xxxv. 5, where the cognate abstract noun is used, the context (see xxxv. 6) suggests that the word is active. This may justify us in accepting *God-hating*, though this does not fit easily into Paul's list. The alternative, somewhat hesitantly adopted in the translation, is to adopt the suggestion of A. Pallis (*To the Romans*, 1933) and combine the present word, taken as an attributive adjective, with the word that precedes it.

Good at inventing new forms of evil (undoubtedly the meaning of Paul's two words, ἐφευρετὰς κακῶν) seems at first sight a curious expression because it too stands in a list of specific evils and is in comparison so unspecific as to be vague. There are in fact several parallels, of which the most familiar is probably Vergil's, in *Aeneid*, ii. 164: 'Ulysses, crime-contriver' (*scelerum inuentor*).

The paragraph comes to a close with a verse which reiterates the main point. Sinners are not excusably ignorant but guilty and respon-

32 sible. **They all are men who knew God's righteous ordinance.** This is certainly the correct translation, though the word (δικαίωμα) for 'righteous ordinance' occurs elsewhere with somewhat different meanings (ii. 26; v. 16, 18; viii. 4; for this meaning, see Luke i. 6). The content of the ordinance follows at once: **that those who practise such things as these are worthy of death** (cf. Gen. ii. 17).

The next words raise a problem, which is in part removed in the translation: **Yet they do them, or (for I would include these also) they approve of those who practise them.** A more literal rendering would run: They not only do them, but also approve of those who practise them. The words 'not only . . . but also' suggest an increase in the offence; but to approve of those who sin can scarcely be regarded as worse than sinning (notwithstanding the old suggestion that mere doing may be excused if it is passionate and therefore unpremeditated, whereas approval implies the deliberate choice of evil). The difficulty is brought out by comparison with 1 Clem. xxxv. 6, which runs: Those who practise these things are hateful to God; and not only those who practise them, but also those who approve of them. There is no difficulty in Clement's words, and in the textual tradition of Romans there are traces of attempts to make Paul's equally straightforward. There can, however, be no doubt that he wrote the sentence in the difficult form, and the difficulty can be solved only by looking forward to ii. 1 ff. In his next paragraph Paul proceeds to deal with those who do not approve the sinful actions just described. Before doing so he deals with those who do approve. His 'not only . . . but also' would thus mean: 'I am not speaking only of those who do these things, but also of those who approve – you are all in the same condemnation. And', he continues in ch. ii, 'you who disapprove, who judge – so too are you.' See further on ii. 1.

40

5 JUDGEMENT AND THE CRITIC

CHAPTER ii. 1–11

(1) That means, my good man, that, whoever you are, whenever you act as judge you are without excuse, for in judging someone else you condemn yourself, since you who judge practise the same conduct as he. (2) Now[1] we know that 'God's judgement on those who practise such things is fair'; (3) but, knowing this, do you think, my man, that you, who judge those who practise such things as these and do them yourself, will escape God's judgement? (4) Or is it that you despise the wealth of his kindness, his forbearance and long-suffering, ignoring the fact that God's kindness is intended to lead you to repentance? (5) Yes, with your hardness, your unrepentant heart, you are storing up for yourself wrath which will break forth in the day of wrath, the day when God's just judgement is revealed. (6) As Scripture says, he will render to every man according to his works. (7) To those who with patient endurance look beyond their own well-doing to glory, honour, and incorruption, he will render eternal life. (8) For those who are out for quick and selfish profit on their own account, and disobey the truth and obey unrighteousness, there will be wrath and anger. (9) Tribulation and anguish will fall upon every human soul that works that which is evil – Jew first and Gentile too; (10) glory, honour, and peace will be for everyone who works that which is good – Jew first and Gentile too; (11) for God shows no favouritism.

Paul has argued that the visible degradation of pagan life proves that the wrath of God (one aspect of his righteousness) is now being poured out upon those who have rejected him. But there exist those who join in Paul's condemnation of moral wickedness: can it be that these escape condemnation and are in no need of the Gospel? It is with this question that Paul now deals. It is not till *v.* 17 that he turns specifically to the problem of the Jews; here, as *vv.* 9 ff., 12–16, show, his thought applies to both Gentiles and Jews. He addresses his readers directly, using the second person singular, and an occasional vocative (**My good man,** *v.* 1). These features are characteristic of the so-called diatribe style, affected by philosophical teachers and preachers of the time. It often becomes easier to follow Paul's arguments if the reader imagines the apostle face to face with a heckler, who makes interjections and receives replies which sometimes are

1 ℵ C lat and some other authorities read, 'For we know'. This reading, though well attested, is surely wrong. Paul is not here supporting the statement of *v.* 1, but introducing a new thought.

withering and brusque. It is by no means impossible that some of the arguments in Romans first took shape in this way, in the course of debates in synagogue or market place.

At the beginning of the paragraph the connection of thought is difficult. The first sentence begins with a particle (διό) which normally means 'therefore'. Sometimes, it is true, it is no more than a conjunctive particle, but it is best not to assume that it is without argumentative force unless attempts to explain it otherwise fail. One solution is to regard i. 32b as a parenthesis. The particle then connects with i. 32a: Men know God's verdict on such sinners as are described in i. 29 ff.; *therefore* the man who judges proves himself to be without excuse, for he sins (see below), and in the act of judging proves that he knows what is right. Within this connection there may also be a contrast between those who approve (i. 32b) and those who judge. It is also however possible, and may be better, to look back to the beginning of the preceding paragraph, to i. 18–23. The list of particular evils later in the paragraph, significant as it is, is nevertheless in a sense detachable, and the connection of thought could be: all men have rejected the knowledge of God (and show the fact by their behaviour), refusing him the glory and gratitude that are his due (i. 21), all *therefore* are under his judgement; and this includes those whose rejection of God is more subtle than that of the murderer, thief, or adulterer.

Paul's own words now become clear. **That means that, whoever you are** (Jew or pagan moral philosopher – in view of *vv.* 9, 10 it is very difficult to accept the view that only Jews are in mind here), **whenever you act as judge you are without excuse, for in judging someone else you condemn yourself, since you who judge practise the same conduct as he.** The last clause is fundamental to the argument. The judge is without excuse *if he does wrong*, because *ex hypothesi* he knows the law – he of all men cannot plead ignorance. In fact, says Paul, he does the same things as the man he judges. This cannot mean that the critic also practises homosexual perversions and the like. The moral purity of the Jews was their legitimate boast, and moral philosophers such as Epictetus and Marcus Aurelius may have been prigs but were certainly not hypocrites. Paul's point is that in the very act of judging (ἐν ᾧ κρίνεις) the judge is involved in the same conduct as the man he condemns. Behind all the sins of i. 29 ff. lies the sin of idolatry, which reveals man's ambition to put himself in the place of God and so to be his own Lord. But this is precisely what the judge does, when he assumes the right to condemn his fellow-creatures. All alike fall under the condemnation of i. 21 and are in view of and as stated in i. 19, 20, without excuse.

2   At this point the objector speaks. **Now we know** introduces his complaint: cf. iii. 19; vii. 14. It seems to be a Jew who speaks – it is

perhaps not wrong to say, the Jew in Paul himself. **'God's judgement on those who practise such things is fair'** – that is, there is no favouritism (*v.* 11) in it. Paul agrees; he has just argued that God may justly visit Gentile sinners with wrath. But there is a qualification to come. **But, knowing this, do you think, my man, that you, who** 3 **judge those who practise such things as these and do them yourself, will escape God's judgement?** The second 'you' is emphatic: Do you suppose that *you* of all men will escape? The objector doubtless did suppose this, and not without reason, for the visible handing over to reprobate mind and behaviour (i. 24, 26, 28) which was the token of God's wrath upon Gentile sinners, did not apply to him. He was rather the object of God's kindness. But this was a privilege he had misinterpreted. He is now to be enlightened.

Is it that you despise the wealth of his kindness (χρηστότης), 4 **his forbearance** (cf. iii. 26; ix. 22) **and long-suffering** (μακροθυμία)? The full force of this accusation will be felt if we set beside it words from Wisdom (which Paul evidently knew). At the end of Wisdom xiv stands a list of pagan vices, similar to that which Paul has given in i. 29 ff. The author continues (xv. 1–4): But thou, our God, art gracious (χρηστός) and true, long-suffering (μακρόθυμος), and in mercy ordering all things. For even if we sin, we are thine, knowing thy dominion; but we shall not sin, knowing that we are accounted thine: for to know thee is perfect righteousness, yea, to know thy dominion is the root of immortality. For neither did any evil device of man lead us astray, nor yet the painters' fruitless labour, a form stained with various colours.

This passage describes the critic Paul has in mind. He is (he thinks) superior to the idolater; even if he does sin he avoids the really fundamental sin of idolatry, and he belongs to the people of God, and is thereby assured of salvation. But God shows no such favouritism as is assumed here; judgement looks to deeds, not privilege. The Jew boasts of God's goodness; in fact he despises it, **ignoring the fact that God's kindness is intended to lead you to repentance.** The fact that judgement has not yet begun to be executed upon him (as upon the Gentiles) has led him not to humble gratitude but to boasting (*v.* 17); he has abused God's grace. He will, however, make no profit out of his attitude. **With your hardness, your unrepentant heart** – these 5 correspond exactly to the despising of God's mercy (*v.* 4) – **you are storing up for yourself wrath which will break forth in the day of wrath, the day when God's just judgement is revealed.**

Of course, the Jew was looking forward to a day of wrath (Zeph. i. 15); but for him also that day will be darkness and not light (cf. Amos v. 18). It will be a day when righteous judgement is revealed, and the wrathful sentence of i. 18 is confirmed.

It is the present which is sadly misunderstood by the Jew. (1) It is marked by God's forbearance and mercy, which the Jew takes as a privilege that he possesses in his own right, whereas they ought to bring him to his knees in penitence and gratitude. (2) He supposes that by his cherishing of the law he is storing up for himself merit with God; in fact it is wrath which he is storing up. (3) Paul subtly inverts the common belief that the wicked received their few rewards in this life in order to have unmixed punishment in the next, and the good received their few punishments in this life in order to have unmixed reward in the next. In his view, the virtuous Jews (and other critics of the wicked) are now being spared only that (if they do not repent) they may receive their full share of wrath hereafter.

When the judgement is held, national privilege, and an attitude of
6 moral superiority, will be irrelevant: **As Scripture says, he will render to every man according to his works.** Paul does not himself say that he is quoting Scripture, but there can be little doubt that he intends a reference to be understood; see Ps. lxii. 12; Prov. xxiv. 12; Jer. xvii. 10; in the New Testament compare Matt. xvi. 27; 2 Cor. v. 10; 2 Tim. iv. 14; 1 Pet. i. 17; Rev. ii. 23; xx. 12; xxii. 12. His own Bible tells the Jew that he can appeal only to what he himself has done, not to what others have left undone. This emphasis persists throughout the chapter; see *vv.* 7, 9, 10, 13, etc. Not hearing the law, being the proud and privileged possessor of it, but doing it is what matters.

This emphasis upon works is intelligible in the present context; but is it compatible with Paul's theology of grace and faith? The answer to this serious and important question must inevitably begin, 'It depends on what you mean by works'. The next two verses, which form a balanced couplet, point to Paul's meaning, and demand detailed consideration.

7 Paul deals first with the reward of **eternal life.** This is the opposite of corruption (Gal. vi. 8), and describes not the blessedness of the Christian life in this world but the greater blessedness of life beyond the final judgement. It will be bestowed on **those who with patient endurance look beyond their own well-doing to glory, honour, and incorruption.**

'Patient endurance' (ὑπομονή) occurs frequently in Paul's writings. It is closely related to hope; see especially viii. 24 f.; 1 Thess. i. 3; cf. 1 Cor. xiii. 7. It suggests a readiness to look beyond the present moment, to see the full meaning of the present, and, in particular, of the things men do in the present, not in themselves but in the future, that is (for one who looks upon the future in the biblical manner), in God. Paul's words are very awkwardly co-ordinated – literally the phrase runs 'in patient endurance of (a) good work' – but the meaning appears to be that suggested in the translation. This is confirmed both by the words that follow, and by the parallel sentence in the next verse. Those who view their own activity with patient endurance attest thereby that they are seeking what is not to be found in any human being and doing. Glory and incorruption (to a less extent honour) are matters which are exclusively in God's gift; they are eschatological terms. For glory, see viii. 18, 21; ix. 23; 1 Cor. xv. 43 (where *dis*honour suggests that honour may be regarded as a synonym of glory), and of course the common phrase, 'glory of *God*'; for incorruption, see 1 Cor. xv. 42, 50, 53 f. The reward of eternal life, then, is promised to those who do not regard their good works as an end in themselves, but see them as marks not of human achievement but of hope in God. Their trust is not in their good works, but in God, the only source of glory, honour, and incorruption.

The second member in Paul's couplet deals with the recompense of **wrath and anger**. In this verse the construction changes. One might 8 have expected Paul to put *wrath and anger* in the accusative, writing (in parallel with *v.* 7), *To those ... God will render wrath and anger*. The variation is insignificant; much more important is the question, Who are those who will be visited with wrath and anger? **Those who are out for quick and selfish profit on their own account, and disobey the truth and obey unrighteousness.**

In *v.* 7, the vital word, on which the meaning of the sentence turns, was 'patient endurance'. In *v.* 8 also there is a single Greek word (ἐριθεία) which is vital to the thought, but many English words are needed to express it – 'those who are out for quick and selfish profit on their own account'. The rendering of RV ('them that are factious') was probably based upon the only pre-Christian passages in which the word is known to occur. These are in Aristotle's *Politics* (1302 b 4; 1303 a 14), and refer to the hiring of partisans. The word is derived from ἔριθος, a hireling; ἐριθεύειν, to act as a hireling, to work for pay, to behave as, to show the spirit of, a hireling. A meaning based on this fundamental sense is suitable to all the Pauline passages in which the word is employed (2 Cor. xii. 20; Gal. v. 20; Phil. i. 17; ii. 3). In the first two of these the thought of division, of factiousness, is covered by other words, so that to give this meaning to ἐριθεία is to introduce a measure of repetition. Compare also James iii. 14, 16; Ignatius, *Philad.* viii. 2. It is clear (as the passages in Aristotle demonstrate) that it is possible to hire a claque; men who will do anything, or nearly anything, for appropriate reward can be found and used in the political field, about which Aristotle was writing. Paul however was discussing not politics but theology, and uses an acquaintance with hirelings, which he shares with Aristotle, in a different way. That he is thinking of men who form a faction against God is not a convincing suggestion.[1] It seems very probable that Paul intends by means of this

---

1 Paul's word is not connected with ἔρις (which he uses elsewhere to mean strife, contentiousness), though very many both in antiquity and in more recent times have believed this.

word to describe the motives (the Greek preposition ἐξ suggests that their actions rise *out of* the quality just defined) of those who look on their works as achievements of their own, complete in themselves, by means of which they may acquire rights. This makes them as disobedient to the truth (of God's sovereign lordship) and as prone to unrighteousness (rebellion against their Creator) as the men of i. 18, upon whom God's wrath is with evident justice poured out. They too will be the objects of wrath and anger.

In a second balanced couplet Paul repeats the thought of the last,
9 with one significant addition. **Tribulation and anguish will fall upon every human soul that works that which is evil – Jew first**
10 **and Gentile too; glory, honour, and peace will be for everyone who works that which is good – Jew first and Gentile too.** Tribulation and anguish are the result of wrath and anger (*v.* 8); to glory and honour (*v.* 7) is added peace (see on *v.* 1). The repeated reference in these verses to Jew and Gentile makes it 'clear that what is said in *vv.* 6–8 is said with reference to Jews and Gentiles alike' (Cranfield 149), and it is hard to see why this should not apply also to *vv.* 1–5. In *v.* 4 **forbearance** (ἀνοχή) recalls iii. 26; cf. Acts xiv. 16; xvii. 30.

The analysis of works presupposed by *vv.* 7 f. has the important consequence of dissolving the barrier between Jew and Gentile. The former no longer possesses the exclusive privilege of performing good works done in obedience to the revealed law. The 'good' which God will reward does not consist in 'works of law', but in patient seeking, in looking beyond human activity to its divine complement; the 'bad' which he punishes may include good deeds, 'works of law', done in a servile spirit with a view to profit. Both for good and ill the Jew retains a certain priority (cf. i. 16) – not necessarily an enviable priority; but inevitably must be added – and the Gentile too.

11   This inclusion is ultimately grounded upon the fact that **God shows no favouritism.** His election of the Jews (cf. chs. ix–xi), and the undoubted advantage which they possess (iii. 1 f.), do not mean that they, or any other self-righteous, self-appointed judges of mankind, enjoy an exclusive right to his favour.

6 CONSCIENCE

CHAPTER ii. 12–16

(12) Those who have sinned outside the sphere of the law shall also perish outside the sphere of the law; those who have sinned within the sphere of the law shall be judged by means of the law – (13) for it is not those who listen to the law who are righteous with God; no, it is those who do the law who shall be

**justified. (14) For when Gentiles (who have not the law) do by
nature the things that the law requires, then, since they have not
the law, they are a law for themselves. (15) They show the effect
of the law written in their hearts; their conscience bears witness
with the law, and their inward thoughts in mutual debate accuse or
else excuse them, (16) in the day in which, according to my Gospel,
God judges the secret things of men through Jesus Christ.**

In the preceding paragraph Paul has reached the conclusion that Jew
and Gentile are equal before God. To this statement there is one
evident objection. The difference between Jew and Gentile is not
simply a matter of race, but of religion, or rather, of revelation. God
through Moses gave the law to Israel; this was an advantage the
Gentiles never had. The objection, however, is not insuperable. In i. 19
ff. Paul showed that the Gentile was guilty of a responsible act of
rebellion against the Creator; lack of a special revelation did not excuse
him. In the same way, lack of revealed law is now seen not to open a
way of escape from judgement. The essential difference between Jew
and Gentile did not constitute ground for favourable treatment on one
side or the other. The fact is first laid down in general terms: **Those 12
who have sinned outside the sphere of the law shall also perish
outside the sphere of the law.** The law of Moses is the plainest
statement (outside the Christian revelation) of the claim of God upon
his creatures, but the claim is independent of the statement of it, and
failure to acknowledge the claim can never be anything other than
culpable and the result is simply destruction.

So far a Jewish reader would have applauded Paul. But he
proceeds, **Those who have sinned within the sphere of the law
shall be judged by means of the law.** Instead of *shall perish* Paul now
writes *shall be judged.* Law made judgement possible, and supplies a
means by which man's failure and destruction can be analysed. The
law is not a talisman calculated to preserve those who possess it. It is
an instrument of judgement, and sin is not less sin, but more, when it
is wrought within the sphere of the law (cf. vii. 13). **For it is not those 13
who listen to the law** (for example, Sabbath by Sabbath, in
synagogue) **who are righteous with God; no, it is those who do the
law** (by obeying it) **who shall be justified.** For the contrast between
hearing and doing compare James i. 22. It is also common in Rabbinic
teaching (e.g. *Aboth*, iii. 10: He whose works exceed his wisdom, his
wisdom endures; but he whose wisdom exceeds his works, his wisdom
does not endure), and Paul must have been familiar with it. Elsewhere
he argues that the essence of the law is (as the law itself declares) a
matter of doing; see x. 5, and especially Gal. iii. 10 ff. What the law
commands is good (cf. vii. 12; Gal. iii. 21); if only men would not
merely listen to it but do it, they would be righteous.

It is important to pause for a moment upon the word *righteous* (δίκαιος). We have already considered the meaning of God's righteousness (δικαιοσύνη) (above, pp. 30 f.; further, pp. 69 f.), and pointed out (p. 30) that, in Jewish thought, before salvation could be enjoyed the righteousness of man must also be established. This means that man, arraigned in God's court, must secure from his judge a favourable verdict. The vital question, therefore, which determines man's eternal fate, is how he can achieve this state of 'rightness' with God. The state itself is not a moral quality but a relation – a relation of gracious favour, and peace – between God and man; it could, hypothetically at least, be achieved by a perfect performance of what the law required, but certainly not by mere acquaintance with the contents of the law. The present passage refers only to the sentence, whether of condemnation or acquittal, pronounced at the last judgement; that is, it does not deal with the specifically Christian conception of justification which rests upon the anticipation of the eschatological righteousness of God in the saving event of Jesus Christ. On this much more must be said later (see pp. 73 f., 76 ff.). But it is relevant here to note the parallel between the two clauses of *v.* 13:

> Not those who listen . . . are righteous;
> Those who do . . . shall be justified.

This suggests that 'to be justified' means 'to be (or to be made) righteous'. This is not the common interpretation of Paul's usage, and the point must be discussed in detail later; here the reader may be reminded that 'righteous' describes a relation not a quality, and that accordingly 'to make righteous' does not mean 'to make virtuous', but 'to grant a verdict of acquittal'.

Paul returns to his opening assertion, which, as it stands, is open to objection. Why should the Gentile, who is not instructed by the law in the conduct that God requires, perish? If he cannot be tried in due process of law why should he be punished? Paul himself asserts that apart from the law sin (at least in the sense of positive transgression) cannot exist (v. 13; vii. 7, 9, *et al.*). The answer is that the Gentile is not really outside the sphere of law, though he is of course outside the 14 sphere of the law of Moses. **For when Gentiles (who have not the law) do by nature the things that the law requires, they are a law for themselves;** hence the possibility of sin and judgement. For, whatever modern usage may have made of his phrase, Paul does not mean that the Gentiles are free to make their own rules and do as they please.

It is implied by the construction that Gentiles sometimes do the things which the law requires (literally, the things of the law, τὰ τοῦ νόμου). Paul does not say, If Gentiles were to do...but when, or whenever (ὅταν) Gentiles do the things that the law requires. What are these things? Clearly not the detailed precepts of the Mosaic code: in *vv.* 26 f. Paul says that the 'uncircumcision' (which in the nature of the case does not observe the ritual law) may keep the righteous requirements of the law, and fulfil it. Again, Paul never distinguishes between 'ritual law' and 'moral law'; and in any case to suggest that the Gentiles kept the moral law would make nonsense of Paul's thought as a whole, since in the next chapter he conducts a detailed argument to prove that all men without exception, Jews and Greeks, are 'under sin' (iii. 9; cf. iii. 19, 23; xi. 32; Gal. iii. 22). What the law requires is ultimately neither ceremonial nor moral conformity (though wilful non-conformity would be sin) but believing obedience, or obedient faith (cf. i. 5). This (when the matter is viewed from the human side) is the only tolerable basis of relationship between man and his Creator, and, just as the Gentile finds (or ought to find) the creature–Creator relationship written in the natural universe (i. 19 ff.) so also he finds (or ought to find) it written in his heart. Some, after all, do glorify God and give thanks to him.

When man recognizes and accepts this relationship he may be said to do what the law requires 'by nature' (φύσει).[1] This word arises out of the notion of growth (φύειν, to grow), but comes to mean *the way* things grow, hence what they have (in virtue of their own proper being) become, their nature. Thus there is a nature (φύσις) of an individual (which gives him his individuality), of a genus (in which the several individuals comprising it share), and finally of the cosmos. This inward nature of things Aristotle distinguished from law (νόμος), law being for him convention;[2] but the Stoics taught that true law was rooted in nature.[3] Now the Jews had come to believe that their law was the ground and means of creation,[4] so that the Hellenistic synagogue was able to adopt the Stoic doctrine of 'natural law', with the further proposition that *their* (revealed) law was the supreme expression of natural law (cf. *v.* 20). This notion appears most clearly

---

1 It would be possible to take this word with the earlier part of the sentence: When Gentiles who by nature (i.e., by birth) have not the law...The analogy with Gal. iv. 8 however shows that if Paul had meant this he would probably have written τὰ φύσει μὴ νόμον ἔχοντα.
2 E.g. *Nicomachean Ethics*, 1133 a 30: Money is 'what it is not naturally (φύσει) but by custom or law (νόμῳ)'.
3 E.g. Cicero, *Laws*, I. vi. 8: 'Law is the highest reason (*summa ratio*), planted in nature, which commands those things which are to be done, and prohibits their opposites'.
4 E.g. *Aboth*, iii. 15: '...it was made known to them that to them was given the precious instrument [the law] by which the world was created'.

in Philo,[1] and was evidently of great propaganda value. It can scarcely be doubted that this Stoic-Jewish use of nature was in Paul's mind, though he makes of it something different from what Philo made of it.[2]

There is, then, something, Paul argues, in the very pattern of created existence which should, and sometimes does, lead the Gentiles to an attitude of humble, grateful, dependent creatureliness. When this takes place they are a law for themselves. In saying this Paul draws again upon the language of Hellenistic Judaism. Philo, for example, speaks of the patriarchs (who since they lived before Moses could not know the law in its written form) as themselves 'laws endowed with life and reason' (*Abraham*, 5). Paul does not go as far as this (see the next verse), but far enough to justify what he had said in *vv.* 9 ff.; the Gentile comes into judgement with the Jew, even though the Jew comes first.

The relation between man, nature, and the law requires further
15 elucidation. The Gentiles who do the things required by the law **show the effect of the law written in their hearts**. Some take these Gentiles, who do the things that the law requires and have the effect of the law written in their hearts, to be Gentile Christians. Against this see Wilckens 1. 133, who notes that Paul writes not 'The Gentiles' but 'Gentiles', that is, some, not all. Gentiles therefore cannot be equivalent to Gentile Christians. It is not the law itself that is written in their hearts; this would imply the fulfilment of Jer. xxxi. 33. In the phrase 'the effect of the law' (τὸ ἔργον τοῦ νόμου; contrast Paul's use of ἔργα νόμου, works of the law; see p. 67), the genitive is probably subjective. The law has, as it were, left its stamp upon their minds; this stamp is **their conscience**. Once more, Paul draws on Stoic terminology. By the Stoics, and Philo, the conscience is often described as an accuser, or convictor; in Romans it is a witness (so here, also ix. 1; cf. 2 Cor. i. 12). This is in accord with the etymology of the word, which in ancient use is a backward-looking and judging agent rather than forward-looking and directing. It implies man's ability to detach himself from himself and to view his character and actions independently. He is thus able to act as a witness for or against himself. His conscience is not so much the bar at which his conduct is tried, as a major witness, who can be called on either side as the case may be.

---

1 E.g. *Creation of the World*, 3: 'The world (κόσμος) is in harmony with the law (νόμος), and the law with the world, and . . . the man who observes the law is constituted thereby a loyal citizen of the world (κοσμοπολίτης), regulating his days by the purpose and will of nature (φύσις), in accordance with which the entire world itself also is administered'.
2 It has been suggested that Paul here alludes to the precepts given to Noah (Gen. ix. 1–7), and believed to be binding upon Gentiles. But there is no evidence whatever in support of this. Paul is not interested in Noah, but goes back from Moses to creation.

This role of the conscience appears in the following words: their conscience **bears witness with the law, and their inward thoughts in mutual debate accuse or else excuse them.** This clause is sometimes taken differently, and is said to mean that there are three witnesses: (1) the Gentiles themselves, (2) their consciences, and (3) their inward thoughts. But it is better to take it as suggested here. All that Paul says is that the conscience bears witness with (συμμαρτυρεῖ) – he does not say with what. It suits his argument if we think of the conscience bearing witness with the divine law whose imprint it is; the clause 'their inward thoughts ... excuse them' then describes the operation of conscience. The thoughts enter into debate (this is an attempt to render the obscure Greek μεταξὺ ἀλλήλων); some are for acquittal, some for conviction.

The connection of the next verse with the context is obscure. Many expositors think that it must be taken with *v.* 13, *vv.* 14 f. being regarded either as a parenthesis or as having been misplaced. This view has much to commend it. To say, 'Not hearers but doers of the law shall be justified in the day when God judges ...' makes excellent sense, whereas the alternative (connecting *v.* 16 with *v.* 15) seems to imply that the Gentile conscience comes into operation only at judgement day. But the objection is not serious. Whatever the conscience may do inwardly in men's experience, what matters ultimately is the witness borne by it **in   16 the day in which ... God judges.**

Two problems remain in this verse. In full it runs, In the day in which, **according to my Gospel,** God judges **the secret things of men through Jesus Christ.** How can judgement be part of the Gospel? And what does Paul mean by *my* Gospel (cf. xvi. 25)? The connection between Gospel and judgement is closer than is sometimes recognized; see on i. 16. 'My Gospel' is not that God will judge the world, since all Christians and all Jews believed this; nor is it (as Lagrange suggests) that God will judge the world through Jesus Christ, since all Christians believed this. It is unlikely too that 'my Gospel' is that the heathen also come within the jurisdiction of the Messiah; it is doubtful whether this conviction was peculiar to Paul. The answer to both questions appears to lie in the emphasis laid upon the 'secret things'. God's judgement does not rest upon the observable behaviour of either Gentile or Jew (cf. *v.* 29), but upon the secret things of the heart, the faith which a man has to himself before God (xiv. 22). This is judgement, but it is also good news for the sinner, to whom it opens the prospect of justification by faith.

7 JUDGEMENT AND THE JEW

CHAPTER ii. 17–29

(17) But if you bear the name 'Jew', and put your trust in the law,

and make your boast in God, (18) and know his will, and (instructed by the law) are able to judge what is significant and good; (19) and if you are confident that you are a guide of the blind, a light for those who are in darkness, (20) an instructor of fools, a teacher of babes, provided with the embodiment of knowledge and truth in the law – (21) well then, you who teach your neighbour, do you not teach yourself? you who preach that men ought not to steal, do you steal? (22) you who say that men ought not to commit adultery, do you commit adultery? you who regard an idol as an abomination, do you commit sacrilege? (23) You, who make your boast in the law, by your transgression of the law dishonour God. (24) For (as Scripture says) 'On your account the name of God is blasphemed among the Gentiles'.

(25) This is what I mean. Your circumcision is profitable to you – if you practise the law. But if you are a transgressor of the law, your circumcision is turned into uncircumcision. (26) If then (to take the opposite point of view) an uncircumcised man keeps the righteous requirements of the law, will not his uncircumcision be counted as circumcision? (27) Yes, and the man by race uncircumcised if he fulfils the law will judge you, who, for all your observance of the letter, and your circumcision, are a transgressor of the law. (28) For not the outward Jew is a Jew, nor is outward fleshly circumcision circumcision; (29) but the secret Jew is a Jew, and circumcision of the heart, in spirit not letter, is circumcision. He is a Jew, whose due comes not from men but from God.

All men stand under the judgement of God: the licentious, and the timid who would be licentious if they dared; no less, the moral critics who look with disfavour upon the grossness of their fellow-men. These critics preach virtue, some from the philosopher's platform, some from the pulpit of the synagogue. In *vv.* 1–11 Paul addressed both groups; now he turns to the supreme critic of his fellows, the self-righteous Jew. We should probably not be wrong in the guess that the most notorious example of the class was the unconverted Paul. The paragraph as a whole may properly be headed 'Judgement and the Jew', but towards the end Paul further clarifies the position by introducing the Gentiles again.

17   **But** introduces a formal counterpart to *v.* 12, and indicates that Jews were not exclusively in mind in ii. 1–16. **If you bear the name** 'Jew' – perhaps a contrast is intended with the true Jew, who is a Jew secretly (*v.* 29) – **and put your trust in the law,** literally, rest upon the law. The Jew relies upon the law to provide him with a secure standing before God. It was to provide him with a means of remaining within the God-given convenant that it was given. If further you **make**

your boast in God . . . confident that because of his promises to the fathers of the race you are certain of salvation. These are the grounds of confidence which enable the Jew to face the world, sure that he is in a position to pass sentence on it. The Jew whom Paul has in mind will start from such conviction as that of Wisdom xv. 2, Even if we sin, we are thine, knowing thy power; but we shall not sin, because we know that we are accounted thine. See the whole context in Wisdom. He is wrong at every point. As soon as he boasts of his privileges he loses them (cf. iii. 2; ix. 1–5). As a Jew, he is the supremely vulnerable man. He cannot rest upon the law, because the law accuses him; he cannot glory in God (though there is of course a sense in which this is proper; cf. Jer. ix. 24; 1 Cor. i. 31; 2 Cor. x. 17), because God is his Judge. The next clauses are hardly more than corollaries of what has been said.

If you know his will (literally, *the* will; cf. perhaps 1 Cor. xvi. 12), **18 and (instructed by the law) judge what is significant and good** (an alternative translation of δοκιμάζεις τὰ διαφέροντα is, 'try, have experience of, things that differ', that is, 'be acquainted with, and know the difference between, good and evil'; but this is less probable); **and if you are confident that you are a guide of the blind, a light 19 for those who are in darkness** (cf. Isa. xlii. 6 f.; xlix. 6; Matt. xv. 14; xxiii. 16, 24), **an instructor of fools, a teacher of babes, provided 20 with the embodiment of knowledge and truth in the law –**. The sentence breaks off. Paul has (characteristically) forgotten how it began, and starts again.

The Jew is persuaded that in the (book of the) law he has truth in visible form. Paul does not disagree with him; he himself says little less in vii. 12, 14, though he does not fail to add the complementary negative truth (e.g. vii. 10, 11, 13, 21, 23).

Paul does not disagree; but, with an abrupt break in the construction, faces his compatriot with a fresh challenge. **Well then, you who 21 teach your neighbour, do you not teach yourself?** Since you know the truth, do you not mean to apply it? **You who preach** (κηρύσσειν, the technical term for Christian proclamation, perhaps borrowed from Jewish usage) **that men ought not to steal, do you steal?** The question to be faced here and in the next verse is whether Paul means that the Jew commits theft, adultery, and sacrilege in a literal sense. It is certainly possible to adduce instances of all three, but such instances are beside the point. Paul's argument is lost if he is compelled to rely on comparatively unusual events, and it is simply not true that the average Jewish missionary acted in this way. It was the purity of Jewish ethics (and of Jewish ethical practice as well as Jewish ethical theory) which (together with Jewish monotheism) made the deepest impression on the Gentile world. Paul's point here is the same as in *v.* 1. The fact that the actual crimes were occasionally committed adds of course some vividness to the argument, and the criminals in some sense involved the nation in their guilt; but the nation was inwardly guilty already. When theft, adultery, and sacrilege are strictly and radically understood, there is no man who is not guilty of all three. Compare Matt. v. 21–48, and the Old Testament passages quoted below.

For theft, compare Mal. iii. 8 f. Israel as a whole has robbed God of the honour due to him; even their boasting in God (*v.* 17) is a subtle arrogance which gives to man what is due to God.

22 **You who say that men ought not to commit adultery, do you commit adultery?** For Old Testament parallels see Hos. i–iii *passim*; Jer. iii. 8. Israel as the bride of God can hardly escape the charge of adultery.

You who regard an idol as an abomination (this attitude is written all over Jewish literature), **do you commit sacrilege?**[1] (RV: Dost thou rob temples? – but the word is conclusively proved by inscriptions and papyri to have a wider meaning). The Jew regards an idol with horror because it claims a devotion to which only the true God is entitled; but when he exalts himself as judge and lord over his fellow-creatures he renders this devotion to – himself! Paul's word may have a more specific sense than this (which nevertheless remains as the theological core of what Paul means). 'To rob temples' suggests one who goes about from one religious centre to another, pilfering the offerings of the worshippers. In English however one could equally say 'to be a temple-robber', and understand this with reference only to the Temple in Jerusalem. *Do you profane* the Temple of God himself? This would be no new charge; see especially Jer. vii. 1–15, where the Temple is robbed of its true meaning by worshippers who were willing to supply it with material resources.

The construction changes, and this may well be taken to mean that the next sentence is not a question (though grammatically there is no reason why it should not be one) but a statement summing up the position that has now been reached. It is so taken in the 26th edition of

23 the Nestle-Aland Greek Testament. **You, who make your boast in the law** (cf. *v.* 17), **by your transgression of the law dishonour God.** This is not merely Paul's opinion. It is the verdict of Scripture itself.

24 **For (as Scripture says) 'On your account the name of God is blasphemed among the Gentiles'** (from Isa. lii. 5, quoted after the LXX rather than the Hebrew; cf. Ezek. xxxvi. 20, 23). The greater the privilege, the greater the abuse; the revolt of the people of God is the most subtle, and the most grievous, of all. Given the privilege of acting

---

1 It is interesting to note that theft, adultery, and sacrilege often stand side by side in lists of vices and sins; so, e.g., Philo, *On the Confusion of Languages*, 163 (...when he attempts to commit theft or adultery, or murder or sacrilege...). Except for murder (which is not mentioned here), Philo uses the same words as Paul.

as God's signpost in the world they have chosen to point not to God but
to themselves. The next verse will give a special example.

Up to this point, Paul has dealt with the Jewish privilege of the law
in general terms. Now a particular commandment is invoked – in
response, we may guess, to a Jewish objector, who interrupts Paul's
argument: 'You say that the Jew has no advantage over the Gentile;
but we have what he has not – circumcision and the covenant that it
represents'. Paul replies, **Your circumcision is profitable to you – if** 25
you practise the law. This sentence throws light upon what Paul
means by practising, or doing, the law (cf. *vv.* 14 f.). The Jew would
reply to Paul that the contrast he implies, between circumcision and
'practising the law', is unreal; circumcision is part of the law, and you
cannot 'practise the law' without being circumcised. But for Paul,
'doing the things which the law requires' does not mean carrying out
the detailed precepts written in the Pentateuch, but fulfilling that
relation with God to which the law points; and this proves in the last
resort to be a relation not of legal obedience but of faith (iii. 31; ix. 31,
32; x. 6 ff.). This revolutionary conviction leads to the striking
conclusions stated in the remainder of the paragraph. Thus **if you are**
a transgressor of the law, your circumcision is turned into
uncircumcision. The Jew who boasts of his circumcision as a visible
badge of his superiority, as a certain passport to salvation, thereby
abandons his proper relation with God and automatically his circumcision is annulled; that is, it no longer is circumcision in the only true
sense (*v.* 29) and is no longer a valid mark of the covenant relation.
Outwardly he obeys the law, by being circumcised; inwardly he
transgresses it, by failing to recognize that to which his own
circumcision points, namely, the fact that he belongs completely to
God and has no ground of boasting in himself.

To illuminate the matter further, it is possible **to take the** 26
opposite point of view, and consider the man who does recognize
and adopt the relation with God implied by the law, even though he
stands outside the visible legal framework of Jewish life. **Then** (οὖν)
implies a logical relation between *v.* 25 and *v.* 26. The invalidation of
circumcision by neglect of the (true) requirement of the law implies
its converse. **If an uncircumcised man keeps the righteous**
requirements of the law, will not his uncircumcision be counted
as circumcision? 'Righteous requirements' here translates the plural
of the word (δικαίωμα) translated at i. 32 'righteous ordinance'. The
sense is, 'that which the law requires if a man is to be righteous with
God'; and though one answer to this question is, a complete
performance of everything written in the law (x. 5; cf. Gal. iii. 12; v. 3),
the new answer to which the eschatological activity of God in Jesus
Christ points is – faith. If an uncircumcised Gentile has this faith (and
the 'when' of the parallel in *v.* 14 suggests that the possibility is not

merely hypothetical), outward circumcision becomes irrelevant; God treats him as if he were circumcised, counting him as fully a member of his people as the born Jew. 'Will ... be counted' is significant. The passive conceals (in Semitic manner) a reference to God, and the verb 'to count', or 'to reckon' is one that appears at key-points in the epistle (see especially iv. 3). No mere fiction, but a creative act of God is meant. God, who commanded circumcision, is free to dispense with it.

Paul is not appealing for tolerance of the man who, in his uncircumcision, stands outside the religious framework of the holy
27 people. The Jew must seek, not grant, tolerance. **The man by race** (literally, by nature, the word of *v.* 14; as regards circumcision, the Gentile is still in a state of nature) **uncircumcised if he fulfils the law** (see above on *vv.* 14, 26; Paul nowhere else uses this verb (τελεῖν) of the law; perhaps the best interpretation is 'give full effect to' – 2 Cor. xii. 9; Gal. v. 16; also Rom. x. 4; James ii. 8) **will judge you** (for this use of 'judge' cf. Matt. xii. 41 f.), **who, for all your observance of the letter, and your circumcision** (cf. iv. 11, 13), **are a transgressor of the law.** Again, Paul makes clear beyond all doubt what he means by keeping, and by transgressing, the law. It is possible to neglect so weighty a command as circumcision – and fulfil the law; it is possible to observe the letter of the law, including circumcision – and transgress the law. This is not Rabbinic Judaism, or any other orthodox kind of Judaism. Paul's new Christian conviction, that Jesus, whom the law had cast out, crucified, and cursed, was the risen Lord in heaven, led him to a revaluation of religion, and in particular of the law, the basis of his own national religion, far more radical than is often perceived. He not merely had a new faith, and a new theology; in the light of these he came to the conclusion that the old faith – the Old Testament and Judaism – meant something different from what he had thought. It was not a closed system, complete in itself, requiring only strict and unimaginative obedience; for those who had eyes to see it pointed forward to Christ, and the Gospel which was the power of God unto salvation – for everyone who had faith.

The question is inevitably raised whether Paul's criticism of Judaism is fair. It is a question that will arise more than once in the course of this commentary as it is provoked by various passages in Romans; it has often been answered in the negative. Its complexity however has not always been perceived. It is necessary in the first place to recognize that not two (Judaism and Christianity) but at least three entities are involved: Pauline Christianity, Judaizing Christianity, and Judaism. Of these the third is certainly a complex factor, though a simple division into Hellenistic and Palestinian Judaism does not fit the facts. In the second place, only a very rash (one might almost say, a very ignorant) twentieth-century scholar will suppose that he understands first-century Judaism better than Paul did,

though he is of course entitled to disagree with Paul's judgement of
theological truth. A simple contrast alleging that Paul's was a theology
of grace whereas Judaism was a purely legalistic religion is as false as
the assertion that Paul taught, Let us do evil that good may come (iii.
8). That Paul believed that non-Christian Jews were in some
important matters wrong is evident; it is equally evident that he
continued to think of them as kinsmen and to long for their salvation
(ix. 1–3; x. 1). He was less patient with those who tried to make the
best of both worlds and enjoy both faiths; he was the true radical (see
Context: Festskrift til Peder Borgen (1987), pp. 26–8). The fundamental points of difference between Paul and Judaism have already been
suggested (pp. 7 ff.). Was Jesus Messiah and Lord or not? If he
was, but only if he was, it was reasonable to believe that old things had
passed away and a new creation come to birth (2 Cor. v. 17). The
second question, the answer to which turns in the end on the same
alternative, was asked explicitly by Paul in Gal. iii. 19: Why was the
law given? or, What is the law? (τί οὖν ὁ νόμος;). Given an original
covenant of grace,[1] did the law abrogate it? change it? come into a
subordinate place? What was God's intention in giving the law? The
Epistle to the Romans does not work out a systematic answer to these
questions, but the material necessary if an answer is to be given may
be collected from point to point.

   Paul proceeds to attack the question before him from a new angle.
Words like 'Jew' and 'circumcision' retain great significance, but they
require new definitions, which Paul supplies, negatively and positively, in *vv.* 28 f. The Greek of these verses is elliptical, but the
meaning is not in serious doubt. In the translation the simplest
grammatical supplements are added. **Not the outward Jew is a Jew** 28
(that is, a *real* Jew, under the new definition), **nor is outward fleshly
circumcision circumcision** (that is, *true* circumcision, under the
new definition); **but the secret Jew is a Jew, and circumcision of** 29
the heart, in spirit not letter, is circumcision. By the 'outward Jew'
Paul does not mean simply the circumcised Jew; if he did he would
merely repeat himself in the next clause. The 'outward Jew' is the Jew
marked by 'works of the law', who externalizes his religion and
esteems his membership of the people of God as a visible privilege
which he can parade before the world. He also, of course, as Paul goes
on to say, regards his circumcision as a kind of visible badge or
passport. The real Jew is distinguished not by outward signs but by an
inward obedience, virtually identical with the obedience of faith (i.
5) – what the law really requires (though it is easy to mistake this) is
faith. Circumcision requires a corresponding interpretation; the hint

1 On this see especially E. P. Sanders, *Paul and Palestinian Judaism* (1977), pp.
419–22, *et passim.*

is given by Old Testament passages that speak of the circumcision of the heart (Deut. x. 16; xxx. 6; Jer. iv. 4).

In fact, being a Jew, being circumcised, is a matter of which the truth is known only to God, who looks on the heart. By the 'secret Jew' Paul does not mean a good, modest Jew, who does not boast of his virtues or national status. The decision upon men's modesty, as upon their other virtues and their sins, is God's; the 'secret Jew', who is the true Jew, is the man who is declared to be so by God (see further below).

'Circumcision of the heart' is an Old Testament expression; cf. Deut. x. 16, where it means (as here) man's humble response to God's gracious love and election; and Jer. iv. 4, where it means repentance.

For the contrast between spirit and letter compare vii. 6; 2 Cor. iii. 6 ff. 'Letter' was probably suggested in this verse by its occurrence in *v.* 27 and means 'Letter and no more', a mechanical observance not quickened by faith on man's side, Spirit on God's. In the other passages referred to, 'spirit' means the Holy Spirit, and the possibility that it does so here also cannot be excluded;[1] probably, however, the meaning is more general – 'in a spiritual way'.

Paul concludes: **He is a Jew, whose due** (literally, praise) **comes not from men but from God.** There is a play upon words here; in Hebrew, 'Jew' is *yᵉhudi*, 'praise', *hodayah* (there are other cognate words, including a verbal form *yᵉhodeh*). The translation attempts to bring out this play. But though Paul uses a rhetorical trick his meaning is serious and profound, and points forward to the long discussion of God's elective purpose in chs. ix–xi. It is God, not man, who decides and knows what being a Jew means. All is of God's election, not of man's achievement; and so far as there exist visible traces of his purpose they are to be found not in human rites (even in rites commanded by God himself) but in humility before God, and in the absence of boasting – that is, in *not* judging (from an eminence of supposed superiority).

8 THE ADVANTAGE OF THE JEW

CHAPTER iii. 1–8

(1) What then does the Jew possess which others have not? What profit is there in circumcision? (2) Much in every way. In the first place, they were entrusted with the oracles of God. (3) And what of that? If some have proved unbelieving, will their unbelief

---

1 Cf. Odes of Solomon, xi. 1 f.: 'My heart was circumcised .... For the Most High circumcised me by his Holy Spirit'.

make void the faithfulness of God? (4) Of course not. Rather, let God be found true, though that should mean that every man (to use Scriptural language) be found a liar. Again as Scripture says, 'That thou mayest be proved right when thou speakest, and be victorious when thou enterest into judgement'.

(5) But if (as appears) our unrighteousness demonstrates God's righteousness, what shall we say? Is God, who inflicts his wrath, unjust? (Forgive these human arguments.) (6) Of course not; otherwise, how is God to judge the world? (7) Yes, but[1] if by my falsehood the truth of God increased and thereby increased his glory too, why am I actually judged to be a sinner? (8) And why should we not do evil that good may come of it? (That is what some of our detractors actually allege that we say; they will get what they deserve).

The style of this paragraph is again that of the diatribe. This may be mere literary form, but it is more probable that behind the written matter there lie real debates, though it is possible that to some extent it was Paul's own mind that formulated the objections which he proceeds to brush aside.

The argument of ch. ii seems (to the objector) to lead to the conclusion that the Jew has no advantage over the Gentile, indeed, that he is worse off; there is no good in being a Jew, and no profit (cf. ii. 25) in observing the ordinances of Judaism. **What then** (in view of 1 ch. ii) **does the Jew possess which others have not? What profit is there in circumcision?** If negative answers were returned to these questions the result would be offensive not only (as is often supposed) to Jewish national sentiment but to theology. If the Old Testament is to be believed, God did choose the Jews out of all mankind and did bestow special privileges upon them. To reduce them therefore to the level of other nations is either to accuse the Old Testament of falsehood, or to accuse God of failing to carry out his plans. It is this theological objection to his thesis that Paul is bound to meet.

What then is the advantage of the Jew? Paul answers, **Much in 2 every way.** Just as the objection is not prompted by nationalist sentiment, so Paul's answer is not the victory of patriotism over logic. Paul consistently maintains a real advantage for the Jew, though it is a terrible one. He is first in election, first in judgement, instructed out of the law, judged by means of the law. He stands, as it were, nearer to the scene on which the divine purpose is worked out – a dangerous, but real, privilege (cf. i. 16; ii. 9 f., 12, 18 ff., 25), a blessing that may turn out to be a curse.

1 Instead of 'Yes, but' (δέ), 'for' (γάρ) is strongly supported (by B D G ω); but it gives precisely the wrong connection between *vv.* 6 and 7.

'Much in every way' is a large claim. Paul sets out as if to support it by means of a list. Paul's word (πρῶτον) may be translated, 'Of first importance', but, since God's gifts are all important and can hardly be arranged in order of merit, it is better to take it as **In the first place**, even though the first point is never followed by a second. This is not because he can think of only one 'advantage'–in ix. 4 f. he mentions more; but because his thought is deflected, and he never follows out to its conclusion the argument here begun.

The first advantage in fact turns out to include all the others that might be listed. It is that the Jews **were entrusted with the oracles of God**. In a Jewish context 'oracles' can hardly mean anything other than Scripture, and it was to the Jews that the divine speech recorded in Scripture was given. The parallel in ix. 4 suggests that the *whole* Old Testament is meant. It is therefore not legitimate to restrict the 'oracles' to the law (or the ten commandments), or to the prophecies of the Old Testament (as if the argument were, The Jew gets no good out of the law, but he has after all the messianic promises). To possess the law is itself an advantage. Israel knows the mind of God (cf. ii. 18), and cannot deny the total moral claim which he makes upon his creatures (see *vv.* 10–18).

3   **And what of that?** Paul continues in the brusque personal style of the diatribe. The advantage is one which nothing can destroy, since it depends not upon man but upon God. **If some have proved unbelieving, will their unbelief make void the faithfulness of**

4   **God? Of course not.** 'The faithfulness of God' translates a phrase (τὴν πίστιν τοῦ θεοῦ) which could, in other contexts, mean 'faith in God'. The analogous phrase is usually translated (e.g. at iii. 22) 'faith in Jesus Christ'. It may be that there are passages where 'the faith' or 'the faithfulness of Jesus Christ' would be a better rendering. Compare i. 17, where 'from (God's) faithfulness to (man's) faith' is at least worthy of consideration. Here the genitive must be possessive (or subjective), and the noun must refer to the quality of faithfulness (to one's promise, or to one's character). God has given his word, and whatever men may do or not do, he will keep it. This is supported from Scripture itself.

Let God be found true, though that should mean that every man (to use Scriptural language) be found a liar. Only the concluding words are drawn from Ps. cxvi. 11. The truth, or faithfulness, of God is to be believed, even though maintaining it (in the teeth of human unfaithfulness) leads to the conclusion that all men are liars. He will always be true to his word, faithful to his promise.

Again as Scripture says, 'That thou mayest be proved right when thou speakest, and be victorious when thou enterest into judgement'. Paul quotes Ps. li. 4, agreeing word for word with the

LXX. The Old Testament affirms that God will always be found in the right over against men. Their untruth and unfaithfulness will serve only to set off his faithfulness. Paul, following the Psalmist, pictures a scene in court, where God and men plead against each other; when this happens, God is sure to win his case and leave the court in the right.[1]

The Jew then has an advantage which he can never lose, since it rests not upon his merit but upon God's faithfulness to his declared word. In saying this, however, Paul has laid himself open to a new objection, brought out and answered in diatribe style.

The objector (we may suppose) speaks: **But if (as appears) our 5 unrighteousness demonstrates God's righteousness, what shall we say?** The connection of thought is best brought out by recalling the part of Ps. li. 4 that Paul does not quote in *v.* 4. It runs: Against thee, thee only, have I sinned, and done that which is evil in thy sight, in order that thou mayest ... (the LXX underlines the sense of purpose). Man's sin contributes to the glory of God. God might well be grateful to sinful man for bringing out more clearly than would otherwise be possible his righteousness and truth. The question may even be raised, **Is God, who inflicts his wrath, unjust?**[2] This sentence in Greek is so worded as to expect the answer No. Logically, a sentence expecting the answer Yes would have been better. Paul's objector is speaking: If my unrighteousness demonstrates God's righteousness, is not God (on your showing) unjust when he punishes me? Paul alters the expression probably out of reverence. He canno bring himself to put on paper even the grammatical implication that God is unjust. Such alterations occur in the Rabbinic writings. Alternatively, but less probably, there is a change of speaker and these words are Paul's own. Paul adds a further apology for carrying human arguments (even though they are not his own) too far: **Forgive these human arguments** (cf. 1 Cor. ix. 8; Gal. iii. 15; also Rom. vi. 19).

The real objection to Paul's case is that it impugns the moral government of the universe and the righteousness of God. It leaves God with no room to vindicate virtue and punish sin. Paul meets it with a direct negative. **Of course not; otherwise** (the same 6 construction, ἐπεί, occurs at xi. 6), **how is God to judge the world?** 'How is God to judge?' retains an ambiguity in the Greek verb. If it is accented in one way (κρίνει) it is in the present tense, How does he judge? if differently (κρινεῖ) it is future, How will he judge? The

---

1 Literally, justified (δικαιωθῇς). Evidently this means not 'counted right', but actually right, the victorious litigant. See pp. 71 ff.
2 The sentence would be neater and more apt if instead of ὁ ἐπιφέρων, 'who inflicts', we could read simply ἐπιφέρων, 'when he inflicts'; but the textual tradition is unanimously in favour of ὁ ἐπιφέρων.

ambiguity cannot be resolved, for there are few accents in the oldest MSS; fortunately the difference scarcely affects the sense: what matters is that God is the Judge. There are at least three ways of taking this rhetorical question. (1) If God is unrighteous how is he to judge...? (2) If God is not to use his wrath how is he to judge...? (3) If God does not punish Jews (as well as Gentiles) how is he to judge the *world*? Of these, (1) is certainly the most likely. We know for a fact that God is the judge of the whole earth, and we can be confident that the judge of the whole earth will do right.

The objector is not yet overcome. He cannot let go the implica-
7 tions of *v.* 4. **Yes, but if by my falsehood the truth of God increased and thereby increased his glory, why am I actually** (if the order of words in Greek is strictly followed, 'I too...'; but this is certainly not the point) **judged to be a sinner?** See n. 1 on p. 59. Paul has replied; the objector does not respond with 'for' (γάρ), but adversatively, 'But if...' The point is unchanged. The objector does not himself wish to draw blasphemous conclusions, but only to point out the dilemma in which Paul appears to be placed by his own uncompromising reference of all things to God. It is easier to bring such complaints against a profound view of the mysterious divine government of the universe than to answer them; this time Paul makes no fresh attempt to answer (see, however, the last clause of *v.* 8).

But what if the practical conclusion from these disputes is drawn? Paul turns to deal with an accusation that had been brought against himself. He is embarrassed by it, and his embarrassment comes out in the tangled construction of his sentence. It is straight-
8 ened out in the translation. **Why should we not do evil that good may come of it?** Why not increase God's goodness by contributing as generously as possible to the stock of human sin? **That is what some of our detractors actually allege that we say; they will get what they deserve.** Evidently Paul had to face the charge that he taught antinomianism, and worse. We need not doubt that some of his contemporaries thought, quite sincerely, that this was what he meant. And it may be that some members of his own churches so far misinterpreted him as to believe and teach that moral evil did not matter (cf. 1 Cor. v. 1–6, especially *v.* 2).

Again, Paul's answer is a simple and vigorous negative. People who will say that will say anything, and they deserve their punishment. The real answer to the question will be given in ch. vi (for the question itself see especially vi. 1, 15). It cannot be given here, because it rests upon truths of the doctrine of justification by faith which have not yet been established. Paul invokes again, as in *v.* 6, the moral government of the universe.

9 ALL HAVE SINNED

CHAPTER iii. 9–20

(9) What then does this amount to? That we Jews do after all stand on a higher plane that the Gentiles? By no means.[1] For we have already brought against both Jews and Greeks the common charge that they are all under the dominion of sin. (10) And this, moreover, is the verdict of Scripture. Hear these words of Scripture: 'There is no righteous man, not even one; (11) there is none with understanding, none that seeks after God. (12) They have all fallen away, all become worthless. There is none that practises kindness; no, there is not even one. (13) Their throat is an open grave, they practise deceit with their tongues, the poison of asps is under their lips. (14) Their mouth is full of cursing and bitterness. (15) Their feet are swift to shed blood, (16) affliction and wretchedness mark their path; (17) the way of peace they have not known. (18) There is no fear of God before their eyes.'

(19) Now we know that all the things the law says, it says to those who fall within its scope, to the intent that every mouth may be shut, and the whole world be brought to trial before God. (20) For (as Scripture itself says), 'By works of law shall no flesh be justified before him'. For in fact it is through the law that the recognition of sin comes.

The opening sentence of this paragraph is notoriously obscure, and it is impossible to feel confident that any one translation represents what Paul intends.

Looking back over his argument, Paul asks: **What then does this** 9 **amount to?** Here we take Paul's first two words (τί οὖν) as a separate interjection. They could be taken with the main verb which follows. The principal reason for not taking them so is that if Paul had constructed his opening question in this way he would have answered it differently (οὐδὲν πάντως – 'nothing at all', instead of οὐ πάντως – 'by no means'). In the variant reading mentioned in the footnote, the first two words must be taken with the (different) main verb.

The main verb (προεχόμεθα) which follows the interjection can be taken in no fewer than three ways; the answer (οὐ πάντως) to the question which it asks can be taken in two ways. Our first task must be to set out the various grammatical possibilities, and then consider which of them represents what Paul wishes to say in the present context.

1 Instead of the text translated above, the Western Text (D G) reads: 'What then do we Jews possess that others have not?' This seems to be an attempt to alleviate the difficulty of a very obscure passage; see the commentary.

(1) The verb. Its form is that of the middle or the passive voice (these are identical in the present tense in Greek). (i) The verb may be taken as having the force of a genuine middle. In this case it means, 'to offer as excuse, as self-defence'. The objection to taking it in this way is that, in this sense, it should have a direct object – one offers *something* as a defence, or excuse. An object might be found in the 'what' with which the verse opens; reason has already been given for taking this 'what' as an independent interjection, but it must be allowed that some possibility remains of taking the sentence in this way. (ii) The verb may be taken as middle with active meaning. It is so taken in the Vulgate (*praecellimus eos*). The meaning, on this view, is, 'Are we better off than they? Have we any advantage over them?' The objection to it is evident. Why, if Paul means this, did he not write the verb in the active voice (προέχομεν)?[1] (iii) The verb may be taken as passive. If it is so taken, the meaning is simply the opposite of that given in (ii): Are we excelled? There seems to be no *grammatical* objection to this.

(2) The answer. Literally rendered, Paul's words are, 'Not altogether' (cf. 1 Cor. v. 10); but there is no question that they were sometimes loosely used as if they stood in the reverse order, that is, they can mean 'Altogether not' (cf. *Diognetus*, ix. 1; Epictetus, *Enchiridion*, i. 5). Only the context can determine the meaning here.

The various grammatical possibilities are now before us. Which is most suitable to the context and to the line of thought which Paul is here pursuing? There is force in the suggestion[2] that the subject of the disputed verb must be the same as that of the verb which follows, 'We have brought the charge' (προητιασάμεθα), that is, the 'we' must refer to Paul himself. On this view, Paul says, ironically, 'What do you think I am doing? Defending (1. i above) the Jews and their privileges? No; I have already charged both Jews and Gentiles . . . '. An objection to this way of taking the verb, however, has already been pointed out, and it is by no means unlike Paul to change subjects in the middle of a verse.

If this suggestion is rejected it seems certain that the subject of the verb must be 'We Jews'.[3] This is supported by the fact that the charge against *Jews and Greeks* is represented as the ground of the statement that precedes it. The issue is not yet, however, closed. It will be well to set out the various possibilities.

1 The Western reading mentioned in the footnote to the translation takes the sentence in this way, but removes its difficulties and ambiguity. It is no doubt a secondary reading, but bears witness to an ancient interpretation.
2 Bauer-Aland, *Wörterbuch*, pp. 1413 f.
3 The suggestion that it should be 'We Christians' is attractive. Whether of Jewish or Gentile origin, even Christians are still open to the charge of sin, and can claim no superiority over their fellow-men. But if this were intended there would probably have been an emphatic 'we' (ἡμεῖς), or some other clear pointer.

(i) Are we Jews indulging in self-defence? Obviously not, for we have charged both Jews and Greeks ....

(ii a) Well, then, since there is advantage in being a Jew (*vv.* 1 f.), do we Jews excel? Not at all, for we have charged both Jews and Greeks ....

(ii b) ... do we Jews excel? Only in a limited degree, for we have charged both Jews and Greeks ....

(iii) The question, Have Jews an advantage over Gentiles? having now been treated, we turn to the converse, Have Gentiles an advantage over Jews, who stand under the law? Not at all, for we have charged both Jews and Gentiles ....

Of these suggestions, (i) is not preferable to that which was rejected above. (iii) introduces a thought which seems to be alien to the context. (ii) remains, and it is in the form (ii a) that it harmonizes best with Paul's thought, which on this theme is fundamentally paradoxical.[1] He has laid it down that the Jew has an advantage which not even his own unbelief and disobedience can take from him. Yet what does this amount to? **That we Jews do after all stand on a higher plane than the Gentiles? By no means. For we have already brought against both Jews and Greeks** (i.e. Gentiles; cf. i. 16) **the common charge that they are all under the dominion of sin.** Discussion of relative privilege is therefore in a sense academic. All without exception are sinners who rightly incur God's wrath. The Jew has an advantage, and he has not an advantage. It is a serious injustice to Paul if we suppose him to have known that theological consistency could allow only the denial of all advantage to the Jew, but to have permitted a sentimental patriotism to lead him from time to time into nationalist parrot-cries which he knew in his heart and mind to be false. The advantage of the Jew is real, but it is an advantage which is (or may at any moment become) at the same time a disadvantage. It consists in knowing (out of Scripture) that before God all talk of 'advantages' is folly and sin.

Paul has already (i. 18–ii. 29) brought his charge against Jews and Greeks; but he would not have it regarded as merely an intellectual analysis of the moral life of the first century. Far more important than

---

1 The reader should consult the splendid discussion in Cranfield, pp. 187–91, which goes into far more detail than is possible here. Cranfield, 'after long hesitation', prefers to take the answer (οὐ πάντως) to mean ' "Not altogether", "Not in every respect" ', noting that this interpretation, unlike the other, does not introduce an element of contradiction into Paul's thought. The view taken here is that Paul is not contradicting himself, but that his thought is paradoxical. There is *a sense* in which the Jew has an advantage. There is *a sense* in which the Jew has no advantage at all. This is not very different from Cranfield's conclusion; it is perhaps a sharper – perhaps a more Pauline – way of putting it.

10   any such analysis is the fact that **this is the verdict of Scripture.** This is the point of the long cento which follows in *vv.* 10–18. Paul may have put the quotations together himself; it is not impossible that he drew them from an already existing florilegium. They require little comment.

    Hear these words of Scripture: 'There is no righteous man, not
11 **even one; there is none with understanding, none that seeks after**
12 **God. They have all fallen away, all become worthless. There is none that practises kindness; no, there is not even one.'** The source of the quotation is either Ps. xiv. 1 ff. or Ps. liii. 1 ff. These passages are almost identical. The main point of interest is that Paul has introduced the word *righteous*, which is in neither the Hebrew nor the LXX Greek of either Psalm. It represents, of course, an essential element in Paul's thought. The ultimately significant question, which underlies the argument of Romans as a whole, is whether man secures a favourable or unfavourable verdict in God's court.

13   **Their throat is an open grave, they practise deceit with their tongues.** From Ps. v. 9.

    The poison of asps is under their lips. From Ps. cxl. 3.

14   **Their mouth is full of cursing and bitterness.** From Ps. x. 7.

15, 16   **Their feet are swift to shed blood, affliction and wretchedness**
17 **mark their path** (literally, paths); **the way of peace they have not known.** From Isa. lix. 7 f.; cf. Prov. i. 16.

18   **There is no fear of God before their eyes.** From Ps. xxxvi. 1.

19   Paul's Old Testament catena is at an end. What is its effect? **We know that all things the law says, it says** (or *speaks* – a different verb from the last, but Paul seems to intend no difference in meaning and the variation does not make pleasing English) **to those who fall within its scope, to the intent that every mouth may be shut, and the whole world brought to trial before God.**

    Paul can on occasion (cf. 1 Cor. xiv. 21) use the word law (as the Rabbis could use the word *torah*) to cover the whole of the Old Testament, the Prophets and the Writings as well as the Pentateuch. 'All the things the law says' may therefore refer to the composite quotation of *vv.* 10–18, regarded as summarizing the content of the Old Testament. But 'those who fall within its scope' (literally, 'those who are in the law') must mean, 'Those who are subject to the law of Moses', that is, Jews. This might determine the earlier use of the word law. There are two possibilities. (i) The Old Testament proves that the Jews, and *a fortiori* all other men, are guilty before God. (ii) The guilt of the Jews is now proved (from the Prophets and Writings), and further we know that the law condemns them too. The latter alternative is very strained, and does not account for the '*every* mouth' and 'the *whole* world' which follow. The former is therefore to be preferred. The change which it implies in Paul's use of *law* is not a serious objection; in fact, it could in each place be translated without serious inaccuracy, 'the Old Testament religion' – which is a ministry of condemnation (2 Cor. iii. 9).

The whole world (this is proved *a fortiori*, as indicated above) is brought to trial before God. In normal Greek usage, the noun coupled with 'brought to trial' should be not the judge but the person wronged; but it can hardly be doubted that here God, though wronged, is primarily the judge. Cf. 'without excuse' in i. 20; ii. 1. No man can answer the charge.

There is no escape from this situation of silent guilt before the God the Judge. **For (as Scripture itself says), 'By works of law shall no** 20 **flesh be justified before him'. For in fact it is through the law that** (not righteousness but) **the recognition of sin comes.** Paul invokes Scripture once more, and quotes Ps. cxliii. 2; but introduces two significant modifications into the text he quotes. (i) He adds 'by works of law'. He cannot deny the possibility of justification altogether (indeed the Psalmist did not wish to do so), since that is the theme of his epistle, and he must therefore define the scope of the negative expressed in the Psalm. 'Works of law' are not good works simply, but works done in obedience to the law and *regarded as*, in themselves, a means of justification. By the highest means (outside the Gospel), no one will be justified. (ii) Paul substitutes 'no flesh' for 'no man living'. No substantial change is made, but the fact that Paul, in writing of the total failure of mankind, should choose, no doubt unthinkingly, the word 'flesh' (σάρξ) is significant for his doctrine of the flesh; see pp. 128 f., 137 ff., 146–9, 152. Here 'flesh' signifies myself in my attempt to justify myself.

Paul had himself believed that righteousness (that is, a correct relation with God) was to be had on legal terms; his profounder Christian insight is that the law points out the meaning and horror of sin; see on vii. 7.

Paul began at i. 18 to describe the manifestation of God's righteousness in wrath which accompanies the manifestation of righteousness in salvation. He first depicts the operation of wrath upon the wilful sinner, then turns aside to consider the case of those who 'approve' and those who 'judge'. Of these 'judges' the supreme representative is the Jew, who takes his stand upon the law, and from that secure eminence deals out instruction to and passes sentence upon mankind. Is he really secure? Is the man of religion in a position to censure the man of the world? Are his privileges as comfortable as they appear?

Paul speaks of judgement. It is of the essence of his message that the time is come for judgement to begin at the house of God. The Jew becomes not the moral tutor but the scapegoat of humanity. His death warrant is, as it were, written into his own birth certificate. The law, the religion of the Old Testament in which he glories, accuses him, in order that the whole world may be found guilty. The Old Testament, though, when it is rightly understood, it offers justification, yet declares justification to be a universal impossibility. The law, which if it had been introduced into a situation not already corrupt would have had a different effect, in fact brings to light not righteousness but sin. As long, therefore, as God's righteousness is manifested and understood in terms of the law it must spell wrath. The only hope for man is that God should find some other means, beyond law and religion, of manifesting his righteousness.

10 THE RIGHTEOUSNESS OF GOD

CHAPTER iii. 21–31

(21) But now in fact God's righteousness has been manifested apart from the law, attested indeed by the law and the prophets, (22) yet God's righteousness manifested through faith in Jesus Christ, and directed to all who have faith. All, for there is no distinction. (23) All have sinned, all lack the glory of God. (24) But they are justified, as a free gift, by God's grace, through the act of redemption which he performed in Christ Jesus. (25) This Christ Jesus God publicly set forth in his bloody sacrificial death as his means of dealing with sin, received through faith. He did this in order to show forth and vindicate his righteousness, because in his forbearance he had passed over, without punishment or remission, the sins men had committed in days gone by. (26) He did it, I say, to show forth and vindicate his righteousness in this present time, so that he might both be righteous himself, and justify the man who relies on faith in Jesus.

(27) If this is what the manifestation of righteousness, and justification, mean, where is boasting?[1] It is excluded. By what kind of law? A law based on works? No, by a law based on faith. (28) (For[2] we reckon that it is by faith, to the exclusion of works of law, that a man is justified). (29) Or does God belong to the

1 G lat have 'Where then is your boasting?' This points to the meaning of the better attested text, which does not contain the pronoun. Paul is addressing the Jew, but the Jew as the prime example of the religious man.
2 'For we reckon' is in ℵ A D G lat; B C ω have 'We reckon therefore'. The former reading gives the right connection between *vv.* 27 and 28; the latter is the ground of the former, not *vice versa*.

Jews only? Is he not the God of the Gentiles also? Of course he is, (30) if indeed God is one, and will justify the circumcision by faith and the uncircumcision through faith.

(31) Do we then, by this insistence upon faith, do away with the law? Certainly not; on the contrary, we establish the law.

At this critical stage (see on *vv.* 19 f.) we find one of the great turning points (cf. v. 20; vi. 22; vii. 6; viii. 1, 9) of the epistle: **But now in fact.** 21 Paul's words in Greek (νυνὶ δέ) could refer to a temporal contrast ('But at the present . . . ') or to a logical contrast ('But as it is . . . '); in fact they refer to both. The contrast is not purely temporal because the manifestation of wrath (i. 18) is an eschatological event taking place in the present; yet there is a temporal contrast, since the law belongs to God's dealings with Israel in old time, and Christians live no longer under the law but under grace (vi. 15), their relation with God determined and established now not by the law but by Christ.

The new, good news is that now, in the present age, **God's righteousness has been manifested apart from the law.** Compare i. 16 f., and for 'God's righteousness' see on those verses. What Paul means by the term appears best from the accounts of the acts of God given in this paragraph. It has two aspects, represented by the two clauses of *v.* 26 (on which see the notes), 'that he might be righteous himself' and 'that he might justify'. That is, it includes an *interior* righteousness, the quality of being right, or righteous, and an *exterior*, or outwardgoing, righteousness, the activity of doing right, of delivering, of setting things and persons right. Both aspects of righteousness are revealed in the Gospel, and in the eschatological events to which it bears witness; moreover, they result in the second sense of righteousness (mentioned on p. 31), since their effect is to bestow on the believer the status of righteousness before God.

In i. 17 Paul said, God's righteousness is (being) revealed (ἀποκαλύπτεται, present tense). Here he says, God's righteousness has been manifested (πεφανέρωται, perfect tense). There is little difference. The present tense emphasizes the continuation of the process in the proclamation of the Gospel, the perfect the fact that the process has a beginning. It will shortly appear that this beginning is to be found in the death of Jesus.

This manifestation of righteousness takes place apart from the law; not because the righteousness of God could not be manifested through the law, but because the righteousness which, when manifested through the law, could only lead to wrath, since the law was abused (cf. iv. 15), has now been manifested in a different way so as to lead to justification. It is because law has been defined out of the manifestation and faith (*v.* 22) defined in, that in this paragraph (contrast i. 18) we hear nothing of wrath.

Though God's righteousness is thus manifested apart from the law, it is nevertheless **attested by the law and the prophets**, that is, by the Old Testament as a whole. Not only do the prophecies point forward to the saving acts which have now taken place, the law itself (if only men would understand it rightly) points in the same direction. That is to say, though God's righteousness in the saving sense that it has in the Gospel is attested by the Old Testament, it must be understood as God's righteousness manifested through faith in Jesus Christ, and directed to all who have faith. *Manifested* is not expressed in Paul's Greek, and it might seem better to supply a different word, such as *enacted* or *operative*; *manifested* however is the word of *v.* 21 and must have preference here, though, of course, more than a mere showing is implied. The old revelation is to be understood in the light of the new, not the new in the light of the old. In this verse one element in the new, non-legal, basis of righteousness appears, namely, faith. The second (grace) is not mentioned till *v.* 24. At first the

22 wording appears repetitious: **through faith, to all who have faith.** The repetition provides a measure of underlining of a vital truth, but Paul is in fact making two points. The manifestation is apprehended through faith; and, secondly, as will be emphasized throughout the paragraph, it is not for Jews only but for all – with the one proviso immediately added, for *all who have faith.* For the meaning of faith see on i. 17 and compare i. 21 (with the note). It can hardly be better defined than as the opposite of man's self-confident or self-despairing attempt to establish a proper relationship between himself and God by legal (that is, by moral or religious) means. Instead of concentrating his hope upon himself he directs it towards God, and in particular towards a creative act of God's grace (see below in the rest of this paragraph, and the discussion of Abraham's faith in ch. iv). 'Faith in Jesus Christ' is trust in him as the creative means of reconciliation provided by God. There thus exists a close inner relationship between saving righteousness and faith; only those who have faith are restored to a true relationship with God, since faith (over against works of law) is the only visible expression of that relationship. The manifestation of righteousness as God's action leads to righteousness understood as the status of righteousness that man receives as God's gift; it is thus directed to all who have faith – All, **for there is no distinction** (διαστολή), that is, between Jew and Gentile. Paul looks back to the argument which culminates in *vv.* 19 f. The Old Testament knows a distinction (διαστολή) between Jew and Gentile (Exod. viii. 19 (23)), but it is law that makes this distinction so that in a situation defined as *apart from law* it ceases to exist; and in respect of sin Jew and Gentile alike stand guilty before God.

23 **All have sinned, all lack the glory of God.** It is half correct to describe this as a reference to the eschatological glory for which man

hopes (v. 2; viii. 18, 30); for man as sinner, and unbelieving, can expect no glory from God. But the present tense (*lack*) is used, and presumably means that man now lacks what he might now have had, that is, the glory with which Adam was created and which he (and all mankind with him) lost through sin. The glorious state of Adam in the Garden of Eden is a common conception in the Rabbinic literature, and in the apocalypses. Man could hardly be blamed for lacking a future thing, but, of course, the future glory may be regarded as the restoration of the lost, original, glory.

We see, then, men, revealed through the unique and ambiguous privilege of Israel as sinners, guilty before God, deprived of glory both as possession and as hope. In the next verse Paul states succinctly what he believes has happened to them. This is the heart of his Gospel, as he expounds it in Romans. See further below, pp. 76 ff.

They are justified, receive the status of righteousness, **as a free** 24 **gift, by God's grace, through the act of redemption which he performed in Christ Jesus.**

No word is more characteristic of Paul's vocabulary than 'to justify' (δικαιοῦν; for other notes see on pp. 60 f., 83 ff., 99 ff.). Before the word itself is discussed it is important to recall (see above, pp. 30 f.) that God's righteousness (δικαιοσύνη) belongs to the realm of eschatology. It is manifested in the 'present time' only by an anticipation of the 'last time'. It implies the verdict of the last judgement, and the verb 'to justify' means an anticipation of this verdict.

Greek verbs of the class to which 'to justify' belongs (verbs in -όω) have normally a factitive, or causative, meaning. For example, from the adjective τυφλός, *blind*, is derived the verb τυφλόω, *to make blind*. Analogy suggests therefore that from 'righteous' (δίκαιος) should be derived a verb 'to make righteous' (δικαιόω). It is, however, very generally recognized that, in Paul's usage, 'to justify' cannot mean 'to make righteous' in an ethical sense – 'to make virtuous'. To mention no other consideration, the epistles depict countless Christians who, though justified, are certainly not perfectly good. Accordingly, it is often pointed out that when the Greek verbal suffix in question (-όω) is attached to adjectives denoting moral qualities the meaning is sometimes not 'to make ...' but 'to count ...', or 'to treat as ...'. From this observation is drawn the most popular modern interpretation of the Pauline verb 'to justify' and the Pauline doctrine of justification. The verb means 'to count, or treat as, righteous'. Justification means that God treats sinful men as if they were of complete and unstained virtue.

Two radical objections may be brought against this interpretation. (i) On the linguistic side, it ignores the fact that behind Paul's Greek verb there lies a Hebrew verb, to which the Greek of the LXX points.

This Hebrew verb (*hitzdiq*) is in the Hiph'il form, which is regularly causative in meaning; it cannot possibly be weakened so far as to mean 'to treat as righteous'. (ii) Doctrinally, it may be said that this account of justification must lead either to Pelagianism (since faith itself will be treated as a righteous work, or at least as righteousness in germ), or to the kind of legal fiction which men feel instinctively is not legitimate even for God, if he be a moral being. Not even he may pretend that black is white.

It is far better, and more in harmony with Paul's teaching as a whole, to suppose that 'to justify' (δικαιοῦν) does mean 'to make righteous', but at the same time to recognize that 'righteous' does not mean 'virtuous', but 'right', 'clear', 'acquitted' in God's court. Justification then means no legal fiction but an act of forgiveness on God's part, described in terms of the proceedings of a law court. Far from being a legal fiction, this is a creative act changing the relation between God and man.

This creative act Paul will very shortly describe, but for the moment he emphasizes that God justifies men *as a free gift, by his grace*. The first phrase is an essential element in Paul's thought; since men are undoubtedly sinners they cannot be justified, or acquitted, on the grounds of any merit of their own. We have seen (p. 70) that it turns upon faith. It arises out of God's grace. Grace (χάρις) is an Old Testament word. In the LXX it translates most often *hen*, sometimes in the later books of the translation *hesed*. This word is more often rendered ἔλεος, mercy, an important fact because, together with the use of *hesed* in post-biblical Hebrew, it shows that *hesed* was in the New Testament period no longer understood in the sense it bore at an earlier time (loyalty to a covenant relation) but means (as *hen* did) favour or love, especially when free and undeserved. In Paul's use grace is undoubtedly the free, gracious favour of God, the love he bestows on men while they are still sinners (v. 8); but characteristically in Paul it conveys the sense of action. Here, for example, it stands in the dative case as the instrument of God's act of justification. It operates (as Paul goes on to say) through the redemption wrought in Christ Jesus; it is thus pre-eminently, though not exclusively, an eschatological term, referring to a unique gracious activity (cf. v. 2, 15; vi. 1).

So far, then, we see God moved by love to perform an act of grace by means of which it becomes possible for him to manifest his righteousness in justification. Justification (like the 'handing over' of i. 24, 26, 28) is a verdict anticipated from the last day. It is the verdict which faith, and only faith, can hear. Outside faith, as outside grace, men can hear (out of the law) only the verdict of guilty, and the sentence of condemnation. This is not to deny that the law was, in itself, a gift of God's grace; it describes the effect of the law in the sinful situation in which, inevitably, it was operating.

It has already been pointed out that even God can declare this unexpected verdict only through a creative act of his own – in Paul's words, through the act of redemption which he performed in Christ Jesus. 'Act of redemption' (ἀπολύτρωσις) is, like righteousness, salvation, and wrath, an eschatological term; see viii. 23 (and cf. Eph. iv. 30; Luke xxi. 28). At Eph. i. 7 (cf. Col. i. 14) redemption is 'through the blood' of Christ; here also connection with the death of Jesus is at hand (see *v.* 25). The word can mean simply 'deliverance', 'liberation'; the act, that is, by which God finally sets men free from bondage to evil powers and to corruption; but the connection with blood and death suggests that it has not completely lost its original sense of 'ransoming', emancipation by the payment of a price; compare Mark x. 45; 1 Pet. i. 18 f.; and especially Gal. iii. 13, Christ redeemed (ἐξηγόρασεν) us from the curse of the law.

Paul still has to explain how the death of Jesus was an act of redemption, capable of rectifying the relations between God and man. He says: **This Christ Jesus God publicly set forth in his bloody** 25 **sacrificial death as his means of dealing with sin, received through faith.** There is scarcely a word in this statement that could not give rise to long discussion.

'Publicly set forth' does not exclude but rather implies the sense of purpose, which the verb (προέθετο) has at i. 13; Eph. i. 9, the only other occurrences of it in the New Testament. This sense is rightly emphasized by Cranfield (pp. 208–10), but what God publicly showed in the public, historical, event of the crucifixion of Jesus was a manifestation of his eternal purpose. It is very doubtful whether the word can mean 'to set forth as a sacrifice', but the notion of sacrifice is contained in the words 'his bloody sacrificial death' (literally, *his blood*, but the shedding of blood implies sacrifice).

The death of Christ, thus understood, or rather, Christ thus dying, became God's 'means of dealing with sin'. This cumbersome phrase translates a single Greek word (ἱλαστήριον). This is derived from a verb (ἱλάσκεσθαι; cf. the compound ἐξιλάσκεσθαι) of which the normal meaning is 'to propitiate', 'to appease'. This verb is employed in the LXX, where, however, it commonly translates a Hebrew verb (*kipper*), whose original meaning is 'to cover over' or 'to wipe off'; hence 'to conceal' or 'to cleanse'. It is sometimes used with sin (or some such word) as its object; its meaning then naturally becomes, 'to expiate'. The common Greek meaning 'to propitiate' becomes practically impossible when, as sometimes happens, God is the subject of the verb. God cannot be said to propitiate man, still less his sin; he cleanses, and forgives, man, and expiates (wipes out) his sin. Derivatives of the form before us here (in -τήριος) generally refer to the means by which, or the place where, an action is carried out. The word itself may be regarded as an adjective in the accusative masculine, agreeing with Christ Jesus (ὅν), or as an accusative neuter, the neuter of the adjective being used as a substantive. Christ crucified was set forth as an 'expiatory person' or as an 'expiatory agency'. We can hardly doubt (since Paul says that God set forth Christ in this capacity) that expiation is in his mind; it would however be wrong to neglect the fact that expiation has, as it were, the effect of propitiation: the sin that might justly have excited God's wrath is expiated (at God's will), and therefore no longer does so. This amounts to the paradoxical claim that God propitiates God. Paradoxical as it is, this assertion comes close to the heart of what Paul has to say, and the paradox is rooted in the nature of God. It is the nature of God to be irreconcilably opposed to sin; it is the nature of God to love sinners and to seek reconciliation with them. No one but God could resolve the problem; and God himself could be faithful to both aspects of his being only at the cost of the Cross.

Christ's death, then, has reconciling power. To say this was not to make a complete innovation in Judaism. For some time, innocent death, and especially the death of martyrs, had been considered to have atoning effect (e.g. 4 Macc. xvii. 20 ff.). It is possible that at this point a reference should be made to the Suffering Servant of Isa. liii; but Paul's language does not require it, and it is doubtful whether this passage had any great effect on his thought. See on iv. 25; viii. 32.

It is, however, possible that another Old Testament symbol is in Paul's mind. The word he employs is used, sometimes alone, sometimes as an adjective qualifying a noun meaning 'cover', to denote the lid of the Ark of the Covenant.[1] This cover was sprinkled with blood by the High Priest on the Day of Atonement; it was here that the gracious God appeared, in thick darkness, once more reconciled with his people. There is much to be said for the traditional view that Paul represented Christ as the true 'mercy-seat'. What else to a Jew represented at once the place and the means of atonement?[2] But we can go with certainty no further than the translation: God set forth Christ as the means of dealing with sin. Other allusions may be no more than overtones.

'Through faith' is not to be connected with 'in his blood'. It is through faith that the act of redemption becomes effective, because faith is the human counterpart of the divine act. See pp. 29, 70.

Paul has now asserted the closest possible connection between the

---

1 The Hebrew is *kapporeth*, from the same root as *kipper*.
2 Cf. 1 Cor. v. 7, where Paul makes a similar passing allusion to the Passover. Professor T. W. Manson (*JTS* xlvi (1945), pp. 1–10) brings out other points of comparison and contrast between this passage and the ceremonies of the Day of Atonement: a public act over against one in the most secret place in the Temple; the blood of Christ over against the blood of an animal; a gift received by faith over against one acting *ex opere operato*.

'act of redemption' necessary if God is to justify sinners, and the death of Jesus; but he has not yet fully answered the question why the death of Christ should be necessary if God is to manifest his righteousness (before the due time) through the Gospel (see pp. 27–32). Why should God set forth Christ crucified as the means of dealing with sin?

He did this in order to show forth and vindicate his righteousness, because in his forbearance he had passed over, without punishment or remission, the sins men had committed in days gone by.

'Show forth and vindicate' represents one Greek word (ἔνδειξις) which possesses precisely the same ambiguity as the English 'demonstrate'. It means both a simple showing forth, and also a proof, effected by showing forth. God reveals his righteousness, and thereby proves that it exists, and that it really is righteousness. This is done through the Cross. But why should it be done at all?

We meet here a major problem of exegesis, to which two quite different solutions have been propounded. The problem turns upon the meaning of two Greek words, rendered in RV 'because of the passing over' (διὰ τὴν πάρεσιν). (i) It is sometimes held that the noun has the meaning 'forgiveness' (that is, it is a synonym of the similarly formed ἄφεσις). If this view of the noun is taken, the preposition must mean 'with a view to'. Paul's meaning thus becomes: Christ died and thereby demonstrated God's righteousness in order to secure forgiveness. (ii) The alternative is to suppose that the noun means not 'forgiveness', the full remission of sins, but a mere 'passing over', or ignoring of sins – pretermission. If this view of the noun is accepted, the preposition may have its more usual meaning, 'because of', 'on account of'. Paul's meaning now becomes: Christ died and thereby manifested God's righteousness because in the past God had merely overlooked men's sins.

(ii) is undoubtedly the preferable alternative, for several reasons. That there is a real difference between the two Greek nouns mentioned above (πάρεσις and ἄφεσις) seems certain,[1] and it is hard to see why, if Paul simply means 'forgiveness', he does not use the ordinary word. Further, (ii) provides better links between this point in the argument and those which precede and follow. The question is why God manifested his righteousness in an act of redemption in Christ crucified. The answer is: In the past he had overlooked men's sins, and decisive action was necessary if his righteousness was to be vindicated. Paul goes on to speak of 'his forbearance'; cf. ii. 4; ix. 22. The meaning is that for purposes of his own God has held his hand when he might have punished (cf. also Acts xiv. 16; xvii. 30).

1 See J. M. Creed, *JTS* xli (1940), pp. 28 ff. See also however W. G. Kümmel, *Heilsgeschehen und Geschichte* (1965), pp. 260–70, who takes the opposite view.

Paul now repeats himself[1] in order to bring out more completely the connection between the death of Christ and righteousness.

26   He did it, I say, to show forth and vindicate his righteousness in this present time, so that he might both be righteous himself, and justify the man who relies on faith in Jesus.

The first fresh point here is the explicit reference to 'the present time'. This contrasts in the first instance with the time of God's forbearance in respect of sins *previously* committed (προγεγονότα), that is, with the past. But the present time is also contrasted with the eschatological future. The manifestation of righteousness proper to the last judgement has been brought forward. The second fresh point is the clear statement of the goal intended in the demonstration of God's righteousness. It was intended to show that God (a) was righteous in himself, and (b) justified the man who relied on faith. Purpose (a) is achieved because the crucifixion shows to the full God's abhorrence of sin and his righteous judgement upon it, and at the same time indicates beyond doubt that his apparent disregard of sin in the past was due not to negligence but to mercy which patiently offered to sinners opportunity for repentance (ii. 4). Purpose (b) is achieved, because, though the crucifixion is an unparalleled demonstration of God's love (v. 8), it can be apprehended as such a demonstration only by faith which, viewing it in the light of the resurrection, sees in it God's act of redemption. Thus (cf. p. 69) the Cross vindicates both the interior and the exterior righteousness of God. The Cross anticipates the results of the last judgement: the Judge of all the earth does right and is seen to do right, and, since he chooses to bear himself, in the person of his Son, the affliction antecedent to the Age to Come, he is able righteously to justify those who believe. There is an additional difference between *v.* 25 and *v.* 26 which is obscured in the translation. *To show forth and vindicate his righteousness* in *v.* 25 translates εἰς ἔνδειξιν τῆς δικαιοσύνης αὐτοῦ, literally *for the demonstration of his righteousness*. In *v.* 26 the Greek words are the same except that for εἰς we now have πρὸς τήν. It is hard to see any difference in meaning.

The present verse (26) brings us to the close of one of the most crucial and concentrated arguments in the whole epistle, and it will be well to look back over it. It has two aspects, each of which is essential to the whole.

Paul's argument is in part an anthropology. We have already traced his analysis of the human situation. The basic ill of mankind, expressed alike in sheer moral evil, in ethical criticism, and in the

---

1 Not so, according to some exegetes, who take the new reference to the demonstration of God's righteousness with his forbearance; he forbore to punish with a view to the future manifestation of his righteousness in Christ.

practice of religion, is the idolatry of self. Man, designed as God's creature to glorify his Creator, chooses rather to glorify himself, and in the end debases himself, because in so doing he contradicts his own essential nature. Obediently or disobediently, he lives 'under the law'. He may deliberately throw off the yoke, or, alternatively, suppose that by doing what he conceives to be 'right' he can secure his own position by establishing 'rights' over against God; in either case he is exercising a will-to-power (which may be described in general terms as a 'will-to-power over his environment' or in religious terms as a 'will-to-power over God') which can only be harmful because it denies the fundamental insecurity of man's position. The cure of this ill is faith, which may (up to a point) be described in terms of the old maxim, 'Know thyself'. Man's primary responsibility is to recognize his own place in the universe, and to respond to his Creator in grateful and obedient creatureliness. The man who so responds is in harmony with the universe of which he is himself a created constituent; he is what he was meant to be and is therefore at peace. He no longer uses his religion as a means to establish his rights over against God, but perceives through it that he stands under God's judgement, and instead of thinking to control God's judgement through his own activity, accepts it and submits to it, and is thereby at peace with God.

But 'Know thyself' is not the Gospel. It is impossible for man as he is to know himself, for man as he is is not 'himself', that is, he is not the person he was intended in God's purpose to be. This true self he cannot *be* but can only *become*, precisely in the moment of self-recognition, or faith. It follows that faith cannot be regarded as one more religious, or psychological, possibility, among, or additional to, all the other possibilities of human existence. Faith is not a human possibility, and comes to man as a gift from outside himself. At this point we see how Paul is driven, not by the fact that he lived in the remote world of the first century but by the inward necessity of his own argument, to add to his anthropological analysis the conception (which may perhaps be described as mythical, in the sense that it speaks of an incursion of the supernatural into the natural) of an act of redemption. Only in consequence of a divine invasion of the closed system of human affairs is it possible for men to believe and to be reconciled to God. In other words, 'they are justified . . . through the act of redemption which God performed in Christ Jesus'.

The centrality in Paul's thought of the doctrine of justification by faith has been questioned, chiefly on the ground that it is bound up with the disputes that arose over Paul's controversies with the Jews (and Judaizers) and his mission to the Gentiles, so that in consequence justification should be viewed in this polemical setting and not as the article by which the church stands or falls, the clue to the true relation between man and God, the foundation on which salvation rests. It is certainly true that it is in Romans and Galatians, and seldom elsewhere, that Paul uses the language of righteousness and kindred words, and that it was in the great theological battles of his career that the doctrine was sharpened and deepened. What this means is that it proved increasingly to be the criterion by which, in Paul's belief, thought and action were to be judged. As we have seen (p. 74), Paul's understanding of justification is rooted in his understanding of God, the God who hates sin and loves sinners, an inward tension that can be reconciled only at unspeakable cost, who calls a people and gives them great privileges which have a way of turning into anti-privileges, so that in the end an elect people may become an elect world. It must be emphasized that justification is not the whole story of God's dealings with mankind, but it is the first chapter without which there would be no story at all. And it is not only a beginning but a dialectical definition of every point in the story, in which man continues to be both sinner and righteous, until the end, when God is all in all. See further, pp. 208 ff.

The climax of his argument passed, Paul turns again to his Jewish
27 hearer. **If this is what the manifestation of righteousness, and justification, mean** (this long protasis represents the one word 'then' (οὖν), which looks back upon the whole argument), **where is boasting?** Boasting is the attitude of the natural man, who seeks to establish his position independently of God, and the only alternative to it (outside faith) is despair. Paul's answer is clear. **It is excluded.** Boasting and faith are mutually exclusive. As long as a man boasts in his own deeds, it is impossible for him to trust in God's act of redemption. He can be justified, that is, rightly related to God, only when he ceases to boast, and believes.

How does boasting come to be excluded? **By what kind of law?** Paul's answer to this question is twofold, and the two parts are separated by *v.* 28, which in modern book production could best be placed in a footnote. This does not mean that it is unimportant; on the contrary, it sums up what is perhaps the most important paragraph in the epistle. *V.* 29 is the continuation of *v.* 27 (though *v.* 28 gives the ground for *v.* 27 b). The parenthesis may be dealt with first; it sums up
28 the argument of i. 15–iii. 26: **We reckon that it is by faith, to the exclusion of works of law, that a man is justified.** What is to be noted here is that Paul sums up his Gospel of the redeeming activity of God as justification (not because 'justification' is itself a complete account of all that God does for men but because it is the *conditio sine qua non* of salvation), and emphasizes that justification comes only by faith. The 'only' (which Origen,[1] not Luther, was the first to bring to

1 *Commentary on the Epistle to the Romans*, iii. 9 (Migne, *Patrologia Graeca*, xiv. 952 D), according to Rufinus's translation. See Luther's 1530 addition to the Preface to Romans in the 1522 New Testament, 'Grund und Ursach der Übersetzung: *Allein* durch den Glauben. Röm. iii. 28.'

the interpretation of this verse) is fully warranted by Paul's own 'to the exclusion of works of law'. If anything other than faith could be the means of justification, then works done in obedience to the law, which was set forth by God himself, and is holy, righteous, good, and spiritual (vii. 12, 14), could justify. If these are excluded, everything is excluded, and faith alone remains. With this parenthetically stated but radically important fact in mind we return to Paul's question.

By what kind of law is boasting excluded? **By a law based on works? No, by a law based on faith.** 'Based on' is a somewhat unsatisfactory way of expressing the Greek genitives (literally, *of works*, *of faith*); *understood as requiring* might be better, though clumsy. Many modern commentators and translators suppose that in this passage the word 'law' (νόμος) should be rendered 'principle'. This is a possible meaning of the Greek word, and it yields good sense. On what principle (Paul asks) is boasting excluded? On the principle of faith, not the principle of works. This rendering is attractive, but cannot be maintained in the face of two weighty objections. (i) The meaning 'principle' is too philosophical for Paul, especially in a passage such as the present, in which Paul has been writing primarily of the Old Testament law. (ii) It is improbable that Paul would change his usage of the word between *v.* 27 and *v.* 28; and we cannot suppose that in *v.* 28 he means, 'to the exclusion of works of principle'. It must, however, be admitted that, since he sets over against each other two 'laws', a law based on works and a law based on faith, he cannot mean simply the Jewish law. The fact (and it will be important to remember it in the discussion of later passages; see especially on vii. 7–25) is that here and elsewhere for Paul law (νόμος) means something like 'religious system', often, of course, though not always, the religious system of Judaism. If, he argues here, religion is a matter of works, boasting is in order, since religious works, moral or ceremonial, may undoubtedly be done and therefore may be boasted of; but if religion has been transformed into a religion of faith, then by definition there are no religious works, and accordingly no ground for boasting. See ix. 30–x. 4, where Paul claims that the Jews have misunderstood the law by supposing that it called for works, not faith.

Paul proceeds to the second part of his answer. **Or does God 29 belong to the Jews only** (that they should boast about him)? **Is he not the God of the Gentiles also?** If God is to justify only on the basis of works done in obedience to the law of Moses he must confine justification to Jews, a fragment of the human race. But he is in fact the God of all, and will therefore justify by faith. The Old Testament itself laid down that boasting before God was intolerable; men might glory *in* God but not *before* him (e.g. Jer. ix. 23 f.). The Old Testament had also laid it down that a special relation existed between God and Israel (e.g. Ex. xix. 5 f.). But the Old Testament was misunderstood if

passages such as these were taken to mean that God was a private possession of the Jews on which they might pride themselves over
30 against the Gentiles. **Of course he is** the God of the Gentiles also, **if indeed God is one**, as the Old Testament itself declares (e.g. Deut. vi. 4).

No Jew would have denied that God is one, and that he is Lord over the Gentiles as well as the Jews. Paul's addition to this common faith follows. Jew and Gentile are equal before God, and neither is in a position to boast, because God **will justify the circumcision by faith and the uncircumcision through faith**. 'By faith' and 'through faith' are not to be distinguished. The change of preposition is only a rhetorical device (cf. iv. 11; v. 10; 1 Cor. xii. 8; 2 Cor. iii. 11), and it is the foundation of Paul's argument that for circumcised and uncircumcised alike there is but one way to justification, the way of faith alone.

It is comparatively easy thus to set aside the natural human desire, which becomes visible in Judaism but is felt universally, to have a ground of boasting; but the exclusion of works of law (*v.* 28)
31 raises a far more serious problem than this (cf. on *v.* 1). **Do we then, by this insistence upon faith, do away with the law?** The objection would be grave enough if 'the law' meant simply the Old Testament (cf. *v.* 19), for the Old Testament is the 'oracles of God' (*v.* 2), and if it were proved wrong God's word would be shown to be untrue. But it is probable that 'law' (as in *vv.* 27 f.) means both more and less than this. It is not simply the written record of God's revelation of himself to man, but the whole system of religious thought and practice based upon this revelation – in a word, the religion of Judaism. Does the Gospel thus cut away the ground from under its own feet? **Certainly not; on the contrary, we establish the law.** Here again, 'the law' is not simply the Old Testament, which Paul believes to be fulfilled in the saving events of the New Testament, and especially in the person of Jesus Christ himself (2 Cor. i. 20). The full meaning of religion is to be found and understood in the Gospel, to which the law *as law* also points. Paul is not, as is sometimes supposed, contradicting himself and his earlier argument about faith over against works of law; he is contradicting the understanding of the law that treats it as an agency by which, on the basis of works, a man may justify himself before God. This is a natural way of understanding the law, but Paul now looks back at it from the vantage ground of the Gospel and sees it in a new light. He does this in various parts of the epistle, for example in the next chapter, in his treatment of Abraham.

'The law' is not simply the Old Testament; but the Old Testament is the visible expression of it, and it is to the Old Testament that Paul now turns to support his emphatic assertion that faith does not do away with the law.

11 ABRAHAM JUSTIFIED BY FAITH
CHAPTER iv. 1–12

(1) What then shall we say that Abraham (on human terms, our ancestor) has found?[1] (2) For if Abraham was justified on the ground of works, then after all he has something to boast of. But in fact before God he has no such ground of boasting. (3) For what does the passage of Scripture say? 'Abraham had faith in God, and that was counted to him as righteousness.' (4) Now to a man who does works, his pay is not 'counted' as a matter of grace, but as a due; (5) but to a man who does no works, but has faith in him who 'justifies the ungodly', his faith is counted as righteousness. (6) It is in this way that David speaks of the blessing of the man to whom God 'counts' righteousness apart from works: (7) 'Blessed are they whose iniquities have been forgiven and whose sins have been covered over; (8) blessed is the man whose[2] sin the Lord will not count'. (9) Is the blessing then valid for the circumcision only? or for the uncircumcision too? For the latter also, for we can say, 'His faith was counted to Abraham as righteousness'. (10) In what state was he then when it was counted? In a state of circumcision, or of uncircumcision? Not in a state of circumcision, but in a state of uncircumcision. (11) And he received the sign of circumcision as a seal of the righteousness which came from faith, the faith he had while still uncircumcised. This was in order that he might be the 'father' of all who, in a state of uncircumcision, have faith, that righteousness may be counted to them, (12) and the 'father' of the circumcision – of those, that is, who do not rely on circumcision only but also follow[3] in the footsteps of the faith our father Abraham had while still uncircumcised.

---

1 The word (εὐρηκέναι) translated 'has found' is placed in this position by one group of MSS (ℵ A D G), in a different place by another group (ω: 'What then shall we say that Abraham our ancestor has found on human terms?'); and is omitted altogether by a third (B 1739: 'What then shall we say of Abraham (on human terms, our ancestor)?'). It is tempting to suggest that the short text is original and that the word which is inserted in different places came into the text from the margin. But Lietzmann is probably right in the view that the text as translated here is original; the reading of ω is an error which produced a senseless text, emended by the omission of the offending word.

2 'Whose sin the Lord will not count'; so B ℵ D G, a strong combination of Western and Alexandrian authorities. Alternatively, but less probably, 'To whom (ᾧ for οὗ the Lord will not count sin' (A C ω). The latter reading is probably due to assimilation to the quotation of Gen. xv. 6 in v. 3.

3 This sense, or any other, can only be obtained by omitting one Greek word (the τοῖς before στοιχοῦσιν). There is no question that this is the right course.

The new paragraph has two links with that which precedes it. There is a link, both verbal and substantial, with iii. 27. 'Boasting and faith are mutually exclusive' (p. 78). But are there no circumstances in which boasting is legitimate? May no one boast? And what does *faith*, *believing*, mean? There is, secondly, a more direct link (though the substantial point is essentially the same) with iii. 31, which was represented above as the transition from Paul's discussion of justification by faith through God's act of redemption in Christ to the present chapter. Paul vigorously denies that his preaching of faith does away with the law; rather, it establishes the law. It is, however, important to understand what he means by this. If he means that he now proposes to re-establish legal means to justification he is contradicting himself, and must be dismissed as a writer who does not understand the words he uses. But the 'law' he establishes is not a religion of legalism, but the religion of the Old Testament *properly understood*.

In any discussion of the Old Testament and its religion, Abraham must be allowed to be a central figure. He was the father of the race (Isa. li. 1 f.), and perfectly righteous (e.g. *Kiddushin*, iv. 14: We find that Abraham our father had performed the whole law before it was given, for it is written, Because that Abraham obeyed my voice and kept my charge, my commandments, my statutes, and my laws (Gen. xxvi. 5)). In particular, he was the type of absolute trust in God (e.g. *Aboth*, v. 3: With ten temptations was Abraham our father tempted, and he stood steadfast in them all). The Hellenistic synagogue pursued the same theme in its own way by representing Abraham as the fulfilment of all the (Greek) virtues (Philo, *Abraham*, 52 ff.; Josephus, *Antiquities*, i. 256).

The present paragraph opens in the style of the diatribe (see p. 41 f.), and we may suppose that the figure of Abraham is invoked by a Jewish objector, or perhaps is invoked within Paul's own mind – he was good at conceiving that kind of objection by whose refutation an argument may often be strengthened and clarified. Wherever the

1 challenge came from, Paul takes it up. **What then shall we say that Abraham (on human terms, our ancestor) has found?** Paul is bound to allow that *on human terms* (literally, *according to the flesh*; on this word see pp. 67) Abraham is the ancestor of the Jewish race; he will have more to say on the question of the descendants of Abraham below (*vv.* 11 f.; ix. 6–13; cf. Gal. iii. 7; iv. 21–31).

The objector is allowed to speak first: You say that men are justified

2 by faith only, and that therefore no boasting is possible; yet if **Abraham was justified on the ground of works, then after all he has something to boast of.** It is clear that Paul must prove the contrary of this, and from Scripture, but he begins by merely stating his case. **But in fact before God he (Abraham) has no such ground of boasting.**

There are two ways of translating this last sentence, and connecting it with that which follows. One is that which is adopted here; the 'for' (γάρ) with which *v.* 3 begins is then a genuinely argumentative particle: Abraham has no ground of boasting before God, *for* Scripture says .... The alternative translation would run: Yes, Abraham would then have some ground for boasting, but on the human level only; not before God. This translation evacuates the particle (γάρ) of argumentative force, and we should have to continue, But what in fact does the Bible say? This is an unsatisfactory rendering of the connecting particle (γάρ) and gives an improbable connection; it is also open to the objection that it introduces a distinction (boasting before God, and before men) which does not seem to be in Paul's mind. It is therefore better to maintain the rendering given here; Cranfield's 'But that is not how God sees him' and Käsemann's 'Doch (stimmt das) nicht vor Gott' are similar. Paul is arguing, and his argument, here at least, is not so disconnected as is sometimes thought.

Abraham then (whatever the Jew may think) cannot boast before God. **For what does the passage of Scripture** (relevant to the 3 matter) **say? 'Abraham had faith in God, and that was counted to him as righteousness'.** The reference is to Gen. xv. 6 (Paul follows the LXX in using the passive ('was counted') rather than the active ('he counted it' – RV)). The force of Paul's 'for' has already been discussed; he is using his quotation as the basis of his proof that not even Abraham was in a position to boast before God. But for this purpose he finds it necessary to establish his own interpretation of the passage, for according to current Jewish interpretation the 'faith' spoken of in it was not faith in Paul's sense but a meritorious work (e.g. 1 Macc. ii. 51 f.: ... the deeds of the fathers.... Was not Abraham found faithful in temptation, and it was reckoned unto him for righteousness? See S.B. iii, pp. 199 ff.; J. B. Lightfoot, *Galatians*, pp. 158–64). If this is what *faith* and *counting* mean, then Abraham has something to boast of before God, and the argument summarized in iii. 28 falls to the ground.

Paul's first step is to fasten upon the verb 'to count'. Evidently, if faith is 'counted' as righteousness it is not itself identical with, but distinguishable from, righteousness. The argument which follows is somewhat hurried, and to some extent confused, but it is possible to make the necessary logical supplements without great difficulty. Paul introduces the word 'pay', or 'reward' (μισθός), to make his point clear, drawing it probably from the LXX of Gen. xv. 1: Thy reward (μισθός) shall be exceedingly great (RV: I am thy shield, and thy exceeding great reward; but see RV mg and RSV). He begins: **To a 4 man who does works, his pay is not 'counted' as a matter of grace, but** is paid **as a due.** The contrast between 'as a matter of grace' and 'as a due' is instructive. 'Works' and 'due' belong together as correlatives; 'faith' and 'grace' similarly correspond, and it is to this pair that 'counting' belongs. It follows that since Abraham had righteousness *counted* to him, he cannot have done works, but must have been the recipient of grace. This is indeed the next stage in the argument, but Paul does not stay to state it; his short cut complicates the argument slightly. Instead of saying, 'But to him who does no works but has faith the reward (pay) is counted as a matter of grace',

5 he takes the next step in his stride: **But to a man who does no works, but has faith in him who 'justifies the ungodly', his faith is counted as righteousness.** This verse presupposes the conclusion already arrived at: faith and works are opposites, and Abraham is to be found among those who do not perform works with a view to justification but put their trust in God himself. This faith is counted as righteousness; that is, God justifies the man who has it, pronouncing over him a favourable verdict.

In this verse, the three words 'justifies the ungodly' are a very striking allusion to the Old Testament. They describe God as doing what the Old Testament forbids. Thus:

> Ex. xxiii. 7: I will not justify the wicked (LXX: Thou shalt not justify the ungodly).
>
> Prov. xvii. 15: He that justifieth the wicked, and he that condemneth the righteous, both of them alike are an abomination unto the Lord. Cf. xxiv. 24.
>
> Isa. v. 23: Woe unto them ... which justify the wicked for a reward, and take away the righteousness of the righteous from him.

The verbal contradiction is striking, though it would, of course, be mistaken to suggest that the Old Testament knows nothing of God's readiness to forgive the sinner. The passages indicate (i) that 'to justify' is a forensic term, which does not mean 'to make (ethically) righteous' but 'to acquit'; and (ii) that Paul is describing a divine act absolutely paradoxical in its mercy and grace. Compare v. 8.

Paul has now reached the second step in the argument by which he establishes his own interpretation of Gen. xv. 6. It consists in the application of a Rabbinical exegetical principle known technically as *g^ezerah shawah*.[1] According to this principle (the second of Hillel's *Middoth*), when the same word occurs in two biblical passages, each can be used to illuminate the other. The word in Gen. xv. 6 that most

---

1 For an account of this exegetical principle, see my *The New Testament Background: Selected Documents* (²1987), pp. 185 f. For its application to Rom. v, see J. Jeremias in *Studia Paulina in honorem J. de Zwaan* (1953; edited by J. N. Sevenster and W. C. van Unnik), pp. 149 ff.

requires elucidation is 'counted'; Paul proceeds to quote another passage in which the same word occurs.

It is in this way that David speaks of the blessing of the man to 6 **whom God 'counts' righteousness apart from works: 'Blessed are** 7 **they whose iniquities have been forgiven and whose sins have been covered over; blessed is the man whose sin the Lord will not** 8 **count'.** The quotation is from Ps. xxxii. 1 f., given in exact agreement with the LXX.

The conclusion to be deduced from this *gᵉzerah shawah* is that the 'counting of righteousness' is equivalent to the 'not-counting of sin'. It becomes clearer and clearer that justification, or the counting of righteousness, is neither the just evaluation of human merit (such as the Jew supposes Abraham to have had), nor the imparting of virtue, but forgiveness or acquittal. The man is justified, whose iniquities have been forgiven and whose sins have been covered over. The last verb recalls the description of Christ crucified as God's means of dealing with sin (see on iii. 25).

So far Paul has used, first, general methods, and, secondly a *gᵉzerah shawah*, to interpret Gen. xv. 6. He now sees an opportunity of carrying his argument yet further by applying his *gᵉzerah shawah*, as it were, in reverse; Gen. xv. 6 can be used to illuminate Ps. xxxii. 1 f.

Is this blessing (the blessing of forgiveness of which David speaks) 9 **then valid for the circumcision only? or for the uncircumcision too?** There is nothing in the Psalm to enable us to answer this question. Indeed, since David was a Jew we might suppose that he was writing of a peculiarly Jewish privilege. But application of the *gᵉzerah shawah* provides a different answer. **For the latter also** (these words are not in the text but are clearly presupposed), **for we can say, 'His faith was counted to Abraham as righteousness'.** The quotation is not, as is sometimes thought, a mere parenthesis, but an essential step in the argument. The word 'counted' takes us from Ps. xxxii to Gen. xv, and the question that could not be answered in regard to the Psalm admits of an easy solution in the other passage. **In what state was he** 10 **then when it was counted? In a state of circumcision, or of uncircumcision? Not in a state of circumcision, but in a state of uncircumcision.** This is a simple statement of fact; the circumcision of Abraham does not take place till Gen. xvii. In terms of religion (though not, of course, of race) he was a Gentile when God counted his faith as righteousness.

V. 11a is a parenthesis to which we must return presently. The argument continues in *v.* 11b.

This was in order that he might be the 'father' of all who, in a 11 **state of uncircumcision, have faith, that righteousness may be counted to them, and the 'father' of the circumcision – of those,** 12 **that is, who do not rely on circumcision only but also follow in the**

footsteps of the faith our father Abraham had while still uncircumcised. Here the word 'father' is taken from the promise made to Abraham which is quoted fully in *v.* 17.

That Abraham is the father of the Jewish people is, of course, a commonplace (*v.* 1). He was also regarded by the Rabbis as the first proselyte, and thus as the father of proselytes (e.g. *M^ekhilta* Ex. xxii. 20 (101a): Abraham called himself a proselyte (*ger*), for it is written, I am a stranger (*ger*) and a sojourner with you (Gen. xxiii. 4)). Paul's words thus bear a superficial similarity to those of the Rabbis; but the substance is completely different. (i) Abraham is not the father of Jews first, and then, in a derivative way, the father of Gentile proselytes also. He is first of all the father of believing Gentiles. (ii) He does not become the father of Gentiles when, and because, they are circumcised as proselytes; he is their father on the ground of their faith. Not outward incorporation into the visible ranks of Israel 'after the flesh' by means of an ancient ceremony, but the trustful and obedient acceptance of God's word admits them to the family of God's people, of which Abraham is father. (iii) In like manner, the privilege of descent from Abraham is accorded to Jews not in virtue of their birth and circumcision but in virtue of their faith (cf. ix. 6–13). They must 'join the ranks' (the words translated 'follow in the footsteps' suggest the metaphor of soldiers walking in file) of faith; and faith is (as the example of Abraham shows) independent of circumcision.

The story of Abraham shows, therefore, not what the Jewish objector (see p. 82) thinks, but that for Jew and Gentile alike there is but one way to justification, the way of faith alone. This result, however, raises acutely the question to which Paul has already given his answer in the parenthesis of *v.* 11a. If Abraham was already justified by faith, and if circumcision in itself cannot justify, why was Abraham circumcised? The references to circumcision in ii. 25–iii. 1 raise but do not answer the question what end the rite of circumcision was intended to serve. Abraham's circumcision was performed in obedience to a divine command (Gen. xvii. 10–14, 23–7). It must therefore have had some good meaning.

Paul's answer is that Abraham **received the sign of circumcision as a seal of the righteousness which came from faith, the faith he had while still uncircumcised.**

'Sign of circumcision' means simply a 'sign consisting in circumcision'. That circumcision was such a sign appears immediately from the biblical text (Gen. xvii. 11), and was universally recognized. It was the badge of Judaism (e.g. Jubilees xv. 26: . . . nor is there any sign on him [the uncircumcised man] that he is the Lord's).

This sign Abraham received as a *seal*. The question raised here is whether 'sign' and 'seal' are synonyms, or 'seal' adds a further thought not contained in 'sign'. It is sometimes stated that the Jews regarded circumcision as more than a sign, a seal which actually conveyed divine grace. This is, however, more easily stated than proved. Perhaps the strongest evidence in support of it is found in the Christian writer Barnabas, who puts into the mouth of a Jewish objector the words (ix. 6), 'The people have been circumcised as a seal'. The Jewish evidence itself is too late to prove that the Jews spoke of circumcision as a seal in New Testament times. It is a reasonable conjecture (though hardly more) that the Jews did so speak; then dropped 'seal' as a description of circumcision when the Christians began to use it for baptism (see J. B. Lightfoot, *Apostolic Fathers*, I. ii, p. 226); and finally revived their old custom when Church and Synagogue had separated. But in any case there is no need to suppose that 'seal' here means more than it does elsewhere in Paul's writings, namely, confirmation. Thus, for example, he writes at 1 Cor. ix. 2, You are the seal of my apostleship in the Lord – that is, the very fact that you are Christians confirms by an evident token the fact that I am an apostle. The Corinthian Christians did not make Paul an apostle, but their existence demonstrated that he was an apostle. In a similar way, Abraham's circumcision did not confer righteousness upon him, and was not a token that he was obliged henceforth to keep the law in order to be justified, but confirmed by a visible sign the fact that he had already been justified by faith. Thus, like the whole paragraph, this parenthesis inverts the argument of Paul's Jewish objector. Abraham's circumcision, rightly understood, confirms not the doctrine of justification by works of law, but that of justification by faith.

12 FAITH AND PROMISE

CHAPTER iv. 13–25

(13) **For the promise that he should be heir of the world was not granted to Abraham or to his seed in the context of law but in the context of the righteousness that comes by faith; (14) for if those who rely on the law are heirs, then faith has been emptied of its meaning and the promise has been brought to nothing. (15) For the law produces wrath; and[1] where there is no law, neither is there transgression. (16) Therefore God's plan was made to rest upon faith in order that it might be a matter of grace, so that the promise might be secure for all the seed – not only to that part of the seed which is able to rely on the law, but also to that which**

1 Instead of 'and' (or 'but' – the Greek is δέ), the Western text and other authorities (D G ω lat pesh) have 'for' (γάρ). This variant may be correct; if not, it is correct interpretation, if, as is probable, the sense is that the law produces wrath by producing transgression.

relies on the faith of Abraham, who is the father of us all (17) (as it is written, 'I have appointed thee as father of many Gentiles'), before God, in whom he believed, God, who quickens the dead and calls into being the things which do not exist. (18) This Abraham believed, hoping against hope, so as to become the 'father of many Gentiles' (according to the Scripture word, 'So shall thy seed be'). (19) He considered[1] without weakening in his faith that his own body was as good as dead (since he was about a hundred years old), and also the dead state of Sarah's womb. (20) He did not waver in unbelief in respect of God's promise but gave God the glory, (21) was fully convinced that what God had promised he had the power also to do, and grew strong in faith. (22) That is why 'it was counted to him for righteousness'. (23) Now it was not on his account only that it was written, 'It was counted to him', (24) but on ours also. Our faith is to be counted to us, who believe in him who raised up from the dead Jesus our Lord, (25) who was delivered up because of the sins we had committed, and raised up because of the justification that was to be granted to us.

The paragraph falls into three parts. The first is *vv.* 13–18: it provides a further argument for the view (already set forth in *vv.* 1–12) that God's relations with Abraham were not on a basis of law. They were based on promise, and the correlates of promise are grace and faith. These are correlates also of each other. In *vv.* 17 f., at the end of the first part, Paul begins to deal with the question what faith (and in particular Abraham's faith) is. He continues this question, and its answer, up to *v.* 22. The remaining part, *vv.* 23 ff., applies to Christians what has hitherto been said about Abraham.

Abraham received a promise. Paul never quotes it exactly or in full, but it is important to have in mind (as Paul doubtless had) the whole of Gen. xxii. 17 f.:

> In blessing I will bless thee, and in multiplying I will multiply thy seed as the stars of the heaven, and as the sand which is upon the sea shore; and thy seed shall possess the gate of his enemies; and in thy seed shall all the nations of the earth be blessed. Cf. also Gen. xii. 3; xviii. 18.

---

1 'He considered': the Western text (D G ω it) contains a negative, 'he did not consider'. Though opposite to each other, both readings give good sense. 'He considered ... and yet did not lose faith', or, 'He was so strong in faith that he did not even consider ...' The latter is perhaps a little more obvious, and does not give as pointed a contrast with *v.* 20 as does the former, which may therefore be preferred. Perhaps also the Western reviser recalled that according to Gen. xxv. 1 ff. Abraham was still to marry Keturah and to have by her six quite non-miraculous children!

Was this promise, like the 'counting' of righteousness (Gen. xv. 6), a matter of faith only, or was it perhaps dependent upon Abraham's observance of the law? Paul can no longer use the argument of *v.* 10, because in Gen. xxii Abraham has already been circumcised. Moreover, the promise follows and is dependent upon an act (the offering of Isaac) which, though Paul might regard it as a signal instance of faith (as in Heb. xi. 17 ff.), was regularly viewed in Judaism as a supremely meritorious work. Perhaps then the promise is a reward for a good work done in obedience to law.

The answer is a direct negative. **The promise that he should be 13 heir of the world was not granted to Abraham or to his seed in the context of law but in the context of the righteousness that comes by faith.** 'Heir of the world' is probably drawn from Gen. xxii. 18 ('all the nations') and xxii. 17, where in the LXX 'shall possess' becomes 'shall inherit'. Paul uses it to summarize the content of the promise. 'In the context of' translates a Greek word (διά) which, with the genitive, means most simply 'through'. It is often used, however, to denote 'attendant circumstances' (e.g. at ii. 27), and the question here is whether the promise falls within the domain of law, or within that of the righteousness of faith.

Having given his answer Paul justifies it by carefully defining his terms. **For if those who rely on the law are heirs, then faith has 14 been emptied of its meaning and the promise has been brought to nothing.** The main point here can be put in the form of counter-questions: What do you mean by a promise? and, What do you mean by faith? It is fundamentally the same as that of *vv.* 4 f. A promise is not a contract of payment to be made for work done. If you do A, I will give you B, is in Paul's view not a promise but a legal or commercial agreement. A promise falls within the sphere of gift, that is, of grace (cf. iii. 24). Again, if a man has made a contract with his employer he knows that his employer as well as himself is legally bound by the contract. He does not *believe* that he will receive his pay; he *knows* that (provided he keeps his side of the contract) he will receive it. If then it should be true that the way to be an heir (in the terms of the promise) is to keep the law, we can only conclude that the terms 'faith' and 'promise' have lost their meaning.

A second argument is added parenthetically in *v.* 15. It interrupts the connection between *vv.* 14 and 16, but may be taken here. Its opening word 'for' looks back to *v.* 13; it is a further ground for the dogmatic pronouncement of that verse.

For the law produces not promise but **wrath; and where there is 15 no law, neither is there transgression.**

Paul seems here to be anticipating material which he brings out more fully in v. 12 ff.; vii. 7–13; see the notes on these passages. The purpose of the law was in part to show how exceedingly sinful sin was

by actually producing and increasing transgression, which of course is
naturally and rightly visited with God's wrath – a very different matter
from his promise. Law, though good in itself (vii. 12, 14), is so closely
bound up with sin and wrath that it is unthinkable that it should be the
basis of the promise.

Paul now returns to the main line of his argument and his thought
becomes clearer, though the new sentence is grammatically imperfect.

16   **Therefore** looks back to *v.* 14, with which *v.* 16 is closely
connected. Paul insists explicitly that promise, faith, and grace belong
inseparably together.

God's plan was made to rest upon faith on man's side **in order
that** on God's **it might be a matter of grace**. A literal translation of
this part of the verse would run, 'Therefore of faith, in order that by
grace'. The supplements made in the translation are justified by the
context. Instead of 'God's plan' it would be possible to supply 'the
promise', but Paul's thought is broadening here, and the wider term is
to be preferred. If, on man's side, the plan rested on, for example,
works of law, God would be obliged to pay the reward under
constraint, not freely; only when we recognize that it rests upon faith
alone, can God's freedom in grace be maintained; only so can God
truly be God. Cf. xi. 32.

Paul continues: all this was done, **so that the promise might be
secure for all the seed – not only to that part of the seed which is
able to rely on the law, but also to that which relies on the faith of
Abraham.** It is clear that if the promise had been based upon law only
those who had the advantage of possessing the law could hope to
inherit the promise. But (as Paul will presently show from Scripture)
the promise was intended for Gentiles as well as Jews; hence it was
necessary that it should not be based on law. Only on the basis of faith
and grace could the promise be secure for all who were destined to
inherit.

17   The argument is closed by the proof that Abraham **is the father of
us all (as it is written, 'I have appointed thee as father of many
Gentiles').** Abraham is the father of *all* – of believing Jews and Gentile
Christians; see on *v.* 11. This is proved by Gen. xvii. 5, where the LXX
renders the word 'nations' by the word which to Paul regularly means
'Gentiles' (ἔθνη). Abraham is thus proved by Scripture itself to be the
father of non-Jews.

Paul's argument is now essentially complete. It is proved that the
promise (like justification) rests upon faith because (a) only grace and
faith are congruous with promise; (b) only on the basis of grace and
faith can Gentiles be admitted (as Scripture demands that they
should) as fellow-heirs with Jews and thus give effect to the truth (iii.
29) that God is not God of the Jews only but of the Gentiles also; and

90

(c) the law (the only serious alternative to grace and faith) is known to produce in practice not promise but wrath. The apostle ties up a loose end by showing that Abraham himself holds his position as father of the 'heirs' not in his own right, but by faith.

Abraham is the father of Jewish and Gentile Christians not in virtue of any human relationship with them but **before God, in whom he believed, God, who quickens the dead and calls into being the things which do not exist.** In this verse and the following Paul has in mind the story of the birth (and perhaps also of the intended sacrifice; cf. Heb. xi. 19, and see below, p. 93) of Isaac, the child of promise. This theme is developed further in *vv.* 19 ff. The God to whom Abraham's faith was directed quickens the dead. Further, he calls into being things which do not exist (this is the only translation of Paul's words that makes sense, and the linguistic difficulty is not insuperable; see Lietzmann,[1] and cf. Barnabas vi. 13); he is the Creator, and faith means reliance upon his creative power. The man who believes has his attention turned away from himself and fixed upon God as the only source of life. It was such faith as this that made Abraham the father of believers, according to the promise.

This Abraham believed, hoping against hope, so as to become 18 **the 'father of many Gentiles' (according to the Scripture word, 'So shall thy seed be').** Paul alludes again to Gen. xvii. 5, and, in the last five words, to Gen. xv. 5.

'Hoping against hope' is a neat rhetorical phrase, which may be compared with 'on the basis of nothing but faith' (i. 17). Literally it runs, 'Against (or, beyond) hope, in hope'. The two 'hope's' are different; it is when human hope is exhausted that God-given hope (cf. viii. 24 f.) comes into effect; in the midst of human death and non-existence it looks to God, who quickens and creates.

In completing his argument about the promise Paul has already, in *vv.* 17 f., begun to discuss the meaning of faith. He carries the discussion further in *vv.* 19 ff., first emphasizing the scene of human death in which faith is exercised. Abraham **considered** (see note 1 on 19 p. 88) **without weakening in his faith that his own body was as good as dead (since he was about a hundred years old), and also the dead state of Sarah's womb** (Sarah was ten years younger than her husband – Gen. xvii. 17). The procreation of new life in these circumstances was impossible. But the promise had been given, and this, not human weakness, was the decisive consideration. **He did not** 20 **waver in unbelief in respect of God's promise, but gave God the**

---

1 And now especially Cranfield and Käsemann. ὡς ὄντα is consecutive, 'so that it is'. For God's creative summons cf. Isa. xlviii. 13. Käsemann gives many parallels and discusses the significance here of the doctrine of *creatio ex nihilo*.

21   **glory, was fully convinced that what God had promised he had
     the power also to do, and grew strong in faith.**

'Not wavering' and 'being fully convinced' appear to correspond;
but in fact the translation of the latter is not certain. The word
(πληροφορεῖν) when used, as here, in the passive, can mean 'to be full
of', and is used with moral attributes (e.g. love, at 1 Clement liv. 1). An
analogous use ('to be full of *the idea of doing* something') points to the
meaning here: Abraham was full (of confidence) that God . . . Compare xiv. 5 and the note.[1]

By his unwavering confidence that God could and would fulfil his
promise Abraham gave glory to God; that is, he did precisely what the
unbelievers of i. 21 did not do. He recognized God as God; the Creator,
as such altogether different from creation, powerful where men are
weak, living where they are dead. Only faith can so give glory to God;
to perform 'works of law' with a view to establishing a claim upon
him, or to throw off all sense of obligation to him, is to dishonour God.

When Paul adds that Abraham grew strong in faith, he does not
mean that on account of his faith Abraham became a strong man, a
forceful 'personality'. It was in his faith that he was strong, unlike
those (mentioned in chs. xiv, xv, where see the notes) who were 'weak
in faith'. These were scrupulous persons, whose faith was still
mingled with legalistic righteousness. Faith (in Paul's sense) grows
stronger as it is unmixed with confidence in any thing or any one other
than God himself.

Paul concludes his argument about Abraham by quoting again the
22   passage from Gen. xv. 6 with which he opened the discussion. **That is
     why** (because Abraham's faith was what it was, the complete
submission to God which is the human reflection of a right relation
with him) **'it was counted to him for righteousness'.**

Paul's discussion of Abraham is nowhere a purely historical
investigation, for Abraham believed, and was justified, not as a private
individual but as the father of believers. At this point, however, Paul
begins to apply in express terms what he has deduced about faith from
23   the story of Abraham to Christian believers in his own age. **Now it
     was not on** Abraham's **account only that it was written, 'It was
     counted to him'** (these key words are intended to bring to mind the
24   whole Old Testament basis of the argument), **but on ours also.** The
principle of justification by faith cannot apply to one man only; if true
at all, it must be universally true. **Our faith is to be counted** (this
futuristic expression looks forward with confidence to God's vindication at the last judgement of those whom he has chosen) **to us, who
believe in him who raised up from the dead Jesus our Lord.** Our
justification is the same as Abraham's, for it is rooted in the free and

1 See the admirable discussion in Bauer-Aland, *Wörterbuch, s.v.*

gracious will of God, who counts faith as righteousness. Our faith is the same as Abraham's, for it is in the same God, whose properties are unchanged – he is the God who brings life out of death. But for Christians this power of the living God can no longer be described in terms of the unexpected birth of Isaac from aged parents. That which the Old Testament foreshadowed has become manifest in the death and resurrection of Jesus, in which God raised up his own Son not from a dead womb but from the grave.

The parallelism between Isaac and Jesus would be even closer if it could be maintained that Paul had in mind the 'binding of Isaac', which from time to time plays an interesting part in Rabbinic theology. Isaac's willingness to be bound and sacrificed led to his being regarded as an important mediatorial figure. It is just possible that this theme is in mind in *v.* 25; rather more likely that it appears in viii. 32. But Paul makes no serious use of it; like the 'Noachian precepts' (see on ii. 14 f.) it is material he might have been expected to use, but in fact leaves out of account. His concern is with Jesus himself, rather than with analogies to him and his experiences;[1] he means to insist that the God in whom Christians believe is indeed the God of Abraham, now made known by an even clearer, and universally valid and effective, demonstration of his life-giving and creative power than was vouchsafed to Abraham.

Having mentioned Jesus and the resurrection Paul winds up the chapter by using what appears to be a Christological formula, though its history before its use by Paul must remain a matter of speculation. **Jesus Christ was delivered up because of the sins we had** 25 **committed, and raised up because of the justification that was to be granted to us.**

In 'delivered up' some see an allusion to Isa. liii. 12 (LXX): His soul was delivered up unto death. This is not impossible, but compare 2 Cor. iv. 11, where the same verb is used in the first person plural present.

The word (διά) which (followed by the accusative) is here twice translated 'because of' may have retrospective or prospective reference. Here it is taken to be retrospective in the first occurrence, prospective in the second. If this change of reference seems too harsh, the word may at its first occurrence also be taken as prospective – 'he was delivered up with a view to dealing with our (future) sins'. It is very unlikely that Paul meant anything so artificial as, 'He died on account of the sins which we had committed, and was raised on account of our justification (which by dying he had already accomplished)'. On the whole, it seems best to translate as here, and to

---

1 The parallel and contrast with Adam in v. 12–21 stands on a different footing; see the notes.

recognize in the doubled 'because of' an attempt at rhetorical antithesis in a credal formula.

The same rhetorical motive accounts for the apparent separation of the death and resurrection of Christ. Paul does not mean to ascribe one consequence to the death, another to the resurrection. The two events jointly were responsible for both consequences.

13 JUSTIFICATION AND SALVATION

CHAPTER v. 1–11

(1) Since then we have been justified on the basis of faith we have[1] peace with God through our Lord Jesus Christ. (2) It is moreover through him that we have gained our access to this grace in which we now stand, and, looking to the future, exult in our hope of the glory of God. (3) Further, we even exult in our afflictions, because we know that affliction produces endurance, (4) and endurance tried character, and tried character hope; (5) and our hope is not one that can put us to shame, for God's love for us has already been poured out in our hearts through the Holy Spirit who was given to us. (6) For while we were still[2] powerless, at the due moment Christ died for us ungodly men. (7) For scarcely will anyone die for a righteous man/for on behalf of a good man someone might even dare to die,[3] (8) but God proves his love for us by the fact that while we were still sinners Christ died for us. (9) Since then we have now been justified at the cost of his blood, much more shall we be saved through him from God's wrath; (10) for if when we were enemies we were reconciled to God through the death of his Son,

1 The great majority of MSS have not 'we have' but 'let us have'. This variant has such an important bearing on the sense of the passage that it must be discussed in the Commentary proper.

2 There is much textual confusion in this verse and only the most important variants can be mentioned here. The text preferred is awkward because it contains the word 'still' (ἔτι) twice. The second occurrence is wanting in many late MSS, but is undoubtedly genuine (it is contained in ℵ A B C D G 33 lat). There is more doubt about the beginning of the verse. 'For still' (ἔτι γάρ) is read by the majority of MSS (ℵ A C D ω 33 Marcion); the main alternatives are 'For to what end' (εἰς τί γάρ), a rhetorical question (G lat); and 'if indeed' (εἴ γε), connecting with the previous verse ('The love of God has been poured out ... if indeed ...; this is read by B sah). It seems, however, likely that these alternatives are attempts to avoid the repeated 'still'; but this reading is not so difficult as to be impossible. Paul wishes to emphasize that Christ died for us while we were still weak; to do so he places the word first in the sentence, and then uses it again in the normal place, perhaps forgetting that he had uttered it (he was dictating; cf. xvi. 22).

3 For the two parallel clauses in this verse, and a possible explanation of their presence in the text, see the exposition below (pp. 98 f.).

much more, now that we have been reconciled, shall we be saved by his life. (11) And not only have we this hope: we even exult in God through our Lord Jesus Christ, through whom we have here and now received reconciliation.

For three and a half chapters Paul has dealt with righteousness, judgement, and justification. He can now presuppose justification, the result of God's gracious act of redemption in Jesus Christ, and proceed to consider some of its consequences. He presupposes it not as a human experience on which men may build, but as an act of God, a stage in God's dealings with his people.

Since then we have been justified on the basis of faith we have   1 peace wth God through our Lord Jesus Christ. The first consequence of justification is peace with God. Indeed, to say that we have peace with God is hardly more than to say that we have been justified, since justification puts an end to the legal strife between Judge and accused. No more than justification is 'peace' an experience; it is an objective status or condition, a relation which exists between God and those whom he justifies. See the parallel between justification and reconciliation in *vv.* 9, 10. Of course, the objective state is reflected in the *feeling* of peace and security which man enjoys when he knows that he is reconciled to God, and peace in biblical and Jewish usage is a comprehensive description of the blessings of salvation (e.g. Isa. xlviii. 18; 2 Thess. iii. 16).

So far it has been assumed that Paul wrote and intended the indicative, 'we have peace'. But (see note (1) on p. 94) there is strong evidence for the view that he wrote 'let us have peace'. The difference between the two words (ἔχομεν, we have; ἔχωμεν, let us have) is slight, and was not noticed in pronunciation in the Hellenistic age. It follows from this that great stress should not be laid upon the strong numerical superiority of the reading 'let us have'.

It may be said at once that, if 'let us have peace' implies that a man who has been justified may thereafter freely choose whether or not he will be at peace with God, Paul could not have intended it. To be justified is to be at peace with God. The Greek verb 'to have' (ἔχειν), however, 'carries a perfect meaning, viz. I enjoy the possession of something already obtained',[1] so that the subjunctive verb may be interpreted as a brachylogy. Paul means: Since we have been justified we have peace; let us therefore enjoy it.

This is a possible interpretation of Paul's thought; but it may be doubted whether it is correct. The context is not hortatory, but indicative. In the next verse, Paul says 'we have gained our access' and 'we now stand'. Perhaps even more important is the fact that in *vv.* 10

---

1 Moule, *Idiom Book*, p. 15; cf. Moulton, *Prolegomena*, p. 110.

and 11 he says 'we were reconciled', 'we have been reconciled', and 'we have here and now received God's act of reconciliation'. He is not urging his readers to do and be what as Christians they ought to do and be, but reminding them of the facts on which all their doing and being rest. It follows that the reading 'we have' may be preferred, though the textual support for 'let us have' is so strong that a measure of doubt will always remain, since 'let us have' (understood as suggested above) is not theologically impossible, though it is theologically less appropriate than the other reading.

If we have peace with God at all it is through our Lord Jesus Christ.
2 **It is moreover through him that we have gained our access to this grace in which we now stand.** Paul restates the position mainly with a view to his next forward step, but it is worth noting in passing his use of the word 'access' (cf. Eph. iii. 12 – it evokes the picture of a worshipper approaching a shrine or holy place in virtue of a sacrifice), and of 'grace'. The latter is not used in exactly the same way as at iii. 24, because Paul here compresses more into it; he means, 'this state determined by the grace of God', that is, the enjoyment of peace with God. The past and the present thus secure, **looking to the future, we exult in our hope of the glory of God.**

Here another grammatical difficulty presents itself. The verb translated 'exult' (καυχώμεθα) could, as far as its form goes, be either indicative (we exult) or subjunctive (let us exult). Only the context can decide between the possibilities; but, as we have seen, the context is clearly indicative.

This Greek verb has earlier (ii. 17, 23; cf. iii. 27; iv. 2) been translated 'boast'.[1] In the earlier passages it was used in a bad sense of men's boastful confidence; but here, used of Christians, it takes a new colour and cannot be satisfactorily translated by the old word. It means a triumphant, rejoicing confidence – in God. The man who has been justified exults in good hope for the future, knowing that he can look forward to nothing less than the glory of God, which all men have lost (iii. 23). For glory as the final eschatological consequence of justification compare viii. 18, 21, 30.

3   Christian exultation, however, is not merely a matter of hope: **we even exult in our afflictions.** This does not mean that the prospect of glory in the future enables Christians to endure afflictions in the present. It is proper that, when a Christian boasts, or exults, he should do so either in hope, or in his afflictions; in hope, because he knows that he is and has nothing of which he can boast, and hope points to that which is entirely in God's hands (cf. viii. 24); and in afflictions, because they humble him and prevent him from having confidence in

---

1 See A. Vanhoye (ed.), *L'Apôtre Paul*, Bibliotheca Ephemeridum Theologicarum Lovaniensium 73 (Leuven, 1986), pp. 363–8.

himself, so that he trusts in God only, and gives glory to him (cf. 2 Cor. xi. 30). There is a further reason for exulting in afflictions. Paul believes that the ministry of Jesus inaugurated the last age of world history, which (as many Jews believed) was to be marked by severe affliction for the people of God before the coming of bliss in the kingdom of God. This affliction Jesus had absorbed in his own person on the cross, that his followers might go free; yet this had not been done so completely that they were exempt from bearing their crosses after him. Paul exults therefore in afflictions, because they are a sign of the last age, and mark out the path to glory. Cf. Col. i. 24.

Paul proceeds to work out the same point in another way. We exult in afflictions **because we know that affliction produces endurance, and endurance tried character, and tried character hope.** For 4 endurance, cf. ii. 7; also viii. 25. It is not simply the ability to support affliction and distress, but the attitude that looks through affliction and distress to find their meaning in God. Correspondingly, tried character is not simply moral worth. The word (δοκιμή) is a rare one, formed from a verb which means 'to test' and, if the test warrants it, 'to approve' (see on ii. 18). Testing and approving are clearly in mind here; and it is God who is the judge, and vouches for the tried character of the man who patiently endures affliction. For the word, cf. Phil. ii. 22.

When God's approval is thus given there is room for hope, not because the man of tried character is a strong and trustworthy person but because in his endurance he has learnt to look not to himself but to God. Christian exultation again finds its basis – in hope. And this is a more secure basis than might at first appear. **Our hope is not one 5 that can put us to shame.** The language is based upon Ps. xxii. 5; xxv. 3, 20. Paul means that our hope (of the glory of God (v. 2)) will not be disappointed, and that we shall therefore not have to bear the shame of having followed a false hope.

How can we be certain of this? Because **God's love for us has already been poured out in our hearts through the Holy Spirit who was given to us.** The relation between the Holy Spirit who now dwells in the Church and in believers, and the eschatological future, is brought out more clearly and at greater length in ch. viii (see especially viii. 23); but already it appears that the gift of the Spirit now is the pledge that our salvation will eventually be complete. The present sentence is, however, obscure in some points.

God's love for us: the Greek is, literally, the love of God, and the genitive might be objective or subjective. Many interpreters (including Augustine) have preferred 'our love for God'; but in v. 8 Paul demonstrates God's love for us, and it is this – not our love for him – that makes us confident in our hope.

The words 'poured out' are generally used of the Spirit; so, for example, at Acts ii. 18, 33; x. 45. All these passages are probably dependent on Joel ii. 28. Paul's meaning would perhaps have been somewhat clearer if he had said that the Spirit had been poured out in our hearts, and that by this means God's love for us had there become fully operative, both in making us aware of its presence, and in transforming us. Those whom he so loves God will not disappoint in the hope they set upon him.

The definite past tense, 'who was given to us', may point to a particular moment at which the Spirit was received; conversion, or baptism, may be in mind. In any case, the gift of the Spirit, like justification (*v.* 1) can be described by a past tense. These are elements in salvation but not the whole of it; they anticipate salvation which as a totality belongs to the future (xiii. 11; note also the future tenses in *vv.* 9, 10).

The next three verses relate the clearest possible proof that God loves men, sinful as they are. The substance of the verses is clear; it is not possible to say so much of their literary arrangement. *V.* 6 enunciates the truth Paul wishes to express; he amplifies it in *vv.* 7 f. In the two clauses of *v.* 7 he virtually repeats himself, as the repeated 'for' (γάρ) shows. This repetition is often passed by without comment. The first 'for' links well with *v.* 6, and so would the second if *v.* 7a were not there, but it seems impossible to take the second 'for' as giving in *v.* 7b the ground of *v.* 7a. It is not impossible that Paul dictated *v.* 7a, thought he could express himself better, and dictated *v.* 7b. But Tertius (xvi. 22) had now put *v.* 7a on his paper, and by an oversight it was never removed. This explanation is by no means certain, but is a good deal better than most attempts to distinguish between *righteous* (δίκαιος) and *good* 6 (ἀγαθός). See further on p. 99. God's love can be relied on, **for while we were still powerless, at the due moment Christ died for us ungodly men.**

'Powerless' may seem rather weak as a synonym of 'ungodly' and 'sinners' (*v.* 8). The point probably is that Christ died for us when we were powerless to help ourselves; we were ungodly and sinful and could do nothing to improve our state.

The 'due moment' is the eschatological moment of the fulfilment of God's promises, 'when the fullness of the time came' (Gal. iv. 4). God's love, revealed in the death of Christ, is thus not mere compassion. It means God's freedom in taking the initiative on behalf of undeserving men, and his faithfulness to his declared word.

There are many parallels in the New Testament to the statement that Christ died for the ungodly; see especially Mark xiv. 24; John x. 11; xi. 50 ff.; Rom. viii. 32; xiv. 15; 1 Cor. xi. 24; xv. 3; 2 Cor. v. 15, 21; Gal. i. 4; ii. 20; Eph. v. 2, 25; 1 Thess. v. 10; 1 Tim. ii. 6; Titus ii. 14; Heb.

ii. 9; x. 12; 1 Pet. ii. 21; iii. 18; 1 John iii. 16.[1] The conviction that Christ died for sinners (or for sin) was undoubtedly central in the thought of the primitive Church, but this is not to say that all Christians understood in the same way how or why he died for sinners. In the present passage Paul himself is not concerned with a rationale of the crucifixion; he stresses only the love revealed in the fact that Christ went to such lengths on our behalf.

He emphasizes the same point by comparing Christ's readiness to die with the unreadiness men would show in more favourable circumstances. **For scarcely will anyone die for a righteous man,** 7 who might be expected to merit such heroic action.

Paul breaks off and starts again (see above, p. 98). **For on behalf of a good man someone might even dare to die.** 'Good man' has the article in Greek; this points out not an individual but a class.[2] It is also possible, though not probable, that the word 'good' is neuter, and that Paul means 'for something good, for a good cause, someone . . .'. These details, however, are insignificant; in the next verse Paul drives home the main point.

God proves (the word used at iii. 5; God 'brings out' the fact of his 8 love, and at the same time 'brings it home' to us) **his love for us by the fact that while we were still sinners Christ died for us.**

'For us' is here taken with 'love'. It is often taken (as 'to us') with 'proves'. For the ambiguity compare 2 Cor. ii. 8. Paul's usage (see Col. i. 4; 1 Thess. iii. 12; Rom. xvi. 1; 2 Cor. iv. 2; v. 12) strongly supports the view taken in the translation.

The verse can hardly be expounded further. The manifestation of God's love is through a historical event; the application of it is by the Holy Spirit (*v.* 5).

The fact of God's love being now established, Paul returns to the main theme of the paragraph. Since God has already done so much for us, we can have a good hope for the future and be confident of final salvation. **Since then we have now been justified at the cost of his blood, much** 9 **more shall we be saved through him from God's wrath.**

As in *v.* 1, justification is presupposed as an event from which conclusions may be drawn. In *v.* 1, the conclusion concerns the present – we have peace; here, the conclusion concerns the future – we shall be saved. Justification has been effected (to translate literally) 'in his blood' (cf. iii. 25). The 'in' may be instrumental ('by means of'), or, reflecting a Hebrew idiom, mean 'at the cost of'. In any case, the reference to blood suggests sacrifice, and this confirms the translation given above. For the thought, see the notes on iii. 25 f.

---

1 In all these passages, as here, the preposition is ὑπέρ, 'on behalf of'.
2 Moule (*Idiom Book*, p. 111) translates, 'for the good type of man', 'for your good man'.

For Paul's teaching on salvation, see on i. 16; xiii. 11. It belongs essentially to the future, and the verb 'to save' is here, as usual, in the future tense (so at v. 10; ix. 27; x. 9, 13; (xi. 14); xi. 26; at xi. 14 it is possibly in the subjunctive (with future meaning); at viii. 24 it is in the aorist indicative, but qualified by 'in hope'). As 'from God's wrath' shows, it refers to the final deliverance at the last judgement; as such it is already guaranteed by justification, in which God anticipates his favourable verdict. For 'wrath' see on i. 18. It is already revealed in the present age, though not against believers, who are not under law (vi. 15), which produces wrath (iv. 15), and are not being progressively handed over to their own wickedness (i. 24, 26, 28), but promised that sin shall not have dominion over them (vi. 14).

The same truth is now differently expressed in an illuminating 10 parallel. **For if when we were enemies we were reconciled to God through the death of his Son, much more, now that we have been reconciled, shall we be saved by his life.** It is important here to notice the introduction of a new term – reconciliation, and the close parallel between this and justification. The two verses (9 and 10) can be set out in outline as follows:

1	Justified	1	Reconciled
2	Through the death of Christ	2	Through the death of Christ
3	We shall be saved.	3	We shall be saved.

Justification and reconciliation are different metaphors describing the same fact. The meaning of the verb 'to reconcile'[1] is determined by the noun 'enemies'; it puts an end to enmity, just as 'to justify' puts an end to legal contention. 'Reconciliation' evokes the picture of men acting as rebels against God their king, and making war upon him; 'justification' that of men who have offended against the law and are therefore arraigned before God their judge.

V. 10 contains two balanced clauses:

We have been reconciled by Christ's death;
We shall be saved by his life (literally, 'in his life'; cf. (in his blood' in *v.* 9).

For the parallelism cf. iv. 25. Here, as there, it is not probable that Paul means to suggest that Christ's death effects one thing, his (resurrec-

---

1 1 Cor. vii. 11 (the reconciliation of estranged husband and wife) is an illuminating parallel. See also v. 11; xi. 15; 2 Cor. v. 18, 19, 20; Col. i. 20; Eph. ii. 16.

tion) life another; that is, the contrast is rhetorical[1] rather than substantial. Paul begins by asserting that reconciliation depends upon the crucifixion; but as he argues from reconciliation to salvation he recalls the corresponding truth that the crucifixion was followed by the resurrection.

Christians, then, stand between two decisive moments in God's work of redemption. Because God has manifested his righteousness, to faith, in Christ crucified, they have been justified and reconciled; because they have been justified and reconciled, they will finally be saved when God brings history to a close. To this end they look forward in hope. Paul, however, cannot end his paragraph without emphasizing again that for Christians the present, even though it be a time of tribulation, is a time to exult in God. **Not only have we this 11 hope: we even exult[2] in God through out Lord Jesus Christ, through whom we have here and now received reconciliation** – that is, have been reconciled to God.

There is little fresh thought in this verse. For 'exult' see on *v.* 2. 'Here and now' (νῦν) describes the anticipation in the present of God's verdict at the judgement, the peace of the kingdom of God. We have been reconciled *now*, therefore we exult *now*. Compare iii. 26 (with the note); also 2 Cor. vi. 2.

14 ADAM AND CHRIST

CHAPTER v. 12–21

(12) Therefore as through one man sin entered the world (and through sin came that man's death), so also death came to all men, because they all sinned. (13) For until the law came, sin was in the world, but where there is no law sin is not taken into account. (14) All the same, from Adam up to Moses death reigned, even over those who had not sinned in such a way as to produce a transgression like Adam's. Now Adam is a type of the Man to Come.

(15) But the act of grace did not after all correspond exactly to

---

1 With this Käsemann (130 f.; English translation, 139) disagrees, arguing for a substantial distinction. 'The life (Lebensmacht) of the living Lord embraces and preserves the community.' But he adds, 'The Christ who died for us also (nunmehr) lives for us, and destroys the threats of the future as he destroyed the evil power of the past.' There is only one Christ; if the Crucified had not risen there would have been no reconciliation; if the Living One had not first died there would be no salvation.

2 In Greek 'exult' is a participle (καυχώμενοι). It is very unlikely that it is an imperatival participle (see on xii. 9), or that it should be connected with *v.* 10. It is better to suppose that through an accidental slip the construction is defective; this is not the only imperfect sentence in Paul's writings.

the act of sin; for if it be true that by the transgression of the One the Many died, much more did the grace of God, and the gracious gift of the One man Jesus Christ, abound for the Many. (16) Again, God's gift was not a mere equivalent of the result that followed from One who sinned; for from one act of transgression began the process of judgement which leads to condemnation, but the act of grace, wrought in the context of many transgressions, leads to justification. (17) For if, by the transgression of the One, death reigned through that One, much more shall those who receive the excess of grace and of the gift of righteousness reign in life through the One Jesus Christ.

(18) Therefore as, through one act of transgression, the result for all men was condemnation, so also through one act of righteousness the result for all men was justification, which leads to life. (19) For as through the disobedience of the One man the Many were made sinners, so also through the obedience of the One the Many shall be made righteous. (20) The law took its subordinate place in order that transgression might multiply; but where sin did multiply, grace abounded all the more, (21) in order that as sin reigned in death so grace also might reign through righteousness, with eternal life its goal, through Jesus Christ our Lord.

12 The new paragraph opens with **Therefore** (διὰ τοῦτο), but it is difficult to see how it, or its first sentence, arises logically out of the preceding sentence or paragraph. There are two possibilities of interpretation. (i) 'Therefore' refers to the protasis with which *v.* 12 begins. The sentence would then run: 'For this reason, namely, that sin and death entered the world through Adam, in like manner sin and death became the fate of all men'. This is possible, but strains Paul's language. (ii) Alternatively, 'therefore' is a particle of transition, indicating only a loose relation between what has gone before and what follows. Such a loose relation can be made out, and this seems the best course to take. A 'loose relation' does not mean 'no relation', but that there is no rigid logical step from the exultation reached in *v.* 11 to the account of the origin of sin and death in *v.* 12.

In *vv.* 1–11 Paul argued that justification and reconciliation carry with them the certainty of future salvation, in which men may confidently exult. He now supports the same conclusion by a different method. It is through Christ that Christians have their hope of salvation. But Christ is the counterpart of Adam, and we can be as sure that we shall share in the consequences of Christ's acts as that we do already share in the consequences of Adam's. What Christ has done has universal validity.

The thought of this paragraph is complicated, and by no means clearly set out. It will be best to follow Paul patiently through it, and at the end to make an attempt to analyse the position he reaches.

As through one man sin entered the world (and through sin came that man's death), so also death came to all men, because they all sinned. This is by no means a universally accepted translation of the verse. Probably the most common view is that Paul here begins a sentence which he does not complete. Thus RSV has:

> Therefore as sin came into the world through one man and death through sin, and so death spread to all men because all men sinned –

Here (according to RSV) Paul breaks off and starts again. Similarly, in a careful discussion, which should be studied, Cranfield, p. 269:

> Wherefore, as through one man sin entered the world, and through sin death, and so death came to all men in turn, because all have sinned –

There is no doubt that this is a straightforward, word-for-word rendering of what Paul wrote. The question turns upon the two words translated by RSV and Cranfield, *and so* (καὶ οὕτως). That this is a correct rendering of these two words is not in question; nor is it in question that, if they are so translated, we are left with a sentence that has no end. This is not impossible; Paul was capable of writing defective sentences. If however Paul had reversed the order of the two words (οὕτως καί) we should translate *so also*; the sentence would then be complete and make good sense. Either he left it incomplete, or he wrote the two words in the 'wrong' order. Neither alternative is impossible, and most have chosen the former; it is however surprising that so many should affirm (correctly) that *as* (ὥσπερ), at the beginning of the sentence, requires a following *so* (οὕτως), and add that no *so* is to be found. There is in the context a *so*, though it appears as καὶ οὕτως and not as οὕτως καί. A third possibility, not identical with but related to that which is accepted here, should be mentioned. If *therefore* (διὰ τοῦτο) points back to the 'blessed state of confidence and hope just described' in v. 1–11, *as* (ὥσπερ) will introduce a *concluding* comparison, and we must supply before it 'it was' or 'Christ wrought'. This interpretation is to be preferred because 'none of the endeavours of Commentators to supply the second limb of the comparison from the following verses have succeeded: and we can hardly suppose such an ellipsis, when the next following comparison (*v.* 16) is rather a *weakening* than a strengthening of the analogy' (Alford, 2, p. 360, giving Mt xxv. 14 as a comparable use of ὥσπερ). See also Black, p. 87.

It need not be said that Paul, a first-century Jew, accepted Gen. i–iii as a straightforward narrative of events that really happened. He also saw in these chapters a theological account of sin which gave him a tool by means of which he could analyse the state of human society and the human heart. But he begins with the narrative. Sin entered the world through the first man, who disobeyed the commandment given him by God. He did this not simply out of longing for a fruit which happened fortuitously to have been forbidden, but in rebellion against his Maker, for the serpent had cast doubt upon God's truthfulness and goodness, and said, 'In the day ye eat thereof ... ye shall be as God' (Gen. iii. 4 f.). That is, Adam endeavoured to set himself in the place of God (cf. p. 37), and in that moment sin was born. At the same time, Adam fell under sentence of death.

So far Paul has been describing the historical events (as he would deem them) of Adam's career, and has established that he was responsible for the entry of sin and death into the world, at least as far as his own person was concerned. But once the connection between sin and death has been established, Paul moves onward: 'So also death came to all men, because they all sinned'. That is, all men sin (cf. iii. 23), and all men die because they sin; but Paul does not add here that they sin, or that they die, because they are physically descended from Adam. Nowhere, even in v. 19, does Paul teach the direct seminal identity between Adam and his descendants which seems to be implied in the nearly contemporary 4 Ezra (especially iii. 7, 8, 21, 22).[1]

Death, then, is the result of sin. But this raises a problem which Paul allows for a moment to divert him from his argument: What if there are men who do not sin? Will they not live for ever? This is not so hypothetical a problem as might appear, for the only means of estimating sin is transgressible law, and where there is no law sin may exist but can give no indication of its presence. Now in fact no general law existed between Adam and Moses,[2] and it might be expected that in that period no deaths would take place. This, however, was not so. Paul notes the anomaly, but without offering a formal explanation.

13 **For until the law came** (with Moses), **sin was in the world, but where there is no law sin is not taken into account** (a commercial
14 term – 'put in the ledger'). **All the same, from Adam up to Moses death reigned, even over those who had not sinned in such a way** (that is, against a law) **as to produce a transgression like Adam's.** This, as was said, is not a formal explanation, but the germ of an explanation lies in the distinction which Paul, unsystematically it is

1 The Latin rendering (*in quo*) of the words (ἐφ' ᾧ) here translated 'because' could be, and was, understood to mean 'in whom'; that is, all men sinned *in* Adam. But this is certainly not the meaning of the Greek.
2 Note that Paul takes no account of the 'Noachian precepts'; see p. 50, n. 2; also *From First Adam to Last*, pp. 23–6.

true, makes between sin and transgression. Sin is an inward disposition of rebellion against God arising out of exaltation of the self. It has always been in the world since Adam's fall because it is inseparably bound up with man's desire to return to the lost state of bliss and immortality, his will to life in and for himself. This is an unavoidable consequence of man's existence in a world which has once turned away from God. But it is not to be identified with the performance of wicked actions. Sin is turned into transgression, and becomes visible and assessable, only when a law is given.

It will be seen that this paragraph, like Paul's sentence on which it is based, leaves open the question of the origin of sin (as distinct from transgression). The raw material of it was, in the language of Genesis, already present in Eden: the snake was there, and so was a tree with desirable fruit (Gen. iii. 6). But there could be no 'desire to return to the lost state of bliss and immortality'; that state had, by definition, not yet been lost. For a theological description of what happened we may return to chapter i. God can only be known as Lord, and a Lord is what man, himself created to have dominion (Gen. i. 26; Ps. viii. 6), will not tolerate. There is an inevitable clash between the finite and the infinite. To say this is, in a sense, to throw the blame for sin back upon God; but Paul will not tolerate the question (ix. 20), Why did you make me like this? If however it was God's intention to lead his creation through disobedience to his mercy (xi. 32), we can understand that kind of universalism that is expressed by 'all in Christ' over against 'all in Adam' (*vv.* 15–19; 1 Cor. xv. 22).

These observations provide us with important hints for the interpretation of the argument that follows. This is conducted simultaneously on two lines, for Paul deals with both Adam and his counterpart, Christ.

Now Adam is a type of the Man to Come.

Paul introduces this remark without warning or explanation; he knew that he was treading familiar ground. In various ways, the first man and the Redeemer had been compared, contrasted, and even identified. An account of these religious speculations would not greatly illuminate the Epistle to the Romans, for Paul takes an independent line. He begins with Jesus, and adopts and adapts such speculative material as he can use.

Adam is a type (τύπος) of Christ. The word means a visible mark left by some object (e.g. John xx. 25). Hence, in metaphor, a type is the mark, a reversed, laterally inverted, mark, which corresponds to the fact that Adam and Christ are reversed images of each other, left in history or nature by the antitype (ἀντίτυπος). Paul's use of the word in 1 Cor. x. 6 (cf. x. 11) shows that this precise definition must not be pressed. Paul is using analogy (rather than, in a strict sense, 'typology'). Adam and Christ were in analogous circumstances and exposed to analogous temptations. Adam fell, Christ did not; but even so the consequences of their acts were analogous. In fact, the best commentary on 'type' is to be found in the series of correspondences, perfect and imperfect, which Paul notes in the following verses.

'The Man to Come' represents a Greek participle (τοῦ μέλλοντος). This may mean no more than the Coming One (cf., e.g., Matt. xi. 3); but the context, and comparison with 1 Cor. xv. 45, suggest that Paul is thinking of Christ as the last Adam. At all events, he proceeds with a series of parallels which throw light on both figures. In fact, it may be said that Adam and Christ interpret each other. But a surprise is in store, for where a comparison would be expected (type corresponding to antitype), we meet with a contrast.

15 **But the act of grace did not after all correspond exactly to the act of sin.** Paul uses in this chapter three words which, if they stood separately, might all be translated 'sin'. Two have already been considered; one, which represents sin in itself, that which determines man's nature as inimical to God (ἁμαρτία); and another, which means 'transgression', an act of disobedience to a revealed command (παράβασις). The third occurs in this verse, and is here translated 'act of sin' (παράπτωμα); it is scarcely to be distinguished from the second word. Over against the act of sin (committed by Adam) stands the act of grace (performed by Christ). 'Act of grace' represents a word (χάρισμα) closely related to the word grace (χάρις) and having the same grammatical form as the word 'act of sin'. It is used elsewhere in the epistle (i. 11; xii. 6; cf. vi. 23) in a different sense, but there can be little doubt that Paul here uses it to express the actualization of grace, just as the other word represents the actualization of sin. The two words stand in rhetorically effective juxtaposition.

But they do not correspond as exact equivalents. The act of grace does not balance the act of sin; it overbalances it. The point is not simply that grace operates more inclusively and intensively than destruction (Lietzmann). Adam was a man who disobeyed God; Jesus was a man who obeyed God, but he was also more than this. His act was not merely an act of human obedience (though it was this); it was also an act of the grace – of God. In several of the following verses we shall find this fact upsetting straightforward analogies between Adam and Christ. These negated analogies are of great importance both Christologically and soteriologically. There is an analogy between the man Adam and the man Jesus; but Jesus is more than man. There is an analogy between the death-dealing effect of Adam's act of transgression and the life-giving effect of Christ's act of righteousness, but the latter more than undoes the former. **For if it be true that by the transgression of the One the Many died, much more did the grace of God, and the gracious gift of the One man Jesus Christ, abound for the Many.**

Here Paul goes further than in *v.* 12; Adam's act of sin is the instrumental cause of universal death. It is true that he says 'the Many died', but by 'many' he can hardly mean anything different from the 'all men' of *v.* 12 (cf. also 1 Cor. xv. 22). This inclusive use of 'many' is Hebraistic; in Old Testament usage 'many' often means not 'many contrasted with all' but 'many contrasted with one or some'.

Adam's act, then, though the act of one man, resulted in the death of the great mass of mankind; over against this, what Christ did, and its effect upon mankind, can only be introduced by means of a 'much more' (cf. 4 Ezra iv. 30 ff.), since these are a matter of divine grace. Paul first describes this as 'the grace of God' (cf. *v.* 20); then he makes another attempt to indicate the actualization of grace, speaking of it this time as 'the gift in grace', a gift, that is, prompted and determined by grace. The content of the gift is not and cannot be defined; it is (like other terms in this passage) simply a convenient way of expressing all that God has done for men through Jesus Christ.

Grace, like death, was for 'the Many'. It cannot be doubted that 'the Many' has the same inclusive sense in both cases; it is occasionally so used in the New Testament of the effects of Christ's death (*v.* 19; Mark x. 45; xiv. 24, and parallels); but it would be as wrong to deduce from these passages a rigid universalism as to suppose that they meant 'many and therefore not all'. The main point is that, like Adam, Christ is the progenitor of a race; only the blessings which the members of the new race derive through their Founder are far greater than the curse which Adam handed down to his children.

In the next verse Paul repeats what is substantially the same thought.

Again, God's gift was not a mere equivalent of the result that 16 followed from One who sinned; for from one act of transgression began the process of judgement which leads to condemnation, but the act of grace, wrought in a context of many transgressions, leads to justification. The verse is full of obscurities, but this translation gives the probable sense. 'From one act of transgression' interprets 'from one'. 'From one transgressor' is a possible alternative, but the parallel expression 'in a context of many transgressions' suggests that the deed rather than the doer forms the correct supplement. The process of judgement inevitably began with the first act of transgression, and since the transgression was real and responsible it inevitably led to condemnation. The act of grace, however, could only take place where sin already abounded (*v.* 20).

Judgement led to condemnation; grace led to justification. 'Justification' here renders a word (δικαίωμα) which elsewhere (i. 32; ii. 26; v. 18; viii. 4) calls for different translations. In using it here Paul is governed by rhetorical considerations; it chimes with 'condemnation' (κατάκριμα). There is, however, no question what he means, and it is significant that 'justification' is made to stand out as the opposite of 'condemnation'; each is a verdict pronounced in a court of law.

A third time Paul stresses the contrast between Adam and Christ.

17 **For if, by the transgression of the One, death reigned through that One, much more shall those who receive the excess of grace and of the gift of righteousness reign in life through the One Jesus Christ.** The clumsiness of the second part of this verse bears witness to Paul's anxiety to stress the superiority of grace to sin, of Christ to Adam. The 'excess of grace' means that grace more than undoes the effects of sin (cf. *v.* 20). The parallelism of the clauses would have been better maintained if Paul had said not that believers should 'reign in life', but that 'life (not death) should reign'. But the sentence as it stands asserts that they who were reigned over by the tyrant shall themselves reign. The 'gift of righteousness' might mean the conferment of righteousness upon man, or the gift which proceeds from God's righteousness. It is scarcely possible to decide between these alternatives; each presupposes the other.

Having now fully brought out the contrast between Adam and Christ, Paul drops for the moment the language of divine grace, and speaks of Christ as obedient Man, the true counterpart of Adam, or disobedient Man.

18 **Therefore as, through one act of transgression, the result for all men was condemnation, so also through one act of righteousness the result for all men was justification, which leads to life.** The sentence as written in Greek lacks verbs, but its meaning is clear. 'Unto condemnation' (εἰς κατάκριμα), and 'unto justification' (εἰς δικαίωσιν), indicate the goal or result of processes which originated 'through one act of transgression' and 'through one act of righteousness' respectively.

'Act of righteousness' translates the troublesome word discussed in the note on *v.* 16. Again, it has come into use for reasons of rhetoric; Paul needs a word of the 'righteous' family to balance 'act of transgression' (παράπτωμα) and this (δικαίωμα) is the obvious one to choose. But when it is employed in this sense it can no longer (in the same sentence) be used to mean 'justification'; accordingly for this purpose Paul chooses another word (δικαίωσις) which he uses elsewhere only at iv. 25.

Justification, and justification only, leads to life. Paul never attempts to bypass this step. Man must be found righteous in God's court, even though it be by the grace of the Judge.

'All men' in this verse corresponds to 'the Many' in *v.* 15; but it is significant that the present verse is so phrased that it is impossible to draw from it any simple arithmetical conclusion about the numbers of the saved and of the lost. 'Condemnation' and 'justification' are in their ordinary use ultimate and mutually exclusive terms. At the last judgement, a man is either condemned, or justified (acquitted). Yet Paul says that the result of Adam's act of transgression is condemnation for all, and the result of Christ's act of righteousness is justification for all. There are two possible ways out of this logical difficulty. One is to suppose that when Paul says 'all men' he means 'all men who are "on Adam's side"' and 'all men who are "on Christ's side"'. All who (with Adam) choose sin will be condemned; all who (with Christ) choose righteousness will be justified. The other way out of the difficulty is harder to state but more probably true. There are two ways of looking at men. They may be considered 'in Adam' (cf. 1 Cor. xv. 22); that is, viewed as independent, self-explanatory persons, members of a race which has cut itself off from its Creator and wages war against him. This is the natural way of looking at the race, and the way in which it is natural for the race to consider itself. Viewed and understood in these terms it can have one end only. But it is also possible (by faith, for this is no human possibility) to see mankind 'in Christ' (cf. 1 Cor. xv. 22), the new Man. Men are then clothed in a righteousness which is not their own, and in virtue of it they can and will be justified. Condemnation and justification are thus both of them universal possibilities, and even universal actualities, in the sense that they point to a dialectical truth which is valid for mankind as a whole, and for each individual man. The resolution of this dialectical duality lies ultimately not with man but with the merciful God (cf. xi. 32), and rests upon what he has now done in Christ.

Paul restates his position once more, in the clearest antithesis of all. **For as through the disobedience of the One man the Many** 19 **were made sinners, so also through the obedience of the One the Many shall be made righteous.**

Through Adam's act the Many were *made* sinners; through Christ's they shall be *made* righteous. For the verb, compare Acts vii. 27; it does not mean 'to count' or 'to reckon'. But the words 'sinners' and 'righteous' are words of relationship, not character. Adam's disobedience did not mean that all men necessarily and without their consent committed particular acts of sin; it meant that they were born into a race which had separated itself from God. Similarly, Christ's obedience did not mean that henceforth men did nothing but righteous acts, but that in Christ they were related to God as Christ himself was related to his Father.

So far throughout this paragraph Paul has spoken of Adam and Christ as if there were no intervening stage in religious history. But this is to overlook a most significant event – the giving of the law (cf. *v.* 14). The Jewish interlocutor might well have asked what place Paul could find for this supreme factor in the national religion. Paul answers that the law cannot stand on the same level as the fall of Adam and redemption through Christ. **The law took its subordinate** 20

place. The verb used here is that of Gal. ii. 4 (... false brethren privily brought in, who *came in privily*). Paul does not mean to speak ill of the law as he does of the false brethren, but merely to indicate that it came in beside what was already in position, and consequently enjoyed an inferior status. This is made more explicit in a parallel passage, Gal. iii. 15–22, in which Paul says that the law was *added* (προσετέθη) to a situation already determined by grace and promise. The fundamental character of the covenant established in this way was not to be abrogated by the addition, made 430 years after God's covenant with Abraham and designed for the limited period between Moses and the coming of the Seed of Abraham to whom the promise applied, of the law. Abraham stands for a personal relation with God resting on faith and grace (iv. 16); the law could offer at best a mediated relation (Gal. iii. 19, 20).[1] Both in Romans (*v.* 20) and in Galatians (iii. 19) Paul connects law with transgression; see below. In this passage Paul gives his own view of the law in relation to the antecedent covenant; the extent to which his view was shared by his Jewish contemporaries is too large a question to be dealt with here.[2]

But why was the law introduced at all? **In order that transgression might multiply.** Compare Gal. iii. 19. As there Paul answers an explicit question, so here he answers an implicit Why? Or What? His answer expresses God's purpose in giving the law. Paul has already shown that where there is no law sin is not reckoned (*v.* 13), for only law can turn invisible sin into visible transgression. But men will never see their sin and feel their guilt, and will never therefore have faith, until their sin becomes transgression. It was therefore the wisdom of God to give the law that transgression might multiply (for the expression cf. Ecclus. xxiii. 3). This he could safely, and without prejudice to morality, do, not only because the law was itself holy, righteous, and good (vii. 12), but also because **where sin did multiply, grace abounded all the more.** Again, as in *vv.* 15, 16, 17, Paul stresses the surplus of grace in Christ over sin in Adam. Man's rebellion cannot be victorious, or God would not be God.

21   This complicated process of sin, law, transgression, and grace moves to its final purpose: **in order that as sin reigned in death so grace also might reign through righteousness, with eternal life its goal, through Jesus Christ our Lord.**

1 Paul is not comparing persons, among whom the latest comer may indeed be the greatest, but modes of relation with God. Promise, grace, and faith had been established as central in God's dealings with men; anything temporarily placed beside them could not share their centrality, though it might well bear witness to it (iii. 21).

2 See especially the work of E. P. Sanders: *Paul and Palestinian Judaism* (London, 1977); *Paul, the Law, and the Jewish People* (Philadelphia, 1983).

Most of the elements of this final pronouncement have appeared at some earlier point in the paragraph. In *vv.* 14 and 17 Paul said that death reigned. He here expresses himself more fully. It was sin that reigned, and sin used death (the 'in' is instrumental) as the instrument of its tyranny. For the connection, see 1 Cor. xv. 56. Through Christ, however, grace reigns (this is perhaps a more cautious way of expressing what is said in *v.* 17 – men do not reign in their own right); because grace reigns righteousness becomes possible, and righteousness leads to eternal life (cf. *v.* 18). Paul uses here the fuller term (eternal life, not life) to emphasize that he is speaking of the life which properly follows (though in Christian belief it may anticipate) the judgement at the end of the age.

This obscure and pregnant paragraph, the difficulty of which has been considerably mitigated by means of the translation (which is in places somewhat paraphrastic and rests on decisions some of which are tentative) but even so remains severe, is at an end. What has Paul said?

His thought goes back to two propositions which are embedded deeply in the gospel tradition. (i) With Jesus the last age, the age of the new creation, has dawned, though it has not been consummated. (ii) Jesus is the Son of man. These two themes Paul works out with heavy stress upon their moral aspect. The ruin of the old creation, as of the old man, Adam, was sin. Sin could never be a private matter, but corrupted the whole race, which consisted of men born out of true relation with God and condemned constantly to worsen their relationship, whether they carelessly ignored it or self-righteously essayed to mend it. Like planets robbed of the centre of their orbit they could not possibly keep a proper course. The more they sought life for themselves, the more they forsook God and plunged into death. Their lot could be changed only by a new creation, from a new beginning. The new Man instead of seeking to develop his own powers, individuality, and freedom subordinated himself utterly to God, and became obedient even unto death (cf. Phil. ii. 6–11). This was possible because he was at once representative Man and the Son of God. Thus the new manhood was from the beginning joined with God; from this relationship sprang the life which the Man had surrendered in going to the Cross.

As in ch. iii (see pp. 76 f.) Paul's doctrine is in part capable of anthropological development. Two types of manhood are portrayed, and it is of decisive importance that man should recognize the truth of his own existence under the word of God. But there is another aspect of Paul's thought which must not be neglected. Only in virtue of divine action can humanity cease to be what it is and become a new humanity in Christ. The scandal of the incarnation and the Cross cannot be avoided.

15 FREE FROM SIN

CHAPTER vi. 1–14

(1) What then shall we say? Are we to go on in sin in order that there may be yet more grace? (2) Of course not: how shall we, men who died to sin, go on living in it? (3) Of (if you want further proof) do you not know that we who were baptized into Christ Jesus were baptized into his death? (4) Through this baptism into his death, we were buried with him in order that, as Christ was raised from the dead in a manifestation of the glory of the Father, so we too might come to exist in the new resurrection life. (5) For if by means of the image of his death we have been joined with his death, then we shall also be joined with his resurrection. (6) And we know this, that our old self was crucified with him in order that our sin-dominated body might be abolished, that we might no longer be slaves to sin – (7) for a dead man is clear from sin. (8) But if we died with Christ, we believe that we shall also live with him, (9) since we know that Christ, now that he has been raised from the dead, can die no more – no longer has death dominion over him. (10) For whereas he died, he died to sin once for all; but whereas he lives, he lives to God.

(11) So do you also consider that you yourselves are dead to sin, but alive to God in Christ Jesus. (12) Let not sin reign in your mortal body so that you obey your body's desires.[1] (13) Do not offer your members to sin, as weapons in the service of unrighteousness, but offer yourselves to God as dead men brought to life, and offer him your members as weapons in the service of righteousness. (14) For sin shall not dominate over you; for you are not under the reign of law, but under the reign of grace.

The juxtaposition in the last verse of ch. v of sin, law, and grace, raises acutely a question already alluded to in iii. 1–8: What is the basis of Christian morality? If justification is by faith, apart from works of the law; if the law (which commands the practice of virtue) occupies only a subordinate place in God's purpose; and if, where sin abounds, grace abounds much more – why should Christians be good? The fact that

---

1 'Your body's desires' (its desires, ταῖς ἐπιθυμίαις αὐτοῦ) is supported by B ℵ A C L vg pesh. 'It' (αὐτῇ, that is, sin) is supported by another strong group of MSS: P⁴⁶ D G it Irenaeus Tertullian. The majority of MSS have a conflate reading – 'it (that is, sin) in its (that is, the body's) desires' (αὐτῇ ἐν ταῖς ἐπιθυμίαις αὐτοῦ) – which is certainly wrong. The Western reading ('it'), though very early, is probably wrong, since it can be explained as due to assimilation to *vv.* 13, 16, 17, 20.

Paul handles this question at such length shows how seriously his doctrine of 'grace and faith alone' must be taken. It is probable that there were in the Pauline churches antinomians who drew the conclusion that sin might be indulged to the full, and adversaries who alleged that this was the logical outcome of the Pauline system. Cf. iii. 8.

In ch. iii Paul answered the question briefly, and on the basis of Jewish presuppositions: God is Judge, and the judge of all the earth will do right. But he has now elaborated the doctrine of justification and redemption, and must give a Christian answer. Throughout this chapter he labours to express it. The answer itself is clear, but Paul does not find it easy to set it out in suitable language.

In the opening verses the style of the diatribe (see pp. 41 f.) reappears. Again, it is not impossible that the style reflects questions that had been put to Paul.

What then (in view of what has been said about sin, law, and 1 grace) **shall we say? Are we to go on in sin in order that there may be yet more grace?** 'In order that' (ἵνα) expresses purpose. Paul contemplates a course of action directed to the end that there may be more grace – surely (it might be argued) a desirable end. The answer follows immediately. **Of course not: how shall we, men who died to 2 sin, go on living in it?** Paul does not use the ordinary relative (οἵ – 'we who died') but a specialized form (οἵτινες), which gives the sense 'We who in our essential nature, i.e., just because we are Christians, died'. We cannot as Christians go on living in sin because as Christians we have died to sin; as far as sin is concerned, we are dead. The definite past tense, 'we died', points to a particular moment; conversion and (as the next verse shows) baptism must be in mind.

Paul has now stated the basic fact upon which his rejection of the question of *v.* 1 rests. He must still elucidate the manner in which Christians have died, and the clearest way of doing this is by reference to baptism, which he is evidently able to assume as a rite familiar to all his readers.

Or (if you want further proof) do you not know that we who 3 were baptized into Christ Jesus were baptized into his death?

Paul appeals to what is, or ought to be, common knowledge among Christians. How far did this common knowledge extend? To the practice of baptism? To the belief that baptism into Christ involved baptism into his death? To the further conclusions drawn by Paul from the notion of baptism into death? The answer to this question will depend in large part on the view taken of the origin of Paul's doctrine of baptism. If baptism into Christ's death means what it is taken in this commentary to mean, the idea will probably have originated before and independently of Paul, though beyond question he saw more clearly into its implications than any of his contemporaries.

Baptism was into Christ Jesus. This is probably an abbreviated form of the fuller 'into the name of Christ Jesus', and will therefore have a meaning less mystical than realist. 'Into the name of' means 'so as to become the property of', and those who are baptized into the name of Christ become Christ's men (cf. 1 Cor. x. 2; i. 13). Baptized Christians are thus the adherents, the property, of one whose death, resurrection, and ascension marked the dawn of the Age to Come. Baptism thus finds its setting in Christian eschatology; but Christian eschatology is no simple matter, for though, in some sense, the Age to Come has come, it is manifest that the present age still persists, and that the general resurrection and renewal of creation have not yet taken place. It follows that baptism is the gateway not to heaven, or to the fully 'realized' kingdom of God, but to a life which is empirically related both to the present age, which is marked by sin and death, and to the Age to Come, which is 'righteousness, peace, and joy in the Holy Spirit' (xiv. 17). This fact lies behind much of the present paragraph; but we must allow Paul to develop it in his own way.

The point that Paul developed, or possibly introduced, in the understanding of baptism arose out of his insistence that Christ must always be understood as Christ crucified and interpreted in terms of crucifixion and resurrection. It followed from this that baptism into Christ must mean 'baptism into Christ crucified'; there was no other Christ. Baptism into Christ was baptism into his death. It has often been argued that the doctrine of initiation by sacramental death and resurrection is of Hellenistic origin; and there are real parallels between the language of Paul and that of some of the Hellenized oriental cults. That Paul knew, and on occasion used, something of their religious terminology is probable, but this is not to say that he drew his doctrine from this source.[1] The 'messianic affliction' (see p. 76) was probably the starting-point of Paul's understanding of the Cross, as it had been for Christians before him. It remained true that before the people of God could enter the Age to Come they must pass through affliction and resurrection; but since Christ had died and been raised from the dead this transition could be in part anticipated by faith and expressed in baptism. In this fact lies the root of Paul's doctrine of baptism. It is for this reason that, though baptism always retains for him the double pattern of death and resurrection, he handles the latter element very cautiously. In this chapter, for example, references to the resurrection of Christians are regularly in the future tense, or in the imperative or subjunctive mood. There is no sacramental *opus operatum* by means of which Christians can assure

---

1 On this question see especially G. Wagner, *Pauline Baptism and the Pagan Mysteries* (Edinburgh and London, 1967), and A. J. M. Wedderburn, *Baptism and Resurrection* (Tübingen, 1988).

themselves, independently of faith and of their own moral serious-
ness, that they have risen from death to enjoy the life of the Age to
Come.

So far (in *v.* 3) Paul has simply used the practice of baptism to
support his assertion (in *v.* 2) that Christians have died. The reference
to baptism carries him further.

Through this baptism into his death, we were buried with him 4
(Paul makes use of the picture suggested by the practice of baptism by
immersion) **in order that, as Christ was raised from the dead in a
manifestation of the glory of the Father, so we too might come to
exist in the new resurrection life.**

For Paul 'glory' is a word with a predominantly eschatological
meaning (e.g. ii. 7, 10; iii. 23; v. 2; viii. 17, 21); glory is that which will
be revealed at the last day. When therefore Paul says that Christ was
raised from the dead 'through the glory of the Father' he means that
the resurrection was an eschatological event, ushering in the time of
the fulfilment of God's purpose. Only for this reason can it have as its
consequence that we too should (to translate literally) 'walk in
newness of life'. *Walk* as a term descriptive of moral and inward
conduct has a Hebrew background, but newness (καινότης), an
abstract noun, does not suggest Semitic origin. The Syriac paraphrase
(*in new life*), therefore, is probably not an adequate rendering of
Paul's thought: he means that Christians live in a new situation (cf.
the *new creation* of 2 Cor. v. 17); and this is characterized by life (*of
life*, ζωῆς, is epexegetic–so Wilckens 2, p. 13). The expression is
probably Paul's own and it is not easy to find an English translation
that brings out its full force. The word *resurrection* is intended to
represent the new circumstances brought about by Christ's death and
resurrection, but it must be remembered that the new resurrection
life (cf. *eternal life*, v. 21; vi. 22 f.), though anticipated in the present
(*v.* 4), is consummated only in the future (*vv.* 5, 8, *et al.*).

In the next verse Paul repeats and supports his assertion that
baptism means not only death but also resurrection. **For if by means** 5
of the image of his death (that is, baptism) **we have been joined
with his death, then we shall also be joined with** (that is, share) **his
resurrection.**

The word here translated 'joined with' means literally 'grown
together with' (σύμφυτος). The process of grafting may be in mind (cf.
xi. 17 ff. and John xv. 1–5 – though the word is not used in either of
these passages). The construction is obscure, for a literal rendering of
the first clause would run, 'If we have grown together with the
likeness of his death'; and it is hard to see how one can grow together
with a likeness. One solution is to supply a pronoun, 'him'. The
meaning then is, 'If we have grown together *with him* in, or by means
of, the likeness of his death', the 'likeness of his death' being baptism.

This interpretation, however, is not entirely satisfactory in the context, for the balance of the two clauses requires that one should speak of dying with Christ, the other of being raised with him. The word 'death' must in all probability be repeated, so that the meaning is, 'through the image (or imitation) of his death we have come to be joined with his death' – that is, to die with him. Baptism implies such a total commitment to Christ that it carries with it this double union with him, in death and in resurrection.

Of the second clause, Paul writes only 'We shall be of his resurrection also'. The whole framework of the preceding clause must be repeated: Through the likeness of his resurrection (the other aspect of baptism) we shall be joined with his resurrection; that is, we shall be raised with him. Paul breaks the parallelism by using the future. This might be a purely 'logical' future, as in the proposition: If A is true then B will follow. But this would not agree with the undoubtedly temporal future of *v.* 8. In fact, Paul is always cautious of expressions which might suggest that the Christian has already reached his goal, and to say in so many words 'We have died with Christ and we have been raised with Christ' would be to invite if not actually to commit the error condemned in 2 Tim. ii. 18. It is true that in Col. iii. 1 a past tense of the indicative (συνηγέρθητε, aorist) is used: 'If then you were raised with Christ . . . '. On this two observations may be made. One is that the authorship of Colossians is disputed. The matter cannot be discussed here, but it is at least arguable that a Deuteropauline author failed to show Pauline caution. Second, and more important, if the whole passage (iii. 1–4) is read, it appears that the past, baptismal, resurrection is strictly qualified. 'Your life has been hidden with Christ in God'; it will be manifested in glory when Christ is manifested. It is implied that at present it is not to be clearly seen; it is apprehended by faith rather than by sight. In the meantime, Christians are urged to put off the 'old man' and to put on the 'new man' (iii. 9, 10). This, though differently expressed, is not very different from Romans vi. See E. Lohse, *Die Briefe an die Kolosser und an Philemon* (Göttingen, 1968), pp. 192–6.

So far Paul has simply elicited the fact that Christian existence is rooted in a death and resurrection dependent upon Christ's. He has not yet demonstrated the relevance of this fact to the question of *v.* 1. This he now proceeds to do. *Vv.* 6 f. deal with death, *vv.* 8 ff. with life; in *vv.* 11 ff. he holds the two together and brings out their practical consequences; *v.* 14 is a transition to a new line of argument.

What is the significance of the death Christians die by faith in
6 baptism? **We know this, that our old self was crucified with him in order that our sin-dominated body** (cf. viii. 3) **might be abolished,**
7 **that we might no longer be slaves to sin – for a dead man is clear from sin.** The essential substance of this conviction is clear: death

with Christ is an ethical experience, affecting the relation between man and sin, the latter being understood in both its pre-ethical roots and its ethical expression.

The 'old self' is literally the 'old man'. Compare Col. iii. 9 f. (Eph. iv. 22, 24). The interpretation which commends itself by its simplicity is that the 'old man' is the nature of the unconverted man, which upon conversion and baptism is replaced by a new nature, the 'new man'. But careful reading of Col. iii, and of the present passage, makes this interpretation impossible. In Colossians it is the Christian readers of the letter who are told to put off the old man, and to put on the new. Here in Romans Christians are told that they must *consider* themselves to be dead to sin and alive to God (*v.* 11). It is much more exact to say that the 'old man' is Adam – or rather, ourselves in union with Adam, and that the 'new man' is Christ – or rather, ourselves in union with Christ. Compare Gal. iii. 27; 1 Cor. xv. 22, 47 ff. Old and new are not simply in sequence but concurrent.

The old, Adamic, self was crucified with Christ. In his crucifixion Jesus endured the messianic affliction, and it is by sharing this affliction in union with Christ that the descendants of Adam participate in the New Creation of which the New Adam is the head. This, however, is no mystical or metaphysical process. Its purpose is the abolition of the sin-ridden body which men have from Adam. From his time, sin and death reigned (v. 14, 17, 21); human nature (for Paul's word 'body' means hardly less than this) correspondingly passed into slavery (cf. *vv.* 6c, 16, 17, 18, 19, 20, 22). Baptismal 'death' accordingly is a step towards the putting out of action of this sin-dominated aspect or element of humanity. The more remote consequence is that 'we' should no longer be in servitude to sin. That is, 'we' are distinguishable from the sin-controlled side of our being.

And (to translate literally) the man who has died has been justified from sin. There are two possible interpretations here. (i) 'Justify' may have its usual forensic meaning: death pays all debts. (ii) 'Justify' means 'to free from sin (actually)'. This meaning does occur (e.g. Ecclus. xxvi. 29; *Corpus Hermeticum* xiii. 9; perhaps Acts xiii. 38 f.; 1 Cor. vi. 11). It is not, however, right to distinguish sharply between these alternatives. The second is suggested by *vv.* 6 and 10; but there follows immediately *v.* 11 (consider yourselves dead). Thus (i) is true absolutely – the man who has died with Christ by faith has been justified; and (ii) ought to be in process of realization.

Paul has thus worked out his point as far as baptismal *death* is concerned. But as in the story of Jesus, so also in baptism and Christian experience, death leads to life. **But if we died with Christ, 8 we believe that we shall also live with him, since we know that 9 Christ, now that he has been raised from the dead, can die no more – no longer has death dominion over him.**

For the future tense 'we shall live' compare the future 'we shall be' in *v.* 5. It is primarily a real future and points to the resurrection; but as in *v.* 7 it is important not to make over-sharp distinctions. 'The formula "with Christ" is used in the sacramental (vi. 8; Col. ii. 13, 20) and in the eschatological (2 Cor. iv. 14; xiii. 4; Phil. i. 23; 1 Thess. iv. 14, 17; v. 10; Col. iii. 3, 4) sense' (Lietzmann). This is not surprising if it be true that Paul's view of baptism is primarily eschatological. But it must be noted that the 'we shall live' (whether present sacramental or future eschatological) rests upon 'we believe', whereas the resurrection of Christ is introduced by 'we know' (*v.* 9). The life of the Christian with Christ can be experienced and recognized only by faith; it is not capable of direct observation.

V. 9 emphasizes that the resurrection of Christ was an eschatological event, an anticipation of the resurrection of the last day; hence Christ will not die again. He (and he alone) has begun the resurrection life of the Age to Come; but those who are joined with him in his death and resurrection anticipate it by faith.

We come now to the crucial stage in Paul's argument. The question of *v.* 1 is not yet answered. We must ask, What sort of death did Christ, and do Christians, die? And what sort of life does Christ, and do 10 Christians, live? **Whereas he died, he died to sin once for all; but whereas he lives, he lives to God.** Christ died to sin because he died sinless, because he died rather than sin (by disobeying his Father), and because he died in a context of sin. He was raised from the dead by the glory of the Father (*v.* 4), in order that he might continue to live to God only; he never lived otherwise. He was completely obedient to, and completely dependent upon, God.

So far, Paul has described the death and life of Christ; but all that he has said is, *mutatis mutandis*, applicable to the death and life of Christians. It follows that a Christian (a) is dead as far as sin is concerned; (b) has been raised from the dead to new life; and (c) in this new life belongs to God. If this be true it is clear at once that any talk of continuing in sin (*v.* 1) is a contradiction of Christian first principles.

It is also of course clear that Christians do not live a sinless and immortal life in heaven with Christ. Faith and baptism do not in this life effect their own full meaning. In particular, they leave room for ethical effort, in which Christians endeavour actually to achieve (with the aid of the Spirit, given in baptism) the life to which baptism points. Paul's next step is to urge his readers to realize in this way that which 11 is already true for them by faith. **So do you also consider that you yourselves are dead to sin, but alive to God in Christ Jesus.** The word 'consider' (λογίζεσθαι) is the same as that used to denote God's 'reckoning' of righteousness to Abraham (Gen. xv. 6; Rom. iv. 3). Christians are no more visibly dead and risen than Abraham was visibly righteous. Outwardly they appear as other men; but *in Christ Jesus* they are newly related to God. It is important to understand what this means for it sums up much of the teaching of this paragraph. 'In Christ' is itself a Pauline phrase of central but disputed significance. It is best explained as originating neither in mysticism nor in the realistic ideas of sacramental communion, nor in the idea of the Church as an institution, but in primitive Christian eschatology. The death and resurrection of Jesus were eschatological events, effecting the transition from this age to the Age to Come. Believers could take advantage of this transition, but the transference from the one age to the other could take place only 'in Christ'. Those who belonged to him by faith passed through death and resurrection and so came to be alive to God. Paul urges his readers to look upon themselves, and to understand their activity, in this light. What this means in practice is expressed in plain terms in *vv.* 12 f.

Let not sin reign in your mortal body so that you obey your 12 **body's desires.** 'In Christ' men are dead to sin and alive to God. This is (if the expression may be allowed) sacramentally and eschatologically true; but neither the efficacy of the sacrament, nor the anticipation of the eschatological future, alters the fact that men in this world have mortal bodies, conditioned by the present age, not the Age to Come; and in these bodies sin is ever at hand. Hence the form of Paul's exhortation; sin must not be allowed to reign; the desires which are naturally engendered in a personality belonging to this age must not be obeyed (cf. xii. 1 f.).

Do not offer your members (not simply *limbs*, but the various 13 faculties of the mortal body) **to sin, as weapons in the service of unrighteousness** (this word is used in an ethical sense, not corresponding exactly to Paul's most characteristic use of 'righteousness'), **but offer yourselves to God as dead men brought to life, and offer him your members as weapons in the service of righteousness.**

It is impossible to be certain of the translation 'weapons'. The word (ὅπλα) means (i) ship's tackle; (ii) tools, instruments of any kind, (iii) weapons. Compare xiii. 12. Either (ii) or (iii) would make good sense; 2 Cor. vi. 7; x. 4 point to (iii).

Sin, as the parallelism shows (...to sin...in the service of unrighteousness...to God...in the service of righteousness), is almost personified. This is not unusual in Paul; see especially vii. 8, 9, 11, 13.

The real force of Paul's injunction lies in the phrase 'as dead men brought to life'. The 'as' is not easy to define. It is neither 'as if you were' nor 'as in fact you are'; or perhaps rather it is both of these. In one sense, Paul's readers have already been raised from the dead. In another, they are still waiting for this to take place. If they had not died and been raised by faith there would be no point in bidding them

forsake sin and live to God; if they had already died and been raised up
at the last day there would equally, though for another reason, be no
point in bidding them forsake sin and live to God. It is because they
stand between these two moments in the history of redemption that
Christian moral exhortation has its place. It can be given with
14 confidence, because **sin shall not dominate over you; for you are
not under the reign of law, but under the reign of grace.**

'Sin shall not dominate (κυριεύσει) over you' (for the future cf. *vv.* 5
and 8) might almost be translated, 'sin shall not be your lord (κύριος)'.
For the Christian there is only one Lord, and he has offered himself to
God in the service of righteousness (*v.* 13). Sin has lost its power
because the Christian does not live under law, in which the strength of
sin resides (1 Cor. xv. 56). Law opens the way to the upward striving
of human religion and morality, and therefore colours all human
activity with sin, for it represents man's attempt to scale God's throne.
Those who live under the reign of grace, however, have given full
scope to God's freedom, since instead of pressing upward towards God
they humbly wait for his descent in love. Ultimately, therefore,
justification by faith, which means living under grace, though it is
rooted in a region of divine–human relations which lies beyond
morals, becomes the one hope of a truly moral life. Even so, however,
the future 'shall not dominate' remains a future.

The last remark will provide the occasion for a review of the
paragraph (*vv.* 1–14) as a whole. It is a paragraph to which the
modern reader is apt to bring his own questions, forgetting that they
are not necessarily the questions Paul intended to answer. The
modern reader, for example, wishes to know what relation exists
between sacrament and faith, and whether, and to what extent, Paul
believed that Christians could be free from sin.

When questions such as these are raised, it is particularly
important to recall that Paul's thought, like that of primitive
Christianity as a whole, was cast in an eschatological mould, and that
he believed himself to be living 'between the times', in a world which
was swiftly passing; the age in which he wrote formed a bridge
between the old world and the new. The death and resurrection of
Jesus were eschatological events – the messianic affliction and the
manifestation of God's glory. The practice, and the efficacy, of
baptism were rooted in these eschatological events; baptism is not
simply a religious rite, but springs out of the fact that an hour has
struck on the world clock. Christian eschatology is paradoxical, as
Jewish eschatology is not; the Christian life, and Christian rites, are
paradoxical, as Jewish life and rites are not. It is of the essence of
Christian life that men are *simul justi, simul peccatores,* at the same
time righteous and sinners. They are righteous in Christ, sinners in
themselves (or, in Adam). Because Christ is now hidden from men's

eyes in heaven until his *parousia*, the holiness and righteousness of Christians, which are not their own but his, are hidden, and the body of sin is all too clearly visible. In the meantime, however, the 'powers of the age to come' could – and must – be expressed in ethical terms; here indeed was the only visible indication that Christians belonged to the new age.

Baptism was no contradiction but an expression of the 'obedience of faith' (i. 5). To turn it therefore into a supposedly justifying 'work' was automatically to empty it of its true meaning. Any attempt to drive a wedge between baptism and justification will do no justice to Paul's thought – unless indeed we are to suppose that Paul was incapable of theological consistency. The relation between the two is most easily seen in the eschatological context in which Paul himself conceived them. Baptism represents an anticipated passage through the final affliction and consequent resurrection, in union with the dying and rising Christ, into an anticipation of the life of the Age to Come. Justification means a verdict of acquittal anticipated from the last judgement, and thus an anticipation of the life of the Age to Come (see p. 72). The two are different expressions of the same thing, or at least of two very closely related things, though it is fair to add that whereas baptism without faith and justification would be unintelligible, faith and justification without baptism would remain intelligible. Paul[1] never uses the word *sacrament*, and it is not easy (perhaps not desirable) to accommodate his thought to subsequent sacramental theology (though in some respects he provides the raw material of it). He found baptism in existence as the church's rite of initiation, the means by which a believer publicly confessed his allegiance to Christ and accepted membership in the people of Christ.

> Candidate and community confess together that the total renewal of man which has taken place in Jesus Christ is their own renewal, their own sanctification for God, not as their work but as His, not as a self-sanctification which they have undertaken or are preparing to undertake, but as the sanctification for God which has come to them, as to all men, in Jesus Christ. They confess this in baptism. They there say Yes together, not to their own good will, not to their faith, but in great thankfulness to the divine conclusion of peace, to the valid, absolutely trustworthy and victorious Yes which God has spoken to man, and hence to them too. They say Yes to this Yes.'[2]

1 The same is true of the New Testament as a whole; see my *Church, Ministry, and Sacraments in the New Testament* (Exeter, 1985), pp. 55–7.
2 K. Barth, *Church Dogmatics* IV, 4 (1969), 161.

This Yes involves a human renunciation and a human response, but spoken in this context it is inseparable from the divine affirmation and action, which are operative precisely so far as the human partners recognize that they are dead and that their action in baptism is, as it were, a non-action which means 'I no longer live, Christ lives in me' (Gal. ii. 20). Rightly understood, baptism safeguards the doctrine of justification by faith (iii. 28); it has in history (from the first century, in Corinth,[1] and onwards) proved all too easy to understand it wrongly.

16 IN BONDAGE TO RIGHTEOUSNESS

CHAPTER vi. 15–23

(15) What then? Are we to sin because we are not under the reign of law but under the reign of grace? Certainly not. (16) Do you not know that when you offer yourselves to someone as slaves, to obey him, then you are slaves of him whom you obey? This is true, whether the master be sin (slavery to him ends in death), or obedience (slavery to him ends in righteousness). (17) Thanks be to God! You were indeed slaves of sin, but from the heart you gave your obedience to that Christian doctrine to which as slaves you were handed over. (18) You were liberated from sin, and you were made slaves to righteousness. (19) (I am giving all this in a human illustration because your understanding is only human.) The point of the matter is this: Just as in the past you offered your members to uncleanness and iniquity as their slaves (with the result of producing iniquity), so now offer your members to righteousness as its slaves (the result of this will be sanctification). (20) These are mutually exclusive attitudes; for when you were slaves of sin, you were free men in respect of righteousness. (21) And what fruit then did you reap of that? – Things of which you now are ashamed, for their end is death. (22) But now you have been freed from sin, and have become slaves to God. Accordingly your fruit proves to be sanctification, and the ultimate result will be eternal life. (23) For the wage paid by sin is death; but the gift freely given by God is eternal life in Christ Jesus our Lord.

In *v.* 14 Paul found the ground of the Christian's freedom from sin in

1 See *1 Corinthians*, pp. 219–29.

the fact that he is no longer under the reign of law. He had already
shown (in ch. v), and is to show again (in ch. vii), that it is through the
law that sin fastens its grip upon men, because the law awakens
desire, and turns all men's striving, and especially their striving for
life and God, into sin. If then for the law is substituted grace, sin will
inevitably lose its hold.

This is Paul's argument; but it could be reversed, and he now,
reverting to the rhetorical style of the diatribe, proceeds to meet the
possible objection. **What then?** It is the law which directs us to do   15
what is right (vii. 12, 14); do away with the law and you do away with
morality. The more sin abounds, the more grace abounds (v.20); life
under grace invites the multiplication of sin. **Are we** then **to sin
because we are not under the reign of law but under the reign of
grace?** There is – apparently – a double reason why Christians should
consider themselves free to sin, a negative reason (they are no longer
under the law), and a positive reason (they are under grace). It is only
the latter that is developed and refuted here; the theme of law will be
taken up again in ch. vii.

There could be no more complete misconception of Christian
freedom. It is simply not true that Christians, free though they are
from the law as a means of salvation, are under no obligation to God
(cf. 1 Cor. ix. 21). **Do you not know that when you offer yourselves**   16
**to someone as slaves, to obey him, then you are slaves of him
whom you obey?** This is a general principle, to which no one can
take exception. Behind it probably lies the practice whereby men
applied to be taken into slavery in order to secure a livelihood; but
the construction of the sentence is obscure because the writer has
put too much into it. The obscurity, which is somewhat mitigated in
the translation, arises through the addition of 'obedience' to slavery.
Paul introduces this additional matter because it is important to
him to show that obedience has a place in the system of grace and
faith (cf. i. 5); indeed, it would not be wrong to say that the whole
of ch. vi is an attempt to vindicate that place. In saying this, however,
we have already advanced to the application of Paul's general
principle.

**This is true, whether the master be sin (slavery to him ends in
death), or obedience (slavery to him ends in righteousness).**
Paul assumes that men will be slaves, and obedient, to a good
master or a bad. Independence is impossible. 'The man who imagines
he is free, because he acknowledges no god but his own ego, is
deluded; for the service of one's own ego is the very essence of the
slavery of sin' (Cranfield, p. 323). Fortunately there is no question
which side the readers of the epistle have taken. **Thanks be to God!**   17
You were indeed slaves of sin (cf. John viii. 34; also Rom. iii. 19 f.)
but from the heart you gave your obedience to that Christian

doctrine (literally, pattern of teaching – Christian (not specifically Pauline) teaching, for the Roman Christians were not Paul's converts) **to which as slaves you were handed over.** The last verb is curious but significant. One expects the doctrine to be handed over (the verb – παραδιδόναι – is used for the transmission of traditions; 1 Cor. xi. 23; xv. 3) to the hearers, not the hearers to the doctrine. But Christians are not (like the Rabbis) masters of a tradition; they are themselves created by the word of God, and remain in subjection to it. In fact, though being a Christian means on the one hand emancipa-

18 tion, on the other it means enslavement. **You were liberated from sin, and you were made slaves to righteousness.** Righteousness remains important to the Christian; the only righteousness he has given up is his own, and that in order that he may be in subjection to God's righteousness – which is not less but greater than human righteousness (cf. Matt. v. 20).

Looking forward, perhaps, to *v.* 19 b, rather than backward, Paul

19 inserts an apologetic parenthesis. **I am giving all this in a human illustration** (cf. iii. 5; 1 Cor. ix. 8; Gal. iii. 15) **because your understanding is only human.** The last clause has an almost exact verbal parallel in Gal. iv. 13 (cf. 1 Tim. v. 23), but the sense there is different. Literally it runs, 'because of the weakness of your flesh'. Paul's use of the term flesh will be considered later (see pp. 128 f., 137 f.); at this point it has no special theological meaning but simply refers to the frailty of human nature, which cannot grasp profound truth unless it is presented in human analogies. The analogy follows.

The point of the matter is this: Just as in the past you offered your members to uncleanness and iniquity as their slaves (with the result of producing iniquity), so now offer your members to righteousness as its slaves (the result of this will be sanctifica- tion).

This verse adds little fresh substance to what has already been said two or three times in this chapter. Paul as a pastor doubtless knew well that such injunctions cannot be repeated too frequently. What in *v.* 17 was stated in a past tense of the indicative (you gave your obedience) is now restated in an imperative (offer your members). An initial redirection of obedience must be constantly renewed.

The 'members' are again (as in *v.* 13) the faculties (not the limbs simply). If they are in service to uncleanness and iniquity, the result will be iniquity; if they are in service to (God's) righteousness, the result will be sanctification. The parallel with iniquity suggests that 'sanctification' has here an ethical sense; this agrees with the use of the same word in 1 Thess. iv. 3–7. Submission to the righteousness of God is not itself a matter of ethics, but it has its issue in ethical purity.

Compromise between sin and righteousness is impossible. A man

20 cannot serve two masters. **These are mutually exclusive attitudes;**

124

for when you were slaves of sin you were free men in respect of righteousness, that is, you acknowledged no obligation to it. The first five words are not in Paul's Greek, but the 'for' (γάρ) with which the next sentence begins seems to presuppose some such remark. An alternative way of taking the 'for' is to suppose that *vv.* 20, 21 together supply the basis of the command in *v.* 19 b: Offer your members to righteousness, *for* your previous freedom in respect of righteousness issued only in shame and could lead only to death. This however would require in *v.* 20 'When you were slaves of sin and free in respect of righteousness', and in *v.* 21 leaves 'then' (οὖν) unexplained. Paul continues: this freedom in respect of righteousness brought no advantage to you.

What fruit then did you reap of that? Things of which you now 21 **are ashamed, for their end is death** (cf. *v.* 23; i. 32; v. 12 f.).

There are two ways, both grammatically possible, of punctuating this sentence. The question mark may be placed after 'that', or after 'ashamed'. If the latter alternative is accepted, the answer to the question must be supplied: What fruit did you reap of those things of which you now are ashamed? None; for their end is death. This does not fit the context well and the parallel verse (22) distinguishes between the near and remote consequences of a course of action (the fruit is sanctification, the ultimate result eternal life), thus strongly supporting a similar distinction in *v.* 21, where the translation given here may be confidently accepted.

But now (this may be a logical or a temporal contrast – or 22 perhaps both; cf. iii. 21, and note) **you have been freed from sin** (as lord; cf. *v* 14), **and have become slaves to God. Accordingly your fruit proves to be** (that is, in the end issues in) **sanctification** (as at *v.* 19), **and the ultimate result will be eternal life.** 'Fruit' here recalls Gal. v. 22 f. The inward obedience of faith has visible exterior consequences.

For the wage paid by sin is death (cf. Gen. ii. 17); **but the gift** 23 **freely given by God is eternal life in Christ Jesus our Lord.** For the contrast, compare iv. 4. Sin is personified, as at *v.* 13.

The 'gift freely given' (χάρισμα) is not used as at i. 11, or at v. 15. It is the supreme spiritual gift, the total result of grace, as far as man is concerned.

The old servitude to sin was under the reign of law, and sin accordingly paid a wage, as a matter of debt or obligation; the new servitude to God (a servitude no less serious for this reason) is under the reign of grace, and God accordingly gives a gift of grace, namely eternal life. If man is to receive anything other than death it will not be as a reward (even though he now serves righteousness) but a free gift in Christ.

17 FREE FROM THE LAW

CHAPTER vii. 1–6

(1) To put this matter of freedom from the law in another way: you surely cannot fail to know, brethren, for I speak to men who know the law, that the law has dominion over a man for such time as he is alive. (2) For (to take an example) the married woman is bound by law to her husband as long as he is alive; but if her husband dies, she is done with the law of her husband. (3) See what this means. If while her husband is alive she gives herself to another man, she will be styled an adulteress; but if her husband dies she is free from the law, so as not to be an adulteress if she gives herself to another man. (4) So, my brethren, to interpret the illustration: with reference to the law you were put to death through the body of Christ, that you might give yourselves to an Other – namely, to him who was raised from the dead – in order that we might bear offspring to God. (5) For when we were in the flesh, the passions bound up with sins and engendered through the law wrought in our members that we might bear offspring to death. (6) But now we are done with the law since we died to that by which we were held fast, so that we serve God our master in a new life marked by the gift of the Spirit, not the old life, which was marked only by observance of the written law.

The paragraph vi. 1–14 concluded with the statement, You are not under the reign of law, but under the reign of grace. The next paragraph, vi. 15–23, dealt with an objection: Men who are no longer under the reign of law will no longer be obliged to serve God. On the contrary (says Paul), the Christian is bound to the service of righteousness; indeed he alone, since he is in subjection to the righteousness of God (not his own), can serve God fruitfully, and see sanctification and eternal life result from his service. The present paragraph makes substantially the same point, by means of a fresh analogy, in which Paul begins an analysis (it will be continued in the next paragraph) of the effect of law and of liberation from it.

1   **To put this matter of freedom from the law in another way: you surely cannot fail to know** (for the expression cf. vi. 3), **brethren, for I speak to men who know the law, that the law has dominion over a man for such time as he is alive.**

It is probable that *law* in this verse refers to the law of the Old Testament, preserved and developed in Judaism. It need not for this reason be assumed that these words are addressed to Jews (for the racial composition of the Roman church see on i. 6, and the Introduction, p. 6). Gentile Christians also knew the law (i.e., the Old Testament), though it may be that here and elsewhere Paul exaggerates their knowledge. Some think that Paul, writing to Christians in Rome, was referring to Roman law. This is very improbable. The student of ancient history (and of law) is taught to think highly of the Roman legal system, but it is doubtful whether the Roman *plebs* shared his interest or this valuation. Roman law in any case was irrelevant to Paul's argument and to his analogy. It is the divine law of the Old Testament that rules over man – till death. The principle 'death pays all debts' was of course widely recognized, but that the dead are not under obligation to the law was not frequently expressed in Judaism, though Ps. lxxxviii. 5 (RV: cast off among the dead; PBV: free among the dead; LXX (lxxxvii. 5): ἐν νεκροῖς ἐλεύθερος) was sometimes taken to have this meaning, and death was dreaded in part because it meant that one would no longer have the joy and privilege of observing Torah.

Law then is for the living, and obligation to law ceases only at death. Paul now proceeds to his analogy.

For (to take an example) the married woman (the adjective – in 2 Greek ὕπανδρος – may itself include the idea of subordination; cf. Num. v. 20, 29 (LXX)) **is bound by law to her husband as long as he is alive.** This states fairly the position of the Jewish wife, not of the Roman. For what Roman practice became under the Empire see J. Carcopino, *La vie quotidienne à Rome à l'apogée de L'Empire* (1939), pp. 123 f.; but under Jewish law a woman had no right to divorce her husband; the only way of escape from marriage was the death of her husband (or, of course, his decision to divorce her). **But if her husband dies, she is done with** (cf. *v.* 6; Gal. v. 4) **the law of her husband.** The last five words are a literal rendering (of τοῦ νόμου τοῦ ἀνδρός), and the intended meaning is not clear. Probably the best way to understand them is as referring to *the law which establishes her husband's rights.* Another possibility would be *the rule of her husband, law* (νόμος) standing for his authority over her. A neat way of taking Paul's words is to suppose that Paul is already allowing the interpretation to invade the analogy and means *she is done with the law, that is, in my analogy, with her husband,* husband being in explanatory apposition with law. None of these explanations is entirely satisfactory.

See what this means. If while her husband is alive she gives 3 herself to another man, she will be styled an adulteress; but if her husband dies she is free from the law (here the word must refer to the law that establishes her husband's exclusive rights), **so as not to be an adulteress if she gives herself to another man.**

In this verse Paul is not simply illustrating the position of the married woman; the 'other man', to whom she cannot legally be joined during the lifetime of her husband, is mentioned in view of the development of the image and the interpretation that follow.

127

4   So, my brethren, to interpret the illustration: with reference to the law you were put to death through the body of Christ. The last five words are very difficult. An easy interpretation would take *the body of Christ* (τὸ σῶμα τοῦ χριστοῦ) to mean the Church; 'your death to law (conversion) came about through your entry into the Church'. But in Romans (see xii. 5, and the note) the body of Christ has not yet become a technical term for the church. The phrase cannot mean 'through union with Christ' (in baptism or any other way) since this is the next step to be described (*that you might give yourselves to an Other*). It seems necessary to take *the body of Christ* to refer to the human physical body of Jesus, which was killed in the crucifixion and raised up in the resurrection. The closest parallels are in 1 Cor. x. 16; xi. 24, 27 (29). The analogy is imperfect. In marriage, the husband dies and the wife is free. In Christian life, the law does not die (as analogy would require); Christ dies, and by faith Christians die with him. All Paul needs for his purpose is a death; but his argument would of course make no sense if he could not assume both that Christ's death on the cross was followed by the resurrection, and that our death by faith in baptism was followed by a new life. Because this is so, Paul can continue: Our relation of bondage to the law has been broken off by a death, **that you might give yourselves to an Other – namely, to him who was raised from the dead – in order that we might bear offspring to God.** The change from the second person (*you*) to the first (*we*) is harsh but readily understandable. What Paul is saying is applicable not only to his readers in Rome but to himself and to all Christians, and he begins (perhaps unnecessarily) to express this point. The old relation to law has been supplanted by a new relation to Christ. In vi. 21 f. Paul used the image of 'fruit bearing' in quite general terms, but when he employs it in the present context it can hardly be doubted that he has in mind the birth of children. We are joined to Christ (for he not only died but was raised from the dead), but the children are born 'to God'. This dative is probably due to the careless use of metaphor; but it is the sort of carelessness that is significant. What Christ does is the work of God. The actions of Christians are the result of their union with Christ.

The prospect of fruitful union with Christ prompts Paul to look back at the old condition of union with the law. Again, there is a significant confusion, this time of sin, law, and death.

5   **For when we were in the flesh, the passions bound up with sins and engendered through the law wrought in our members that we might bear offspring to death.** (The subject-matter of this verse reappears, at much greater length, in *vv.* 7–25.)

It is implied that we are no longer 'in the flesh'. The same implication is found at viii. 9; Gal. iii. 3; v. 24; but Paul and other Christians are still 'in the flesh' at 2 Cor. iv. 11; x. 3; Gal. ii. 20; Phil. i.

22, 24. It is impossible to escape the conclusion that Paul uses the word 'flesh' (σάρξ) in at least two senses.[1] Here it is used to denote the state in which men are dominated by law, sin, and death. In the terms of this paragraph, it might be described as the state of marriage with the law. The effect of this union was that passions bound up with (due to, or leading to – perhaps both) sins were at work in the organs of our human nature (see on vi. 13). The passions were themselves due to the law (cf. *v.* 9), and in the 'marriage' of man and law (outside the sphere of grace) they resulted in death. 'Death', even if taken to be personified, is not a good parallel to 'God' in *v.* 4; compare, however, vi. 21, 'their end is death'. This is Paul's meaning here.

That the good law of God should give rise to sinful passions is a striking – one might say a shocking – assertion. Paul makes no attempt to explain it here, but the question is inescapable and will be raised at vii. 7 and dealt with in the ensuing paragraph. Such was your state – before Christ and under law. **But now** (the contrast is both **6** temporal and logical; cf. iii. 21; vi. 22; xi. 30) **we are done with the law** (cf. *v.* 2) **since we died to that by which we were held fast.** In the analogy of *vv.* 2 f. the husband died. Freedom through death is the essential point. For the image of men imprisoned by the law cf. Gal. iii. 22 f.

Release through the death of Christ means **that we serve God our master** (no object is expressed in Greek) **in a new life marked by the gift of the Spirit, not the old life, which was marked only by observance of the written law** – literally, 'in newness of Spirit and not oldness of letter'.

The Christian is not exempt from service to God (Paul's verb means service as a slave). Obedience is central in Christian freedom (cf. ch. vi, *passim*).

The meaning of 'newness of Spirit' is clear enough; the life of union with Christ has for its visible mark the fruit of the Spirit. 'Oldness of letter' has been described as a rhetorical imitative formation; but though the choice of 'oldness' is no doubt due to rhetorical considerations, the phrase as a whole is substantial. The old life was marked by subservience to the requirements of the letter of the law. This was of course true pre-eminently of the Jew, but true also in some degree of every man who practised religion seriously. For 'newness' see on vi. 4; for the contrast of *letter* and *Spirit* see on ii. 27, 29.

---

1 It is also true that, even when 'flesh' is used in a bad sense, Christians are both in and not in the flesh, just as they are both sinful and free from sin. Cf. pp. 120 f. For Paul's understanding of 'flesh' (σάρξ) see further *Freedom and Obligation*, pp. 71–7.

18 THE LAW AND SIN

CHAPTER vii. 7-25

(7) In view of this, what shall we say? That the law is sin? Certainly not. Yet it is true that it is only through the law that I came to know sin; for indeed I should not know desire if the law did not say, 'Thou shalt not desire'. (8) But in fact sin seized its opportunity through the commandment and thereby produced in me every kind of desire – for apart from law, sin is dead. (9) And apart from law I was alive once; but when the commandment came, sin sprang to life (10) and I died; and the very commandment that was directed towards life resulted for me in death. (11) For sin took its opportunity, deceived me by means of the commandment, and – again by means of it – killed me. (12) So the law then is holy, and the commandment is holy, righteous, and good. (13) Did then that which in itself is good prove in my case to be death? No indeed. The fact is that sin, in order that it might be shown up as sin, used that good thing to bring forth death for me. Sin did this in order that, by means of the commandment, it might be shown up as exceedingly sinful.

(14) There is no question of the goodness of the law, for we know that it is spiritual; but I am a man of flesh, sold as a slave so as to be under the power of sin. (15) For the works I do are incomprehensible to me, for I do not practise what I wish; on the contrary, I do what I hate. (16) But if I do what I do not wish, then it follows that I agree with the law, admitting it to be right and good. (17) But what in fact is happening is that it is not I that do my works, but sin which dwells in me. (18) For I know that there dwells no good thing in me – I should say, in my flesh. For I can always wish, but never actually achieve, a really good work; (19) for I do not do the good I wish to do; rather, the evil I do not wish to do I practise. (20) But if I do what I do not wish to do, that shows that it cannot be I that do it; it must be sin that dwells in me.

(21) What then does this amount to? That there is imposed upon me, who would do what is good and right, a law, to the effect that evil shall always attend me. (22) For in my inner self I agree with God's[1] law, (23) but I observe in my members another law which makes war upon the law which rules in my mind and takes me prisoner to the law of sin which is in my members. (24) Wretched man that I am! who shall deliver me from this

---

1 Instead of 'God's law', B has 'the law of the mind', harmonizing with *v.* 23. But to say, 'Inwardly I agree with the law of my mind', is tautologous.

body of death? (25) **Thanks be to God through Jesus Christ our Lord.**[1]

To sum up then: **I myself with my mind serve God's law, but with the flesh I serve sin's law.**

There is perhaps no chapter in the epistle which has given rise to so many divergent interpretations as this. The most disputed question is, When Paul in this chapter says 'I', what does he mean? Mankind? The Jewish people? Himself as a non-Christian Jew? Himself as a Christian? But it will be well to set this question aside for the moment, partly because it can be answered only on the basis of exact and detailed exegesis, and partly also because to lay too much emphasis upon it is to miss the real intention of the paragraph. Paul does not set out from the question, How may a Christian (or one who is not a Christian) be defined? Still less does he embark upon a psychological account of the feelings and struggles of either regenerate or unregenerate man. He begins from the question, Is the law sin? Earlier passages in the epistle have come near to suggesting that it is; see especially iii. 20; iv. 15; v. 13, 20; vi. 14; vii. 5. No Jew, convinced that the law was the very word of God, could allow such passages to fall from his pen without being compelled to consider whether he was consistent in his opinions. Accordingly Paul makes what is strictly speaking a digression from the main line of his thought (viii. 1 resumes vii. 6), though it is a digression which in the end leads back to the central theme, a digression which not only in the end leads back to the central theme but is never far away from it. The problem is one that Paul could not avoid if he was to maintain his integrity as a Christian thinker.

The question is thrown up bluntly, in the form of the diatribe (see p. 41). **In view of this** (the contrast between the new life in grace 7 and the old life in the letter of the law – v. 6), **what shall we say? That the law is sin?** See above; the question was inevitable. Paul is in no doubt, however, that the answer is, **Certainly not.** This answer is no more to be dismissed as misplaced Jewish nationalism than that of iii. 2. The law is the word of God, a gift of his grace to his chosen and favoured people; see vv. 12, 14 below; also ix. 4. The law in itself is not sin, but it is impossible to deny a certain connection between it and sin. This raises the question of the place of law in the purpose of God. **It is true that it is only through the law that I came to know sin.** Compare iii. 20; v. 13. The inward rebellion against the Creator in the

---

1 There are several variants, of which that adopted in the text is almost certainly right. 'I give thanks to God' (אA ω pesh Origen) is probably due to an accidental mechanical error; 'The grace of God' (D lat) and 'The grace of the Lord' (G) are attempts (based on the fact that Greek uses the same word (χάρις) for 'thanks' and 'grace') to supply a definite answer to the question, 'Who shall deliver me?'.

interests of self that is the root of sin exists everywhere, and everywhere there exists enough of the rudiments of religion to make it responsible and blameworthy (cf. i. 19 ff.). But only where the law, religion in the form of the command of the living God, exists, can sin emerge in perceptible and measurable form. The law turns sin into transgression (see p. 105). This, however, does not exhaust Paul's meaning. 'Knowing sin' does not mean merely perceiving its existence, but experiencing it. In iii. 20 Paul had spoken of the *recognition*, or perception (ἐπίγνωσις) of sin; he now uses the simple verb *know* (ἔγνων). The law is not simply a reagent by which the presence of sin may be detected; it is a catalyst which aids or even initiates the action of sin upon man. This opinion Paul supports by means of an example.

For indeed I should not know desire if the law did not say, 'Thou shalt not desire'. Paul refers to the tenth commandment, Ex. xx. 17; Deut. v. 21; but he quotes only the verb of the prohibition, omitting the objects which the Old Testament supplies (thy neighbour's house, etc.). The word itself, both noun and verb, is in non-biblical Greek as neutral in meaning as the English 'desire'; only the context can determine whether it is good or bad. The good sense occurs in the New Testament (e.g. Luke xxii. 15), but the bad predominates; and, ultimately, for the reason Paul exposes by omitting to supply an object of desire. It is of course wrong to desire (covet) one's neighbour's wife; but behind this guilty desire, shown to be guilty by its object, lies a desire which is guilty in itself, independently of its object, and sinful though quite possibly respectable, or indeed religious. Desire means precisely that exaltation of the *ego* which we have seen to be of the essence of sin (see pp. 36, 104). Regardless of his place in creation, and of God's command, man desires, and his desire becomes the law of his being. He, rather than God, becomes Lord. This the law cannot tolerate. Its form is God's command, and its basis is God's right as Lord to command. It emphasizes man's creatureliness. Its fundamental requirement, illustrated in a great variety of particular precepts and prohibitions, might be summed up in two clauses: Thou shalt not desire – Thou shalt obey; and if both are left without objects their meaning becomes not less but more clear. The inexactness of Paul's quotation is not due to carelessness or to the wish to abbreviate, but contributes significantly to his own meaning, and to the understanding of the commandment that he quotes.

Another small observation in this sentence will also prove significant. In *v.* 7 b and *v.* 7 c Paul uses different verbs, in different tenses, for 'know'. In *v.* 7 b the verb is aorist, in *v.* 7 c, imperfect.[1] The two

---

1 Strictly speaking, the pluperfect ᾔδειν, used, as regularly in Greek, with the force of the imperfect.

sentences, if strictly interpreted, should accordingly have different meanings: (a) I should not have come to know sin if I had not come to know it through the law; (b) I should not now know desire, if the law did not now say ... If it were right, either grammatically or theologically, to make a strict temporal contrast, (a) would refer to a point in the past, an event belonging to the time before Paul's conversion, (b) to the present, Paul's experience as a Christian man. The very fact, however, that (a) and (b) stand side by side makes such a differentiation difficult. The 'I' in this verse means man, perceiving and participating in sin. The two clauses together amount perhaps to 'I should never have known ... ' – no precise limits being attached to this knowledge, whether forward or backward. Men can be religious, and, in particular, they can be Jews, both before and after their conversion.

How does the law convey knowledge of sin? So far as knowledge means 'perception' the answer is easy. The law provides commandments, and sin shows itself by transgressing them. But if knowledge means 'experience' the answer is not so plain. The law forbids sin; how can it 'engender' it (*v.* 5)? The answer seems to be that it is in the law that man becomes aware of his limitations, and of his status as a creature over against the Creator, who addresses him with authority and requires his obedience. Sin is man's reaction against these limitations, his affirmation of himself and of his own will-to-life in the face of the 'Thou shalt not' of the law. The law itself is not sin, but it supplies the raw material of sin. Paul, however, has a different metaphor.

The law is not itself sin, **but in fact sin seized its opportunity** 8 **through the commandment;** Paul does not here say *law* because, as the next words show, he is still thinking of the last commandment of the Ten, the prohibition of *desire*. The word here translated 'opportunity' means literally 'point of departure', and is often used in military contexts to denote the origin of a war. Sin and law are clearly differentiated, though closely connected. Sin aimed against man an attack which law never intended, and was able to use law in its approach. It **thereby produced in me every kind of desire,** because law had created the conditions in which desire (see above) could operate. Apart from law, the desire would not have been apparent, **for apart from law, sin is dead** – that is, inactive; sin was present, but not counted (v. 13); indeed, not countable.

The allusion of v. 13 suggests one possible interpretation of this verse, and of *vv.* 9 ff. They may be understood as pointing to the story of Adam; indeed, if Paul is not actually telling this story he is at least using it to bring out his point. Sin – the serpent – was in the Garden even before man, but had no opportunity of attacking the man until the command 'Thou shalt not eat of it' (Gen. ii. 17) had been given. It was precisely by means of this command, the prototype of all law and religion, that the serpent tempted man. The command marked out the difference between man and God, creature and Creator, which is the theme of religion. The serpent was able to represent this as humiliating to man. 'The difference is not ultimate; transgress the command and you shall be as God' (Gen. iii. 4 f.). Man's will to live was thus turned into sin, and from sin into transgression. The woman, soon joined by the man, saw that the forbidden tree was 'to be *desired*' (Gen. iii. 6).[1]

It is possible that Paul is not simply describing the fate of Adam, which he had read in the Old Testament, but telling his own story in the light of Genesis. The tenth commandment proved to be the psychological means by which sin was stirred to activity within his own experience. It has often been pointed out that to prohibit some course of action is to awaken desire to pursue it. It may be therefore that Paul is thinking of an occasion in his youth when the legal prohibition awakened revolt within his soul, not simply in the sense that he discovered what fun it can be to break a rule but in the sense pointed out above: the passion for independence, for autonomy, that is unwilling to acknowledge a *Lord* (cf. i. 21).

The next verse looks even more like autobiography. When sin is 9 dead (*v.* 8), man can live. **Apart from law I was alive once; but when** 10 **the commandment came, sin sprang to life and I died.**

The autobiographical interpretation would run as follows. In the first innocence of youth Paul was alive. Death is the consequence of sin (vi. 23), and there was at that time no sin to incur it. Life is from God, and there was nothing to interrupt the child's natural and instinctive communion with him. Then came the moment when the Jewish boy became a 'Son of the Commandment' (*bar mitzwah*), and assumed responsibility before the law. With this new legal responsibility sin took its place in the boy's experience. The forbidden world appeared upon his horizon, and he longed to enter it. He desired to gratify himself and to achieve independence of the God who placed unwelcome restraint upon him. This was death.

When we turn back to the narrative of Gen. iii, all that need be added is precise reference to the warning, 'In the day that thou eatest thereof thou shalt surely die' (Gen. ii. 17; cf. iii. 19).

It will be well at this point to set out clearly the various lines of interpretation that have been and may be offered here. (a) There is a purely autobiographical interpretation. Paul speaks of his early childhood, and of the end that was put to it by an awareness of the law and of his responsibility to it. As soon as law entered his experience, so

---

1 This point is missed in the Greek of the LXX translation; if Paul had it in mind he must have been recalling the Hebrew text.

also did sin. (b) is a variant of (a): Paul is not writing of his own but of the whole Jewish experience. This is what being a Jew, aware of the divine law, means. He uses the first person singular in order to add greater vividness to his discussion. (c) Paul gives an exposition of the story of Adam, the universal Man, based on the story of Creation, Command, and Fall in Gen. i–iii. (d) Paul is combining two or more of these lines of thought. This seems in fact to be correct. Allusions to Genesis are not verbal, but at various points it is impossible to mistake the figure of Adam. At the same time, Paul would not have expressed the story of Adam in terms of the first personal pronoun had he not recognized that it applied to him; he knew the truth of 2 Baruch liv. 19, Each one of us is his own Adam. And he knew it not because he was a unique individual, Saul of Tarsus, but because he was a Jew, born under the law.

At the end of the verse the process is summarized: **the very commandment that was directed towards life resulted for me in death.** Paul achieves brevity by leaving out middle steps. The commandment was intended not to produce life, for this it could not do (Gal. iii. 21), but to preserve life, by restraining man from evil courses that could issue in death. This was true of the command of Gen. ii. 17, which, if observed, would have saved Adam from death; it was true of the law under whose sway the Jewish boy entered; see for example Deut. xxx. 15–20. The commandment resulted in death precisely because it was aimed at life, and that under threat of penalties; resisted by sin, the sanctions of Gen. ii. 17 and Deut. xxx. 15–20 came into effect. Life is that to which the law points when it directs man to be content with the place in creation that God has accorded him. But all these well-intentioned institutions have produced a race under sentence of death, and already the cancer of corrupting bondage (viii. 21) is felt and seen in human affairs; it suffices to refer to i. 18–iii. 20.

The commandment achieved this unintended result not because of a defect in itself but through the attack, and the deceitfulness, of sin, which in what follows is almost personified. It could not be made clearer that, whatever law may be, it is not to be identified with sin. **For sin took its opportunity** (cf. *v.* 8), **deceived me by means of the** 11 **commandment, and – again by means of it – killed me.** This is almost a quotation from Gen. iii. 13, to which Paul alludes again at 2 Cor. xi. 3 (cf. 1 Tim. ii. 14). It was the commandment that gave the serpent (who contributes not a little to the personification of sin) his opportunity. The commandment singled out the forbidden tree and its property of giving divine knowledge; and this last in turn made it easy to twist the warning, Ye shall not surely die. Law, which begins by drawing attention to the gulf that separates man from God, is shaped by man into a bridge across the gulf. *Sin*, not law, killed me, contradicting the purpose of the law. This is man's abuse of the religion (pp. 52 f.) that is instinctive to him, never a greater abuse than when a law, a religion, that is no human instinct but the word of God is so misused. The law is a good gift and a reason for thankfulness (ix. 4), but it is no ground for boasting (ii. 17).

12   The law then is absolved; it is not sin. **The law then is holy, and the commandment is holy, righteous, and good.** Scripture is holy (i. 2) because it comes from God; whatever may be true of other religions and of other codes of morals, those in the Old Testament are the word of God himself. The 'commandment' suggests the special enactments of the Mosaic code (and perhaps Gen. ii. 17). These too are holy; they are righteous, in that they command what is right (cf. Gal. iii. 21); and they are good, that is, beneficent in their intention. Paul's argument hitherto has evidently been intended to vindicate this holy, righteous, and beneficent character of the law.

13   What then is wrong? **Did that which in itself is good** (Prov. iv. 2 was sometimes made the basis of an identification of the law with 'the good') **prove in my case to be death?** The question must be asked, because death has in fact resulted (*vv.* 10 f.). But the answer is clear: **No indeed.** The fault does not lie with the law *in itself.* **The fact is that sin, in order that it might be shown up as sin, used that good thing** (the law) **to bring forth death for me.** The fault lies entirely with sin, again personified. Paul writes here what may be described as a kind of myth, in which sin and law are described, and behave, as persons, one taking advantage of the other. We shall shortly see that Paul the mythographer becomes his own demythologizer. The means by which sin took advantage of the situation created by law have already been brought out in the preceding verses and need not be repeated now. It is to be noted that this verse betrays not the least interest in psychology; Paul simply states that sin led to death – the doom of creation separated from the Creator; and that this happened in order that sin might stand out in its true colours. The serpent had promised (Gen. iii. 5) that men should be as God; but the rebellion begun with the highest conceivable hope ended in condemnation and death. Sin might appear as human progress, or in any other attractive guise; but death proved it to be – nothing but sin. The most damning feature of its disclosure was the fact that sin had used in its death-dealing work God's good gift, the law. **Sin did this in order that, by means of the commandment, it might be shown up as exceedingly sinful.** The second purpose clause is parallel to the first, but goes further. Sin, in its deceitful use of law and commandment, is revealed not merely in its true colours but in the worst possible light. The purpose was God's (cf. v. 20; also Gal. iii. 19), and it showed a second use of the law.

One point in Paul's argument is not perfectly clear; he has not shown whether law precedes sin (as the condition in which it appears), or follows it (with the intention of unmasking its true character). He seems to think of it both ways. It is, however, unfair to expect perfect clarity here, where clarity could be attained only by plunging more deeply into mythological speech than Paul intends to do. He has brought out the subtle interrelation of law and sin; the holiness of the former and the exceeding sinfulness of the latter. It is not too much to suppose that it was precisely these points that he intended to bring out.

But he has not yet done with the matter. Law and sin are still engaged in conflict, and their battle-ground is human life. Their mutual relations may be observed further in this field. This is the point at which Paul must demythologize his story of personified abstracts. What he has to say is not unlike an existential account of human nature and its struggles, but the process retains from the myth an objective element which complements the subjective.

There is no question of the goodness of the law (this clause, 14 which is not in the Greek, is to be understood as the necessary antecedent of the 'for' (γάρ) that follows), **for we know that it is spiritual,** that is, in its origin; it is from God. This was axiomatic in Judaism (e.g. *Sanhedrin*, x. 1: These are they that have no share in the world to come: he that says . . . that the law is not from heaven [God]). Because it is spiritual in origin, the law is spiritual in character, and in its mode of contact with men. Those to whom it is merely a matter of 'letter' (vii. 6) cannot understand it; neither can they who are not themselves spiritual.

It is here that difficulty arises. The law comes from God, for whom and of whom it speaks. But I am determined by *flesh*, humanity that has decided that it has no room for God (viii. 7). **I am a man of flesh, sold as a slave so as to be under the power of sin.** It will be noticed that Paul no longer speaks in the past tenses of *vv.* 7, 8, 9, 10, 11, 13, but in the present; this continues to the end of the chapter.

We have already seen (p. 129) that Paul uses the word 'flesh' in at least two senses; sometimes it merely describes the physical aspect of human life, and sometimes it takes on a darker tone, and describes a proclivity to sin by which all men are affected, their natural tendency to regard themselves as self-sufficient and self-determining. From this Christians are delivered, but their deliverance is never in this life so complete that Paul finds it unnecessary to warn them against the flesh, and exhort them not to live in accordance with it (viii. 12). Those who belong to Christ, the crucified Christ, have crucified the flesh, along with its passions and desires (Gal. v. 24); but the moral process of destruction has still to be completed.

What flesh (in the bad sense) means appears clearly in this verse. I have been sold (as a slave) in such a way as to come under the power of sin. Sin has dominion over me (cf. vi. 14). This dominion is given vivid rhetorical expression in the next verses; for the moment we may recall that Paul is still emphasizing the central point: the law is not at fault. Not the spiritual law, but carnal, sin-dominated man is the cause

15 of death. This even sinful man must admit. **For the works I do are incomprehensible to me** (not, 'I do not know what I am doing', for Paul knows only too well; but 'I do not recognize and approve'), **for I do not practise** (it is doubtful whether Paul means to distinguish between 'practise' and 'do'; cf. i. 32) **what I wish; on the contrary I**

16 **do what I hate. But if I do what I do not wish, then it follows that I agree with the law, admitting it to be right and good** (one adjective only in Greek, not that of v. 12). I am a slave (v. 14); any slave is likely from time to time to find himself doing things he does not wish to do. He does them because his master forces him to do them, and his master must therefore take moral responsibility for them. I would rather do what the law commands, but a stronger power forbids.

Commentators usually quote in illustration of these verses Ovid's words (*Metamorphoses*, vii. 20 f.), *uideo meliora proboque, deteriora sequor*. There is an even closer verbal parallel in Epictetus (II. xxvi. 1–4): the sinner does not wish to sin ... the thief ... does not do what he wishes and does what he does not wish. Neither Ovid, however, nor Epictetus (but the whole paragraph is worth study) says exactly what Paul is saying here. It is assumed that the measure of Paul's actions is the law, and that they do not conform to this standard. Unless his words are simply tautologous, he must mean that there is within himself an independent authority which confirms the judgement of the external law. But Paul has already spoken of such an independent (though allied) authority, namely, the conscience (see ii. 15). The very fact that I am unhappy about my own deeds confirms that the law is just and good. Is the law sin? Certainly not; it is confirmed by conscience.

A further point now emerges. We find man in a state of rebellion against God, and under sentence of death. For this unhappy situation the law is not to blame. But neither, it now appears, am 'I', for I agree with the law, and disapprove of the sins which I myself commit. Who

17 then is to blame? **What in fact is happening is that it is not I that do my works, but sin which dwells in me.** Sin is personified as an evil power which takes up its residence within human nature, and there controls man's actions.

Having come upon this fresh point in the course of an argument directed to a different end (that of exonerating the law), Paul proceeds to develop it through the next three verses, coming back in v. 20 to the conclusion he has already announced in v. 17. In fact, vv. 18, 19, 20 cover very nearly the same ground as vv. 15, 16, 17. It seems possible that they are alternative versions. Compare v. 7; it may be that having dictated *vv.* 15–17 Paul thought he could improve on what he had said and dictated *vv.* 18–20. The stenographer, however, had already got the first version on paper and did not delete it. The fault must lie with sin, **for I know that there dwells no good thing in me** (he must 18 correct himself, for he has just said that 'I' agree with the law and wish to do what is good) – **I should say, in my flesh.**

There is here an apparent distinction between 'I' and 'my flesh'. *Flesh* is clearly evil, but it is not evil because it is material, a part of the body; and it is evil as a perversion of good. It recalls the 'evil inclination' of rabbinic Judaism, which, though it inclined man to sin, was not wholly evil and possessed certain virtues. Here it must suffice to note that there is an element in human nature so completely under the power of sin that not only is there no good in it, it corrupts all man's activity. How do we know that this is so? By observing (as in *vv.* 15 f.) the sheer moral incompetence of man: **For I can always wish, but never actually achieve, a really good work; for I do not do the** 19 **good I wish to do; rather, the evil I do not wish to do I practise.** The conclusion is the same as that of *v.* 17: **But if I do what I do not** 20 **wish to do, that shows that it cannot be I that do it; it must be sin that dwells in me.**

The effect of this reiterated conclusion is to emphasize the distinction between the true self – 'I' – and the sin-dominated flesh, which has its way and carries out actions of which 'I' disapprove, and does not carry out the good actions of which 'I' approve. Yet this sin-dominated flesh is also 'I'. Man is at the same time righteous and sinful (Luther).

Paul has now advanced beyond his original proposition (that the law so far from being sin is in all respects good) in two matters. (a) Equally blameless with the law is the conscience, which, in agreement with the law, condemns evil behaviour. (b) Evil behaviour is caused by sin, a personal power residing in and dominating the flesh. The digression is coming to its close, and in *vv.* 21–5 Paul sums up its meaning. It is unfortunate, in the interests of clarity, that in doing so he introduces new metaphors and psychological terms. The new terms do, however, bring out important new points.

What then does this amount to? That there is imposed upon 21 **me, who would do what is good and right, a law, to the effect that evil shall always attend me.** This verse describes in fresh terms the state described in *vv.* 15 f., 18 b–20 a: but it is complicated by the use of the word 'law'. Of this, several interpretations have been given; the most important are the following.

(i) Throughout the chapter 'law' means the law of Moses. This verse then means, 'This is what I find the law – a life under the law – to come to in my experience: when I wish to do good, evil is present with me' (Denney). This interpretation finds support in *vv.* 8, 11.

(ii) 'Law' (νόμος) means 'rule' or 'principle'. For this suggestion and an objection to it see on iii. 27. It seems most improbable that in the course of a long and profound discussion of the meaning of law (νόμος), in the sense of Torah, the Mosaic law and its developments, Paul would suddenly drop in a use of law (νόμος) that meant something in all respects different.

(iii) 'Law' here stands for a law-like rule, which as an evil double of the Mosaic law can bear the same name. Thus there are *two* laws; the true law of Moses, and the base imitation of this which is the work of sin. This interpretation is strikingly confirmed by *v.* 23, where two 'laws' are mentioned side by side.

Of these interpretations, (i) and (iii) are perhaps not as far apart as at first sight appears; but the sharp antithesis of *v.* 23 requires (iii), or something very much like it. It must be remembered that Paul, in these concluding verses of the chapter, is closing the last gaps in his argument that the law is not in itself responsible for the evil state of mankind. He has asserted that the law is holy. He has shown that this is attested by the conscience. He has accused sin of being the corrupting influence which takes advantage of the law to attack men. Yet, when all this is said, the law still looks like an enemy. It is under the rule of law that sin and death flourish. It would have been simpler for students of the epistle if Paul had here reverted to the language of ch. ii, and shown that the trouble arises not through the use but through the abuse of the law, and that the law ministers to sin only when men, instead of being humbled by it, use it as an instrument of self-glorification. But Paul does not do this. He says (*v.* 23) that sin produces a counterfeit law, which makes war upon the true law, takes man captive and so works its will with him. Religion which, especially in its Old Testament form, ought to keep man in a state of humble dependence before the Creator becomes (in its perverted form) the watchword of his revolt.

As often happens, Paul states his case first, and then proceeds to support it with a 'for' sentence.

22, 23   **For in my inner self I agree with God's law, but I observe in my members** (cf. vi. 13) **another law which makes war upon the law which rules in my mind** (evidently the same as God's law which is approved by my inner self, *v.* 22) **and takes me prisoner** (as a prisoner of war) **to the law of sin** (the 'other law') **which is in my members.**

The two laws mentioned in these verses have already been discussed, but attention must be given to the psychological terms introduced.

The 'inner self', or 'inward man' (ὁ ἔσω ἄνθρωπος), is a term which recurs in 2 Cor. iv. 16 (cf. Eph. iii. 16). In these passages it refers to the interior Christian life. Its meaning cannot be substantially different here; it is synonymous, or almost synonymous, with the 'I' that would do good and hates evil (*vv.* 14–17, 19 f.), and the 'mind' of *vv.* 23, 25. 2 Cor. iv. 16, however, gives a further pointer, for it is set in an evidently eschatological context. The 'inward man' belongs to the Age to Come, just as the 'outward man' belongs to the present age, and is therefore doomed to perish. That is, the 'inward' or invisible man is also the 'new man' implied by vi. 6. It is the new creation, which by faith, given visible expression in baptism, Christians have experienced, and which ethically they must continually be instructed to put into practice; in fact, it is Christ himself, whom Christians have 'put on' (Gal. iii. 27), and whom they must still 'put on' (xiii. 14). 'Paul takes over the language of the Hellenistic-dualistic way of thinking but remoulds it to modes of expression of his own anthropology which is Christian, and determined on soteriological-eschatological lines'.[1]

Little would be gained by an attempt to distinguish between the 'mind' and the 'inner self'. Again, Paul is dependent on Hellenistic terminology, but even where he appears to borrow most he is in fact writing independently. So far from the intelligence being essentially good, it can become 'unfit' (i. 28).

On the 'members' (μέλη) see on vi. 13, though here there is a different emphasis. In vi. 13 the members are thought of as a differentiation of the *body* (σῶμα), which is made up of a number of effective instruments, all of which must no longer be offered in the service of sin but henceforth to God in the service of righteousness. Here the same members (the means by which I do things) are a differentiation of the *flesh* (σάρξ), myself not in neutrality but taking my own side against God. To this self the law of sin corresponds.

To sum up: the mind is able to conceive a pure religion, in which all life is ordered in accordance with its proper place in creation. In a covenant of law man recognizes his indebtedness to, and his total dependence on, God, whom he loves and serves with all his heart and soul. But this is not religion as it exists, even within Judaism and the Old Testament. For sin has taken possession of the law ('the law of sin', *v.* 23), and made out of it a subtle perversion of law. If by 'law' the inquirer means this perversion, then the law is sin; and from it there is no visible means of escape.

No wonder that Paul cries out: **Wretched man that I am! who** 24 **shall deliver me from this body of death?** 'The body of this death' is grammatically possible but scarcely makes sense. Paul means the body or human nature which through sin and law has fallen under the dominion of death.

The source of Paul's wretchedness is clear. Man has become a battle-ground between the true law of God, holy, righteous, good,

1 J. Behm, in *TWNT*, ii, p. 697.

spiritual, requiring the obedience of faith, and sin's law, a counterfeit of the true law, so perverted by sin that (to take the most fundamental examples) instead of ending *desire* (*v.* 7) it provokes it (*v.* 8), and by suggesting the response of works provokes disobedience masquerading as righteousness (ix. 31 f.). The wretchedness is due to conflict, but it is not the conflict of a 'divided self'. It means that man's last hope, in the word of God, has become a broken reed; worse, it has become an enemy. Through sin, the word of God in the law has become not a comfort but an accusation. Man needs not law but deliverance, a new creation (Gal. iii. 21; vi. 15; 2 Cor. v. 17).

Paul writes as a Christian, and he knows the answer to his own question – knows it so well that with unstudied dramatic aposiopesis he does not express it in words. **Thanks be to God through Jesus Christ our Lord!** Christ, and Christ alone, is the answer.

25

Those who interpret this paragraph on psychological lines almost always feel obliged to transfer *v.* 25 b to a different place, or to omit it altogether. These, however, are expedients to which resort may be had only if the words in question prove quite unintelligible where they stand. But this is not so. They are an apt summary of the paragraph. There are two laws; there are two aspects of human nature. The mind (see the note on *vv.* 22, 23) recognizes and serves the law of God, the flesh – human nature living in and for this age – recognizes the law that sin has fashioned for this age.

To sum up then: I myself with my mind serve God's law, but with the flesh I serve sin's law.

We must return to the questions posed at the beginning of our discussion of this paragraph, but it will be necessary first to recall three important facts.

(i) In passages where Paul certainly describes his life before his conversion there is no trace of spiritual conflict or of a 'divided self'. Gal. i. 13 f. and Phil. iii. 4 ff. depict a Jew practising his religion more successfully than any of his contemporaries, blameless in his observance of the law, and entirely satisfied with his own righteousness.

(ii) Ch. vi has already made clear the ambiguous position of the Christian in this world. In baptism, by faith, he has died with Christ to sin, and been raised with him to live a new life. Yet, true as this is, it is still necessary for the apostle to urge him to do what he has already done – to die to sin, and to offer himself to God as one whom God has raised from the dead. He is, and he is not, free from sin; he lives, and he does not live, for God; he is at the same time a righteous man and a sinner (cf. p. 120). This ambiguous personal position reflects the eschatological situation. The Age to Come has dawned, in the life, death, and resurrection of Jesus; but the present age has not passed. The two exist uneasily side by side, and Christians still look earnestly for the redemption of the body (viii. 23), knowing that they have been saved in hope (viii. 24).

(iii) 'The use of the 1st and 2nd person singular as representing any one in general, in order to express some truth of general validity in vivid style by using the example of a single person, as though he were present, is not as common in Greek as in other languages, and in literature seems first to occur in the late classical period (as a peculiarity of vivid colloquial speech). In the New Testament Paul presents a few examples' (BDR § 281).

In addition to these facts it must be remembered that, as the exegesis has brought out, the primary question in Paul's mind here is not psychological or anthropological, but concerns the meaning of law and religion. Is the law sin? If not, how came it to be so closely connected with sin? How did God's good gift, and man's highest achievement in understanding and feeling, prove to be man's death sentence?

In answering these questions Paul is incidentally involved in an analysis of human nature. It is true that the analysis is not merely academic; Paul wrote what he smartingly did feel. But it is human nature, and not Paul's nature, with which he deals; and it is human nature on earth, and not in heaven, that he describes. The insights of this paragraph are Christian insights. The paragraph itself does not tell the whole story of the Christian life, but it is written from within the Christian life to account for the role of law in man's experience. Paul's account of law, though based upon the Jewish understanding of law, is not that of Judaism. It has been transformed by two considerations, a negative and a positive. The negative consideration is the recognition that sin (it is hard not to follow Paul's method of personification, which makes the matter much easier to state) has entered the process, corrupted the 'good thing', and made of it something other than the means of remaining within God's gracious covenant. The positive consideration is the act of God who manifested his righteousness in the life, death, and resurrection of Jesus. It is in the light of this act that Paul understands sin and the law. As a Christian he has learned to interpret the law by the Gospel, and he never works in the opposite direction. A simple 'covenantal nomism'[1] is not for him, though he recognizes the law as a good gift from God to his people (ix. 4). It is not a means by which the covenant may be sustained but an illumination of the promise, which, as grace, must always be predominant. The law could not change this, the basis of God's dealings with his people (Gal. iii. 17). Discussion of the role of

1 The words are those of E. P. Sanders, *Paul and Palestinian Judaism* (London, 1977). They cast much light on the Judaism out of which Paul moved to become a Christian; see Introduction, p. 9.

the law, originating in the question, Is the law sin? thus brings Paul back to his account of salvation.

19 LIFE IN THE SPIRIT

CHAPTER viii. 1–11

(1) It follows therefore that those who are in Christ Jesus fall now under no condemnation whatever. (2) For in Christ Jesus the law of the life-giving Spirit has set thee free[1] from the law of sin and death. (3) For this liberation, which the law could never effect because it was weak through the flesh, God brought about when, by sending his own Son in the form of flesh which had passed under sin's rule, and to deal with sin, he condemned sin in the flesh, (4) in order that the law's requirement (that we should be righteous) might be fulfilled in us, whose lives are determined not by the flesh but by the Spirit. (5) For those whose lives are determined by the flesh set their minds on the affairs of the flesh, while those whose lives are determined by the Spirit set their minds on the affairs of the Spirit. (6) This contrariety is absolute; for to have one's mind set on the flesh results in death, but to have one's mind set on the Spirit results in life and peace. (7) A mind set on the flesh results in death, because it is in a state of enmity against God, for it is not in subjection to the law of God, nor indeed can it be. (8) It follows that those who are in the flesh cannot please God. (9) But you are not in the flesh but in the Spirit, if, as is indeed the case, the Spirit of God dwells in you. And if anyone has not the Spirit that comes from Christ, he is not Christ's. (10) But if Christ is in you, the body on the one hand is dead on account of sin, but the Spirit on the other is at work giving life because you are righteous before God; (11) and if the Spirit of him who raised up Jesus from the dead dwells in you,

---

1 This translates the text (ἠλευθέρωσέν σε) of many of the best MSS (B ℵ F G it pesh) and early Latin fathers (Tertullian, Ambrosiaster). The majority of MSS (A C D ω vg sah) have 'has set me free' (ἠλευθέρωσέν με); a few have 'has set us free'; and there is slight evidence (mainly from Origen) for the use of the verb without any object pronoun. 'Us' is a generalization designed to make it clear that Paul's words apply to all Christian readers of the letter; this is certainly secondary. 'Me' assimilates this statement to the use of the first person singular in vii.7–25; this too will be secondary. The fact that the sentence runs more easily with a pronoun than without argues in favour of the short text; it would be more natural for copyists to add a pronoun than to remove one, and there might have been accidental repetition of the last syllable of ἠλευθέρωσε. The evidence in favour of the short text, however, is very slight, and haplography rather than dittography may have taken place. Fortunately the variation makes no difference whatever to the meaning of the sentence.

then he who raised Christ Jesus from the dead will quicken your mortal bodies too, through his Spirit, who dwells in you.

The question that Paul was obliged to raise at vii. 7 – Is the law sin? – has now been dealt with in a paragraph which, though of the greatest interest and importance, must be described as a digression from the main line of argument. Paul now, using the insights and some of the language that his digression has produced, returns to the point reached at vii. 6. **It follows therefore** (not from vii. 25 but from vii. 6) **that those who are in Christ Jesus fall now** (cf. the 'now' of vii. 6, with the note) **under no condemnation whatever.** It is the law that leads to condemnation, both because sin fastens its grip upon man through the law, and because judgement takes place on the basis of law. Christians, however, are dead to the law and therefore escape judgement. They are dead to the law not because they have decided to ignore it, but because they have died with Christ (vi. 3); hence it is those who are in Christ who are not condemned. Compare v. 16, 18: the act of the first Adam leads to condemnation, but the act of the new Adam leads to acquittal (justification). For the phrase 'in Christ' see vi. 11 and xii. 5, with the notes. Christians share the death and resurrection of Christ and so pass in him into the Age to Come. This observation is of fundamental importance. Paul does not say that Christians are free from condemnation because they are sinless, but because they are in Christ; that is, he is still speaking of justification and its consequences. Since the absence of condemnation is equivalent to justification there is a close parallel between viii. 1 and v. 1, and indeed between the paragraphs which these verses respectively begin. Among the consequences of justification, hardly mentioned in the epistle up to this point (but see vii. 6, which is in fact the beginning of this paragraph) is the gift of the Spirit. To be in Christ is to have passed with him through apocalyptic affliction and resurrection into the Age to Come, or rather, into an anticipation within this Age of the Age to Come. This anticipation is brought about by the Spirit (see especially viii. 23).

That it is their freedom from the law that releases Christians from condemnation is confirmed but also clarified by the next verse, of which it seems best to give a fairly literal translation. **For in Christs Jesus the law of the life-giving Spirit has set thee free from the law of sin and death.** As in vii. 23, 25, two laws oppose each other. The second is clearly the law of Moses, not in its pristine form but as it has been possessed and abused by sin and in consequence leads to death. The first is harder to define. The words *in Christ Jesus*, taken adverbially with *set free*, determine the field in which liberation takes place and the means, or agency, by which it is achieved. Liberation, redemption (cf. iii. 24), is his act; but his act was attested by the law as

well as by the prophets (iii. 21), and, as the second *law* is the old law
perverted, the first *law* is the old law fulfilled in Christ and in the
righteousness of faith (cf. x. 4, 6–8). The old law was already *spiritual*
(vii. 14); it had been taken in terms of *letter* (vii. 6), it is now to be
taken in terms of *Spirit* – the Spirit of God, who is defined comprehen-
sively by the genitive *of life*. As law and sin produce death, the Spirit
produces life (*v.* 6, below). This is not simply a matter of reinterpreta-
tion; a new dispensation has replaced the old. 'The law of the Spirit is
nothing other than the Spirit himself in his ruling function in the
sphere of Christ' (Käsemann, English translation 215 f.; German, 207).
For a full account of alternative ways of understanding this difficult
sentence see Cranfield 373–8.

The new way liberates from the old, which acts as a tyrannical
master; compare vi. 18, 22; vii. 3, 24. It is evident that this liberation
could never have been won for men by the law of Moses, which was
not able to give life (Gal. iii. 21), and had itself passed under the
control of sin. To attempt to use it as a way of salvation was to
misapply it, and to fall into sin. Liberation could come only through a
3 new and creative act of God. **This liberation, which the law could
never effect because it was weak through the flesh, God brought
about.** The flesh was committed to 'sin's law', and was bound
therefore to paralyse the divine law. 'Brought about' has no equivalent
in the Greek, but some such supplement is required in order to
complete the construction, which Paul breaks off when he reaches
the word 'God', going on to say at once what it was that God had
done. The sentence can be translated without this supplement, if we
take the opening clause as constituting a sort of explanatory parallel
to the main sentence. God condemned sin in the flesh . . . a thing that
the law could not do (literally, the law's impossibility, τὸ ἀδύνατον
τοῦ νόμου). But it is better to take 'the law's impossibility' to refer
back to the liberation of *v.* 2; of course the law could not undo the
bondage for which it was in part responsible.

God effected liberation **when, by sending his own Son in the
form of flesh which had passed under sin's rule, and to deal with
sin, he condemned sin in the flesh.**

Jesus Christ was *sent* by his Father; he was neither a man who
discovered the truth about God, nor a heavenly rebel, like Prome-
theus, but a divine envoy, whose authority resided not in himself but
in him who sent him. Paul's assertion here contains the root of the
doctrine of the Incarnation; but as he continues he raises acutely one
of its most difficult problems. If Jesus Christ was on the one hand
God's own Son, on the other he was man. But in what relation did he
stand to the humanity he came to redeem? Paul's words, literally
translated, are that Christ was sent 'in the likeness (ὁμοίωμα) of flesh
of sin'. Paul certainly does not mean that Christ was sinful like the rest

of mankind (2 Cor. v. 21), or that he was a man only in appearance – his insistence upon the Cross as a real event makes it impossible to think that he believed in a docetic Christ. One possible suggestion is that Paul distinguished between flesh as it was created by God, and 'flesh of sin', that is, flesh which had fallen under the dominion of sin. Christ (on this view) had perfect, unfallen flesh, which nevertheless was indistinguishable in appearance from 'flesh of sin'; he came in flesh, so that the incarnation was perfectly real, but only *in the likeness* of 'flesh of sin', so that he remained sinless.

It is doubtful, however, whether this is what Paul means. The word 'form' or 'likeness' (ὁμοίωμα) has already been used several times in the epistle (i. 23; v. 14; vi. 5), and in none of these places does it mean simply 'imitation'. Compare also Phil. ii. 7, where Paul certainly does not mean to say that Christ only appeared to be a man. We are probably justified therefore in our translation, and in deducing that Christ took precisely the same fallen nature that we ourselves have, and that he remained sinless because he constantly overcame a proclivity to sin. It must be remembered that for Paul *flesh* (σάρξ) in theological use does not refer to the material constituent of human existence but to the manner of human existence as it has, since the entry of sin, come in fact to be. It is the nature of fallen man, living in this world, to be wrapped up in himself. He is conditioned to this kind of existence by the human environment in which he finds himself. Christ found himself in the same human environment as all his fellow men and experienced the same pressures that they feel; yet he remained without sin, living a theocentric existence in an anthropo-centric, egocentric, environment. It was in this environment – *in the flesh* – that sin had to be condemned and defeated if it was to be condemned and defeated at all.

The Son of God was sent 'to deal with sin'; compare iii. 25. As in iii. 25 there may be a reference to the lid of the Ark, and to the Day of Atonement, so here there may be an allusion to the Old Testament sin-offering. Paul uses a simple prepositional phrase (περὶ ἁμαρτίας) which means 'concerning sin'; but this phrase was sometimes used in the LXX to translate a Hebrew word *(ḥaṭṭath)* which means sometimes 'sin' and sometimes 'sin-offering'. On the whole it seems more probable that Paul means here nothing more precise than in Gal. i. 4.

The work of Christ was the beginning of the fulfilment of God's eschatological purposes; for this reason its effect could also be described as the condemnation of sin (not of sinners, *v.* 1). Judgement has begun, and the Cross left no doubt of the attitude of God towards sin (cf. iii. 25 f., and the note). But the judgement was not merely negative; it was made **in order that the law's requirement (that we 4 should be righteous) might be fulfilled in us, whose lives are**

determined not by the flesh but by the Spirit. 'The law's requirement (that we should be righteous)' translates the same word as is discussed on i. 32; ii. 26; v. 16, 18. The closest parallel to the present use is ii. 26 ('righteous requirement'). Here the thought is not so much that what the law requires is righteous, as that what the law requires is righteousness. The law tells us that God has the right to summon us to his court, and that he requires that we be found righteous.

Paul would be consistent with what he has written earlier if he wrote here that this requirement is fulfilled in us who rely not on works of law but on faith. But now he is looking at the same truth from a different angle, and describes the same contrast in terms of flesh and Spirit.

5   **Those whose lives are determined by the flesh set their minds on the affairs of the flesh, while those whose lives are determined by the Spirit set their minds on the affairs of the Spirit.** This verse is a definition. To have one's life 'determined by the flesh' is not simply to live a corporeal existence (Christ himself did this) but to have one's gaze focused upon all that flesh means, and limited thereby to this world; 'to have one's mind set' (for this meaning of the word cf. Mark viii. 33; Rom. xii. 16; Phil. iii. 19; iv. 2) upon existence apart from God. Correspondingly, to be determined by the Spirit is to have one's gaze focused upon that which cannot be seen, upon that invisible Other who alone gives meaning and authority to existence. Compare ii. 7 f.

6   The consequence follows at once. **This contrariety is absolute** (this supplement is required by the 'for' (γάρ) which follows); **for to have one's mind set on the flesh results in death, but to have one's mind set on the Spirit results in life and peace.** To confine oneself within the circle of this world is inevitably to cut oneself off from the only source of life, and therefore to court death. To be determined by that which is God and not oneself means life and peace, not only as subjective experiences but as objective relationship with God.

7   Further, **a mind set on the flesh results in death, because it is in a state of enmity against God, for it is not in subjection to the law of God** (it represents the law which is in my members and makes war
8   upon the law of my mind; cf. vii. 23), **nor indeed can it be. It follows that those who are in the flesh cannot please God.** For the flesh to be obedient to God is a contradiction in terms, for 'flesh' in this context means a mind from which God is excluded. It is certain that in *v.* 8 'those who are in the flesh' means 'those who are determined by the flesh'. Elsewhere Paul uses the expression otherwise; so, for example, at i. 3; ix. 5; 2 Cor. iv. 11; x. 3; Gal. ii. 20. But *v.* 9 shows beyond dispute that it cannot here mean 'living a bodily life'. The present verse almost amounts to, 'Those who are living to please themselves (not simply in a "carnal" sense) cannot also please God'.

The word 'please' is itself significant. It is wrong to 'please oneself' (xv. 1, 3); 'pleasing men' is dangerous and often wrong (1 Cor. vii. 33 f.; Gal. i. 10; 1 Thess. ii. 4), but we ought to please God and our neighbour (xv. 2; 1 Cor. x. 33; 1 Thess. ii. 15; iv. 1). 'Being in the flesh' may almost be defined as 'pleasing (not God but) oneself'.

What has just been said does not apply to the Christian readers of the epistle. **You are not in the flesh** (that is, you are not determined **9** **by the flesh) but in the Spirit, if, as is indeed the case, the Spirit of God dwells in you.** Paul is in process of developing a new definition of the Christian life. When he speaks of dying and rising with Christ, and of justification, he is using terms eschatological in origin; now he speaks of the Spirit, contrasting the invisible activity of God himself with the visible world of the flesh. Christians are men whose lives are directed from a source outside themselves. This leads to a fundamental definition: **if anyone has not the Spirit that comes from Christ, he is not Christ's.** It is not a matter of being 'spiritual' (in a pious, or pietistic, sense) but of being open to the transforming action described in *vv.* 10, 11, which is the result of entering with Christ upon the (anticipation of) the Age to Come. It is idle to seek a distinction between 'Spirit of God' and 'Spirit of Christ'. Each is a correct description of what Paul means. The Spirit is the Spirit of God; and it is only through Christ that the Spirit is known and received. A more serious question is raised in the next verse, where Paul continues, **But 10 if Christ is in you, the body on the one hand is dead on account of sin, but the Spirit on the other is at work giving life because you are righteous before God.** In *v.* 9, The Spirit of God dwells in you; in *v.* 10, Christ is in you. Some interpreters of the epistle have maintained that Paul here simply identifies, because he cannot distinguish, the Spirit and the heavenly Christ (cf. 2 Cor. iii. 17, where the same confusion is sometimes said to occur; see *2 Corinthians*, p. 123). But the identification is not demanded by Paul's words, and is flatly contradicted by the words 'Spirit of Christ' in *v.* 9. What Paul means is that 'Spirit in you' is impossible apart from 'Christ in you'. Union with Christ is the only way into the life of the Age to Come, of which the distinguishing mark is the Spirit.

If Christ is in you, two consequences follow. On the one hand your body is dead. 'Your body' is 'you', and you are dead; for this see vi. 2–11; vii. 1–6. Of course it remains true that this baptismal death must be constantly realized (vi. 11), and may well be experienced in persecution (viii. 36). Compare also *vv.* 12 f., where Paul finds it necessary to warn his readers against living under the authority of the flesh.

On the other hand, while the body is dead, the Spirit (of God) is life-giving. Paul does not mean that the (human) spirit is alive, and imply thereby a strict dichotomy of body and spirit. If he meant this he would have said, 'The spirit is alive', not 'the spirit is life' (a literal rendering of his words). Compare the contrast of 1 Cor. xv. 45; also John vi. 63, the Spirit is that which gives life.

The human self is dead – to sin; the Spirit is able to give life – because of justification, because, that is, man is now rightly related to God in whose gift the Spirit lies. All the graces of the Christian life are the consequences of, and depend upon, justification. And the vista of life in the Spirit extends as far as the general

11 resurrection. **If the Spirit of him who raised up Jesus from the dead dwells in you, then he who raised Christ Jesus from the dead will quicken your mortal bodies too, through his Spirit, who dwells in you.**

The resurrection of Christ was an eschatological act (see on vi. 4), which marked the beginning of the Age to Come. This age was running to its close, and at its end death would be destroyed (1 Cor. xv. 26). The first event was the pledge of the last, and they were connected by the presence and activity of the Holy Spirit (see further on *v.* 23), who brought the life-giving activity of God to bear upon every stage of the intervening period (cf. 2 Cor. iii. 18), so that even our *mortal* bodies (cf. vi. 12; 2 Cor. iv. 11) are transformed and quickened.

20 THE HOPE OF GLORY
CHAPTER viii. 12–30

(12) In consequence of this, brethren, we are men under obligation; but our obligation is not to the flesh, to allow our lives to be determined by it. (13) For if you do live under the authority of the flesh you are doomed to death; but if by the Spirit you put to death the activities of the body, you will live. (14) For those who allow themselves to be directed in this way by the Spirit of God are the sons of God. (15) For the Spirit you received was not one which brings into bondage and reduces you again to a state of fear. No, it was the Spirit that anticipates our adoption as sons, the Spirit in which we cry out, Abba (Father). (16) The Spirit himself in this way bears witness with our spirit that we are children of God; (17) and if children, then heirs too – heirs of God and joint-heirs with Christ, if (as is true) we suffer with him that in turn we may be glorified with him.

(18) The glory is as sure as the suffering, for I consider that the sufferings of the present time are not worthy to be compared with the glory that is to be revealed in and for us. (19) So great is this glory that the whole created world is looking eagerly forward to the disclosure of the sons of God. (20) For the creation was

subjected to a vain life under inferior spiritual powers. This was not creation's own choice, but was done by the One who subjected it, and qualified by hope; (21) because the creation itself also shall be liberated from the corrupting bondage in which it lies, to attain the freedom which accompanies the glory of the children of God.

(22) For we know that the whole creation with one consent groans and travails up to this moment. (23) And not the creation only: we ourselves also, who have the first-fruits of the Spirit, we ourselves also groan inwardly, while we still look forward to our adoption as God's children, the redemption of our body. (24) For we were saved in this hope. And hope really means hope; for a hope you can see is no hope at all – for why does anyone endure patiently for what he can see?[1] (25) No; if we hope for what we cannot see, then we wait for it with patient endurance. (26) In the same way, the Spirit also helps us in our weakness; for we do not even know what are the proper prayers to offer, but the Spirit himself intercedes on our behalf with groans that do not need expression in speech. (27) For God who searches men's hearts knows without words what the Spirit means, for he intercedes for the saints as God himself wills. (28) And we know that all things co-operate[2] for good to those who love God, to those, that is, who are called in accordance with his purpose. (29) For those whom he foreknew, he also fore-ordained to bear the same image as his Son, so that he might be the eldest in a large company of brothers; (30) and those whom he fore-ordained he also called; and those whom he called he also justified; and those whom he justified he also glorified.

The last paragraph moved to the same absolute distinction between life and death as is found, for example, in vi. 4. As there, so here also Paul finds it necessary to make clear to his readers that conversion and baptism are not an end but a beginning. Dying and rising with Christ are not an *opus operatum* working automatically to produce a sinless and immortal Christian. 'You are not in the flesh but in the Spirit' (*v.* 9); but this fact must be expressed in a series of choices and decisions, which, of course, can only be made in the Spirit. Final glory is guaranteed by the present co-operation of the Spirit. In what follows

---

1 The text here is very confused and has been transmitted in at least six forms. The text translated is probably correct (see Lietzmann); but the general sense of the passage is in any case not in doubt. Hope must not be glossed, or robbed of its full force by sight.

2 Some excellent authorities (P[46] B A sah Origen) supply 'God' as the subject of the verb 'to co-operate'. Others (including ℵ C D G ω) omit. For the possible translations that result from the variants see the commentary.

viii. 9 is worked out first (in *vv.* 12, 13) in terms of the ethical obligations that it lays upon Christians, and next (in the rest of the paragraph) in terms of the hope and encouragement that it gives them.

12   **In consequence of this, brethren, we are men under obligation** – not 'debtors', for no actual debt is involved; see on i. 14. We are under obligation as men raised from the dead; compare vi. 13. **But our obligation is not to the flesh, to allow our lives to be determined by it.** So far in this chapter the flesh has been constantly referred to. The variety of phrases used shows that we are not dealing with a technical term in the proper sense, yet the fundamental meaning remains constant. Life determined by the flesh is life concentrated on the self, human life in and for itself, apart from God. Such life can have only one end, namely death, because of the principle laid down in vi. 23 and because it is by definition cut off from God, who is the

13 source of life. **For if you do live under the authority of the flesh you are doomed to death.** Paul does not use the simple future, You will die, but a word often used to denote an 'event which will surely happen in consequence of God's decision';[1] compare iv. 24; 1 Thess. iii. 4. He who seeks his life shall lose it; he who does not die by faith will die eternally. **But if by the Spirit you put to death the activities of the body, you will live.** 'The activities of the body' are the same as 'your members which are upon the earth' in Col. iii. 5. To put these to death is truly to 'consider oneself dead to sin' (vi. 11; cf. vii. 4), and can be done only 'by the Spirit'. The reference here is not to the human

14 spirit but to the Spirit of God, as is confirmed by the **For** (γάρ) with which *v.* 14 begins. This is the way that leads from the resurrection of baptism to the resurrection at the last day – 'you will live'.

Throughout the rest of this long paragraph Paul is concerned with this way. He begins here with an injunction to his readers to follow the way of life, and not the way of death, and proceeds to give them an assurance of the certainty of final salvation, and to comfort them in the afflictions that must precede it.

Those who allow themselves to be directed in this way by the Spirit of God are the sons of God. Paul does not often speak of direction (literally, 'being led') by the Spirit, but there is a close parallel in Gal. v. 18. The word (ἄγειν) is not infrequently used of the passions; here Paul is thinking of life under the control not of self but of God. Again it is only rarely that Paul describes Christians as sons of God – apart from this verse, only at *v.* 19; 2 Cor. vi. 18 (a quotation of 2 Sam. vii. 14); Gal. iii. 26; iv. 6 f. The last of these is a close parallel. Paul is interested in sons as heirs (see further on *v.* 17), and in sonship as a relationship which guarantees future salvation, and is established

1 Bauer-Aland, *Wörterbuch, s.v.* μέλλω.

in the present through the Holy Spirit, who anticipates the future (see on *v.* 23). The actual process of begetting does not interest him; unlike some New Testament writers, but like the Rabbis, he does not describe conversion and baptism in terms of regeneration. The argument of this verse is not carried forward until *v.* 17; the next two verses (15, 16) confirm the fact that we are God's sons.

For the Spirit you received was not one which brings into 15 **bondage and reduces you again to a state of fear.** Paul does not mean that there exists such a 'spirit of bondage'; the phrase is a rhetorical formation based upon 'Spirit of adoption', which is mentioned shortly. The old life was marked by fear. The contrast is not so much between those who look upon God as master, tyrant, or judge, and those who approach him as Father with the confidence of children, as between those who have no hope for the future, and those who can confidently look forward to life and glory.

No, it was the Spirit that anticipates our adoption as sons, the Spirit in which we cry out, Abba (Father). *V.* 23 makes quite clear that our adoption (a legal term belonging to the Hellenistic age, but not found in the LXX, doubtless because the Jews did not practise adoption; cf. ix. 4; Gal. iv. 5; Eph. i. 5) lies in the future. The 'Spirit of adoption' is therefore not 'the Spirit which actually effects adoption' but 'the Spirit which anticipates adoption', which brings forward into the present what is properly an eschatological event. We may compare justification, which is properly the verdict at the last judgement but is anticipated by faith through God's manifestation of his righteousness.

It is in the Spirit that we cry out to God as Father. The word Abba (Mark xiv. 36; Gal. iv. 6) is Aramaic, but a word commonly found not in liturgical but in colloquial use. That it occurs twice in Paul's Greek writings is a striking fact, which may be due to the impression made by Jesus' direct and unconventional approach to the Father. It corresponds exactly to the opening of the Lord's Prayer in the Lucan form (Luke xi. 2), and Paul's reference here may be to the use of this prayer in Christian worship – the very fact that you can address God as Abba proves that the Spirit is at work among you and that you are God's children. Alternatively, he may refer to Spirit-inspired prayers (cf. 1 Cor. xiv. 15). This is supported by the use of the violent word, 'cry out'. But the contrast between a liturgical prayer and a free prayer spontaneously inspired by the Spirit may well have been less marked in the first century than it is in the twentieth. Certainly the Spirit was at work in both; how else could men address God as their Father? Thus **the Spirit himself in this way bears witness with our** 16 **spirit that we are children of God.**

In *vv.* 15 and 16 it is possible to put a full stop after '... as sons'; the translation would then continue, 'In that we cry out, Abba (Father), the Spirit himself . . . '. Whether or no this be the correct construction, it gives the sense. The word 'to bear witness with' is used at ii. 15 and ix. 1; both of the conscience; this means, as was pointed out above (p. 50) that man has the ability 'to detach himself from himself'. His conscience can make an independent judgement of his actions. The meaning here is similar. I am confident, because of my faith in Christ, that I am God's child; the Spirit confirms this by putting the word Abba on my lips – and there is further confirmation in the fact that my fellow Christians pray in the same way. The two witnesses (cf. Deut. xix. 15), my own conscious faith and the direct action of the Spirit, confirm each other's testimonies. The content of the Spirit's witness is that we are God's children; this word is hardly more frequent than 'sons'; vv. 16, 17, 21; ix. 8; Phil. ii. 15. It serves to bring Paul back to his main theme, which is not the phenomenon of inspiration but the

17 objective consequences of sonship: **if children, then heirs too.** Paul is still concerned to demonstrate the certainty of future salvation, and argues that if we are heirs of God our inheritance is secure. Of course the analogy is imperfect. Ordinarily an heir enters upon his inheritance only at the death of the testator; but the language of inheriting can be adopted here because in the Old Testament the word 'inheritance' is regularly used of that which God gives to his people (especially the land of Israel).

We are not God's heirs in our own right but only as **joint-heirs with Christ.** The explanation of Paul's point here is to be found in his treatment of Abraham in ch. iv, and, still more clearly, in his discussion of the same theme in Gal. iii. 6–iv. 7. In the latter passage it is argued (see especially iii. 16) that Christ alone is the true 'seed of Abraham' – the heir of the promise. Others may become sons of God *in Christ Jesus* (iii. 26); this is effected by putting on Christ in baptism (iii. 27). Thus believers become the seed of Abraham, and heirs according to promise (iii. 29).

That we are joint-heirs with Christ appears **if (as is true) we suffer with him that in turn we may be glorified with him.** It is important to notice how the basic principle of vi. 8 is expanded here. Christ by enduring the messianic affliction made it possible for men to enter the messianic kingdom by sharing his sufferings by faith, and, especially, in baptism, where they die and rise again with him. But this union with Christ's death does not exhaust the matter. We have just seen (v. 13) that Christians must put to death the activities of the body by renouncing a life directed by the flesh; Paul now implies that the suffering of tribulation and persecution may also be indicative of union with Christ (cf. Col. i. 24). The process initiated in common suffering cannot but end in common glory.

18 Here is a firm basis for consolation and encouragement. **The glory is as sure as the suffering** (this supplement is required by the 'for'

(γάρ) which follows), **for I consider that the sufferings of the present time** (cf. iii. 26 – this is the unique moment of eschatological time anticipated in the present) **are not worthy to be compared with the glory that is to be revealed in and for us.** *In and for* represents one Greek preposition (εἰς) whose basic meaning is *into*, though it often expresses direction or intended goal. The glory is destined for us, and we shall have it (as now we do not have it, iii. 23). For 'glory' as a description of the future see commentary on ii. 7; iii. 23; v. 2; it is preceded by the time of affliction, in which Christians are allowed the privilege (Phil. i. 29) of sharing. Paul now goes on to describe the interim period, showing how Christians should take courage both from the prospect of glory and from the assistance already given them by the Holy Spirit.

So great is this glory that the whole created world is looking 19 **eagerly forward to the disclosure of the sons of God.** The present is a time of concealment (cf. Col. iii. 3 f.). Though they have the Spirit of adoption (*v.* 15), Christians are not manifestly living as the children of God: they still sin and suffer, and will die. 'Disclosure' is the noun cognate with the verb translated 'reveal' in *v.* 18. When it does not mean 'vision' it refers to an eschatological revelation (ii. 5; xvi. 25; 1 Cor. i. 7; 2 Thess. i. 7). Usually it is Christ who is revealed; but compare 1 Thess. iv. 16 f.; 1 Cor. xv. 23; also Deut. xxxiii. 2, and the apocalyptic passages dependent on it (e.g. Zech. xiv. 5 (LXX); 1 Enoch i. 9, quoted in Jude 14). Paul introduces the point here because his main object in mentioning the creation is to emphasize the certainty of future salvation for Christians. He is not concerned with creation for its own sake, but evidently feels that the matter requires some further explanation.

For the creation was subjected to a vain life under inferior 20 **spiritual powers;** literally, to vanity (ματαιότης). The English reader recalls at once passages such as Eccles. i. 2, but in the LXX this and related words sometimes refer to the gods of the heathen (e.g. Ps. xxxi. 6). Paul would doubtless agree that creation apart from Christ could have only an unreal existence, but would himself express this more concretely as subjection to what he describes as the 'elements of the world' (e.g. Gal. iv. 9). Thus the whole universe needed redemption. Paul's language here may owe something to current gnosticism and astrology, according to which all creation lying below the planetary spheres was enslaved to the celestial powers which moved above it; but he makes no concession to dualism. It is reasonable to ask whether it was simply by being created that the created universe was in this way made subject to vanity or whether subjection was the result of a culpable fall, through which creation lost its pristine freedom and entered into bondage which it had brought upon itself. No clear answer can be read out of the text; the

next sentence is compatible with both alternatives. **This was not creation's own choice, but was done by the One who subjected it, and qualified by hope.** Creation always remained under the control
21 of the supreme God, and was therefore never without hope. **Because the creation itself also** (that is, in addition to Christians) **shall be liberated from the corrupting bondage in which it lies, to attain the freedom which accompanies the glory of the children of God.**

'Corrupting bondage' is, literally translated, 'bondage of corruption'. Creation is in bondage because it was subjected (*v*. 20); it is not exactly in bondage *to* corruption (though it is not impossible that Paul personifies 'corruption'); it is in bondage to corrupt powers, and this bondage is inevitably corrupting. Compare 1 Cor. xv. 42, 50.

Over against this corrupting bondage stands (again, to translate literally) the 'freedom of the glory of the children of God'. This string of genitives is inelegant, but 'of glory' is not to be taken as adjectival. The 'glory of the children of God' is an independent concept (see on *v*. 18), which can be contrasted with corruption (cf. 1 Cor. xv. 43). Out of this (eschatological) glory arises freedom (from corruption, death, and sin).

Paul now begins to move back from creation to the Church.

22 **For we know that the whole creation with one consent groans and travails up to this moment** (the decisive moment, when God's purposes are fulfilled; cf. *v*. 18). For 'groaning' cf. *v*. 23 and 2 Cor. v. 2, 4); the cognate noun is used in *v*. 26. It is tempting to translate 'groans and travails *with us*'; but this would make nonsense of *v*. 23, where our groaning is mentioned over against (though along with) that of creation.

23 **And not the creation only: we ourselves also, who have the first-fruits of the Spirit, we ourselves also groan inwardly, while we still look forward to our adoption as God's children, the redemption of our body.** Creation can do nothing but wait and hope – and groan. We too wait and hope and groan, even though we have an advantage denied to creation; we have the Spirit. How the Spirit helps us will be hinted at in *vv*. 26 f. For the moment it is important to note that the Spirit is described as *first-fruits* (for the word, cf. xi. 16; xvi. 5), the first portion of the harvest, regarded both as a first instalment and as a pledge of the final delivery of the whole. The Holy Spirit is thus regarded as an anticipation of final salvation, and a pledge that we who have the Spirit shall in the end be saved. (Cf. the use of the similar word *earnest* in 2 Cor. i. 22; v. 5). In this interpretation *of the Spirit* (τοῦ πνεύματος) is taken as an appositional genitive (first-fruits, consisting of ...); it is grammatically possible to take the genitive as partitive: part (the first-fruits) of the Spirit is given now, with the implication that a further part of the Spirit is to come in the future. This way of regarding the Spirit as

given in instalments does not, however, seem to correspond with Paul's view.

Possession of the Spirit is a great privilege, but it is not God's final gift, for which Christians still look eagerly forward. Adoption is evidently (cf. *v.* 15) our final acceptance into God's family, and of this the redemption of our body must be a synonym. For the word 'redemption' compare iii. 24; 1 Cor. i. 30; Col. i. 14. In none of these passages is 'of the body' attached. It may be doubted whether the 'reference is to the whole mass of fallen human nature in which we share as men';[1] the parallel in 2 Cor. v. 4 suggests rather an individual interpretation. Paul certainly does not mean 'the redemption of the Church', for the Church is never the body *of us* but the body *of Christ*. The deeds of the body must be put to death (*v.* 13); but in the end the body will be redeemed. This is to be understood in the light of 1 Cor. xv. 35–49. Man's future is not a disembodied state; there will be continuity between the present life and the life to come, and man will not be left without a suitable set of instruments to express his *ego*, but there will also be discontinuity: no longer a natural body but a spiritual body. Those who die before the *parousia* will be raised up incorruptible, and those who survive till the *parousia* will be instantly changed. In each case there will be a transformation – the redemption of the body. See 1 Cor. xv. 51–5.

We were saved in this hope. The verb 'to save' is almost always 24 used in the future; see on v. 9. The past tense used here is possible only because it is immediately qualified by hope. The hope, of course, is no forlorn, but a confident, hope, supported by the Holy Spirit. Yet it is true we have not been saved absolutely, but only in hope. Paul underlines this. **And hope really means hope; for a hope you can see is no hope at all – for why does anyone endure patiently for what he can see?** The point here is clear, notwithstanding the textual confusion mentioned above (p. 151, n. 1). It is, however, significant (if we may rely on the text) that Paul uses the words 'endure patiently'; see on ii. 7. The attitude of hope means that Christians put no confidence in themselves but look steadily beyond themselves to find the fulfilment of their own selves and actions in God. **No; if we hope for 25 what we cannot see, then we wait for it with patient endurance.** To live as a Christian is to walk by faith, not by sight (2 Cor. v. 7), to find the meaning of life in God's future, rather than in the present.

But even in the present we are not abandoned. **In the same way, 26 the Spirit also helps us in our weakness.** Paul proceeds to an example of the Spirit's aid. **We do not even know what are the proper prayers to offer, but the Spirit himself intercedes on our behalf with groans that do not need expression in speech.** Why

1 J. A. T. Robinson, *The Body* (1952), p. 30.

157

does Paul choose this example? Possibly because prayer is the most
elementary of religious duties: we are so weak that we do not even
know how to pray. This may be the correct answer, but a different one
will account for more of Paul's words, some of which recall
(Lietzmann, *ad loc.*) the language of gnostic religion. Man does not
know the secret prayers which alone can give him access to God;
when he has been initiated, the divine Spirit speaks through his mouth
the correct formula, which may never be communicated to, and
indeed would not be understood by, the public. It is certain that Paul
does not mean what the gnostics meant; for him, prayer is no formula,
nor are men saved by repeating unintelligible words. He borrows at
most the notion of an indwelling God described as Spirit, and so
introduces the notion of prayer as the Spirit's activity. The Spirit
actually makes intercession for us. It is uncertain whether Paul means
unspoken or *unspeakable* groans. Compare 2 Cor. xii. 4. There may be
a reference here to speaking with tongues (1 Cor. xii, xiv), but it seems
on the whole more probable that the point is that communion
between Spirit (-filled worshipper) and God is immediate and needs
27 no spoken word. This is supported by the next verse. **For God who
searches men's hearts** (cf., e.g., Jer. xvii. 10) **knows without words
what the Spirit means, for** (or, namely that) **he intercedes for the
saints** (see on i. 7) **as God himself wills** (cf. *v.* 26; and 2 Cor. vii. 9 ff.).

The activity of the Spirit on our behalf points to the ultimate
security in God of those whom he has chosen. The presence of the
Spirit, the first-fruits, is a proof that the Age to Come has dawned, and
28 that its consummation cannot be long delayed. **We know that all things
co-operate for good to those who love God.** On the text of this
passage see p. 151, n. 2. The sentence may be taken in several different
ways. If the text that includes the word *God* (ὁ θεός) is accepted, the
translation is clear; *God* must be the subject of the verb (συνεργεῖ)
and in this compound verb the preposition (σύν) will govern the dative
those who love God (τοῖς ἀγαπῶσιν τὸν θεόν): We know that God co-
operates for good in all things with those who love God. If the noun
God is to be omitted several possibilities arise. (i) It may simply be
replaced by the pronoun *He*: We know that he (=God) co-operates,
etc. (ii) The subject of the verb may be taken from the preceding
sentence – the Spirit: We know that he (=the Spirit) co-operates, etc.
(iii) The subject of the verb may be *all things* (πάντα, which as a
neuter plural will in Greek take a singular verb): We know that all
things co-operate for good to those who love God. The last, the text
and construction of AV, has been attacked as attributing to Paul an
evolutionary optimism foreign to his thought; but it is less harsh as a
rendering of the Greek,[1] and though Paul was not an evolutionary

1 See W. L. Knox, *St Paul and the Church of the Gentiles* (1939), p. 105, n. 2.

optimist he did believe that Christ had overcome and was overcoming (*vv.* 35, 38 f.; 1 Cor. xv. 24–8; Col. ii. 15) the powers of evil, and that the last period of world history was speeding to a close that would bring salvation to the elect (xiii. 11).

Paul does not often describe Christians as 'those who love God'. For him, love generally describes the relation of God to men, while for the relation of men to God he reserves the term faith. In this he displays an accurate use of words, for men can never love God (who is altogether worthy of our regard) in the sense in which God loves us, his enemies (v. 8). It is evidently appropriate to speak of love for God, and both Testaments provide examples; it is a grateful, trustful love. But Paul cannot allow himself to leave the impression that men may exercise an initiative which properly belongs to God alone. Those who love God are more searchingly defined as **those who are called in accordance with his purpose.**

For 'called' see on i. 1, 6. 'Calling' is the realization in history of God's eternal *purpose* (cf. ix. 11; also Eph. i. 11; iii. 11). It is here, in God's purpose, not in experience, even the experience of the Spirit, that the ultimate assurance of salvation rests. This purpose and its realization are analysed in the next two verses. *V.* 29 deals with what may be called the pre-temporal (or extra-temporal) aspects of the process, *v.* 30 with the temporal, though it also looks beyond history to the final glory.

Those whom he foreknew (cf. xi. 2), **he also fore-ordained to** 29 **bear the same image as his Son, so that he might be the eldest in a large company of brothers.**

It is not easy to distinguish between 'foreknew' and 'fore-ordained'; God's knowledge must surely involve ordination, since men and things must be and become what he knows them to be. The slightly ambiguous phraseology may serve as a warning that we are dealing here not with a rigidly thought out and expressed determinist philosophy, but with a profound religious conviction. To say this, however, does not mean that predestination is to be emptied of its meaning.[1] The history and personal make-up of the Church are not due to chance or to arbitrary human choices, but represent the working out of God's plan. Only here can peace and security be found. Our own intentions, like our own virtues, are far too insecure to stand the tests of time and judgement.

God's intention is that Christ shall be the eldest (cf. Col. i. 18; i. 15 is less close) of many brothers, who become joint-heirs (cf. *v.* 17) with him, and so enter with him into his inheritance. This picture of Christ as the eldest in the family explains what is meant by 'bearing the same image as his Son'. 'Image' is for Paul primarily an eschatological word

1 On this subject see especially chs. ix–xi.

(though this is not inconsistent with its origin in Gen. i. 27). Compare
1 Cor. xv. 49; 2 Cor. iii. 18; iv. 4; Col. i. 15; iii. 10. When God's purpose is
fully realized we shall share Christ's glorious body in God's likeness.
At present we are conformed (συμμορφιζόμενοι) to his death (Phil. iii.
10); we shall be conformed (σύμμορφοι, used by Paul in the present
verse) to the body of his glory (Phil. iii. 21).

30 Predestination is worked out in time: **those whom he fore-
ordained he also called.** See above on *v.* 28; also i. 1, 6. Calling brings
God's purpose into time. In human terms, calling is conversion;
compare 1 Cor. vii. 18; Gal. i. 6; Col. iii. 15; 1 Thess. iv. 7. Man becomes
aware of the predestinating love of God. **Those whom he called he
also justified,** because they responded in faith to his call. Life and
glory are impossible apart from the righteousness conferred in
justification (see pp. 30 ff.). With justification Paul has reached the
present; but so sure is his confidence, and so certain the purpose of
God, that he can go on to describe a future event in a past tense: **those
whom he justified he also glorified.** For glory as the final
consummation of God's saving purpose, see pp.44 f. Beyond this there
is no more to say.

Predestination is the most comfortable of all Christian doctrines, if
men will accept it in its biblical form, and not attempt to pry into it
with questions which it does not set out to answer. It is not a
'quantitative limitation of God's action, but its qualitative definition',[1]
the final statement of the truth that justification, and, in the end,
salvation also, are by grace alone, and through faith alone.

21 A HYMN OF TRIUMPH

CHAPTER viii. 31–9

**(31) In conclusion, then, what shall we say of all these things? If
God is on our side, who is against us? (32) God did not spare his
own Son, but on behalf of us all delivered him up; how then can
he fail to bestow upon us all things, with him? (33) Who can bring
a charge against God's elect? God – who justifies us? (34) Who
condemns us? Christ Jesus – who died, or rather was raised, who
is at the right hand of God, who actually is interceding on our
behalf? (35) Who shall separate us from the love of Christ? Shall
affliction, or anguish, or persecution, or famine, or nakedness, or
danger, or the sword? (36) These things are foretold as our lot, as
it is written, 'For thy sake we are put to death every day, we were
reckoned as sheep due for slaughter'. (37) True; but in all these**

---

1 K. Barth, *The Epistle to the Romans* (English translation by E. C. Hoskyns,
1933), p. 346.

things we are more than conquerors through him who loved us. (38) For I am confident that neither death nor life, neither angels nor their princes, neither things present nor things to come, nor spiritual powers, (39) whether above or below the level of the earth, nor any other created thing, shall be able to separate us from the love of God which is in Christ Jesus our Lord.

From the beginning of ch. v, though not without digressions, Paul has set out the grounds of Christian hope, and indicated the corresponding lines of Christian action in the present. He now draws the matter to a close, and in the opening verse of the present paragraph, which is in the rhetorical style of the diatribe, and full of passionate eloquence, he states the essence of his argument.

In conclusion, then, what shall we say of all these things? If 31 God is on our side, who is against us? The question is not whether we are on God's side, but whether he is on ours. If he is, we may be exposed to perils and pains of every kind, but none can ever endanger our salvation. That God is 'for us' is proved by the fact of Jesus Christ, and it is to him that we must cling, as the pledge that God will give us every good thing. God did not spare his own Son, but on behalf of 32 us all delivered him up; how then can he fail to bestow upon us all things, with him?

In these words Paul seems to allude to the story of Abraham and Isaac which was mentioned in the note on iv. 24 f. (p. 93), and to do so much more clearly than at that point. Paul's word *spared* (the verb φείδεσθαι) is that used in the LXX at Gen. xxii. 12, 16 (. . . because you did not spare . . .), and it is probable that he would be familiar with Jewish thought about the 'binding of Isaac'. He does not, however, develop it, or make it a starting-point in his theology. It is at most a passing allusion, the same sort of allusion as that to the Passover (in 1 Cor. v. 7; see *1 Corinthians*, pp. 128 f.) and that to the Day of Atonement which may lie behind iii. 25 (see p. 74). It is however a degree less probable than these. The word 'Passover' puts the allusion beyond doubt, and the word (ἱλαστήριον) used in iii. 25, and used in the LXX to denote the 'mercy-seat', is less common and more distinctive than 'spare'. An allusion to Isaac remains more probable than one to the Suffering Servant (see Isa. liii. 12 (LXX)). The meaning is in any case clear and independent of any allusion. In the Cross God displays such love (v. 8) that we cannot doubt his willingness to give us any good thing.

In the next two verses Paul expresses himself in the forensic language of the earlier chapters of the epistle. Their general drift is clear – those whom God justifies, through Christ crucified and risen, no accuser can imperil; but the construction is obscure. The translation adopted here, prompted by the many rhetorical questions

161

in the context (*vv.* 31, 32, 35), assumes that each clause is to be
33 punctuated with a question mark. **Who can bring a charge against**
34 **God's elect? God – who justifies us? Who condemns us? Christ**
Jesus – who died, or rather was raised, who is at the right hand of
God, who actually is interceding on our behalf?

There are two alternative possibilities. (i) There are two questions,
with two ironical answers, thus: Who can bring a charge? God – who
justifies! Who condemns? Christ – who died! (ii) The words 'God who
justifies; who condemns?' may have been drawn from Isa. l. 8 ff., and
should therefore be taken together. We now have one major question
with two answers. Who can bring a charge? God, who justifies (who
then can condemn?)! Christ, who died! Of these, (ii) seems unnecessarily complicated, and the irony of (i) is scarcely Pauline. Neither,
however, can be dismissed as impossible, and neither would affect the
sense of the passage.

The details of the two verses require little comment. If 'Who shall
bring a charge?' is to have a positive answer, Satan must be meant; the
scene is that of the last judgement. The 'elect' is not a common
Pauline description of Christians; elsewhere only at xvi. 13 (in a
different sense) and Col. iii. 12. Election, however, is presupposed by
calling.

In his account of Christ in *v.* 34 Paul may be dependent on a
Christological formula; this is suggested by the parallel participles
(died – was raised) and by the balanced relative clauses. Paul has
already shown that the Spirit intercedes within us (*v.* 27); in heaven,
Christ (who is also judge; see ii. 16) intercedes for the elect. Paul here
reflects Jewish ideas of the Messiah as an intercessor.[1]

To speak of Christ in this way suggests the rhetorical questions of
35 *v.* 35. **Who shall separate us from the love of Christ** (that is, Christ's
love for us)? **Shall affliction** (in which we exult, v. 3), **or anguish, or**
persecution, or famine, or nakedness, or danger, or the sword?
Should it be inferred from these words that persecution had already
fallen upon the Roman church? It is not impossible that the expulsion
of the Jews from Rome under Claudius (Acts xviii. 2), when they
rioted 'at the instigation of Chrestus' (Suetonius, *Claudius* 25), was in
some way connected with the foundation of the church in Rome (see
Introduction, p. 5 f.); it may well have been accompanied by a
measure of violence. It is however more probable that Paul's words
reflect his own experiences (though of course he had not yet
experienced the sword) and the general insecurity and unpopularity
of Christians, which, in Rome, were to culminate in Nero's attack
(Tacitus, *Annals* xv. 44: ... per flagitia invisos ...). For Paul himself
see 1 Cor. iv. 10–13; 2 Cor. iv. 8–12; vi. 4–10; xi. 23–7. But such perils

1 See Nils Johansson, *Parakletoi* (1940).

can never separate us from the love of Christ. Why, **these things 36 are foretold as our lot** (these words, not in the Greek, must be added as the presupposition of the quotation that follows), **as it is written, 'For thy sake we are put to death every day, we were reckoned as sheep due for slaughter'**. The quotation is from Ps. xliv. 22. The sufferings of Christians, like those of Christ, were foretold. This meant that they did not fall outside God's providence; the situation, however unpleasant, was not out of his control. More than that, suffering had a positive significance as part of the messianic affliction (see pp. 76, 114, and cf. Col. i. 24) foretold as a necessary preliminary to the glorious future blessedness. Notwithstanding the picture of the slaughtered sheep there is no reference to Isa. liii. 7.

Suffering and persecution are not mere evils which Christians must expect and endure as best they can; they are the scene of the overwhelming victory which Christians are winning through Christ. **True** (we suffer constantly); **but in all these things we are more 37 than conquerors** (Paul uses a somewhat uncommon verb to intensify the idea of victory) **through him who loved us.**

In his final affirmation of God's love Paul turns to what his readers probably regarded as their chief and most dangerous enemies, the astrological powers by which (as many in the Hellenistic world believed) the destiny of mankind was controlled. Not even these lords of destiny (Paul asserts) can separate the Christian from the love of God, though Paul's words become merely rhetorical nonsense if it was not believed that these spiritual powers existed and were inimical to the people of God (see xiii. 1 and the note). They constituted a serious threat, but a threat the Christian readers need not fear, **For I am 38 confident that neither death nor life** (Paul was not certain that all Christians would have to face death before the return of Christ; see 1 Thess. iv. 15; 1 Cor. xv. 51 f.), **neither angels nor their princes** (for the last word – ἀρχαί – see 1 Cor. xv. 24; Col. i. 16; ii. 10, 15), **neither things present nor things to come, nor spiritual powers, whether 39 above or below the level of the earth** (here Paul uses technical astronomical – or astrological – terms), **nor any other created thing, shall be able to separate us from the love of God which is in Christ Jesus our Lord.**

Of course not; for Christ Jesus is – the Lord. He is Lord over all spiritual powers, for he has triumphed over them in the Cross (Col. ii. 15); he is Lord over life and death, for he was crucified, and raised from the dead; he is Lord over things present and things to come, for it was in him that God elected us in love, and it is with him that we shall enter into God's glory beyond history. In Christ Jesus, God is *for us*; and it is in Christ Jesus that we know him and trust him.

22 THE UNBELIEF OF ISRAEL

CHAPTER ix. 1–5

(1) I am speaking the truth in Christ; it is no lie; my conscience
bears me witness in the Holy Spirit (2) when I say that I feel in my
heart great grief and ceaseless pain. (3) For I could wish that I
myself were separated by a curse from Christ if that would
benefit my brethren, my human kinsmen (4) – the Israelites.
They were made God's sons, they were shown his glory, with
them he made the covenants,[1] to them he gave the law and the
temple worship and the promises,[2] (5) to them belong the fathers
of the race and from them (on the human side) springs the Christ
himself – Blessed for ever be God, who stands over the whole
process![3] Amen.

That viii. 38 f. forms the impressive close of one division of the epistle,
and that ix. 1 opens a new theme, cannot be disputed. But the
connection between chs. i–viii and chs. ix–xi is much closer than is
sometimes recognized; for chs. i–viii are not so much concerned with
an 'experience of salvation' as with the character and deeds of God
who is the source of salvation, and chs. ix–xi are not at all concerned
with Paul's patriotic sentiments but with the character and deeds of
God who elected the Jews and now calls the Gentiles. In the second as
in the first half of the epistle Paul writes about God and his strange
mercy in offering to men justification on the basis of faith alone, but
his portrayal of divine freedom and grace is determined by the
different contexts in which it is set.

The basic fact which, though it is never actually mentioned, lies
behind every verse in the opening paragraph, and sets in motion the
whole long argument of chs. ix–xi, is that, notwithstanding her
privileges, and his apostolic labour, Israel has rejected the Gospel Paul
preached. The movement of his thought is clear. In the last verses of
ch. viii he sings with moving eloquence the love of God bestowed
freely and invincibly upon sinful man from foreknowledge to glory.
The dictation is ended; and in the silence he reflects: He came unto his
own, and they that were his own received him not. Disappointed and
1 bitter, he continues: **I am speaking the truth in Christ; it is no lie;**
2 **my conscience bears me witness in the Holy Spirit when I say that
I feel in my heart great grief and ceaseless pain.**

1 There is very strong evidence (P⁴⁶ B D G) for the singular, 'the covenant',
and this may be the original reading: but the plural (in ℵ C it syr) is the harder
reading, and on that ground may be preferred. On the meaning of the two
readings see the commentary.
2 There is some evidence ((P⁴⁶) D (G)) for the singular, 'the promise'. See the
commentary.
3 Or, the Christ himself, who is over all, God blessed for ever.

Perhaps as the Jewish 'apostle of the Gentiles' (xi. 13) he had been accused of indifference to the fate of his compatriots; perhaps the vehement assertion of truthfulness is no more than a mark of the energy and feeling with which he writes (cf. 2 Cor. i. 23; ii. 17; xi. 31; xii. 19; Gal. i. 20). His conscience is clear in the matter; compare ii. 15, where, as here, conscience is mentioned as a joint-witness. Evidently Paul thought of the conscience as an almost independent party in any dispute (see p. 50), capable of standing over against a man to accuse or acquit him of falsehood. Paul does not, however, simply appeal to what is, after all, part of himself. He speaks the truth *in Christ*, and his conscience bears witness *in the Holy Spirit*. In comparison with these divine witnesses (viii. 26, 34) the verdict of his own conscience is unimportant (1 Cor. iv. 4).

So far from being an unfeeling apostate, Paul is racked with pain at the thought of Israel's unbelief. Further, like the best of all Jews, Moses (Ex. xxxii. 31 f.), he is willing to sacrifice himself for his people's good. **I could wish that I myself were separated by a curse from Christ if that would benefit my brethren, my human** 3 **kinsmen – the Israelites.** The grammatical construction of the 4 sentence shows that Paul recognizes that his wish is scarcely capable of fulfilment. The verb is in the imperfect, the so-called desiderative imperfect, which 'seems to soften a remark, and make it more vague or more diffident or polite ... *I could almost pray to be accursed*' (Moule, *Idiom Book*, p. 9). The verb may mean *to pray*, but it can also mean *to wish* and this seems the more likely sense here.

'Separated by a curse from Christ' is literally 'anathema from Christ'; compare 1 Cor. xvi. 22; Gal. i. 8 f. The word *anathema* is found in the LXX as the equivalent of *ḥerem*, 'thing or person devoted (to destruction or sacred use and therefore secluded from profane use)'.[1] Here, of course, destruction is in mind; to be separated from Christ is to be consigned to damnation. Similar forms of speech were current among the Rabbis; for example, *Negaim*, ii. 1: R. Ishmael says: The children of Israel (may I make atonement for them!) are ... This expression was often little more than a formality, but the formality no doubt originated in, and could revert to, something seriously meant. See *New Testament Essays*, pp. 22–4. In the background lies the desire of Moses to make expiation for his sinful people (Ex. xxxii. 32).

The Jews are Paul's kinsmen, but only *on human terms*, for Paul has now been born into a new family (cf. Mark iii. 34 f.). The qualification is significant, and we shall meet it again in the next two verses, in which Paul sets out the privileges of Israel. It supplies too the clue (though this becomes evident only when the whole of chs.

---

1 L. Koehler and W. Baumgartner, *Lexicon in Veteris Testamenti Libros* (1953), *s.v.*

ix–xi are taken into account) to the otherwise insoluble problem
raised by the defection of Israel. Why should those upon whom so
many privileges had been showered reject the manifestation of God's
righteousness in Christ? Precisely because they were content to
evaluate their privileges on a purely human level. Thus, for example,
the law was their proud possession, of which they could boast; they
failed to see that in it was written their own judgement before God (cf.
ii. 17–29). Similarly the temple worship became a monument of self-
congratulation; they did not consider that it spoke to them of the
holiness of him who was God and not man. Even the Messiah was to be
one of their own children, whom – provided he was a good Jew – they
would be pleased to approve. All this is not explicit, but it can be read
between the lines of *vv.* 4 f. Those who seem now to have been
rejected by God **were made God's sons, they were shown his glory,
with them he made the covenants, to them he gave the law and**
5 **the temple worship and the promises; to them belong the fathers
of the race and from them (on the human side) springs the Christ
himself – Blessed for ever be God, who stands over the whole
process!**

'They were made God's sons' by adoption. The word is used in viii.
15, 23, in a different sense. The sequence of privileges described in
these verses suggests that Paul here thinks of sonship as a status
conferred upon Israel at the Exodus; compare Ex. iv. 22; Hosea xi. 1.

The glory of God also suggests the Exodus. It was manifested in the
pillars of cloud and fire at the crossing of the Red Sea, which was a
glorious act of deliverance (Ex. xv. 6, 11) and in the theophany at
Mount Sinai (Ex. xxiv. 16 f.; xxxiii. 18). When the tabernacle was built
it was filled with the glory of the Lord (Ex. xl. 34 f.).

If the singular 'covenant' (see p. 164, n. 1) is read the reference is
evidently to the covenant made at Mount Sinai. This makes excellent
sense, for this covenant was of course the basis of Israel's national and
religious life. The plural, however, also makes good sense. There were
several covenants – with Adam, with Noah, with Abraham, and with
David, as well as that made through Moses – and it is possible that Paul
refers to these; but it is more likely that (like other Jewish writers; see
S.B. iii. 262) he distinguished three covenants within the great
covenant of the Exodus – a covenant at Horeb, a second in the plains of
Moab, and a third at Mounts Gerizim and Ebal.

The bestowal of the law and the establishment of the temple cultus
were the pre-eminent privileges of Israel. 'By three things is the world
maintained: by the law, by the temple worship, and by deeds of loving-
kindness' (*Aboth*, i. 2). These two gifts accompanied the establishment
of the covenant.

Along with these provisions Israel was given also the promises (or
'the promise' singular, summarizing the many predictions – see

p. 164, n. 2) of an even more glorious future. Promises understood as
messianic are no doubt intended. It is worth noting that all the
privileges mentioned in *v.* 4 can be understood as promises. For
adoption and glory see viii. 15, 23; ii. 7. The past covenants point to the
new covenant (Jer. xxxi. 31; 1 Cor. xi. 25). The temple worship
suggested the language of iii. 25, and the law itself, rightly understood,
pointed forward to the Gospel, as did the patriarchs (see especially ch.
iv).

Last in the list of privileges comes the fact that the Messiah
himself, so far as human descent goes, was to be a Jew. For the same
claim, and the same limitation, compare i. 3. This sums up the truth
that God had chosen Israel to be the scene upon which his saving
purpose should be worked out. This was what made Israel's present
rejection doubly offensive. What was evidently God's purpose seemed
to have failed altogether in its effect. It is not Jewish nationalism, but a
glaring theological paradox that sets in motion the argument of chs.
ix–xi (cf. on iii. 1 f.).

Before, however, we can turn to this argument we must consider
one of the most difficult questions of exegesis in the epistle.

As it is here translated the doxology with which the paragraph
concludes is independent of the preceding sentence and refers to God
the Father. It would, however, be grammatically easier to unite it with
the preceding words as a relative clause referring to Christ. There are
two possibilities: (1) From them . . . springs the Christ himself, who is
over all, God blessed for ever; (2) from them . . . springs the Christ
himself, who is God over all, blessed for ever. A third possibility is to
introduce a stop within the doxology itself, and render: . . . Christ, who
is over all. Blessed be God for ever. It is very hard to decide between
these possibilities. The reader who is in a position to use it should
consult the exhaustive discussion in Cranfield, pp. 464–70.

The objection to the first is grammatical and stylistic. Pauline
doxologies are usually connected with the context and do not stand (as
does this one, in our translation) in complete asyndeton. At Rom. i. 25;
2 Cor. xi. 31, for example, where doxologies are addressed to God the
Father, they arise out of the preceding words. Moreover, if Paul
wished to say 'Blessed be God', he should have placed the word
'blessed' (εὐλογητός) first in the sentence, as he does not; and the
participle (ὤν) would be superfluous in the phrase 'he who is God over
all'.

The objection to the second is theological. Nowhere else in any
epistle does Paul call Christ God. Even Phil. ii. 6 is not a real parallel.
In fact, Paul, 'high' as his Christology is, is reserved in the use of
strictly divine titles for Christ. Is it likely that he would here run
counter to his general practice and use the word God? It may not be
likely but it cannot be held to be impossible; this verse might be an

extension of the partial parallel in i. 3 f. Perhaps Paul wishes to say that Christ was in human terms a Jew, but in fact God. This way of taking the sentence is accepted by Cranfield, in the form '... Christ, who is over all, God blessed for ever'.

The third possibility has little to commend it, but there is a proposed emendation of the text which is worth consideration. By a very slight alteration of the Greek (substituting ὧν ὁ for ὁ ὤν, in Greek uncials ΩΝΟ for ΟΩΝ) it is possible to obtain, '*Whose is* the supreme God, blessed for ever'. This has the advantage of giving a clause parallel to those that have preceded: Whose is the adoption ... whose are the fathers ... of whom is the Christ ... whose is God ... It is true that Paul has denied that God is God of the Jews only (iii. 29) but the Old Testament itself declares that 'they shall be my people, and I will be their God' (e.g. Jer. xxiv. 7), and a special relationship with God was both the foundation and the consummation of Israel's privilege. The emendation is attractive, but it too is open to objection, and since the text of the MSS is not so difficult as to be impossible it is wise to retain it, and to leave open the question whether it refers to Christ or to God the Father. Paul's Christology does not in the end depend upon an answer to this question.

23 GOD'S ELECTIVE PURPOSE
CHAPTER ix. 6–13

(6) But it is not as though the word of God itself had failed. For not all who are descended from Israel are truly Israel. (7) Nor are all the children of Abraham counted as his seed; rather, as Scripture says, 'Your descendants through Isaac shall be called your seed'. (8) That is, it is not the children of Abraham's flesh, born in the course of nature, who are children of God; it is the children who come by promise who are counted as his seed. (9) For the promise runs thus: 'I will come at this time and Sarah shall have a son'. (10) Further: when Rebecca conceived through intercourse with one man, Isaac our father, (11) before the two children had been born, before they had done anything good or evil, in order that God's elective purpose might stand firm, (12) resting as it does not on works but on God who calls, it was said to her, 'The greater shall serve the less'; (13) as again it is written, 'Jacob I loved, but Esau I hated'.

The introductory paragraph (*vv.* 1–5) has sharpened the problem. Since God has so clearly given Israel a position of unique privilege, does not Israel's defection mean that God's intention has broken down? The word of promise has been proved false by history. God's foreknowledge (viii. 29) has been shown to be in error. Paul's blunt negative answer to this question, which is so evident to him that he does not stop to state it, is supported by an analysis of the meaning of Israel.

But it is not as though the word of God itself (cf. iii. 2) had **6 failed. For not all who are descended from Israel are truly Israel.** If the word Israel is understood in a mechanical sense it cannot be disputed that the majority of Israel have, to all appearance, set aside God's word, which has accordingly (at least for the present) failed. But Israel is not a term like Ammon, Moab, Greece, or Rome. 'Israel' cannot be defined in terms of physical descent, or understood simply 'on the human side' (v. 5); it is created not by blood and soil, but by the promise of God, and therefore exists within the limits of God's freedom. If he were bound by physical descent, he would be unfree, and no longer God. But he is not so bound, as Scripture itself proves – a vital point to Paul. Consider first Abraham, the father of the race.

Nor are all the children of Abraham counted as his seed; 7 rather, as Scripture says, 'Your descendants through Isaac shall be called your seed'.

In the first part of this verse there can be no question that 'the children of Abraham' is subject and 'seed' predicate; this is strongly suggested by the plural verb (εἰσίν); and v. 7a carries v. 6b with it. In both clauses the phrase with 'all' is subject. Paul is denying a universal assertion: it is not true that all who appear, or claim, to be Israel are truly the seed of Abraham. This is not guaranteed by physical descent.

For 'seed of Abraham' compare iv. 13, 16, 18; Gal. iii. 16, 19, 29; (2 Cor. xi. 22). The passages in Galatians are particularly important, for they show that though Paul recognizes 'seed' as a collective term he believes that it is focused upon the one descendant of Abraham, Christ. That is to say, behind the difficult theological development of vv. 6–13 lies thought that is fundamentally Christological and soteriological. The 'seed' arose through promise (v. 8), and accordingly to the 'seed' belongs the promise made to Abraham (iv. 13; Gal. iii. 16). It is *in Christ* that the promises of God are fulfilled. Thus the thought of v. 4 receives a severe qualification: the promises do indeed belong to Israel, but – what is Israel?

Paul proceeds to illustrate his point by quoting Gen. xxi. 12, which means that for purposes of inheritance the divine promises made to Abraham shall operate on the line proceeding from him through Isaac. **That is, it is not the children of Abraham's flesh, born in the 8 course of nature, who are children of God; it is the children who come by promise who are counted as his seed.**

Abraham had several children in addition to Isaac (Gen. xxv. 1–4); here it is Ishmael who is primarily in mind (cf. Gal. iv. 21–31).

The word 'counted' is of fundamental importance in this epistle. It has already occurred in several contexts, but especially in the quotation from Gen. xv. 6 (Rom. iv. 3). It points to the creative freedom of God, who creates 'righteousness' by 'counting' it, and annuls sin by not 'counting' it (iv. 6, 8). He can raise up sons to Abraham out of stones (Matt. iii. 9; Luke iii. 8), and freely determines what is 'seed' and what is not.

'Seed', thus understood in the light of the creative freedom of God, is necessarily bound up with 'promise'. Ishmael was a true son of Abraham, with as much of his father's blood in his veins as Isaac had; but he was a child of the flesh, not of promise. Isaac's birth, which took place in the context of human death and sterility (iv. 19), depended entirely upon God's gracious promise.

9   As a footnote, Paul adds a precise reference: **For the promise runs thus: 'I will come at this time and Sarah shall have a son'** (Gen. xviii. 10, 14; cf. xvii. 21).

So far Paul has based his argument upon the story of Abraham; and it is open to an objection. Ishmael and Isaac (it could be argued) had one father, but Ishmael's mother was the bondwoman Hagar, Isaac's the princess Sarah (cf. Gal. iv. 21-31, where however the explanation is different; see *Freedom and Obligation*, pp. 27 f., and *Rechtfertigung, Festschrift für Ernst Käsemann* (Tübingen and Göttingen, 1976), pp. 1-16). This difference could account for the fact that Abraham's seed was reckoned through the one and not the other. Paul answers this objection by proceeding to the next generation.

10   **Further: when Rebecca conceived** (Gen. xxv. 21) **through intercourse with one man** (the *one* is emphatic), **Isaac our father**
11   (for the patriarchs as 'fathers' cf. *v.* 5), **before the two children** (Esau and Jacob) **had been born, before they had done anything good or evil, in order that God's elective purpose might stand**
12   **firm, resting as it does not on works but on God who calls, it was said to her** (Gen. xxv. 23), **'The greater shall serve the less'** (the original Hebrew could be correctly translated, 'The elder shall serve the younger' (so RV); the Greek could not in itself mean this, and Paul
13   probably gave to the Greek its proper Greek meaning); **as again it is written** (Mal. i. 2 f.), **'Jacob I loved, but Esau I hated'** (the Hebrew idiom means, 'I preferred Jacob to Esau'; but Paul may again have taken the words literally).

In this story, as in that of Abraham, we have to do with two brothers. Not only have they the same father; they have also the same mother, and their origin goes back to the same moment of conception. The distinction between the twins is expressed between conception and birth. God's freedom is absolute. No antecedent ancestry, and no subsequent virtue or sin, controls it. Whatever happens, God's purpose, which operates on the basis of election, stands firm. This marks out the theme of chs. ix–xi. God has a purpose; it works by a process of election; and it cannot fail. When viewed from the human side this means that not works but the call of God is decisive. Works and calling are co-ordinated here, just as, earlier in the epistle, works and faith are co-ordinate. Evidently calling and faith correspond; faith is the answer to God's call – as the example of Abraham makes clear. Not works but faith leads to justification; not works but God's call admits to the promise. These are different ways of expressing the same truth.

So far Paul has simply established his argument in terms of events that happened in remote antiquity; but the first-century Jew – and the twentieth-century Christian – cannot escape the consequences of the argument. For what Paul has established is the freedom of God in grace. It is impossible for his Jewish interlocutor to reply: Very well! I am descended from Abraham, through Isaac (not Ishmael), and Jacob (not Esau); therefore I must stand within the promise. To argue in this way is to say: God was free in the days of the patriarchs, but he is no longer free now – which is absurd. God, if he be still God, still operates on the basis of his 'elective purpose'. The Church can never draw a simple boundary line between itself and the world, nor can it connect itself with the divine promise by means of a simple line of succession.

It is important to recall here that the seed of Abraham contracted till it became ultimately Christ (Gal. iii. 16), and was subsequently expanded to include those who were in Christ (see on vi. 11). This means that election does not take place (as might at first appear from Paul's examples) arbitrarily or fortuitously; it takes place always and only *in Christ*. They are elect who are in him; they who are elect are in him (cf. Gal. iii. 29). It is failure to remember this that causes confusion over Paul's doctrine of election and predestination. But the point must be pursued in the next paragraph.

24 GOD'S SOVEREIGNTY
CHAPTER ix. 14–29

(14) What then shall we say? Is there unrighteousness in God's dealings? No, indeed. (15) For he says to Moses, 'I will have mercy on whomsoever I do have mercy, and I will pity whomsoever I do pity'. (16) So then everything depends, not on man who exercises his will or like an athlete runs to a goal, but on the merciful God. (17) For God in Scripture says to Pharaoh, 'For this very purpose did I raise thee up, namely that in thee I might demonstrate my power, and that my name might be proclaimed in all the earth'.

(18) So then he has mercy on whom he wills, and whom he wills he 'hardens'.

(19) Of course you will say to me, If this is so,[1] why does he still make complaints? For who can resist his will? (20) Yes, but,[2] my dear sir, who are you to answer back to God? What, will the model say to the modeller, Why did you make me like this? (21) Has not the potter a right over the clay, to make out of the same lump one vessel designed for noble, one for ignoble use? (22) But what if God with great long-suffering 'endured the vessels of wrath', 'prepared for destruction', because he wished to show forth his wrath and to make known his power, (23) and moreover did so in order to make known the wealth of his glory for the vessels of mercy, which beforehand he made ready for glory – (24) us, those whom he called, not only from among the Jews but from among the Gentiles too? (25) That this calling of Gentiles as well as Jews was intended is shown in Scripture, as God says in the book of Hosea: 'That which was not my people I will call my people, and her that was not beloved I will call beloved'; (26) 'and it shall come to pass that in the place where it was said to them, You are not my people, there shall they be called sons of the living God'. (27) And Isaiah cries out concerning Israel, 'Though the number of the children of Israel should be as the sand of the sea, yet it is the remnant of them that will be saved, (28) for the Lord will bring his word to pass upon the earth, accomplishing it and determining it'. (29) This accords further with what Isaiah said earlier, 'If the Lord Sabaoth had not left us a seed, we should have become like Sodom, and we should have been made like Gomorrah'.

Paul resumes his argument in the question-and-answer style of the diatribe, as he often does when an objection has to be faced. If the fundamental fact (see p. 169) that Christ is the seed of Abraham, and that men are elected in him, is lost sight of, the assertions of *vv.* 6–13 are open to objection. To distinguish between unborn twin infants, to love the one and hate the other, even to prefer the one to the other, is unjust. This is the verdict of the conscience, and if Paul can appeal to conscience when it suits his case he is bound to listen to it when it does not. It seems therefore to follow that, on Paul's showing, God is unjust. This is unthinkable, and the objector will infer that the argument

1 'If this is so' is an addition made in the translation to bring out the sense. It could be regarded as a translation of 'then' (οὖν) if this word be read ('Why *then* does he . . . ?'), with P⁴⁶ B D G.

2 'Yes, but' represents the Greek μενοῦνγε. This is read before 'My dear sir' (ὦ ἄνθρωπε) by the the majority of MSS (ω), and after it by ℵ A (B); it is omitted altogether by P⁴⁶ D G lat – perhaps rightly.

which leads to such a conclusion is false. **What then shall we say? Is** 14 **there unrighteousness in God's dealings?** Paul is as eager as any man to deny such a suggestion **No, indeed.** But how can the objection be met?[1]

Paul defends his position in *vv.* 15 f.; at least, he appears to do so, but it is often held that in fact he does no such thing, but merely reiterates his offensive views in shriller tones. But this judgement fails to do justice to Paul. He begins with an Old Testament quotation, introduced by the words, **For he** (the subject must be God, as *v.* 14 15 suggests; cf. *v.* 17) **says to Moses.** *For* (γάρ) explains the question in *v.* 14. God's righteousness is called in question by the fact that Scripture speaks of him as it does. The quotation, from Ex. xxxiii. 19, runs '**I will have mercy on whomsoever I do have mercy, and I will pity whomsoever I do pity.**' From this assertion of the divine freedom and initiative Paul concludes, **So then everything depends, not on man** 16 **who exercises his will or like an athlete runs to a goal, but on the merciful God.**

The point to note is that these verses emphasize not only the freedom of God, but his mercy. If God does anything at all for sinful man, it is of his mercy. If he does nothing, he is not unjust, for man deserves nothing. Mercy (ἔλεος; verb, ἐλεεῖν) is the key-note of chs. ix–xi, as will appear at point after point in the commentary. Here, where the word first occurs, it may suffice to recall its Old Testament background (in the LXX it translates the Hebrew ḥesed which is also rendered χάρις, *grace*) and to point onwards to the last occurrence: God has shut up all men to disobedience, in order that he may deal with all men in mercy (xi. 32). In chs. i–viii Paul has dealt with the divine act of grace and redemption by virtue of which men may be justified, and in the end saved, through faith alone. Behind this process lies an attitude or attribute of God which is occasionally described as love (v. 8) but more characteristically as *mercy*. It is because God is merciful that justification by faith is possible. And God is determined to treat men on the basis of mercy; indeed, if he treated them otherwise none would survive. But if his dealings with them are to be governed by his mercy they cannot be determined by man's will, or earnest striving towards a goal. Elsewhere (1 Cor. ix. 24, 26; Gal. v. 7; Phil. ii. 16; (iii. 12)) Paul uses the metaphor of running a race (common in the Stoic diatribe) in a good sense – Christians must run so as to win the prize; but never in such a way as to suggest that salvation, or the mercy which grants salvation, rests upon man's achievement. Everything depends (one might almost say, God's mercy depends), not upon man, but only upon the merciful God.

---

1 It is worth noting that Paul finds it necessary to demonstrate that God is righteous. See iii. 26, and the notes.

So far, then, Paul has argued that his conception of the absolute predestinating sovereignty of God is necessary if God's dealings with men are to be seen to rest solely upon his mercy. He now presses his point further still on the basis of another text in Exodus. Election necessarily implies non-election; if some are chosen, others must remain unchosen. Paul (quoting the Old Testament) goes further. The non-elect, or some of them, are hardened so that a positive response to God becomes impossible for them.

17 **For God in Scripture** (literally, Scripture – the written word being almost personified) **says to Pharaoh, 'For this very purpose did I raise thee up, namely that in thee I might demonstrate my power, and that my name might be proclaimed in all the earth'.** Paul's quotation follows neither the Hebrew nor the Greek of Ex. ix. 16 exactly, but gives their substance.

The new quotation allows two fresh points to be made. Pharaoh, who doubtless thinks himself master of the situation in Egypt, has in fact been brought on the scene by God for two purposes; (i) in order that God may manifest his power; (ii) in order that God's name may be universally proclaimed. Pharaoh exists not to further his own ends, but God's; and God's ends are the carrying out of a mighty act of salvation, and the publication of this act of salvation among all men. Historically, Pharaoh supplied the occasion for the deliverance of the people; if there had been no 'Pharaoh of the oppression' there would have been no Exodus, and the proclamation of the Exodus (in Scripture, and in the Passover service) would never have taken place. Paul's interpretation of this history is as clear as the history itself, though it involves the transference of imagery from Pharaoh to Israel. In the present time, Israel (like Pharaoh in his) exists for a double purpose, (i) to provide the occasion or context for a divine act of deliverance – that in which men are freed from the law, and thereby from sin and death; (ii) to act so as to cause the publication of God's act of deliverance through all the world – which took place precisely because Israel rejected the Gospel (xi. 11, 15, 19, 25; cf. Acts xiii. 46; xviii. 6; xxviii. 28). Thus, as Pharaoh's plans were overruled to God's ends, so Israel's self-will is to be overruled to God's ends; and his ends are merciful.

18 Paul sums up the position reached so far: **So then he has mercy on whom he wills, and whom he wills he 'hardens'** (this word is suggested by the story of Pharaoh, and occurs at Ex. iv. 21; vii. 3; ix. 12; xiv. 4, 17). It is true that 'hardening' introduces a sharpness that was not apparent in *vv.* 15 f.; but it cannot be understood apart from the thought of *v.* 17, which has just been explained. It does not necessarily imply final rejection, but points out the way in which God has, in his wisdom, decided to work out his purposes, which are governed from first to last by mercy.

Nevertheless, 'hardening' is an offensive word, and objection again breaks out. No doubt Paul had encountered it more than once. **Of 19 course you will say to me, If this is so, why does he still make complaints? For who can resist his will?** (cf. Wisd. xii. 12). The gravamen of the objection lies not in the injured national sentiment of the Jew, but in the implication that the moral government of the universe is at fault. If God treats men as Paul supposes, they have no moral responsibility; God himself has no business to condemn as a sinner a man whom he himself has hardened. Paul replies in more Old Testament imagery.

Yes, but, my dear sir, who are you to answer back to God? 20 Man's sense of moral responsibility has not the ultimate value he attaches to it; it gives him no right to question God's dealings. He can never be anything other than God's creature, and his wisest course is not to pass judgement upon his Creator, but to accept his position with humility. **What, will the model say to the modeller, Why did you make me like this? Has not the potter a right over the clay, to 21 make out of the same lump one vessel designed for noble, one for ignoble use?** In these verses there are echoes of Isa. xxix. 16; xlv. 9 f.; lxiv. 7; Wisd. xii. 12; compare also Jer. xviii. 1–6. 'Vessel' (σκεῦος) in *v.* 21 is used literally, of a vessel made by a potter; but the transition to the metaphor of *vv.* 22 f. is easy, since the corresponding Hebrew word (*kᵉli*, and the Greek word in Judaizing Greek) has a very wide range of meaning, including persons and even abstract ideas.

Paul argues that, just as a potter is not dictated to by the clay he uses but may fashion it as he pleases, so God has perfect liberty to make what he wills of the humanity he has created, and man has no more right to answer back than the potter's clay. 'It is a well-worn illustration. But the trouble is that a man is not a pot; he *will* ask, "Why did you make me like this?" and he will not be bludgeoned into silence. It is the weakest point in the whole epistle' (Dodd, p. 159). But the argument is perhaps not so weak, or the analogy so remote, as at first appears. Of course man is not a pot, and obstinate questionings arise in his mind. It is because the mind asks questions about the divine government of the universe that works like Romans are written. To stress this point, however, is to emphasize a detail in the analogy instead of the major comparison, which is between the final responsibility of the potter for what he produces, and the final responsibility of God for what he does in history. 'Everything depends, not on man who exercises his will ... but on the merciful God' (*v.*16). The question of *v.* 19 is wrongly framed, for God is not making complaints against men who have had no opportunity of being good, but commending his love to wilful rebels in the death of his Son (v. 8). The doctrine of apparent double predestination implies not a crude numerical division within the human race but a profound definition of God and of his purpose for men in terms of mercy (cf. p. 160).

It is to be noted further that in *v.* 21 Paul speaks of vessels designed for noble and ignoble use respectively. This distinction seems to reflect the different roles played by Israel and Pharaoh respectively in the story of the Exodus; and it is not unimportant that Pharaoh (as *v.* 17 already implies) is regarded as standing within God's purpose, which is a purpose of mercy. His place in it may be an ignoble one, but it is within and not outside it. Once more, however, the following verses, with their reference to 'vessels of wrath, prepared for destruction', sharpen the contrast.

The next three verses (22 ff.) raise very difficult linguistic questions, which must be attended to before an exposition can be attempted. In the translation, one view of the construction is adopted; in the notes an attempt will be made to justify it.

22   **But what if God with great long-suffering 'endured the vessels of wrath'** (cf. Jer. l. 25, xxvii. 25 LXX), **'prepared for destruction'** (cf. Isa. liv. 16, LXX), **because he wished to show forth his wrath and to**
23   **make known his power, and moreover did so in order to make known the wealth of his glory for the vessels of mercy, which**
24   **beforehand he made ready for glory – us, those whom he called, not only from among the Jews but from among the Gentiles too?**

Three separate problems may be distinguished here. (i) The whole passage is in the form of a conditional sentence with a protasis (if-clause) but no apodosis. This is not a serious difficulty. Greek sometimes expresses by means of an if-clause what in English we express by saying 'What if ... ?' (e.g. John vi. 62). The construction is rhetorical in style, 'What if this is so?' being used in the present case for 'Why should this not be so?'; that is, 'This is in fact so, and there is no reason why it should not be so'.

(ii) *V.* 24 is loosely attached to what precedes, but here again there is no serious difficulty. The two relative clauses ('which he made ready' and 'us, those whom he called') are both in explanatory apposition to 'vessels of mercy'.

(iii) The main difficulty lies in the participle (θέλων) here translated 'because he wished', and in the conjunction (ἵνα) here translated 'in order to'. (a) The participle may be causal ('because he wished') or concessive ('though he wished'). The latter has been supported by a reference to ii. 4: God wished to show forth his wrath and make known his power, yet instead displayed long-suffering to the vessels of wrath with a view to bringing them to repentance. But it will be recalled that the whole of i. 18–iii. 20 describes the eschatological manifestation of God's wrath (see especially on i. 18–32), mitigated in such a way – by God's long-suffering – that sinners are not instantly consigned to destruction. The former way of taking the participle may therefore be preferred, especially because it also makes possible the better explanation of the conjunction, and the most convincing interpretation of 'to show forth his wrath and to make known his power'. (b) If the participle is taken as concessive, it becomes necessary to couple the conjunction (καὶ ἵνα) with 'with great long-suffering' ('... with great long-suffering and with the intention of making known'). This is very awkward grammatically and does not seem to make good sense. Alternatively, if the participle is causal the conjunction (expressing purpose) will be parallel to it ('... on the one hand wishing to show his wrath upon A, ... and on the other to make known his mercy upon B'). This seems preferable on every ground.

It remains to ask what Paul means by these three verses. It is important to bear in mind several facts which have already been established. (i) Paul represents the present as an eschatological age, in which God, through the death and resurrection of Jesus, is manifesting his righteousness in such a way as to anticipate the last judgement. A verdict of 'Guilty' is expressed in the hardening of the unbelieving, and of 'justified' in the peace and joy of those who have faith. (ii) Paul has used the example of Pharaoh (*vv.* 17 f.), whom God raised up and hardened in order to show forth his power and to cause his name to be proclaimed in all the earth. (iii) What is said about Pharaoh is transferred to Israel, whose hardening and unbelief have furnished the occasion for a demonstration of God's power and for the worldwide publication of the Gospel.

It is in the framework of these facts that *vv.* 22 ff. must be understood. *Endured* is the one main verb (the only indicative) in *vv.* 22 f. and indicates the fundamental direction of Paul's thought. It would have been easy for him to write that God intended to show his wrath and power in the destruction of vessels of wrath apt for destruction and to show the wealth of his glory towards vessels of mercy, created for glory. He does not do so, but declares that God endured, put up with, vessels of wrath, and makes no comparable statement about vessels of mercy. The verses may be outlined thus: (a) God endured ... (b) because he wished ... (c) in order to ... Clause (c) is comparatively easy to understand. What God has done, he has done in order to show his mercy towards those whom he calls, both Jews and Gentiles. Clause (a) also can be fairly readily understood. God's endurance and long-suffering refer to the fact that he has not yet instituted the last judgement and brought in the day of wrath (ii. 5); he seeks to lead men to repentance (ii. 4). His long-suffering applies to all, for all (iii. 20) would fare ill if judgement according to works (ii. 6) were set up at once. 'Vessels of wrath prepared for destruction' may apply as well to Jews as Gentiles (*vv.* 27, 29). Between these fixed points, clause (*b*) seems to mean that God

177

wished to reveal both his wrathful judgement against sin, and his saving power. But this is precisely what Paul has already said in iii. 26, a most important parallel. What then if this is the purpose that lies behind God's election? In glory and in wrath he is manifesting his righteousness, and all his actions are rooted in the mercy with which alone he will deal with men. Cf. xi. 32.

The remaining verses of this paragraph do not require lengthy exposition. Paul uses a series of Old Testament quotations to prove (i) that God means to call Gentiles, and (ii) that he calls only a remnant and not the whole of Israel. It appears also that designation as 'vessels of wrath' and 'vessels of mercy' is not irreversible.

25 First come two passages from Hosea. **That this calling of Gentiles as well as Jews was intended is shown in Scripture** (a supplement, to explain the following 'as'), **as God says in the book of Hosea: 'That which was not my people I will call my people, and her that was not beloved I will call beloved'** (Hosea ii. 23, somewhat loosely
26 quoted); **'and it shall come to pass that in the place where it was said to them, You are not my people, there shall they be called sons of the living God'** (Hosea i. 10). Paul of course refers mainly to the call of Gentiles; it is, however, possible that he is also thinking (as Hosea did) of the temporary lapse of Israel and their subsequent return, that is, of the possibility that 'vessels of wrath' might become 'vessels of mercy'.

27 Two passages from Isaiah follow. **Isaiah cries out concerning Israel, 'Though the number of the children of Israel should be as the sand of the sea, yet it is the remnant of them that will be**
28 **saved, for the Lord will bring his word to pass upon the earth,**
29 **accomplishing it and determining it'** (Isa. x. 22 f.). **This accords further with what Isaiah said earlier, 'If the Lord Sabaoth** (this word is a transliteration, used by the LXX as by Paul, of the Hebrew word for 'hosts'; it has now become virtually a name) **had not left us a seed, we should have become like Sodom, and we should have been made like Gomorrah'** (Isa. i. 9); that is, in view of the election of Israel, there is a possibility, corresponding to that mentioned above, that 'vessels of mercy' may become 'vessels of wrath'.

It is unlikely that Paul quoted the word 'seed' without remembering the use he had made of it elsewhere (see p. 169). The remnant and the seed alike were reduced to one – Jesus Christ; henceforth the elect people of God were elect in *him*. This fact reminds us that behind Paul's discussion there lies the historical background formed by the ministry of Jesus; his rejection and crucifixion by Israel, which thereby disavowed its own place in God's plan; and the election of a new Israel in Christ to take the place of the old. These were the events of the last age, which reflected the mind and character of God; but they were not the end itself, and the reflection in consequence remains something of a riddle (αἴνιγμα, 1 Cor. xiii. 12). The story of election is obscured by the brokenness of history, and God is hidden as well as revealed in its events. The time is still to come when men shall know as they have been known.

The profoundest problem in history is the unbelief of Israel, God's elect people. In this chapter Paul has been talking round the problem in the light of God's freedom and mercy. He will now attack it head on.

25 WHY ISRAEL STUMBLED

CHAPTER ix. 30–3[1]

(30) What then shall we say? This, that Gentiles, who do not make righteousness their aim, have attained righteousness – the righteousness, of course, that rests on faith; (31) but that Israel, whose aim is a law purporting to give righteousness, never reached that law. (32) Why? Because they did not pursue their aim by faith, but as if it could be reached by works. They stumbled against the stone set for stumbling – (33) as it is written, 'Behold I lay in Zion a stone for stumbling and a rock for tripping; and he who believes upon it[2] shall not be put to shame'.

The facts have now been laid bare. God, in the pursuit of his elective purpose, has caused the partial rejection of Israel, and the election into the messianic people of the last age of a number of Gentiles. So far Paul has been content to say that God has the right to treat men in this way, and that what has happened was in fact predicted in the Old Testament; but the question cannot fail to be asked, How did Israel come to make the astounding blunder of rejecting the Messiah? The answer is first stated in this paragraph, in terms – righteousness, faith, law – that Paul has used earlier, and then developed in ch. x, before Paul returns in ch. xi to consider the full meaning of God's elective purpose.

What then shall we say? The sum of the matter is **this, that 30 Gentiles** (not *the* Gentiles – as RV; there is no article in the Greek, and the Gentiles as a whole were not yet included in the Church), **who do not make righteousness their aim, have attained righteousness – the righteousness, of course, that rests on faith.** For the various meanings of *righteousness* see pp. 50 f. It would not be correct to say that (all) Gentiles did not make moral righteousness their aim, or

1 I have considered some aspects of Romans ix. 30–x. 21 in greater detail in *Die Israelfrage nach Röm 9–11*, Monographische Reihe von "Benedictina", Biblisch-ökumenische Abteilung 3 (Rome, 1977), pp. 99–121.
2 The Greek pronoun (αὐτῷ) could equally be translated 'him'.

that all had now achieved it. *Righteousness* here must refer to the right, harmonious relation with God from which alone life and salvation can spring. It is God's gift and is received by faith. It had not been a concern of the Gentile world, though its inharmonious and sinful life bore witness – to those who had ears to hear – to the lack of it. It was only under the preaching of the Gospel that they had discovered faith, stumbling upon it unexpectedly.

So much for the Gentiles who had become Christians. Of the Jews it
31 must be said **that Israel, whose aim is a law purporting to give righteousness, never reached that law.** This verse has often been misunderstood, perhaps under the influence of x. 5, and taken to mean that Israel pursued righteousness, made righteousness their aim. So even Calvin (p. 217): 'In the first part of the verse he has, I think, put *law of righteousness* by hypallage to mean *righteousness of the law*, and when he repeats the phrase in the second clause, he has understood it in a different sense to mean the form or rule of righteousness.' But Paul does not say that Israel made *righteousness* their aim, but (to translate literally) a *law of righteousness*. The law of Moses was itself righteous (vii. 12), and it could have produced righteousness (a) if it had been done (x. 5; Gal. iii. 10), and (b) if it had been able to give life (vii. 10; Gal. iii. 21). These two conditions amount to much the same thing, and they mean that the law, though good, is misused if treated as a means of attaining righteousness. This was the mistake made by the Jews. It is proper to seek righteousness, that is, a proper relation with God; and the law itself is a good thing. But to seek righteousness by means of works done in obedience to the law, may produce at most human righteousness, not God's (x. 3).

In fact, Israel did not even reach the law after which they strove.
32 **Why? Because they did not pursue their aim by faith, but as if it could be reached by works.** It is sometimes supposed that Paul has now changed his expression and thinks of the Jews as aiming at righteousness, but it is much more probable that he is following out what he has said in *v.* 31. Israel aimed at (literally, *pursued*, διώκων) the law, Israel did not reach (ἔφθασεν) the law; Why? because they did not pursue the law by faith (understanding νόμον ἐδίωκεν with οὐκ ἐκ πίστεως), as they should have done. Here is the second of the two great keys to the mystery of Israel's rejection. The first is that God willed it; the second, that Israel sought the right goal by the wrong means. Paul cannot bring himself to say, They sought it by *works*; this is to him so manifest an absurdity that he says, *as if it could be reached by works* (ὡς ἐξ ἔργων). To seek by works the right relation with God to which the law pointed is not merely contrary to Paul's own doctrine; it is contrary to the true meaning of the law itself (though in view of all the precepts contained in the law it is a natural enough error). See x. 6 ff. Thus Israel, in their ill-directed search for

righteousness, **stumbled against the stone set for stumbling.** Paul returns to the fundamental explanation of Israel's defection: it was willed by God. It may be possible to give a psychological or anthropological account of what took place, but this would only describe the mechanism used by God, who provided the stone for Israel to trip over.

The 'stone of stumbling' is a phrase drawn from the Old Testament; but in providing the reference Paul combines two passages. **As it is written, 'Behold I lay in Zion a stone for** 33 **stumbling and a rock for tripping** (cf. Isa. viii. 14); **and he who believes upon it** (see p. 179, n. 2) **shall not be put to shame'** (Isa. xxviii. 16, LXX).

Isa. xxviii. 16 is quoted again at x. 11; and a similar composite quotation occurs in 1 Pet. ii. 6 ff. (where Ps. cxviii. 22 is also included). This fact has led some to think that Paul and the author of 1 Peter may both have drawn upon a Testimony Book (or collection of Old Testament proof-texts) in which the passages were already combined. This may be so; but Paul was not unfamiliar with the Old Testament, and it must be supposed that he knew what he was doing when he used the composite quotation, which contains in germ the argument developed in x. 1–13. Three points may be distinguished.

(i) It is the man who has faith who is not put to shame. This *sola fide* was, historically speaking, the primary source of scandal to the Jews (cf. 1 Cor. i. 22 f.). They preferred the way of law, by means of which they hoped to establish their own righteousness, and to avoid submitting to God's (x. 3). Here we are driven back to the theme of God's mercy, for only faith is the proper response to mercy.

(ii) There are two ways in which the *stone* may be understood. (a) It is most easily understood to refer to Christ himself. It was Christ whom the Jews found offensive, and had rejected; if they had believed in him they would not have been exposed to the shame of seeing Gentiles take their place as the people of God; positively, they would have been justified, saved. (b) Alternatively, however, the *stone* may be the law. The Jews stumbled over this in not seeing that what it called for was faith; had they rightly understood it they would have found righteousness in it. Ultimately the two interpretations tend to come together in view of x. 4.

(iii) All these truths, as the quotation itself shows, have the authority of Scripture. The Jews' own Bible proclaims the offensive Christ, whose obscurity and suffering scandalized his own people (*v.* 5), just as it commends, even through the law, the way of faith.

There is no need to develop these themes here, since they are continued in ch. x.

26 THE RIGHTEOUSNESS OF MEN AND THE RIGHTEOUSNESS OF GOD

CHAPTER x. 1–13

(1) Whatever may be the cause of their unbelief, brethren, my own heart's will, and my supplication to God, are on their behalf, and are that they may be saved. (2) For I bear them witness that they have an enthusiasm for God, but it is not informed with understanding. (3) For precisely because they did not understand God's righteousness, and sought to establish their own, they did not submit themselves to the righteousness of God. (4) For Christ, by realizing righteousness for every believer, proves to be the end of the law.

(5) For Moses writes of the righteousness which has its root in the law, that 'the man who has done it shall live by it'. (6) But the righteousness which has its root in faith speaks thus: 'Do not say in your heart, Who shall ascend into heaven?' (that is, to bring Christ down); (7) 'or, Who shall descend into the abyss?' (that is, to bring Christ up from the dead). (8) No; what does it say? 'The word is near you, in your mouth and in your heart' (that is, the word of faith which we preach). (9) And the word is to this effect, namely, that if 'with your mouth' you confess Jesus as Lord, and if 'with your heart' you believe that God raised him from the dead, you shall be saved. (10) For faith works in the heart to produce righteousness, and confession in the mouth to produce salvation. (11) For Scripture says, 'No one who believes in him will be put to shame'. (12) For there is no distinction between Jew and Greek; the same Lord is Lord of all, and he abounds in wealth to all who call upon him. (13) For 'whosoever shall call upon the name of the Lord shall be saved'.

How did the most religious of all peoples come to reject their own Messiah, for whose coming they had so long waited? Paul has already given his answers to this question (see pp. 180 ff.); now he analyses them further. But first of all he emphasizes afresh (cf. ix. 1 f.) his own

1 longing for the salvation of Israel. **Whatever may be the cause of their unbelief** (this supplement is an attempt to bring out the meaning of the particle (μέν) which opens the paragraph, and means 'so far as it depends on my wish'[1]), **brethren, my own heart's will** (this rather than 'wish' seems to be the meaning; cf. Eph. i. 5), **and my supplication to God, are on their behalf** (taking 'on their behalf' as a predicate – with the Vulgate, *fit pro illis*), **and are that they may be saved.** The last word looks beyond (and therefore includes) the

1 BDR § 447, n.14.

process of justification up to the salvation of Israel at the last day. Nothing Paul has said about God's sovereign electing grace, and no Scripture prediction that only a remnant of Israel shall be saved, can alter his desire for the salvation of all Israel.

For I bear them witness (cf. 2 Cor. viii. 3; Gal. iv. 15; Col. iv. 13) 2 **that they have an enthusiasm for God, but it is not informed with understanding.** This takes up ix. 30–3. The words of Judah b. Tema, Be strong as the leopard and swift as the eagle, fleet as the gazelle and brave as the lion to do the will of thy father which is in heaven (*Aboth*, v. 20), are no more than characteristic of Judaism at its best. No nation had given itself to God with such devoted and courageous zeal as Israel; yet it was also true that the eternal decree which had determined Israel's unbelief could be traced in sins and errors for which Israel was responsible – an interplay of predestination and human responsibility characteristic of the Bible, and not to be disposed of in the interests of simplicity on the one side or the other.

Israel's religious enthusiasm is misdirected. **For precisely be-** 3 **cause they did not understand God's righteousness, and sought to establish their own, they did not submit themselves to the righteousness of God.** There is a close parallel to this verse in Phil. iii. 9 (righteousness from God, ἐκ θεοῦ), which strongly suggests that, in Romans, the genitive 'of God', and the genitive substitute 'their own' (τὴν ἰδίαν), denote *origin* rather than *possession*. There is a righteousness which comes from God as his gift, and there is (or, at least, there may be thought to be) a righteousness which men evolve out of themselves by works done in obedience to the law.

Now the Jews have rightly perceived (cf. ix. 31) that religion is a matter of righteousness – man cannot stand in the presence of God the righteous judge without righteousness; but they have not seen that, if their own beliefs are to be taken seriously, the only righteousness which can be of the slightest use is God's own. Man can never make himself God, and can never produce a righteousness capable of satisfying God's requirements. It is true that God had given the Jews a law, but in thinking that their own obedience to it could secure their standing in God's court they misunderstood God's intention. What was required was not that they should be perfectly obedient to the law and so 'establish their own righteousness', but that they should 'submit to God's righteousness'; that is, acknowledge him as the righteous and merciful God and leave their fate in his hands. Here again is the contrast between 'works' and 'faith', for man's 'own righteousness' can be nothing other than a righteousness based on works of law, and God's righteousness can be accepted only by faith. The law stated the goal correctly, but suggested (by its form) the wrong way to reach it. The man who seeks to establish his own righteousness, however virtuous he may be, can be only a rebellious creature of God, for he is pressing himself into the Judge's throne; the man who accepts God's verdict and submits to God's righteousness thereby automatically harmonizes himself with the universe, since he falls into his appointed place as a dependent creature.

Yet this is not the whole truth. The contrast of the principles of faith and works can up to a point be expressed in anthropological terms, but Paul never (cf. pp. 76 f., 111) supposes that these terms can express it completely. Man does not of himself decide to put an end to his legal relation with God and to live henceforth by faith. This can take place not at man's choice, but only through God's initiative. **For** (γάρ, establishing v. 3, and showing additionally why the old effort after legal righteousness should be abandoned) **Christ, by realizing righteousness for every believer, proves to be the end of the law.** 'Christ' means God's act in history, by which he introduced the Age to Come, and brought to an end the old order of relations between God and man, since it is in Christ that men are henceforth related to God. Hence Christ is the 'end of the law'. Paul's word (τέλος) may mean not only 'termination' but also 'purpose', or 'intention', or 'goal'; and there is no reason why two, or even all, of these should not be combined. A goal is an achieved intention, and when an object has served its purpose it may be discarded. The key to the present passage is to be found in the words 'by realizing righteousness' (literally, 'unto righteousness', εἰς δικαιοσύνην – 'unto', εἰς, expressing purpose, or goal). Christ is the end of the law, with a view not to anarchy but righteousness. He puts an end to the law, not by destroying all that the law stood for but by realizing it. The law never was an effective means of attaining righteousness, but, since it was righteous (vii. 12; also ix. 31) it did always bear witness to God's righteousness. This, however, has now actually been manifested in Christ (i. 16 f.; iii. 21).

Thus Christ is the end of the law; but he is the end of the law – for every believer. We saw that the opposites, 'works' and 'faith', do not simply lie within human choice; it was necessary that a divine act should take place. Yet the corresponding truth is also valid. The divine act, when once it has taken place, is appropriated by faith. The second pair of opposites, law and Christ, does not form a simple chronological sequence, for, as the story of Abraham shows (ch. iv), faith was possible 'before Christ', and, as the story of the Jews constantly pressed home upon Paul, allegiance to the principle of works remained possible 'after Christ'. Apart from Christ, and apart from faith, the curse of the law (Gal. iii. 13; cf. Rom. iv. 15) still holds sway. The law thus continues to carry out a negative purpose; its call for righteousness and its threat of punishment may drive men to Christ. It also has a positive purpose, indicating how God is to be obeyed and served (cf. xiii. 8–10).

The next nine verses (5–13) are devoted to a contrast between the

4

righteousness which comes through the law, and that which is based on faith. As Paul has pointed out already (see p. 69), the law itself points to a non-legal righteousness; in the present paragraph he develops this point.

Law itself is inextricably bound up with works, for a law exists only to be obeyed (cf. ii. 25 ff.). **For Moses writes of the righteousness** 5 **which has its root in the law, that 'the man who has done it shall live by it'.** The same quotation (from Lev. xviii. 5) is used at Gal. iii. 12. Paul no doubt found it a convenient way of summarizing, in the law's own words, what he understood the law to mean. The whole law includes Lev. xix. 18 (Rom. xiii. 8–10); see above on *v.* 4. To do this is to have righteousness. But also the new righteousness, which is by faith, is mentioned in the law itself, and Paul proceeds to quote Deut. xxx. 12 ff., with interspersed and appended comments.

In this passage, the Deuteronomic writer claims that the law is not too difficult to fulfil. Like the author of Leviticus (see *v.* 5), he too speaks of 'doing', and adds that there is no reason why the law should not be done. In point of fact, it is doubtful whether he did think of the law in a strictly 'nomistic' way; Deuteronomy is full of the notion that God's relations with his people rest upon grace. Paul, however, strikes out a fresh interpretation of the passage which seems to have no Jewish parallel, though it is worth noting that in 1 Bar. iii. 29 f. the words of Deuteronomy are taken to apply to Wisdom. So here, Paul supposes that they refer to Christ, though he takes the speaker to be the righteousness of God (*v.* 6), here described as the righteousness which has its root in faith. He supplies his interpretation of the verses quoted in three clauses (*vv.* 6, 7, 8), each introduced by the words 'that is' (τοῦτ' ἔστιν). This recalls the interpretative formula 'its interpretation is' (*pishro*) used in the Qumran MSS (e.g. 1 Q pHab 2.10 f.: Hab. i. 6 is quoted; then, Its interpretation is of the Kittim . . .).

But the righteousness which has its root in faith speaks thus: 6 **'Do not say in your heart, Who shall ascend into heaven?'** (that is, **to bring Christ down).** 'Bringing Christ down from heaven' means to precipitate the incarnation. This has already taken place; the Messiah has appeared, and it is therefore impossible to hasten his coming (as some devout Jews thought to do) by perfect obedience to the law and penitence for its transgression. The divine act of redemption (iii. 24) has already been performed, not as a reward for legal righteousness but as an act of sheer grace.

It is equally wrong to say, **'Who shall descend into the abyss?'** 7 **(that is, to bring Christ up from the dead).** Paul's words here differ from all known forms of the text of Deut. xxx. 13 (RV: Who shall go over the sea for us?). His freedom suggests that he is not using his quotation as a rigid proof of what he asserts, but as a rhetorical form. The variation in the quotation was no doubt suggested by the interpretation of the previous clause. The counterpart of bringing Christ down from heaven is not crossing the sea, but bringing Christ up from the underworld (the abode of the dead). This also is sheer impossibility, since the resurrection has already happened and Christ has ascended into heaven. This means that the eschatological conditions have been realized; the Age to Come has dawned; the Gospel has come into being through the manifestation of God's righteousness (i. 17; iii. 21).

The righteousness of faith, then, does not mean that man must initiate the process of salvation, or, by good works or repentance, induce God to act. No; **what does it say? 'The word is near you, in your mouth and in your heart' (that is, the word of faith which we preach).** Paul's *word* agrees with Deut. xxx. 14 (*dabar*; ῥῆμα), but xxx. 11 makes clear that the *word* in Deuteronomy is a command. Paul's conversion of this into the *word of faith* is justified so far as he is right in thinking that it was in the end the response of faith that the law sought. Faith, as a divine possibility, is an immediate possibility. That which man might seek in heaven and hell in vain is at his side. Faith alone is what God seeks, and that he himself provides. The 'word of faith' means the Gospel, as preached by Paul; compare Eph. v. 26; vi. 17; Heb. vi. 5; 1 Pet. i. 25 b; if, as is possible, *v.* 9 suggests baptism, the first of these parallels may be the most relevant. But the 'word of faith' does not itself refer (as is often supposed) to a baptismal confession of faith, for it is something 'we preach' – that is, the Gospel message itself, not the summary of this message in a symbol. It follows that the first word (ὅτι) of the next sentence is to be translated not 'for' but 'that'; the good news is that (*v.* 13) everyone who calls upon the name of the Lord shall be saved.

9   **The word of faith is to this effect, namely, that if 'with your mouth' you confess Jesus as Lord, and if 'with your heart' you believe that God raised him from the dead, you shall be saved.**

The formulation of this verse is due to Deut. xxx. 14 (in thy mouth and in thy heart). No distinction is to be drawn between the confession and the faith; the confession is believed and the faith confessed. The Old Testament passage also suggests (though it certainly did not create) the content of faith – Christ the heavenly Lord, Christ crucified and risen.

The word 'confess' (ὁμολογεῖν) has several meanings in New Testament Greek, as in modern English. Here evidently it means to 'declare', 'profess', 'avow', 'proclaim'. For the double accusative (Jesus *as* Lord) compare John ix. 22; for similar use of the verb see, for example, 1 John iv. 2, 15; for the cognate noun, Heb. iii. 1; iv. 14; x. 23; 1 Tim. vi. 12. The verb suggests that Paul may be using a recognized formula, and this is confirmed by 1 Cor. xii. 3. The form of the sentence, 'If thou shalt confess . . . and believe . . . thou shalt be saved' suggests that the formula may be a baptismal confession.

The profession 'Jesus is Lord' is undoubtedly one of the oldest expressions of Christian belief. It has been suggested[1] that it arose in time of persecution as the Christian reply to the insistence of the state religion that 'Caesar is Lord',[2] but this seems improbable. (i) The Aramaic-speaking Church seems to have called Jesus Marana, our Lord (1 Cor. xvi. 22; *Didache*, x. 6; cf. Rev. xxii. 20). At first, during the life of Jesus, this may well have meant no more than 'Teacher'; but as soon as Christians, after the resurrection, said, 'Marana *tha*' (Our Lord, *come*), begging their absent *Mar* to return from heaven, they were addressing not a Rabbi but a heavenly being. (ii) In the non-Jewish world, the word 'Christ' (χριστός) was unintelligible, and speedily became (as it already is in the Pauline epistles) scarcely more than a proper name. The notion of divine kingship (more or less bound up with Messiahship) was now expressed by Greek-speaking Jews and Gentiles alike by the term Lord (κύριος). (iii) Lord (κύριος) was the natural correlative term for men who knew themselves to be slaves (δοῦλοι); compare i. 1 and the note.

Along with the first article, Jesus is Lord, goes the second, God raised him from the dead. This provides a very important qualification, or corrective. In the Hellenistic world it was very easy for the figure of Jesus, as the divine Lord and Saviour, to become assimilated to the 'gods many and lords many' (1 Cor. viii. 5 f. – Paul associates Christ with even as he distinguishes him from these lords) which peopled that world; he might well seem no more than another 'divine man', the centre of yet another oriental-Hellenistic cult. By insisting upon this second clause, Paul does two things. (i) He emphasizes again the true Christian subordinationism (see pp. 21 f.). Christ is not an independent demigod, but one who was what he was only in virtue of his ordination by and unbroken union with the Father. His ministry, and his death, had their effect only through the seal laid upon them when God raised him from the dead. The Christian faith therefore is not one cult among many, nor is Christ one 'lord' among many; he is, and the Church accordingly rests upon, the one unique act and self-revelation of God. (ii) At the same time, Paul reasserts the primitive Christian eschatology. The significance of Jesus is that in him God began to put into effect the Age to Come. Jesus is confessed and believed as one who stands both within and outside history; not primarily as a teacher (Paul shows no interest in him in this role) but as the source of supernatural life.

---

1 O. Cullmann, *Die ersten christlichen Glaubensbekenntnisse* (1943), pp. 22 f.
2 Cf. *Mart. Pol.* viii. 2: What harm is there in saying 'Caesar is Lord' and in sacrificing and in the accompanying rites, and so being saved (διασώζεσθαι)?

Hence he adds: You shall be saved. For Paul's conception of salvation see pp. 28 f., 100; as usual, the verb 'to save' is used in the future tense. Paul means that believers, already justified, will be saved at the last day; though, of course, he does not deny that preliminary effects of salvation are already apparent through the work of the Holy Spirit.

The shape of *v.* 10, like that of *v.* 9, is determined by Deut. xxx. 14; the distinction between faith and its effect, and confession and

10   its effect, is rhetorical only. **For faith works in the heart to produce righteousness, and confession in the mouth to produce salvation.** In this neat rhetorical summary of *vv.* 6–9, Paul uses some of his key-terms (faith, righteousness, salvation), and works back to the theme, central to his argument in this chapter, that righteousness is by faith only, so that the Jews who sought it by means of the law were doomed to failure and rejection. This is

11   supported by another quotation: **For Scripture says, 'No one who believes in him will be put to shame'.** The passage is taken from Isa. xxviii. 16, already used at ix. 33; here Paul has slightly modified it (by adding $\pi\hat{\alpha}\varsigma$ – 'all' – in Greek) so as to make it more universal in scope. He does this perhaps under the influence of the words he is about to quote in *v.* 13, but also because his argument requires it. In the back of his mind, the dominant question is still, Why have the Jews been rejected? And a major part of the answer to this question is (see ch. xi), In order that the Gospel may be preached to *all*, Gentiles as well as Jews. Paul proceeds to emphasize this.

12   **For there is no distinction between Jew and Greek** (that is, Gentile); **the same Lord** (confessed in the Christian faith, *v.* 9) **is Lord of all** (cf. iii. 29 f.), **and he abounds in wealth to all who call upon him.** At iii. 22 Paul spoke of the absence of 'distinction' between Jew and Greek in a negative sense – all without distinction have sinned. Here he makes the corresponding positive statement – all without distinction have the same Lord, and enjoy the rich resources of his goodness and glory (cf. ii. 4; ix. 23: God's 'wealth' is a favourite thought of Paul's; cf. xi. 33; 1 Cor. i. 5; Phil. iv. 19; Col. i. 27; iii. 16). 'Calling upon God' implies, and is the outward expression of, faith (cf. *v.* 14). Paul draws the word from the quotation used in the next verse, which is already in his mind.

13   **For 'whosoever shall call upon the name of the Lord shall be saved'.** Compare *v.* 11 and the note – Paul has in mind the extension of the Gospel beyond Judaism. Here there is no need to modify the Old Testament material, and Paul quotes exactly the LXX version of Joel ii. 32, but reinterprets it so that Lord means Messiah, not God.

27 ISRAEL'S UNBELIEF INEXCUSABLE

CHAPTER x. 14–21

(14) This, however, evokes a new series of problems. How are they to 'call upon' one in whom they have not believed? How are they to believe in one whom they have not heard? How are they to hear without someone to make proclamation? (15) How shall men make proclamation unless they are sent? Yes, but, as it is written, 'How beautiful are the feet of those who bring good news of good things!' (16) Yet not all became obedient to the good news. For Isaiah says, 'Lord, who believed what they heard from us?' (17) Faith then comes as a result of hearing, and hearing comes through the word of Christ. (18) Yes, but I say, Did they not hear? Why, listen: 'Their utterance has gone out into all the earth, and their words have come to the end of the world'. (19) But I say, Did Israel really not know? First Moses says, 'I will stir you up to envy with that which is not a nation, by means of a senseless nation I will provoke you to anger'. (20) And then Isaiah makes bold to say, 'I was found by those who did not seek me, I appeared to those who did not inquire for me'. (21) But of Israel he says, 'I stretched out my hands all day to a disobedient and contradicting people'.

'Whosoever shall call upon the name of the Lord shall be saved' (*v.* 13). This, as an Old Testament pronouncement, was beyond dispute. The trouble was, that Israel had not called upon the name of the Lord (by which title Paul, though not of course Joel, understands Jesus; see above). Where did the fault lie? Paul seeks an answer to this question by constructing a chain of connecting links, and inquiring which link fails.

This evokes a new series of problems (a supplement helpful for 14 the understanding of the following sentences). **How are they to 'call upon' one in whom they have not believed? How are they to believe in one whom they have not heard? How are they to hear without someone to make proclamation? How shall men make** 15 **proclamation unless they are sent?**

Most of the links in this chain are self-evident and require no comment. It goes without saying that men will only call (for salvation) upon one in whom they believe. In the next clause it is right to translate strictly, 'whom (not *of whom*) they have not heard'. Christ must be heard either in his own person, or in the person of his preachers, through whom his own word (*v.* 17) is spoken; otherwise faith in him is impossible. Further, those who 'make proclamation' must, if they are to speak the word of Christ, come not of their own choice or on their own authority, but because they are sent. The verb 'sent' (ἀποσταλῶσιν) is cognate with the noun 'apostle' (ἀπόστολος). For the ideas involved see on i. 1. Christian missionaries act under and with the authority of him who sent them. The chain of argument is at an end. Men call on the Lord because they believe; they believe because they hear; they hear because others preach; these preach because they are sent – by the Lord, with whom the whole process begins, as it ends with him.

Paul next shows, from Scripture, that God did not fail to send out authorized preachers (*v.* 15), and adds, a little later, that Israel did not fail to hear and know what was said (*vv.* 18 f.). He anticipates the vital conclusion in *v.* 16. The break in the chain occurs at the link of faith.

How can there be preachers if they are not sent? **Yes, but as it is written, 'How beautiful are the feet of those who bring good news of good things!'** Some commentators regard this quotation (in which Paul is nearer to the Hebrew than to the LXX version of Isa. lii. 7) as a mere ornament, but it is better to take it as a step in the argument. If there had been no preachers, Israel could not have been blamed for unbelief; but in fact Scripture itself shows that there are those who preach the Gospel (bring good news), and since their existence is noted in Scripture, and with approval, it cannot be doubted that they are true apostles.

In the next verse Paul leaps to his conclusion, though it might more appropriately have been placed later; it is presupposed, and might
16 have been stated here rather than in *v.* 18, that Israel did hear. **Yet not all became obedient to the good news.** The break in the chain consisted only in Israel's unbelief, for which Israel was responsible, since she had not only heard but also known (*vv.* 18 f.) God's plan. That 'disobedience' means unbelief is shown by the quotation that follows; compare i. 5 and the note. **For Isaiah says, 'Lord, who believed what they heard from us?'** (Isa. liii. 1). The prophetic and the apostolic witness to Christ have gone unheeded.

17   **Faith then comes as a result of hearing, and hearing comes through the word of Christ.** Paul here uses the word 'hearing' (ἀκοή) in the sense it commonly has in his writings, that is, of the process or faculty of hearing. The same word is differently employed (as 'report', that is, 'what they heard') in the previous verse, where Paul has taken both the word and the meaning it bears from the Old Testament. The preachers speak the word *of Christ*; see on *v.* 14.

It has often been remarked that this verse (17) would come more appropriately after *v.* 15 a. It is undoubtedly true that a rearrangement would improve the logic of the paragraph, for *v.* 17 summarizes the chain of connections given in *vv.* 14 f., and so would prepare the way for *v.* 16, with its disclosure that the chain was broken in the link of faith. This, however, is not a sufficient reason for rearranging the text. Paul leaps ahead to his main point, and then returns to fill up a gap in the argument. He will fill up more gaps in *vv.* 18 f.

Yes, but I say, Did they (Israel) **not hear?** If it could be 18 established that they did not, they would at once be exonerated from the guilt of not believing. But this is not so. **Why, listen: 'Their utterance has gone out into all the earth, and their words have come to the end of the world'.** Ps. xix. 4 appears to refer to the witness of God's creation. Paul takes it to apply to the Christian mission, and to be already fulfilled. For this 'universal' preaching of the Gospel, compare xv. 19, 23; also Mark xiii. 10; xiv. 9. Israel has heard the Christian message of salvation; no excuse for her unbelief can be found here.

Paul can go further. Israel ought to have understood the theme of God's righteousness and mercy, for first the law (*v.* 19) and then the prophets (*vv.* 20 f.). declared it. And (*v.* 20) Gentiles did hear – and believe.

But I say, Did Israel really not know? First Moses says, 'I will 19 stir you up to envy with that which is not a nation, by means of a senseless nation I will provoke you to anger' (Deut. xxxii. 21). That is to say, unbelieving Israel will be put to shame by believing Gentiles. This theme will prove to be an important part of the argument of ch. xi; see especially xi. 11 f., 28.

After the law, the prophets. **And then Isaiah makes bold to say** 20 (perhaps, *grows even bolder* – than Moses – *and says*), **'I was found by those who did not seek me, I appeared to those who did not inquire for me',** that is, the Gentiles; compare ix. 30. The quotation has an apt continuation. **But of Israel he says, 'I stretched out my 21 hands all day to a disobedient and contradicting people'.** The reference is to Isa. lxv. 1 f. The paradox of the Gentiles' faith will be matched by the paradox of Israel's disobedience. Through the Son, both in his own incarnate person and by means of his apostles, God has pleaded with Israel, and met with nothing (or little more than nothing – see xi. 5) but rebuffs. Both the pleading and the rebuffs, as the reference to Scripture shows, formed part of his eternal purpose.

28 THE REMNANT
CHAPTER xi. 1–10

(1) With all this in mind, I am bound to ask this question, Has God cast off his people?[1] **Certainly not. Why, I myself am an Israelite, of the seed of Abraham, of the tribe of Benjamin. (2)**

---

1 P[46] A D* add 'whom he foreknew'. This reading is an assimilation to *v.* 2, and incorrect.

God has not cast off his people, whom he foreknew. Do you not know what the Scripture says in the story of Elijah, how he appeals to God against Israel? (3) 'Lord,' he says, 'they have killed thy prophets, they have digged down thine altars, and I alone am left; and they seek my life.' (4) But what does the divine oracle say to him? 'I have left myself 7000 men who have not bowed the knee to Baal.' (5) So also at the present time there has come into being such a remnant, based on a gracious act of election. (6) But note that if this act is done by grace it does not depend on works; otherwise grace would no longer be grace.[1] (7) What then? What Israel seeks after, Israel did not attain – but the elect remnant attained it, while the rest were hardened, (8) as it is written, 'God gave them a spirit of slumber, eyes not to see and ears not to hear, up to this day'. (9) And David says, 'Let their table become a snare and a trap, an offence and a recompense to them; (10) let their eyes be darkened so as not to see; bow down their backs for ever'.

If Israel is a disobedient and contradicting people (x. 21), totally unresponsive to God's appeals, it might seem that God has no recourse but to wash his hands of her. And at first glance this appears to be what has happened, for the rejection of Israel has been shown to be no accident of history but God's eternal plan, foretold in Scripture. But this would be far too simple a reading of the circumstances. The Old Testament contains far more than predictions of Israel's fall.

1   With all this (x. 14–21) in mind, I am bound to ask this question, Has God cast off his people? The language of this verse (and of *v.* 2) is based on Ps. xciv. 14. The question is raised again at *v.* 11. It is similar to that of iii. 3 and a special form of ix. 6. God's foreknowledge and election of Israel are expressed in his word, and, if the foreknowledge proved to be in error and the election were revoked, God's word would indeed have fallen to the ground and lost all credibility. The answer here is as clear as in the other passages: **Certainly not.** It may be established on theological grounds (as in iii. 3), but here Paul bases it upon a simple matter of fact, **Why, I myself am an Israelite, of the seed of Abraham, of the tribe of Benjamin.**

It is possible that by these words Paul means, 'God cast off his people? How could I, a Jew myself, even entertain such a thought?'; but it is much more likely that he means, 'God cannot have cast off his people (as a whole), for I myself am both a Jew and a Christian; this proves that Christian Jews may exist'. The answer is based not on

---

1 The text translated here is that of P[46] ℵ A D G lat. B ω pesh add 'But if it depends on works it is no longer grace; otherwise the work is no longer work (B has, no longer grace)'. This is almost certainly a secondary expansion, intended to complete the sense but in fact obscuring it.

national pride (which, though some have thought so, plays no part in these chapters) but on the historical facts of the Christian mission, which Paul throughout his argument does not lose sight of. They are so intertwined with his theological interpretation that it is impossible to assign priority to either.

In other passages Paul speaks of his Jewish origin: 2 Cor. xi. 22; Phil. iii. 5 f.; also Gal. i. 13 f.; ii. 15. Compare also Acts xxii. 3; xxiii. 6; xxvi. 5. He mentions it here, without boasting (ii. 17), as a fact relevant to his argument. The word 'seed' is used without the special sense it has in ix. 7; Paul means simply, 'descended from Abraham'.

The existence of Jewish Christians, such as Paul, proves that **God 2 has not cast off his people, whom he foreknew.** For God's foreknowledge compare viii. 29. Paul refers to the many passages in the Old Testament which speak of God's election of Israel to be his own people in a special sense (see on ix. 5). God will not go back on his ancient choice (cf. *v.* 29). See on *v.* 1.

The existence of Jewish Christians is not a full answer to Paul's problem, since they are a small minority of the nation as a whole. This very fact, however, suggests a line for advance. There are important Old Testament precedents for the presence of such a minority within an apostate people. Of these, Paul quotes only one. As early as the time of Elijah and the national apostasy under Ahab there remained a faithful remnant.

Do you not know what the Scripture says in the story of Elijah (literally, *in Elijah*, a curious expression which reflects a usage of Rabbinic Hebrew), **how he appeals to God** (Paul's word, ἐντυγχά- νειν, often has the sense 'to intercede' (e.g. viii. 27, 34); but in itself it means only 'to have dealings with', and takes its sense from the context) **against Israel?** '**Lord,**' he says, '**they have killed thy 3 prophets, they have digged down thine altars, and I alone am left; and they seek my life.**' Paul gives the sense of 1 Kings xix. 10. So far the story seems to speak of a uniformly successful revolt against God. Only Elijah has resisted it, and he will soon be dead. But this, though it was Elijah's own impression of the situation, was false. **What does 4 the divine oracle say to him? 'I have left myself 7000 men who have not bowed the knee to Baal.'** Again Paul gives the sense, rather than the words, of 1 Kings xix. 18. Elijah was not alone; 7000 other Israelites were as faithful as he. The nation was not totally apostate; a substantial proportion had kept faith.

So much for the historical illustration. The application is clear. **So 5 also at the present time** (see on iii. 26) **there has come into being such a remnant.** It is impossible to bring out in English the fact that the Greek word for 'remnant' (λεῖμμα) is cognate with the verb 'to leave' (*v.* 4, κατέλιπον); in the translation, the word 'such' is introduced in order to make the connection. The body of Jewish

Christians, exceptions to the general unbelief of their race, form a group analogous with the 7000 who refused to worship Baal.

At this point Paul introduces, in *vv.* 5 b, 6, what at first sight appears to be a parenthesis. In fact, like some other similar notes (e.g. iii. 28), it proves to contain the core of the argument, emphasizing his primary contention, that God's dealings with men are based not upon works but upon grace. The remnant was **based on a gracious act of election** (literally, according to election of grace, κατ' ἐκλογὴν χάριτος). For election, see on ix. 11. The existence of a remnant – a nation within a nation – can be due only to an act of choice (ἐκλέγεσθαι), and the choice (ἐκλογή) must therefore have sprung from God's freedom, or grace. Thus 'remnant' is a word that spells grace, as the distinction (see ch. ix) between Isaac and Ishmael, Jacob and Esau, spells mercy. In itself the remnant is not 'better' than the rest of Israel, any more than Isaac was 'better' than Ishmael, or Jacob than Esau; but it consists of the 'vessels of mercy' (ix. 23), whom God chose as the vehicles of his glory.

6   **But note** (Paul develops the point for his readers' better understanding of the whole matter) **that if this act is done by grace it does not depend on works; otherwise grace would no longer be grace.** As the last clause shows, Paul is here defining his terms rather than offering a constructive argument. If you confuse such opposites as faith and works, then words will simply lose their meaning. Paul does not, of course, deny that the remnant had performed 'works of law' – he had performed many himself (Gal. i. 14; Phil. iii. 6) – but insists that the election was not *dependent* upon them, since God's choices are eternal as he is eternal, and the election is therefore antecedent to all works. That is why it is by grace. Thus the logical basis of the latter part of the verse ('grace would no longer be grace') may be said to rest upon a time-sequence: election cannot take place both before and after the performance of works.

But it is time to return to direct consideration of the theological significance of the paradoxical events of the primitive Christian 7 mission. **What then?** Paul pulls himself back into line with a rhetorical question. **What Israel seeks after, Israel did not attain – but the elect remnant attained it, while the rest were hardened.** The object of 'seeks after' and 'attained' is nowhere expressed, but may be supplied from ix. 30 ff.; x. 3. It is, in the last resort, righteousness, the proper relation between man and God (or people and God), in which alone are life and salvation. This righteousness they sought by means of the 'law of righteousness', but this they had misunderstood, supposing (as Paul himself had done – Phil. iii. 9) that it was to be achieved by a faultless performance of works, whereas the law itself, correctly understood, required faith. Paul has already said that Israel as a whole has, through seeking it by means of works, failed to achieve this goal, though the Gentiles, who, in the nature of the case, could reach it by faith alone, had achieved it. He now adds to the Gentiles, and subtracts from the people as a whole, the elect remnant, who also, like the Gentiles, attained it, not because they had not shared in Israel's error – Paul had shared it to the full – but because they had learned to count their gains loss and to receive it as part of the act of grace by which they were constituted.

The rest of Israel (that is, Israel less the remnant) stood outside this relation and consequently were 'hardened'. For this important biblical word compare *v.* 25; ix. 18 (a different word in Greek); and Isa. vi. 10. It is incorrect to stress the use of the passive voice – 'they were hardened' – as if Paul were unwilling to commit himself to the view that God himself had hardened men. If they were hardened, it was because someone hardened them, and there is no doubt who is the subject of the active verb in the next verse. Moreover, the use of a passive instead of an active verb with God as subject is a common Jewish reverential expedient for avoiding the use of the divine name. It is impossible here to distinguish between 'hardened because disobedient' and 'disobedient because hardened'; the two processes are concurrent. Because those Israelites who were not of the remnant stood outside the relation of grace, the more they sought righteousness (as all Jews did – x. 3) the further they fell away from it. Their religious enthusiasm was turned to sin. Paul does not shrink from the conclusion that it was God's will (determined ultimately by his mercy) that this should be so, and confirms the conclusion by Old Testament quotations.

They were hardened, **as it is written, 'God gave them a spirit of** 8 **slumber, eyes not to see and ears not to hear, up to this day'.** Paul sharpens Deut. xxix. 4 by placing the negative with the infinitives, instead of with 'gave'.

And David says, 'Let their table become a snare and a trap, an 9 **offence and a recompense to them; let their eyes be darkened so** 10 **as not to see; bow down their backs for ever'** (Ps. lxix. 22 f.). It was no doubt the reference to unseeing eyes that attracted Paul to the passage, and he probably understood the obscure words about their 'table' and their 'backs' in a corresponding sense. Their table is their table-fellowship: the unity and interrelatedness created by the law and so highly valued in Judaism were no more than a delusion since they were a union in sin (iii. 20), not righteousness. The bent back is a symbol of bondage; compare Gal. iv. 25.

It seems that Paul has reached his conclusion. The answer to the question of xi. 1 is that God has not cast off his people *as a whole*; he has hardened and cast off some, but he will save an elect remnant. Paul however cannot leave the matter there.

29 THE UNFOLDING OF GOD'S PLAN
CHAPTER xi. 11–24

(11) I must repeat my question then: Did they stumble so as to fall altogether? Certainly not. What has happened is this. By their stumble, salvation has come to the Gentiles, in order to provoke them (the Jews) to envy. (12) But if their stumble has thus come to mean the wealth of the world, and the cutting down of their numbers has led to the wealth of the Gentiles, it will mean so much more when their numbers are again brought up to full strength.

(13) Now I am speaking to you Gentiles. Precisely because I am a Gentile-apostle, I make much of my office, (14) to see if I may provoke to envy my own flesh and blood, and so save some of them. (15) For if their rejection has resulted in the reconciliation of the world, what will their acceptance be but life from the dead? (16) If the first-fruit is holy, so also is the lump; and if the root is holy, so also are the branches.

(17) But if some of the branches were broken off, and you, a wild olive, were grafted in among them and became a partaker in the rich root of the olive tree,[1] (18) do not boast over the branches; and if you do boast, it is still true that it is not you who bear the root, but the root that bears you. (19) You may say, 'Branches were broken off that I might be grafted in'. (20) True enough: it was for unbelief that they were broken off, and it is by faith that you stand. There is nothing for you to grow boastful about; you should rather show reverent fear. (21) For if God did not spare those that were branches by nature, no more will he spare you.[2] (22) See then God's kindness and severity; severity for those who have fallen, God's kindness for you, if you continue in his kindness; otherwise you too will be cut away. (23) And they too, if they do not continue in their unbelief, will be grafted in, for God is able to graft them in again. (24) For if you were cut out of that which by nature is a wild olive and – contrary to nature –

---

1 'In the rich root of the olive tree'; literally, this is 'of the root of the richness of the olive tree'. This string of genitives was too much for many copyists. Some MSS have 'of the richness of the olive tree' (P[46] D G it Irenaeus), others 'of the root and of the richness of the olive tree' (A ω vg pesh). But the difficult reading is not impossible, and should be adopted. The genitive τῆς πιότητος, *of the richness*, may be taken to be adjectival.

2 'No more will he spare you'. Many MSS (P[46] D G ω lat pesh Irenaeus) read 'lest he spare not you', supplying presumably, out of v. 20, 'one may well fear . . .'. It has been suggested that this is the correct reading, since it is so well supported, gives characteristically Pauline irony, and is the more difficult reading. But *v.* 20 c (You should show reverent fear) is parenthetical, and it is unlikely that it should be followed up in this way. The variant seems to be a secondary weakening of Paul's warning.

grafted into the cultivated olive, so much more will they, who belong by nature to the cultivated olive, be grafted into their own olive tree.

The Old Testament quotations at the end of the preceding paragraph (*vv.* 8 ff.) led Paul a little astray from his point. The paragraph as a whole was designed to prove that God had not finally rejected his people, because, as at other critical junctures in Israel's history, there existed an elect remnant, which owed its standing solely to grace yet stood between the people as a whole and complete apostasy. But the final quotations said nothing of a remnant, but spoke only of the blinding of Israel. Since he has thus been diverted from his theme, Paul is compelled to return to the question of *v.* 1, which he now expresses in other terms. The remnant does not exist simply for its own sake. The essence of the paragraph is contained in *vv.* 11, 12.

I must repeat my question then: Did they stumble so as to fall 11 **altogether?** There is no doubt that the Jews, or the majority of them, have stumbled (cf. ix. 32 f.) and lost their place; the Gentiles are overhauling them. But does this mean that they are now out of the race? that they are for ever outside the sphere of salvation? It is probable that some Christians gave a positive answer to this question; there are passages in the gospels which suggest this (e.g. Matt. xxi. 43; xxvii. 25). But this was not Paul's solution of the problem. He answers his own question: **Certainly not.** What then of the facts? The defection of the Jews is temporary, and while it lasts serves a definite and important purpose.

What has happened is this. By their stumble (elsewhere this word – παράπτωμα – means 'transgression' but here it must be given its more obvious etymological sense), **salvation has come to the Gentiles, in order to provoke them (the Jews) to envy.** 'Has come' is the simplest but perhaps not the happiest of possible translations here, for Paul does not abandon his usual view, that salvation is a future event (see pp. 28 f., 100); but some such word must be supplied (no verb is expressed in the Greek) in order to make clear that Paul is describing a state of affairs which has actually come about in history. It could be said, more fully but more clumsily, that salvation has become a sure hope for the Gentiles because they have already been justified through faith. It was the failure of the mission to the Jews that led to the mission to the Gentiles (cf. Acts xiii. 46; xviii. 6; xxviii. 28), who were thereby brought within the scope of salvation and through the Gospel received the assurance that in due time they would possess it (xiii. 11–14).

This was the immediate result of the Jewish apostasy; it had, however, a further purpose. The inclusion of the Gentiles would provoke the Jews to envy. Paul here alludes to the Old Testament passage (Deut. xxxii. 21) which he quoted at x. 19. There was foreshadowed the argument which is to be developed in this paragraph: Israel, seeking to fulfil by works the law of righteousness, did not believe; the Gospel was accordingly sent to the Gentiles, who accepted righteousness by faith. So far Paul can use past tenses; the next stages must be expressed in terms of purpose and hope. Israel will be provoked to envy by the Gentile attainment of righteousness, and so fly to God's mercy, so that God may in the end bestow righteousness upon her too. The details of this scheme will be unfolded as we proceed.

The point we have reached at present is that by the Jews' stumble the Gentiles have come to be included within the scope of salvation.

12 **But if their stumble has thus come to mean the wealth of the world, and the cutting down of their numbers has led to the wealth of the Gentiles, it will mean so much more when their numbers are again brought up to full strength.** For the verse as a whole compare *v.* 15. It sums up the content of chapters ix–xi.

The translation of this verse is disputed. The first clause is reasonably clear. Of the Jews' *stumble* we have already heard (*v.* 11), and seen that through it salvation reached the Gentiles. The only true wealth was thus conferred upon the whole world. In the second clause, it is made explicit that the beneficiaries are Gentiles; but what happens to Israel? Paul uses a word (ἥττημα), which in strict etymology is derived from a verb (ἡττᾶσθαι) meaning 'defeat'. Accordingly some commentators, quoting Isa. xxxi. 8, translate, 'their defeat has led to the wealth of the Gentiles'. But, whatever may be the witness of etymology, Paul is not here speaking of a defeat of Israel, but of a diminution of their numbers by the rejection of all save a remnant, and it is possible that he (wrongly, no doubt) derived his word from a comparative (ἥττων), meaning 'inferior', 'less', 'smaller'. It is probable that he already has in mind the word (πλήρωμα) translated later in the verse as 'full strength', and required an opposite.

In the third clause, Paul uses a word (πλήρωμα) which is here taken to mean 'full strength', 'complement'. This seems to yield excellent sense (especially when taken with the interpretation of the second clause advocated above), and is consistent with Paul's usage (e.g. *v.* 25; Gal. iv. 4); but some, comparing xiii. 10 (love is the *complete fulfilment* of the law), think that it means, 'when they fulfil the will of God'. That is, Israel's sin has conferred a benefit upon mankind; so much more will their obedience. This is less probable because throughout the chapter Paul is dealing with the totality of Israel, its reduction to a remnant, and its return to totality.

The details of this verse may thus remain in some obscurity, but its main point is clear. Paul looks beyond the advantages conferred on the

Gentiles by the unbelief of Israel to the far greater eschatological bliss which Israel's return will inaugurate. But he is not for the moment addressing himself to Jews and their fortunes. **Now I am speaking to** 13 **you Gentiles** – and Gentiles might think that a long discussion of the remnant of Israel had little to do with them. Paul points out the significance of his work and of his exposition of it. He may also have been answering Jews who complained that in preaching to Gentiles he was wrongly neglecting his own people. **Precisely because I am a Gentile-apostle** (that is, an apostle appointed to preach to Gentiles), **I make much of my office, to see if I may provoke to envy my own** 14 **flesh and blood, and so save some of them.** For Paul's special commission to 'go unto the Gentiles' see especially Gal. i. 16; ii. 7, 9; also Acts ix. 15; xxii. 21; xxvi. 17. The drift of his argument appears to be: I know I am the 'Gentile-apostle', and I know that I am speaking to Gentiles (cf. i. 5, and note). Yet my concern for my fellow-Jews is not derogatory to or inconsistent with my office; in fact, my work among Gentiles – because it is work among Gentiles – is connected with the Jews. The more I make of my Gentile mission the more jealous will the Jews become, and this will lead in the end to what I desire – their salvation.

Paul's hope here seems surprisingly limited, ' . . . and so save *some* of them'. Out of the provocation of Israel as a whole ('my flesh and blood') there may come a few conversions. There is a close parallel in 1 Cor. ix. 22, which illuminates the meaning of 'save', and thus of the verse as a whole. Cf. also 1 Cor. vii. 16. 'Save' here means 'bring to the Christian faith', that is, 'convert'. Evidently, though Paul can hope for the final salvation of all Israel (*v.* 26), he does not hope for it in terms of the actual conversion of all individual Israelites; salvation of them all is a mysterious eschatological event, which is only prefigured in occasional personal conversions.

These conversions, however, few though they may be, truly point to the full return of Israel, which is part of the total hope not of that race only but of the world. **For if their rejection has resulted in the** 15 **reconciliation of the world, what will their acceptance be but life from the dead?** For *reconciliation* in Paul's teaching see v. 10 f., and the notes. Here the idea is perhaps limited (cf. Eph. ii. 16) to the reconciliation of Jew and Gentile in one new people of God. Or it may be that the 'world' means the 'Gentile world'; the meaning would then be that, through the estrangement of Israel the Gentiles have been reconciled to God.

Reconciliation, issuing in peace with God, is in origin an eschatological term, though like other eschatological terms it has been subjected to a Christian revaluation: 'life from the dead' is another such term, and must not be understood in a pietistic sense. Paul means that the final return of Israel (*v.* 26) will be the signal for the resurrection, the last stage of the eschatological process initiated by the death and resurrection of Jesus. The full conversion of Israel therefore stands on the boundary of history.

The next verse forms the transition from *vv.* 11–15 to the elaborate allegory of the olive tree in *vv.* 17–24, though the connection with the latter is verbal rather than substantial. Paul is arguing for the certainty of the ultimate salvation of Israel, but, as will appear, the exact basis of his argument is not clear.

16   **If the first fruit** (ἀπαρχή) **is holy, so also is the lump** (φύραμα). The origin of the metaphor is to be found in Num. xv. 18–21: Of the first (LXX: ἀπαρχήν, the first-fruits) of your dough (LXX: φυράματος, lump) ye shall offer up a cake for an heave offering . . . Of the first of your dough ye shall give unto the Lord an heave offering throughout your generations. See also Neh. x. 37; Ezek. xliv. 30. The dedication of the first-fruit loaf released the whole for general consumption; in fact, it would be not inaccurate to say, in terms of primitive religion, that the sanctification of the first-fruit loaf 'de-sanctified' the remainder and so made it available for common use. But Paul's meaning is clear, even though technically open to objection. The pious Israelite might well feel that the bread he ate, though not sacrificial bread, was sanctified by that which had been taken from it for holy purposes. *God* intends that the people shall have their bread; *they* recognize that, though they have made it, it comes from him.

A second metaphor follows. **If the root is holy, so also are the branches.** The meaning is the same. You cannot divide a living organism, such as a tree; the trunk and branches which grow from holy roots must themselves be holy.

So much for the metaphors. What does Paul intend them to convey? That the 'lump' and the 'branches' signify Israel as a whole is clear. Many commentators, drawing *v.* 28 into comparison, suppose that 'first-fruit' and 'root' signify the fathers of the Jewish race. This, however, is not the most probable interpretation. Paul is not yet speaking of the relation of Israel to the patriarchs, but of the remnant; as we have just seen (on *v.* 14) he regards the few Jewish Christians as the pledge of the eventual salvation of all Israel. This is precisely what he brings out metaphorically in this verse, if 'first-fruit' and 'root' refer to the Jewish Christians. This seems the most likely view, though it is not impossible that behind the Jewish Christians Paul sees the figure of Christ himself, whom he actually describes as the 'first-fruit' in 1 Cor. xv. 20. There is Rabbinic precedent for describing Adam as the 'first-fruit loaf',[1] and as Adam was the head of the old humanity so Christ was head of the new (v. 12–21; cf. 1 Cor. xv. 21 ff., 48 f.). If Paul is thinking here of Christ himself as the first-fruits he is

1 See S.B., iv. 667 f.

only sharpening a thought which is in any case inherent in his argument: the fact that first-fruits and root exist is in itself a mark of God's grace; no claim upon him is established.

It is the root and branch metaphor that suggests to Paul the allegory of the olive tree. This is inserted (cf. *v.* 13) mainly for the benefit of Gentiles. Their own place in the saving process is described, and when Paul speaks also of that of the Jews it is in the first instance for the better understanding, and consequent humility, of the Gentiles. One remark on the allegory as a whole may be made here. Paul knows, and explicitly states, that he is describing a process that is contrary to nature (*v.* 24). The conclusion sometimes drawn that he was a townsman unfamiliar with country life and agricultural practices is therefore absurd. It is equally wide of the mark to suggest that he was too careless or unskilful to handle his metaphor correctly. He is speaking not of nature but of grace, and his metaphor takes its origin not in husbandry but in theological and historical fact. Whether, or how far, in this it resembles or differs from the gospel parables is a question which cannot be handled here. Paul at least is not deducing theology from natural processes. There is no argument from nature to grace.

But if some of the branches were broken off, and you, a wild 17 **olive, were grafted in among them and became a partaker in the rich root of the olive tree, do not boast over the branches.** The 18 language is technical, even though the process is 'contrary to nature' (*v.* 24). The branches broken off are of course unbelieving Jews; the wild olive branches grafted in are believing (i.e. Christian) Gentiles, who henceforth belong to the main stock of the people of God. As such they enjoy the privileges and benefits described as the 'rich root of the olive tree' (for this phrase see p. 196, n. 1). In practice these amount to the supernatural life of the people of God in the last age, alluded to in ch. vi. These privileges, however, give the Gentile Christian no ground for boasting over the unbelieving Jew, for he possesses them by grace, not by right, still less by merit. Moreover, **if you do boast, it is still true that** (these words are inserted to fill a gap in a sentence which, in Greek, is elliptical, and meaningless if translated literally) **it is not you who bear the root, but the root that bears you.** In other words, the Jews really are the people of God, because the Old Testament really is true (cf. iii. 2 f.). Christian Jews are not grafted into paganism, but Christian Gentiles are grafted into Israel. Accordingly, the Gentile who feels disposed to boast (the Greek present tense can bear this meaning) should remember not only that he stands by grace alone but also that the privilege he has acquired is – that of being an Israelite. But he is not yet silenced.

You may say ... no doubt Gentile Christians had said this. Again 19 the style recalls that of the diatribe (see p. 41). **'Branches were**

broken off that I might be grafted in'. The implication is, 'God prefers me (a Gentile) to the Jews'. To the statement of fact, but not to 20 the implication, Paul replies, **True enough: it was for unbelief that they were broken off, and it is by faith that you stand.** The mission to and inclusion of the Gentiles did not take place because God had grown tired of the Jews and wished for a change. The Jewish 'branches' were broken off because they did not believe (x. 16 f.); the Gentile 'branches' were grafted in not because they were superior in religion or morals (they were not) but because they received the Gospel with faith. **There is nothing** here **for you to grow boastful about; you should rather show reverent fear.**

'To grow boastful' (ὑψηλὰ φρονεῖν): the same expression is used at xii. 16, but in a different sense. What is common to the two is the idea of being 'above oneself'. The proper attitude for the Gentile Christian, as indeed for any Christian, is 'reverent fear', for he must recognize that there is in himself absolutely nothing which can secure his position with God. The moment he begins to grow boastful he ceases to have faith (humble dependence upon God), and therefore himself 21 becomes a candidate for 'cutting off'. **For if God did not spare those that were branches by nature, no more will he spare you.** The fault of the Jews lay in their boastfulness and self-confidence (ii. 17 f.); if the Gentiles fall into the same ways they will share the same fate. There is no hope, no peace, and no security for man but in faith only.

22   The whole process is a revelation of the nature of God. **See then God's kindness and severity; severity for those who have fallen, God's kindness for you, if you continue in his kindness; otherwise you too will be cut away.** Kindness and severity are equally attributes of God, just as grace and wrath are equally activities of God. Paul does not mean that God is kind and severe in an arbitrary way (though this is what a superficial reading of his account of God's dealings might suggest). God is always God; his kindness and his severity are correlates of faith and unbelief (*v.* 20), for it was on account of unbelief that some (the rejected Jews) 'fell', and it was on account of faith that believing Gentiles were attributed to Israel. This correlation appears clearly from the fact that both the kindness and the severity are reversible. For 'you', the kindness lasts – as long as you abide in it. The meaning of this is given by ii. 4 f. To abide in God's kindness is to continue in repentance and faith; an unrepentant heart turns kindness to severity. If the Christian Gentile treats his privileges as the Jew formerly treated his, then he too will be cut out of the olive tree.

23   This process also operates in the reverse direction. **And they too, if they do not continue in their unbelief, will be grafted in.** It was unbelief that excluded them; when unbelief is gone, exclusion is at an end. When the unrepentant heart repents and accepts God's judge-

ment whatever it be, severity becomes kindness. This is not to say that man can at any time determine his own acceptance or rejection with God; they will be grafted in because **God is able to graft them in again.** Why should he not? To graft branches once cut from a cultivated olive back into a cultivated olive is a far more natural process than grafting branches of wild olive into a cultivated olive. **For if you were cut out of that which by nature is a wild olive and –** **– 24** **contrary to nature – grafted into the cultivated olive, so much more will they, who belong by nature to the cultivated olive, be grafted into their own olive tree.** It will be easier – if such things can be compared – to bring back to the holy people a Jew born into the covenants of grace, endowed with the law (which did after all bear witness to the manifestation of God's righteousness by grace through faith – iii. 21), and instructed by the messianic prophecies, than to introduce for the first time a Gentile whose only advantage was the dim vestige of religion which warned him that the world of which he was part was not his but God's (i. 20).

It is at this point that Paul reminds his readers that the process he is describing is an unnatural one. Certainly, in historical terms it is a very strange one. Almighty God chooses a people to be his own: to know and serve him, and to represent him in the world. His relations with them are determined entirely by grace, but they use the law he has given them to pervert these relations; legal relations, they think, will give them greater freedom. Accordingly, when God, in fulfilment of his promise, sends them his Son, they reject and kill him. The message of this gracious act is now taken beyond the chosen people to the Gentiles, some of whom accept it, and take advantage of the universal act of grace performed in the death and resurrection of Jesus to enter into gracious relations with God (that is, to be justified by faith). The chosen people who have now (with few exceptions) lost their position see Gentiles standing in that relation with God which they once enjoyed, are stung to envy and to repentance, and so return not to supplant but to join the Gentiles in the relation of grace. All these events are to be regarded as due to the sovereign freedom and elective purpose of God himself.

When the story is told in this way it is difficult not to conclude that the kindness and severity of God are disposed in arbitrary fashion. But it must be remembered that Paul – inevitably, in view of his belief that the purposes of God would in a very short time be brought to a full close – writes in what must be called a mythological manner; that is, he expresses what he has to say about God and his eternal purposes in historical, or quasi-historical, terms. History did not come to an end when he thought it would do so, and it is consistent with this fact that the reunion of Jew and Gentile within one Church or people has not taken place. History still runs its course, and it is a course which

neither Paul nor any other in the first century was able to foresee. But
two points are clear. (i) The matters on which Paul commits himself
are truths which lie beyond history, because they are truths about
God. It will be recalled that, on p. 160, it was pointed out that his
doctrine of predestination implies a 'qualitative definition' rather than
a 'quantitative limitation' of God's action. God is kind and God is
severe; when we view him through Jesus Christ we see his kindness,
when we try to approach him in some other way – through, for
example, a legalistic religion – we see his severity. (This point is
developed in the next paragraph). (ii) When the meta-historical truths
with which Paul is concerned impinge upon history, they do so, in
every generation, in the pattern Paul describes. For him, it was an
affair of Jew and Gentile; but, though it will always need the Old
Testament to give it force, precision, and a firm anchorage in history,
Paul's account of the affair issues in a picture of the religious and the
irreligious man. The former lives in an atmosphere which should
constantly remind him that God is in heaven and he upon earth
(Eccles. v. 2); but in this atmosphere he makes himself at home and
domesticates his God. The irreligious man stumbles by accident (as he
may think) upon the terror and the grace of God, and supplants his
brother, because he knows he has no virtue and no piety to offer to his
Maker, but trusts the grace he has glimpsed in Christ. And the
religious man, or Pharisee, learns with painful inward struggle that he
must divest himself of his pride, count his gains loss and his boasts
dung, in order to be found in Christ, with a righteousness not of his
own fabrication but from God (Phil. iii. 8 f.).

30 GOD'S PLAN COMPLETE

CHAPTER xi. 25–32

(25) For, brethren, I do not wish you not to know this divine
secret, lest you be wise – in your own conceit. The secret is that a
partial hardening has fallen upon Israel, and will remain until
the full number of the Gentiles has come in; (26) when this is
done, all Israel will be saved, as it is written, 'Out of Zion shall
come a deliverer, and he shall remove from Jacob all his
impieties; (27) and this is the covenant I will make with them,
when I take away their sins'. (28) As far as the present results of
the preaching of the Gospel go, they are enemies – for your
advantage; when you bear in mind the fact of God's election, they
are beloved, on account of the fathers; (29) for God does not go
back on his acts of grace and his calling. (30) For as you formerly
were disobedient to God, but now (corresponding to their
disobedience) have received his mercy, (31) so they also now

**(corresponding to the mercy you have received) have become
disobedient, in order that they too may now[1] receive God's
mercy. (32) For God has shut up all men to disobedience, in order
that he may deal with all men in mercy.**

The allegory of the olive tree ended, Paul sets out *expressis verbis* the
mystery of the divine purpose, and draws to a close the long discussion
of chs. ix–xi. Two words are significant for the meaning of the
paragraph as a whole: secret and mercy. What Paul describes is not a
simple historical process already visible to the human eye. It can be
perceived and understood only by divine revelation. In due course it
will be worked out on the plane of history, but so far it is a mystery
concealed in heaven and disclosed only to the elect (see on *v.* 25). The
meaning of the secret is God's mercy. His treatment of the Gentiles (i.
18–32) and of the Jews (ii. 17–24; ix. 32 f.; xi. 7–10), when viewed
simply on the historical plane so far as history has yet run its course,
may seem to spell anything but mercy – wrath, judgement, vengeance,
neglect (cf. iii. 25). But when God is all in all, he will be recognized
as – God who has mercy (ix. 16), and already this truth is declared in
the Gospel.

This piece of Pauline apocalyptic is not set in motion by the desire
to parade 'visions and revelations' (2 Cor. xii. 1), or by mere curiosity
about the future and the number of the saved. As is usual with Paul,
the motivation is practical; he is repeating and clarifying *vv.* 11, 12.
For (that is, I have given you this allegory of the olive tree *because*), 25
brethren, I do not wish you not to know (cf. i. 13) **this divine
secret, lest you be wise – in your own conceit.** Paul is still
addressing Gentiles (*v.* 13), who might be inclined to mock at
unbelieving Israel, and to congratulate themselves upon their adher-
ence to the Gospel. How much wiser they had been than the Jews,
who had rejected it! But the man who thus congratulates himself is
wise only in his own estimation (cf. xii. 16; Prov. iii. 7). He fails to
recognize (a) that the acceptance of the Gospel implies no merit on his
part but is by faith only (*v.* 20); (b) that his faith is itself the result of
God's initiative and mercy (ix. 16); and (c) that his faith and inclusion
within the people of God are but one provisional (see *v.* 21) stage in
the unfolding of God's complete and all-embracing purpose.

From this self-delusion the Gentile may be delivered by the
disclosure of God's secret, or mystery. This word is used again at xvi.
25, but in a somewhat different sense; there it refers to the whole plan
of salvation in Jesus Christ which was kept secret until the proper

---

1 'Now', which is found in B ℵ D*, is omitted by P[46] A G ω; 33 sah substitute
'subsequently'. 'Now' is a very difficult, but Pauline, reading (see the notes),
and the variants must be regarded as secondary 'improvements'.

moment of revelation. At 2 Thess. ii. 7 it is the 'mystery of iniquity'; at Col. i. 26 f. it recalls Rom. xvi. 25 and the present passage. The most illuminating parallel, however, is 1 Cor. xv. 51, where the mystery is an apocalyptic secret, which the seer is able to make known for the enlightenment of the elect. Here Paul imparts to his readers the secret which makes sense of the otherwise inexplicable course of the last age.

The content of the secret, hinted at in *vv.* 7, 12, and in the allegory, is now stated. **The secret is that a partial hardening has fallen upon Israel, and will remain until the full number of the Gentiles has come in; when this is done, all Israel will be saved.** 'Partial' renders a phrase which recurs in xv. 15, 24; 2 Cor. i. 14; it may be adjectival (as, apparently, here), or adverbial. The 'hardening' (cf. *v.* 7) was only partial, since there was a remnant that believed; that is, the hardening was *partial* in the sense that it was only a part (though the larger part) of Israel that was hardened. Through this hardening arose the Gentile mission (*vv.* 11, 28), and it will continue until its purpose is complete. But what does the 'full number of the Gentiles' mean? From *v.* 12 it appears that it must mean 'totality' or 'complement'; but this might mean either 'all Gentiles that ever were born' or 'all Gentiles intended by God to belong to the elect'. Only the context as a whole can decide between these alternatives, which indeed cannot be taken as strict alternatives, since the 'number intended by God' might be identical with the 'total number'.

Paul continues with the assertion that *all Israel will be saved.* This sentence contains two problems. It is introduced by the words *And so* (καὶ οὕτως). This may be taken in one of three ways: (1) it may simply express continuity of operation; (2) it may mean, At that time (when the full number of Gentiles has come in); (3) it may mean, In this way (as the effect of God's calling of the Gentiles). It suits the context to combine (2) and (3), which are quite compatible: When the Gentiles, because the Gentiles, have been included in God's people. The second problem is the meaning of *All Israel.* In what sense does Paul mean 'all Israel'? 'Israel as a whole' or 'each several Israelite'? There is an interesting parallel to Paul's words in *Sanhedrin*, x. 1: All Israelites have a share in the world to come. This statement certainly does not refer to each several Israelite, for it proceeds to enumerate a long list of exceptions: from 'all Israel' must be subtracted all Sadducees, heretics, magicians, the licentious, and many more. It means that Israel as a whole is destined for eternal life in the Age to Come. This, of course, does not prove that Paul's meaning was the same; but when his two statements, about Gentiles and Jews, are taken together, it seems probable that he is thinking in representative terms (see on the rest of this paragraph, and on xv. 19); first the remnant of Israel, then Gentiles, finally Israel as a whole.

That Israel will be delivered, by the removal of sin, is proved from Scripture: **as it is written, 'Out of Zion shall come a deliverer, and he shall remove from Jacob all his** (these two words are a sense-addition to the Greek – it is clearly not intended that the deliverer will remove only some, or some other) **impieties; and this is the 27 covenant I will make with them, when I take away their sins'.** This is a composite quotation, from Isa. lix. 20 and xxvii. 9; compare Ps. xiv. 7; Jer. xxxi. 33. It may be (cf. ix. 33) that Paul drew it from a Testimony Book, or that he himself, subconsciously perhaps, combined the two passages.

The two verses make the same point: God has not done with Israel, but is preparing a new covenant of salvation in which Israel's sins will be done away. It is because Scripture itself affirms this that Paul can predict that 'all Israel will be saved'.

The paragraph is brought to an end with two balanced sentences, each constructed on the same pattern. Each contains a pair of antithetical clauses explained by a 'for' (γάρ) clause. Thus:

$$
\begin{cases}
\text{A – Enemies, for your advantage } (v.\ 28) \\
\text{B – Beloved, on account of the fathers } (v.\ 28)
\end{cases}
$$
$$\text{C – For God does not} \ldots (v.\ 29)$$
$$
\begin{cases}
\text{A' – You once} \ldots \text{but now } (v.\ 30) \\
\text{B' – They now} \ldots \text{but now } (v.\ 31)
\end{cases}
$$
$$\text{C' – For God has shut up} \ldots (v.\ 32)$$

The rhetorical pattern suggests that Paul is writing with care as well as feeling, and his words must be carefully marked.

In relation to God the Jews are at the present time both enemies and beloved. **As far as the present results of the preaching of the 28 Gospel go, they are enemies – for your advantage.** This is simply a statement of the facts which have already been described. The Gospel was preached to the Jews, and they rejected it, thereby placing themselves under God's wrath, since the law, which they preferred to the way of faith, produces wrath (iv. 15). Their rejection of the Gospel, however, led to the mission to the Gentiles, and thereby turned out to be to the advantage of the Gentiles. But this is not the whole truth; **when you bear in mind the fact of God's election, they are beloved, on account of the fathers.** 'If some have proved unbelieving, will their unbelief make void the faithfulness of God?' (iii. 3). They are the race whom God elected to be his peculiar people, and their election rests in no way upon their merits or achievements. It is true that when Paul says that they are beloved 'on account of the fathers' his language recalls the Rabbinic doctrine of the merit (*zᵉkuth*) of the fathers, which forms a treasury upon which their sinful descendants can draw; but the resemblance is only superficial, for

Paul is not speaking of human merit but of divine election. To say that they are loved *because* they are their fathers' children would contradict chapter ix. The key is the *fact of God's election* (κατὰ τὴν ἐκλογήν). It is not the merits of the fathers but God's electing grace that is in question. Paul proceeds to underline this.

29   **For God does not go back on his acts of grace** (for this meaning of the word–χάρισμα–see on v. 16) **and his calling.** This is the explanation not simply of God's love for Israel, but also of the paradoxical fact that the same people may be at the same time enemies and beloved. It is at this point also that we may go back to ix. 6–13 and take up Paul's argument about God's freedom in election, and the true Israel. It is often supposed that Paul here contradicts what he has said in ch. ix: here, the Jews are beloved *on account of the fathers*, whereas there it is proved that God is not bound by any human line of descent and is free to call and create his people as he pleases. The underlying truth which connects the two apparently contradictory lines of thought is that, for God, freedom is freedom to act in grace, and that since he is ever the same he never regrets or revokes the acts of grace which he performs, and never annuls the vocation he prepares for men and nations. Israel is always *called*. This is quite the reverse of saying that men by their descent, nationality, or other qualifications, are able to establish a claim upon God and so limit his freedom. If (to put the matter in a paradox) God's freedom is limited at all, it is limited only in the fact of his being God – the gracious God who delights in mercy, and whose wrath (as we shall presently see) exists to serve the ends of his mercy.

The final period (*vv.* 30 ff.) is parallel to the last (*vv.* 28 f.), but goes
30   perhaps deeper. It starts from the same historical circumstances. **For as you formerly were disobedient to God** – that is, as Gentiles, rebelling against your Creator (i. 18–21, 28) – **but now (corresponding to their disobedience) have received his mercy** – in accepting the Gospel now proclaimed to the Gentiles by Paul and his coll-
31   eagues – , **so they** – the Jews – **also now (corresponding to the mercy you have received) have become disobedient** – in rejecting the Gospel preached first of all (i. 16) to them – **in order that they too may now receive God's mercy.**

For Jew and Gentile alike, the end of the road is God's mercy; and for each the road leads through disobedience. The Gentile story, told in *v.* 30, is straightforward and needs little comment. The phrase 'corresponding to their disobedience' translates a Greek dative, which is sometimes taken in a simple instrumental (cf. *v.* 20) and sometimes in a temporal sense.[1] But, both here and in the next verse ('corresponding to the mercy you have received'), more is involved than

---

1 See Moule, *Idiom Book*, p. 44.

mere instrumentality and temporality. In each case, behind disobedience and mercy, stands the same sovereign divine activity (Gaugler, ii. p. 209). God wills and enacts the one as he wills and enacts the other.

The case of the Jews is less simple. They stumbled (ix. 32 f.) at the appointed stone of stumbling – Christ, the requirement of faith, and of nothing other than faith, for justification, and the extension of the Gospel to the heathen world. The present age ('now') means for them disobedience, since they have rejected the Messiah God sent them. This we have heard before, and that Jewish disbelief led to Gentile faith, and leads to the apprehension of mercy. But now two further points are added, (a) an 'in order that' (ἵνα), and (b) a 'now' (νῦν). Apparently, then, the unbelief of the Jews was a necessary stage on the way to faith – they disbelieved, and disobeyed, *in order that* they might believe; and their return to faith, and their resumption into the people of God, is to take place *now*, in the present age. On the first of these points more will be said below; it is only the disobedient who can know the mercy of God. The second introduces what has been described as an 'almost intolerable eschatological tension' (Barth, *op. cit.* p. 417). Not only the unbelief, but also the return of the Jews is *now*. It is no doubt true that Paul expected the full eschatological end to fall within his own generation (see xiii. 11 f.; 1 Thess. iv. 15; 1 Cor. xv. 51); but it seems in the highest degree unlikely that he actually contemplated a successful operation of rapid missionary work, culminating, in the very near future, in the conversion of every single Jew. He is, rather, speaking of the End, of that which is beyond history and beyond all human understanding, of God all in all, the merciful God. It is the unique, and unenviable, privilege of the men of religion that they are at once believers and disbelievers, and stand at once under the wrath and mercy of God. They live not in the truth but on the edge of it; in the half-light before dawn. When their religion asserts itself and its independent effectiveness, they are lost; when it denies itself, and circumcision of the flesh is seen to point to circumcision of the heart, they are redeemed. And they must share the damnation of the disobedient if they are to be justified in the mercy of God.

For God has shut up all men to disobedience, in order that he may 32 **deal with all men in mercy.** That is, God has brought men into a position which merits nothing but his wrath in order that his relations with them may be marked by nothing but mercy. God's rejections, punishments, and abandonments (i. 24, 26, 28) are rightly understood as the foil of his mercy. Only sinners can be the objects of his mercy, and only those who know that they are sinners can know that they are loved. The righteous 'need no repentance' (Luke xv. 7) and cannot know what it is to be forgiven. Every man must be damned if he is to be justified.

Here at length the full meaning of Paul's 'double predestination' is revealed. God has predestinated *all men* to wrath and he has predestinated *all men* to mercy. If they were not predestinated to the former they could not be predestinated to the latter. It is true that the stress here does not lie on the 'all men' but on the 'disobedience' and the 'mercy'; Paul does not intend to make a definite pronouncement about the ultimate destiny of each individual man. But the hope of mankind is more, not less, secure because it is rooted in the truth about God, rather than in a truth about man himself.

Paul expresses almost the same truth in similar words in Gal. iii. 22: The Scripture hath shut up all things under sin, that the promise by faith in Jesus Christ might be given to them that believe. For faith is man's assent to the mercy which came to action in Jesus Christ, and the opposite of the disobedience which refuses God's mercy by seeking to deserve his favour.

31 THE PRAISE OF GOD

CHAPTER xi. 33–6

(33) O the depth of God's wealth and wisdom and knowledge! How unsearchable are his judgements! How his ways baffle our attempts to track them down! (34) For 'Who has known the mind of the Lord? Who has been his counsellor?' (35) 'Who first gave to him, that recompense might be made him?' (36) For of him and through him and unto him are all things. To him be the glory for ever. Amen.

Precisely because Paul sees that the tangled problems of existence and history find their solution not in man but in God, the chapter ends with an ascription of praise to God.

33   **O the depth of God's wealth and wisdom and knowledge!** It is possible to make 'wisdom' and 'knowledge' dependent upon 'wealth': ' ... the depth of God's wealth both of wisdom and of knowledge'; but it seems better to treat all these words as independent. For God's wealth compare ii. 4; ix. 23; Col. i. 27. God is of infinite resource, and his plans rest upon infinite wisdom and knowledge.

How unsearchable are his judgements! How his ways baffle our attempts to track them down! Who would have thought of the means just described by which his mercy is brought to bear on all men? But he whom men cannot find when they seek him has freely and graciously revealed himself and his purposes in Christ.

34   Two Old Testament quotations follow. **For 'Who has known the mind of the Lord? Who has been his counsellor?'** (Isa. xl. 13

(LXX)). This quotation emphasizes the profundity and inscrutability of God's counsels.

The second quotation takes up a different point: God acts in grace, and it is therefore impossible to build up a store of merit with him by reason of which one may claim a reward; whatever he gives he gives freely. With God, man never earns a recompense; he can only be loved and treated with mercy. **'Who first gave to him, that recompense** 35 **might be made him?'** (Job xli. 11 (not LXX)).

God is the source of all wisdom and of all love: **For of him and** 36 **through him and unto him are all things.**

It is sometimes maintained that in this verse Paul employs a formula drawn from Hellenistic mysticism and theology.[1] Stated in this form, the hypothesis is unnecessary. Paul's propositions, that all things are from, through, and unto God, are axioms of biblical theology, and he himself has emphasized them, especially in chs. ix–xi, as strongly as any biblical writer. The whole process of salvation, including its negative aspects of disobedience and wrath, is due to God's initiative. He remains in control of the process from beginning to end, putting his eternal purposes into effect through the acts of the Son and the Spirit. And all things find their end in him, for he has 'shut up all men to disobedience, in order that he may deal with all men in mercy', while the 'creation itself also shall be liberated from the corrupting bondage in which it lies' (viii. 21), and 'all things co-operate for good to those who love God' (viii. 28). It remains, however, a true and valid observation that there are close verbal parallels to Paul's words in Stoic writers,[2] and it is quite likely that Paul chose to express his biblical faith in Stoic words, which originally bore a quite different meaning. The connecting link is no doubt to be found in Hellenistic Judaism.[3]

The God in whose mercy all things originate, and in whose mercy all things end, is the only proper object of worship and praise: **To him be the glory for ever.** The *sola gratia* and *sola fide* of these eleven chapters can issue only in this *soli Deo gloria*. What it means to give glory to God, and how far removed this is from mere pious ejaculations, will appear in chs. xii–xvi.

---

1 In addition to the commentaries see especially E. Norden, *Agnostos Theos* (1913), pp. 240–50.

2 E.g. M. Aurelius, iv. 23: 'All that is in tune with thee, O Universe (κόσμος), is in tune with me! Nothing that is in due time for thee is too early or too late for me! All that thy seasons bring, O Nature (φύσις), is fruit for me! From thee are all things, in thee are all things, unto thee are all things.'

3 There are several examples in Philo, e.g. *The Special Laws*, i. 208: 'The division of the animal into its limbs [Philo is allegorizing sacrificial regulations] indicates either that all things are one or that they come from one and return to one'.

32 THE GROUND OF CHRISTIAN ETHICS

CHAPTER xii. 1, 2

(1) I exhort you, therefore, brethren, by God's mercies, to offer your bodies as a living sacrifice, holy and well-pleasing to God; this is the spiritual worship you owe him. (2) And do not be conformed to this age, but be transformed by the renewing of your mind, that you may try and approve what is the will of God, what (that is) is good and acceptable and perfect.

It is pointed out in most commentaries that a major division of the epistle falls between chs. xi and xii; chs. i–xi form the dogmatic part of the epistle, chs. xii and xiii (or xii–xv) the ethical. There is, of course, a measure of truth in this observation; but it is a serious mistake to treat the two parts of the epistle as distinct from each other. Paul's dogmatic teaching is misunderstood if it is not seen to require ethical action, and his ethical teaching cannot be grasped if it is not recognized that it rests at every point upon the dogmatics. So far from its being a contradiction of the doctrine of justification by faith (good works returning, as it were, by a back door after their formal expulsion), it is best understood as an exposition of the obedience which is an essential element in faith (i. 5), and of the gratitude which redeemed and justified man is bound to feel towards the merciful God.

This connection between Paul's dogmatics and his ethics is
1 emphasized by the opening words: **I exhort you, therefore, brethren** (i. 13), **by God's mercies.** The word 'therefore' (οὖν) can be, and sometimes is, treated as no more than a transition-particle, but since it is supported by the appeal to the mercies of God it seems best to give it its normal meaning. For 'the mercies of God' forms a not inadequate summary of what is contained in chs. i–xi, and especially in chs. ix–xi, though it should be noted that the word (οἰκτιρμός) that Paul uses here has not been used earlier in the epistle, though the cognate verb (οἰκτίρειν) is used at ix. 15 in the quotation of Exod. xxxiii. 19. The use of a different word from that which is characteristic especially of chs. ix–xi suggests that Paul has in mind the argument of the whole epistle, and the whole truth about God, rather than the last few verses only. In Paul's view, the proper response to the kind of argument conducted there is not to speculate upon the eternal decrees, or one's own place in the scheme of salvation, but to be obedient. Obedience well summarizes the following words, in which Paul exhorts his readers to **offer your bodies as a living sacrifice, holy and well-pleasing to God.**

The language throughout this clause is sacrificial; not only the word 'sacrifice' itself, but also 'offer', 'holy', and 'well-pleasing' are technical terms. Paul however uses sacrificial, 'religious' language in what may be called a secularized sense; it has little to do with formal worship, and a great deal to do with behaviour in everyday life. It is consistent with this that he goes on to refer to *your bodies*; by 'body' (σῶμα) Paul means the whole human person, including its means of expressing itself in common life (cf. vi. 6, 12). The 'mercies of God' on the one hand move men to offer him what is essentially a sacrifice of thanksgiving; on the other, it is through these mercies, and not through any merit of their own, that men are able to bring a sacrifice to God.

It is not quite certain how the last words of the verse are to be constructed. It is possible to take them (as here) in apposition to 'sacrifice': **this is the spiritual worship you owe him**. It is also possible, though perhaps less likely, that they are in apposition to the whole sentence: I beseech you ... to offer your bodies ... in such a way that this is the spiritual worship you owe. The difference is not great.

It is hardly possible to find a satisfactory rendering of the words here translated 'spiritual worship' (λογικὴ λατρεία); compare 1 Pet. ii. 2, 5. Etymologically, the adjective means, 'pertaining to the logos, or reason', and was therefore naturally applied, especially by the Stoics, to that which related man to God. Thus, in a famous passage, Epictetus declared, 'If I were a nightingale I would do what is proper to a nightingale ...; but in fact I am a rational (λογικός) creature, so I must praise God' (*Discourses*, I, xvi. 20 f.). In the *Corpus Hermeticum* a hymn of praise to God is called a rational or spiritual sacrifice (λογικὴ θυσία; xiii. 19, 21). Paul means, a worship consisting not in outward rites but in the movement of man's inward being, resulting in concrete outward action. This is better described as 'spiritual worship' than as 'rational', for Paul is not thinking of what is meant in modern English by 'rational'.

The Hellenistic parallels do not prove that Paul's thought was based on Stoic material. The Old Testament itself knows inward as well as material sacrifice (e.g. Ps. li. 17). This was not forgotten in later Judaism. For example, Deut. xi. 13 (... to serve him with (the Hebrew might be translated *in*) your heart ...) was interpreted to mean that as there was a service of the altar (cf. ix. 4), so there was also a service in the heart (prayer, *Sifre Deuteronomy*, 11. 13 (41)). R. Johanan ben Zakkai taught, after the destruction of the Temple in AD 70, that merciful action is a means of atonement equal to the sacrifices of the Temple (*Aboth d. R. Nathan* 2d, based on Hos. vi. 6), and it was believed that in the age to come, when other sacrifices ceased, the sacrifice of praise would continue for ever (*Pesiqta* 79a). It was probably with examples such as these in mind that Paul wrote of the Christian's spiritual worship; but his phrase (especially the adjective) looks back to Stoic language, mediated through the Hellenistic synagogue.[1]

All men owe obedience to God, though the Christian, with a clearer perception of God's mercies, is under a special obligation. Paul now proceeds to an exhortation based upon a unique Christian conviction. It is expressed in eschatological form; in fact, all the exhortation of chs. xii, xiii is contained within an eschatological framework, for xii. 2 bids Christians not to be conformed to this age, and xiii. 11–14 points to the new day which is at hand.

2   **Do not be conformed to this age, but be transformed by the renewing of your mind.** The 'mercies of God' are the ground of the Christian's self-sacrifice to God; but they are also the record of the way (traced out in chs. i–xi) in which God has brought his eternal purposes to their fulfilment in Christ. Paul never goes so far as to say that the Age to Come has come; for him, 'this age' is still, as in Jewish apocalyptic, the existing framework of human and demonic society. But, since the life, death, and resurrection of Jesus, 'this age' can no longer be the regulative principle of life for those who have died and been raised with Jesus (vi. 3 ff.). *In Christ* they have entered the new age; already they have received the first-fruits of the Spirit (viii. 23), and are under obligation not to the flesh but to the Spirit (viii. 12). In the present verse Paul expresses this truth in new terms.

An attempt is sometimes made to distinguish between 'conformed' (συσχηματίζεσθαι) and 'transformed (μεταμορφοῦσθαι). The former is said to refer to outward form only, the latter to inward being. The attempt is probably baseless: (a) conformity to this age is no superficial matter; (b) Pauline usage does not support a difference between the two verbs (cf. 2 Cor. iii. 18 with Phil. iii. 21).

Being conformed to this age results in an 'unfit mind' (i. 28). To recognize and share the act of redemption accomplished in the death and resurrection of Jesus means the renewing of the mind. Paul's use of this word (νοῦς), notwithstanding a superficial resemblance, differs radically from that of the Greek writers. The mind is not necessarily good; it must be renewed. 'Renewal' is used at Titus iii. 5 for that which is wrought in baptism; the cognate verb is used at 2 Cor. iv. 16; Col. iii. 10. These passages are instructive. Paul is able to speak of a radical renewal of human nature because the old age is disappearing and the new age is at hand; the renewal which is begun in conversion and baptism and advanced with every Christian decision taken ends in the glory of God.

In this world, renewal is most clearly shown in moral life. Its aim is

---

1 Philo, for example, writes: 'The soul . . . ought to honour God not irrationally (ἀλόγως) nor ignorantly, but with knowledge and reason (λόγῳ)' (*Special Laws*, i. 209).

that you may try and approve what is the will of God, what (that is) is good and acceptable and perfect. For 'try and approve' see pp. 53, 97; more than testing is implied. The Christian finds out the will of God not to contemplate it but to do it. It goes without saying that what is known to be God's will is – perfect. Paul knows no other moral criterion than this. For the mind's recognition of the will (or law) of God, compare vii. 25; it is the renewed mind (not mind as such) that is capable of this recognition. Compare also i. 21, 24, 26, 28; the mind of fallen and unredeemed man is incapable of valid moral (and theological) distinctions and understanding. And even the renewed mind needs a good deal of instruction: hence the detailed advice and exhortation of the following paragraphs.

33 THE CHRISTIAN OFFERING

CHAPTER xii. 3–21

(3) For, through the grace God gave me, I tell you, every one, not to think more highly of yourselves than you ought to think, but to be sober-minded about yourselves, as God has given to each of you a measure of faith. (4) For as we have many members in one body, and all the members do not have the same function, (5) so we, who are many, are one body in Christ, and severally members of one another. (6) Since then we have gifts of grace differing according to the grace God has given us, if the gift be prophecy, let us exercise it according to the proportion of faith; (7) if it be ministry, let us attend to our ministry; if one be a teacher, let him attend to his teaching; (8) if an exhorter, to his exhortation; the man who practises charity, let him do it whole-heartedly, let the president act with zeal, let the man who does acts of mercy do them with cheerfulness. (9) Let your love be free from dissimulation. Abhor that which is evil; cleave to that which is good. (10) With the love that befits a brotherhood be affectionate to one another; give each to other the higher rank in honour; (11) do not allow your Christian zeal to slacken; be fervent in the Spirit, serve the Lord,[1] (12) rejoice in hope, show endurance in

---

1 Instead of 'serve the Lord' (κυρίῳ) the Western text (D* G it Ambrosiaster) has 'serve the time' (καιρῷ). This may be a mechanical blunder; the two Greek words are similar. It has however been discussed and defended in an important Durham University dissertation (1988) by J. L. North. Dr North shows that the expression (which superficially appears to commend 'time-serving') not only has a respectable history in Greek ethical usage but is also often associated with other ethical terms and concepts used in the present passage. It is to be hoped that Dr North's evidence and argument will be published.

affliction, persevere in prayer. (13) Minister to the needs[1] of the
saints, practise hospitality with enthusiasm. (14) Bless those who
persecute you, bless and do not curse them. (15) Rejoice with
those who rejoice, weep with those who weep. (16) Have a
common mind; do not set your mind on exalted things, but keep
company with the humble; 'do not be wise in your own
estimation'. (17) Return no one evil for evil; plan to lead an
honest life before all men. (18) If it be possible – that is, as far as it
rests with you – live at peace with all men. (19) Do not avenge
yourselves, beloved, but leave room to God's wrath; for it is
written, 'Vengeance is mine, I will recompense, saith the Lord'.
(20) Rather, 'if your enemy is hungry, feed him; if he is thirsty,
give him drink; for by doing this you will heap up burning coals
upon his head'. (21) Do not be overcome by evil, but overcome
evil with good.

This paragraph illustrates the principles laid down in *vv.* 1 f. It is not a
complete account of Christian ethics, and it is not a Christian
casuistry, for it is in no sense legalistic; yet it covers a wide field, and
touches the order and conduct of church life in addition to more
evidently moral questions.

The first sentence is closely linked with *vv.* 1 f. by means of a 'for';
Paul is about to give an authoritative exposition of his ethical first
3 principles, and states the ground of his authority for doing so. **For,
through the grace God gave me** (cf. i. 5), **I tell you, every one.**
Grace (χάρις) is given to every Christian (*v.* 6); without it the Christian
life cannot exist. The fundamental meaning of *grace* appears in
passages such as iii. 24; it is the undeserved but active favour of God,
which is directed equally to all. It is however received in different
forms and with different effects; these specific gifts and acts of grace
are often described (e.g. in *v.* 6; see the note) by a related word
(χάρισμα), not used in the present verse. The special grace given to
Paul fits him for the work of an apostle (cf. i. 5) and for building up the
churches (cf. 2 Cor. xiii. 10). This includes the speaking of truths
which may possibly be unwelcome to those who hear them. He has in
mind here the possibility that one group of Christians may think
themselves superior to others – as, for example, Gentile to Jewish
Christians (cf. xi. 18 ff.) – and therefore charges them **not to think
more highly of yourselves than you ought to think, but to be**

1 Again the Western text (D* G it) diverges, and instead of 'needs' (χρείαις) has
'remembrances' (μνείαις) – that is, the remembering of the saints and their
needs in prayer. This is not impossible, but the reference to hospitality which
follows makes it more likely that Paul wrote 'needs' and that the variant arose
through a mechanical slip in copying.

sober-minded about yourselves. An injunction of this kind probably implies that there were Christians in Rome who did think too highly of themselves. They may have been Gentiles, or, possibly, Christians who possessed special and showy 'gifts of grace' (*v.* 6) and despised others (cf. 1 Corinthians *passim*). Such pride belongs to 'this age', after which Christians must not fashion themselves (*v.* 2). Sober-mindedness is one of the Greek virtues, mentioned by Aristotle (*Nicomachean Ethics*, 1117 b 13) next after courage; it means soundness of mind, prudence, discretion; moderation, especially with regard to things of sense. Paul (as the context shows) uses the word differently, and establishes it not in general ethics but in the words, **as God has given to each of you a measure of faith.** Compare *v.* 6 and Eph. iv. 7. 'Faith' is used here in a sense somewhat different from that which it has in the rest of the epistle, and more akin to that of 1 Cor. xiii, where faith is a power given by God to do certain things (for example, to remove mountains). Men's opinions of themselves should be in proportion not to their natural capacities but to God's gifts; if this is so they will never (even though God calls them to be apostles) be boastful, for they will remember that they have nothing they have not received (1 Cor. iv. 7). The man who is humble before God is unlikely to be arrogant before his fellow-creatures.

The reason why Christians should be not arrogant but humble and loving to one another is now expressed in a new way. **For as we have 4 many members in one body, and all the members do not have the same function, so we, who are many, are one body in Christ, and 5 severally members of one another.** The metaphor of the body, used to describe a group of men who have common interests and activities, was not infrequent in antiquity. An example often quoted is the speech put by Livy (ii. 32) into the mouth of Menenius Agrippa on the occasion of the secession of the Roman *plebs.* Senate and people, Agrippa argued, could no more dispense with each other than stomach and limbs; they formed a unity within one body. One aspect of Pauline usage cannot easily be paralleled; this is the description of the Church as the body *of Christ.* This phrase, however, does not occur in Romans, where (as the 'as ... so' shows) we have no more than simile or analogy. It is implied by *v.* 4 that Christians have diverse functions corresponding to the gifts of grace given to them; these are all necessary to the proper working of the body of which all are parts; so that there is no room for any to think too highly of himself or to despise another (1 Cor. xii. 12–31). The phrase 'one body in Christ' is, however, a stage on the way to 'the body of Christ', and it is important to note the origin of the latter term (Eph. iv. 12; cf. Col. i. 18; ii. 19; iii. 15). Evidently it is closely related to the Pauline 'in Christ' (see p. 119), and its setting is accordingly not so much sacramental (Dodd, pp. 194 f.) as eschatological. It was the body of Christ which died in the messianic affliction and rose to life in the Age to Come; those who are to share in this process must enter into and become part of the 'body of Christ' (understood now in a new, extended sense). There is, of course, a very close relation between this and the Pauline doctrines of baptism (vi. 3–11; Gal. iii. 27) and of the eucharist (1 Cor. x. 16 f.); but the relation, if it may be set out in a diagram, is not

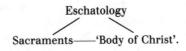

Sacramental ideas and language

|

'Body of Christ'

but

Eschatology

Sacraments——'Body of Christ'.

These considerations, which show the background of Paul's use of the term *body*, make clearly visible the importance of unity and the dreadful consequences of the lack of it. To fall out of unity, out of the one body, is to fall back into the old world of sin and death.

The various members of the Church have therefore, not in themselves but in the grace of God, a variety of functions which are to
6 be exercised in unity. **Since then we have gifts of grace differing according to the grace God has given us** (cf. *v.* 3) . . . The word 'gift of grace' (χάρισμα) has occurred several times in different senses (i. 11; v. 15 f.; vi. 23; xi. 29); here it means an actualization, a practical expression, of the grace (χάρις) of God under which the Church stands. In this sense the whole life of the Church, not its ministry only, is 'charismatic'; but the total effect of this passage (cf. 1 Cor. xii–xiv) shows that this supernatural conception of the Church's life does not exclude the notions of discipline and authority.

The construction of this passage is obscure. *V.* 6 begins with a participle, and up to the full stop which must be placed at the end of *v.* 8 there is no finite verb. It is possible to construct the participle (having, ἔχοντες) with *v.* 5: We are one body in Christ, having gifts . . . . But it is better to take it as the introduction of a new sentence, and to supply imperatives (as the new form of clause beginning with 'if one be . . .' requires): Having (that is, since we have) gifts, let us . . . God's gifts are not given for the self-congratulation of those who receive them, but for employment in the building up of the body.

There follows a series of gifts, some of which suggest, more or less clearly, ministerial office (for detailed discussion see below). These are prophecy, ministry (διακονία), teaching, and exhortation; we may add the reference to 'the president'. It is, however, quite impossible to

regard this as a list of ministers; there was no special order of those
who practised charity, or of those who did acts of mercy; charity and
mercy were expected of all Christians. The present list should be
compared with that of 1 Cor. xii. 8 ff., rather than that of 1 Cor. xii. 28.
To Paul, the Spirit suggests primarily function and activity, rather
than office.

**If the gift be prophecy, let us exercise it according to the
proportion of faith.** For New Testament prophecy, see especially 1
Cor. xii and xiv, where it is distinguished from glossolalia, not
mentioned here. It was expressed in inspired but intelligible speech,
and sometimes though not always included prediction of future events
(e.g. Acts xi. 27 f.). Like Old Testament prophecy it was primarily an
immediate communication of God's word to his people, through
human lips. Paul urges prophets to do their work according to the
proportion of faith. It is possible to translate, 'of *the* faith', 'faith'
representing the content of Christian truth, the Christian religion.
Proportion (ἀναλογία) will then be taken in the sense (possibly akin to
that of *measure*, μέτρον, in *v.* 3) of *standard.* A variation of this, in
which *faith* is taken as *fides qua*, the faith with which one believes, is
accepted by Cranfield: 'the prophets are to prophesy in accordance
with the standard which they possess in their apprehension of, and
response to, the grace of God in Jesus Christ' (p. 621). This is an
attractive view, but may seem to read a great deal out of one word. It
is perhaps better to take *proportion* in much the same sense as
measure in *v.* 3: prophetic utterances, like men's estimates of
themselves and of their fellows, are to be regulated not by self-esteem
but by the faith which finds its authority in God alone. Like other
Christians, the prophet must be sober-minded about his own activities
and his own importance. God has equipped him with faith for his task;
he must employ it to the full but not seek to go beyond it.

If it be ministry, let us attend to our ministry. The word 7
'ministry' (διακονία) means simply 'service' (xv. 31), but it is already
on the way to becoming a technical term. It is impossible to find a
precise rendering for it here, but probably service to the needy is
meant (cf. 'he who practises charity', 'he who does acts of mercy').
For the word 'minister' (deacon, διάκονος) in the New Testament see
especially xvi. 1; 1 Cor. iii. 5; 2 Cor. iii. 6; vi. 4; xi. 23; Eph. iii. 7; vi. 21;
Phil. i. 1; Col. i. 7, 23, 25; iv. 7; 1 Tim. iii. 8, 12; iv. 6.[1]

If one be a teacher (the construction changes, showing that Paul
is now giving injunctions to various groups), **let him attend to his
teaching; if an exhorter, to his exhortation.** Exhortation, especially 8
when placed beside teaching, suggests the work of the preacher; but it

1 See my *Church, Ministry, and Sacraments in the New Testament* (1985),
Index, s.v. *diakonos.*

would be wrong to deduce an absolute distinction between teaching and preaching, just as it would be wrong to distinguish between practising charity and doing acts of mercy. Each means a communication, effected in different ways, of the truth of the Gospel to the hearer; in the one it is explained, in the other applied. Yet it could never be explained without application or applied without explanation.

The man who practises charity (that is, imparts what he has to others), **let him do it whole-heartedly.** Paul several times (especially 2 Cor. viii. 2; ix. 11, 13) uses, in connection with giving, the word here translated 'whole-heartedly' (and its cognates). The meaning is probably not 'with liberality' but 'being without *arrière-pensée* in one's gifts'.

Let the president act with zeal. It is uncertain whether this clause refers to an office. 'The president' translates a participle. The verb in question is used in quite untechnical fashion at Titus iii. 8, 14; in 1 Tim. iii. 4, 5, 12 it is used in a transitional sense – Church officers must be able to *preside* satisfactorily over their own households; otherwise they will not be able to preside over the church of God. In 1 Thess. v. 12; 1 Tim. v. 17 it is used of those who preside over churches. It is certain that in Romans (and 1 Thessalonians) it does not describe any office with precision; it rather refers to a function which may have been exercised by several persons, perhaps jointly or in turn. There is no indication whether the 'president' presided at a service (like the Synagogue service) of preaching and teaching, at the eucharist, or in a church meeting convened for deliberative or disciplinary purposes.

Let the man who does acts of mercy do them with cheerfulness. Paul's phrase recalls the 'deeds of love' often emphasized in Rabbinic writings (e.g. *Aboth*, i. 2, quoted on p. 166). 'Cheerfulness' points in the same direction (cf., e.g., *Leviticus Rabbah*, xxxiv. 9: When a man gives alms he should do it with a joyful heart). To a Christian, 9 kindness is a delight, not a duty. Paul adds, **Let your love be free from dissimulation.** Of course, if love is not spontaneous it cannot be cheerfully expressed.

There now follows (*vv.* 9–13) a series of clauses containing only participles, with no finite verb. It is evident and undisputed that these participles must be understood as imperatives – 'Abhor', 'cleave', etc. But why should participles be used in this way? It has been argued[1] that in Hellenistic Greek a usage had grown up in which the participle could stand for the imperative. Satisfactory evidence for this belief, however, has not been adduced. An attractive alternative explanation[2]

1 Moulton, *Prolegomena*, p. 182.
2 See D. Daube, Appended Note, 'Participle and Imperative in 1 Peter', in E. G. Selwyn, *The First Epistle of St Peter* (1946).

begins from the observation that in Rabbinic Hebrew participles are used to express, not direct commands, but rules and codes. The participles in Romans (and in 1 Pet. ii. 18; iii. 1, 7 ff.; iv. 7–10) occur in similar codes, and it seems not improbable that they represent original Hebrew participles. If this be a correct linguistic explanation it will follow that the material in *vv.* 9–13 goes back to a Semitic source originating in very primitive Christian circles. These verses present a very interesting picture of early Christian life, but call for little explanation; they illustrate various aspects of the general command of love (xiii. 8 ff.).

Abhor that which is evil; cleave to that which is good. With the 10 **love that befits a brotherhood** (this word – φιλαδελφία – seems not to have been used metaphorically before the time of the New Testament) **be affectionate to one another; give each to other the higher rank in honour** (cf. Phil. ii. 3); **do not allow your Christian** 11 (it seems necessary in translation to add this explanatory adjective) **zeal to slacken; be fervent in the Spirit, serve the Lord.**[1] Apollos, who subsequently was further instructed though not rebaptized was, according to Acts xviii. 25, 'fervent in Spirit'. Whatever the meaning in Acts, the parallel with 'the Lord' (if this word be read) shows that here 'Spirit' means not the human spirit but the Holy Spirit. **Rejoice in** 12 **hope, show endurance in affliction, persevere in prayer.** For hope, see p. 96; for endurance, see p. 44; for affliction, see pp. 96 f. Christian life, for all its fervent zeal, can never be so busy a 'doing' that it fails to look beyond all human activity. Christian rejoicing, which endures through affliction, is rooted in the Christian hope of what God will do, and at all times the Christian looks beyond his immediate environment to God in prayer.

Minister to the needs of the saints. 'Minister to' is literally 'share 13 in', 'partake of'. The verb is one which Paul regularly uses in the context of Christian charity (xv. 27; Gal. vi. 6; Phil. iv. 15). The cognate noun is used more generally, but compare xv. 26. For 'the saints' see on i. 7; it is unlikely that there is here a special reference to the Jerusalem church (see xv. 25 f., 31).

Practise hospitality with enthusiasm. This was evidently a very important Christian duty in the early Church; compare Heb. xiii. 2; 1 Clement i. 2; x. 7; xi. 1; xii. 1; Hermas, *Mandate*, viii. 10. For the adjective 'hospitable' see, for example, 1 Tim. iii. 2; Titus i. 8.

With the next verse the construction changes abruptly, and the imperatival participles disappear. This may correspond to the fact that Paul is now drawing on a new source. It is possible that this may be (not any of our gospels, which were not yet written, but) the gospel tradition. Certainly the words that follow, **Bless those who persecute** 14

---

1 See note 1 on p. 215.

you, bless and do not curse them, recall a saying from the Sermon on the Mount (Plain).

> Matt. v. 44: Love your enemies, and pray for them that persecute you.
> Luke vi. 28: Bless them that curse you, pray for them that despitefully use you.

Neither verse is quoted precisely, and there are too many parallels in Jewish literature to permit confidence that Paul was using the tradition of the words of Jesus. If he was, why does he not say so, referring to his authority, as he does at 1 Cor. vii. 10; 1 Thess. iv. 15? The same question will arise at *vv.* 17–20; xiii. 9 f. The answer is probably that Paul, unlike some of his contemporaries, did not regard the sayings of Jesus as constituting a new legalism. For him the importance of Jesus was not legislative but historical and theological; accordingly he used material that came to him from the historical tradition, but because it was intrinsically suitable, rather than to establish doctrine.

15   **Rejoice with those who rejoice, weep with those who weep.** Here infinitives are used for imperatives; but this substitution (unlike the use of participles, noted above) has a respectable history in the Greek language. Those who, because they have faith, are no longer self-centred, can show true sympathy with others, since they can rank their neighbours and their affairs above themselves.

16   **Have a common mind** (cf. Phil. ii. 2 – this is a mark of love); **do not set your mind on exalted things, but keep company with the humble.** Here the imperatival participles return, and continue as far as *v.* 19. It would be possible to translate: Condescend to lowly things (taking ταπεινοῖς as neuter). This is suggested by the neuter 'exalted things' (ὑψηλά); but in the New Testament the adjective (ταπεινός) is never used of things but always of persons. Usage of the verb (Gal. ii. 13; 2 Pet. iii. 17), however, is not decisive, and it is impossible to feel confident that either translation is correct to the exclusion of the other. It is well to remember that Greek occasionally allows an ambiguity impossible in English; Paul may have been aware, and may have approved, of both ways of taking his words. Both are supported by the Old Testament quotation that follows. '**Do not be wise in your own estimation.**' See Prov. iii. 7, already alluded to in xi. 25, where it has a particular application to a situation in which Gentile Christians might be inclined to think themselves superior to their Jewish brethren. Here the application is general.

17   **Return no one evil for evil.** Compare Matt. v. 38–42; Luke vi. 29; and see on *v.* 14. **Plan to lead an honest life before all men.** Paul

seems to depend on Prov. iii. 4 (LXX). Christians as such lead a public
life, and it is important that they should not behave in such a way as to
bring discredit upon the faith. The word Paul uses (καλά) is perhaps
stronger than 'honest'; it refers to a life that an honest Greek would
recognize as right and good. The next command is similar (note the
recurrence of 'all men'): **If it be possible – that is, as far as it rests** 18
with you – live at peace with all men. Compare Matt. v. 9. There is
no Christian virtue in provoking strife, whether inside or outside the
Church; limits may, however, be imposed on peaceable relations by
the attitude of others. But even when peace is broken by another, the
Christian is not to seek revenge. **Do not avenge yourselves, beloved,** 19
but leave room to God's wrath. Paul himself writes only 'the wrath',
and, were it not for the quotation that follows, which makes it clear
that he is speaking of God, it would be possible to translate, 'Avoid
wrath'. **For it is written, 'Vengeance is mine, I will recompense,**
saith the Lord'. There are occasions when God's wrath is rightly put
into effect by human agency (xiii. 4), but this is always by special
divine appointment (xiii. 1); no private person is at liberty to assume
that his own vengeful feelings will carry out the divine sentence. Here
Paul's quotation (Deut. xxxii. 35) rests upon the Hebrew text; contrast
v. 17.

Scripture not merely reserves vengeance to God alone; it points out
a more excellent way. **Rather, 'if your enemy is hungry, feed him; if** 20
he is thirsty, give him drink; for by doing this you will heap up
burning coals upon his head'. Again Paul turns to the LXX (of Prov.
xxv. 21 f.). In view of *v.* 21, it can scarcely be doubted that the 'burning
coals' are the fire of remorse. If an enemy is treated in this way he
may well be overcome in the best possible fashion – he may be so
ashamed of his own contrasting behaviour as to become henceforth a
friend. **Do not be overcome by evil, but overcome evil with good.** 21
This is not merely prudential; it is the way God himself has proceeded
against his enemies (cf. v. 8). The mercy of God (to which Paul
appealed at the beginning of this chapter, *v.* 1) will triumph over the
rebellion and disobedience of men (xi. 32); the mercy of those on
whom God has had mercy may similarly prove victorious.

34 AUTHORITIES

CHAPTER xiii. 1–7

(1) Let every one be in subjection to the authorities who rule
over you: for there is no authority that is not ordained by God,
and the authorities which in fact exist have been appointed by
God. (2) It follows that he who sets himself against the authority
resists God's ordinance, and those who resist will be responsible

for their own condemnation. (3) For the rulers are no terror to the man who does good works, but only to the man who does evil. If you wish not to be afraid of the authority, do what is good, and you will have praise from it. (4) For he is God's servant, appointed to promote what is good. But if you do what is evil, you may well fear; it is not for nothing that he bears a sword, for he is God's servant, an instrument of vengeance to carry out God's wrath[1] against the man who practises evil. (5) It is necessary therefore to be in subjection, not only through fear of God's wrath, but also for conscience sake. (6) Moreover, this is why you pay taxes, for these men are God's public servants, attending upon the purpose I have described. (7) Render to all men what is due to them. Pay the tax to him to whom the tax is due, the levy to him to whom the levy is due; pay reverence to him to whom reverence is due, honour to him to whom honour is due.

The new paragraph, a self-contained treatment of a special theme, appears at first to be introduced somewhat abruptly, so that it has been thought by some to be an insertion, interrupting the course of the epistle. In fact it has been prepared for by the exhortations to humility, to live an honest life in the eyes of the world, to live at peace, and to give place to God's wrath, of ch. xii. Obedience to magistrates forms an excellent practical example of all these Christian virtues; and there may well have been good reasons, unknown to us (though the disturbances *impulsore Chresto* (see Introduction, p. 5) come to mind), why this example should have been chosen. For the connection with what follows see p. 229.

1   **Let every one be in subjection to the authorities who rule over you.** In Paul's Greek the word *authorities* (ἐξουσίαι) is qualified by a participle (ὑπερέχουσαι) which is not easy to translate. It can be used alone (οἱ ὑπερέχοντες) to mean *the authorities*. At 1 Peter ii. 13 it is used of the king, or emperor, and is rightly rendered *supreme*. If (as in AV) it is rendered *higher* the reader is left asking, Higher than what (or whom)? It may be best, as here, to paraphrase, though *rule over you* introduces an awkward second person after the third of *every one*. Paul however makes the same change in *v.* 3. So far it has been assumed that the authorities Paul has in mind are human authorities, in particular the governing authority of the Roman Empire under which Paul and his readers lived. This is the view of many

---

1 There is some variation in the order of words here, and the Western Text (D* G it) omits altogether the reference to God's wrath ('he is God's avenging servant against...'). But the reference to wrath was probably found stylistically awkward, given different positions in the sentence, and even omitted for this reason. It represents, however, an essential element in Paul's thought.

commentators, but it has been challenged by Dr O. Cullmann,[1] who argues that the word 'authorities' (ἐξουσίαι) refers not simply to the state itself, but also to the 'invisible angelic powers that stand behind the State government' (*op. cit.* p. 195). This may appear a small distinction; in fact the difference is very great, as appears if two questions are asked (a) Must Christians be in subjection to the magistrates, or to angelic powers? (b) Are the angels or the magistrates of divine appointment?

The matter cannot be decided on purely linguistic grounds. Paul does elsewhere use the same word with the meaning of 'angelic authorities' (e.g. 1 Cor. xv. 24); but it is also used of magisterial authority (e.g. Luke xii. 11). The latter meaning is attested in Greek contemporary with the New Testament; for example, Josephus, *Jewish War*, ii. 350 (The powers (ἐξουσίαι – the Roman procurators of Judaea) should be conciliated by flattery, not irritated). There is thus (at the least) no difficulty in supposing that Paul is here referring to the state, or its administration. There is, of course, no question that he does so in vv. 3–7; and the tone of his references elsewhere (cf. Col. ii. 15) to spiritual-angelic (or perhaps better, demonic) authorities, suggests that it is very unlikely that he would bid his readers be in subjection to them. We may therefore for the moment assume that Paul is speaking simply of the relation of Christians to the state, though the full justification of this view may for the moment be reserved.

The 'every one' of the translation conceals a Semitic expression (*every soul*); and in what follows Paul expresses what is a characteristically Jewish point of view. All should obey the authorities, **for there is no authority that is not ordained by God, and the authorities which in fact exist have been appointed by God.** Many parallels can be cited from Jewish authors, for example, Wisdom vi. 3; Josephus, *Jewish War*, ii. 140 (No ruler attains his office save by the will of God). From the time of Pompey this attitude was given practical effect by the offering of daily sacrifice on behalf of the Roman authorities. Its roots lie in the Old Testament conviction that God is the ruler of all nations and of all history, and it may be described as an aspect of the doctrine of providence, arrived at by taking seriously the fact of God's lordship. In order to protect his creatures from the consequences of unbridled sin he provided them with civil rulers, just as he provides them with sun and rain. The fact that both sun and rain can be excessive and cause damage and suffering through drought and flood does not contradict the fact that God provides an environment in which his creatures can live; the fact

1 *Christ and Time* (English translation, 1951), pp. 191–210.

that authorities may be lax and negligent or tyrannous and overpowering similarly does not contradict God's intention that they should live in peace and well-being. The state thus has its appointed place in the providential order which God has established for the good of mankind. To say this does not confuse the state with the Church, or civil law with the Gospel, any more than it confuses the universe itself, and natural law, with Church and Gospel. The authorities are provisions of the merciful God.

2 **It follows that he who sets himself against the authority resists God's ordinance** (a word etymologically connected with 'appointed' in *v.* 1), **and those who resist will be responsible for their own condemnation.** The first part of this sentence draws an immediate inference from *v.* 1; the second asserts that the resistance to God's ordinance which is implied by resistance to authority does not escape judgement. This is true of resistance to any divine ordinance, but when resistance is offered to the state divine judgement comes into

3 operation at once by means of the state's own judicial procedures. **For the rulers are no terror to the man who does good works** (literally, to the good work), **but only to the man who does evil** (literally, to the evil work). 'The rulers' are the same as 'the authorities', though with a more directly personal reference. The word itself (ἄρχοντες) is capable of the same ambiguity. It is used of spiritual powers (e.g. Eph. ii. 2), and of earthly rulers (e.g. Acts iii. 17). Magistrates may well strike a guilty fear into the heart of the evil-doer, but not into the good. The man whose conscience is clear has nothing to dread. This simple observation points the practical way to an untroubled life. Paul writes colloquially. His opening words may be either a statement or a question: *You wish not to be afraid . . .* , or, *Do you wish not to be afraid . . . ?* Similarly colloquial English might use the positive form with a question mark: *You wish not to be afraid of the authority?* We could then continue, noting another colloquial form of conditional sentence, expressed by means of an imperative, *If you do what is good, you will have . . .* (literally, *Do what is good and you will have . . .*). The translation suggested here gives the meaning and something of the feel of Paul's sentence. **If you wish not to be afraid of the authority, do what is good, and** (Paul passes over to a positive account of the office of the authority) **you will have praise from it** (Paul uses the pronoun appropriate to 'authority', which is feminine in Greek; 'him' would be more natural in English). What Paul means by 'what is good' is not explicit. Abstention from evil is certainly included; it cannot be certainly deduced that the doing of what is socially good is positively intended, but there is no reason why 'good' should be understood in a purely negative and individualist sense. Praise (in the form of statues or inscriptions) was sometimes publicly bestowed upon those who made notable contributions to the welfare

of the state. By encouraging such benefactions, the state could make a positive contribution to the common life; **for he is God's servant, 4 appointed to promote what is good.** The word servant (διάκονος) was in process of becoming a technical Christian term (see xii. 7; xvi. 1); it cannot bear any such sense here, but it is not for that reason without theological significance. Behind the more technical use of the word and its cognates lies, not the idea of service in general, but that of a ministry performed in the first instance by Jesus himself and then by him through the Church, which furthers God's eschatological purpose. In this purpose the state and its representatives have a part to play, alongside that of the apostles and their helpers.

The negative service of the state is as real as the positive. **If you do what is evil, you may well fear; it is not for nothing that he bears a sword, for he is God's servant** (as above, διάκονος), **an instrument of vengeance to carry out God's wrath against the man who practises evil.** God's wrath, which belongs properly to the last day (ii. 5), is capable of being brought forward into the present (i. 18); one means by which this future wrath is anticipated is the magistrate's sword. This last expression recalls the technical term *ius gladii*, by which was meant the authority (possessed by all higher magistrates) of inflicting sentence of death (cf. Tacitus, *Histories*, iii. 68). We saw above that the action of the state was to be regarded as an aspect of God's providence; in this his wrath finds a place, for it represents his resistance to evil. Accordingly the state takes its place as avenger, bringing the wrath of God himself to bear upon evil-doers. It is thus, paradoxically, an instrument of God's long-suffering (ii. 4), for through this partial manifestation of his wrath the power of evil is restrained and its final judgement and defeat deferred; compare 2 Thess. ii. 6 f.

Paul resumes and explains the instruction he first gave in *v.* 1. **It is 5 necessary therefore to be in subjection, not only through fear of God's wrath, but also for conscience sake.** Two facts direct the Christian to give obedience to the authorities. One is that if he fails to do so God's wrath will be visited upon him, by means of the magistrate's sword; the other, that he is bound as a Christian to recognize the divine authority of the state as God's servant, so that his conscience (ii. 15; ix. 1) itself will impel him to render obedience. A particular example follows: **Moreover, this is why you pay taxes. 6** The state requires not merely the good will but the active support of the citizen. **For these men are God's public servants, attending upon the purpose I have described** (that is, of promoting good, and of restraining evil). The word Paul uses here to describe the state authorities (λειτουργοί) was in common use for public officials, and especially for those who carried out public works in the service of the state. The word in itself (although Paul uses it to describe his own office – xv. 16) is not a theological term, but derives theological significance from the genitive, 'of God'. The Roman magistrates, little though they knew it, were public servants not of Rome but of God; it was his work they did. In this fact lay their true authority, and their

7 right to receive their 'dues': **Render to all men what is due to them. Pay the tax** (or tribute, direct taxation) **to him to whom the tax is due, the levy** (indirect taxation, such as customs dues) **to him to whom the levy is due; pay reverence to him to whom reverence is due, honour to him to whom honour is due.** For the teaching of this verse, compare Mark xii. 17 (and parallels); 1 Pet. ii. 17. Honour and respect are due to earthly rulers not because they are powerful and influential *men*, but because they have been appointed by God. It follows that to treat them with less than their due of honour is to dishonour God; and honour without its practical corollary of the due payment of taxes for the maintenance of the authority would be a mockery.

Paul's attitude to the state, that is, to the Roman Empire, under whose authority he lived, was that of many, though not all Jews, and was on the whole that of the primitive Church. It may also be described as that of the *petit bourgeois* under the Empire. It must not be forgotten that Nero, though known to us from such ill-disposed writers as the senatorial historian Tacitus and the Christian Tertullian, was a popular Emperor, especially with the provincials, whose affairs were not badly conducted during his principate. The relief and gratitude which had greeted the re-establishment of a reliable and benevolent state under Augustus had not yet been dissipated. But to view Paul's attitude as a mere expression of lower-class provincial loyalty is quite inadequate. Paul's motive is primarily theological, not sociological, and to be understood it must be placed in the eschatological context of his thought as a whole. For him, as for most ancient thinkers, the world was much less secure, and much nearer to the brink of disaster, than it has appeared in modern times (until, perhaps, very recently). The stable order of society was constantly threatened by demonic powers, and the catastrophes preceding the End could not be far away. To Christians, it was highly desirable (though by no means certain) that ordered life should continue until the return of Christ, when death would be swallowed up in victory. The imperial government acted as a restraining power (2 Thess. ii. 6 f.; this seems the best way to understand this difficult passage) which afforded Christians a peaceful existence and the opportunity of preaching the Gospel. Accordingly it was their duty to maintain the machinery of the state, and to recognize in it God's own appointed means of preserving the stability and moral order of the world, and of putting his wrath into operation before the 'day of wrath'.

If this view of Paul's use of 'authority' is adopted, it is possible to recognize that the New Testament is consistent in its attitude to the state, for when (as in Revelation) the state appears to be the enemy of Christians the fact is that demonic powers have usurped the state's authority. These are the true enemy, and their victory over the state, shown by the rise of persecution, is interpreted as a sign that the end is at hand (Mark xiii. 9–13; Revelation *passim*). Thus Dr Cullmann's interpretation of 'authority' in Rom. xiii (see p. 225) turns out to be almost the exact opposite of the truth: the 'authorities' are the state, appointed by God not as the 'executive agent' (Cullman, *op. cit.* p. 195) of, but as a bulwark against demonic powers.

35 THE LAW OF LOVE

CHAPTER xiii. 8–10

(8) Owe no man anything – but remember the debt of love you owe one another; for he who loves someone other than himself has fulfilled the law. (9) For 'Thou shalt not commit adultery', 'Thou shalt do no murder', 'Thou shalt not steal', 'Thou shalt not covet', and any other commandment there be, are all summed up in this one saying: 'Thou shalt love thy neighbour as thyself'. (10) Love works no harm to the neighbour; that is why love is the complete fulfilment of the law.

Having dealt with the relation of the Christian to the state, Paul concludes (for the present) his treatment of Christian ethics by returning to the all-inclusive command of love. There is a good connection with what precedes, and no ground therefore for regarding xiii. 1–7 as an interpolation (see p. 224). From the precept 'Render to all men what is due to them' Paul passes to its negative corollary: **Owe no man anything** – that is, do not leave your obligations to them 8 unfulfilled. It is not clear how the following words should be translated. The word *owe* (ὀφείλετε) is not repeated but is presumably to be understood in order to introduce an infinitive with its object (τὸ ἀλλήλους ἀγαπᾶν, literally, *to love one another*, or perhaps, *loving one another*). The connecting link is provided by an expression (εἰ μή) which in Paul's writings usually means 'except' (e.g. 1 Cor. i. 14). If this interpretation is accepted, Paul means that the only debt Christians ought to incur is that which they are bound to incur and can never completely discharge – the debt of mutual love. *Owe* need not be repeated in English (any more than ὀφείλετε in Greek); a literal translation would be 'Owe no man anything except to love one another', or '...except loving one another'. We might render: 'Let your only indebtedness be the mutual love you are bound to owe as

Christians'. This would imply a special reference to Christian love within the Church (cf. xii. 10), over against universal love for non-Christians. Of course, Paul does not mean that Christians should love only Christians (xii. 14, 17, 19 ff.); yet there is a unique mutuality of love within the Christian fellowship which has a special significance because it is the unifying force within the Body of Christ (cf. John xiii. 34 f.). It is, however, possible that Paul's conjunction (εἰ μή) should be translated 'but'. If this is done the word translated 'owe' in the opening clause must be considered to take its alternative meaning 'ought' when it is applied to the second clause: 'Owe no man anything – but you ought to love . . . '. The change involved in passing from the notion of 'rendering every man his due' to the positive and sacrificial quality of Christian love seems to justify the choice of the latter alternative, and (in order that the sense of *debt* may not be lost) we may proceed, **But remember the debt of love you owe one another.**

The debt, or obligation, is not constituted by a natural relationship; it is created by the command of God. **For he who loves someone other than himself has fulfilled the law.** What Paul means by 'the law', and the fulfilment of it, must be discussed below (on *v.* 10). In this verse he does not use the word 'neighbour' (*vv.* 9 f.), and his choice of a different word (τὸν ἕτερον, literally, *the other person*) is significant. Just as Christian faith means that a man is prepared to worship and obey God rather than himself, so Christian love means that his attention is directed away from himself and towards those who are essentially – other than himself (cf. Phil. ii. 4). Love for the *neighbour* can too easily be misinterpreted as 'love for the like-minded man who is congenial to me'; love is not Christian love if it cannot include love for the man who differs from me in every way.

What Paul means by the fulfilling of the law begins to appear in the
9 next verse. **For 'Thou shalt not commit adultery'** (Ex. xx. 14; Deut. v. 18), **'Thou shalt do no murder'** (Ex. xx. 13; Deut. v. 17), **'Thou shalt not steal'** (Ex. xx. 15; Deut. v. 19), **'Thou shalt not covet'** (Ex. xx. 17; Deut. v. 21; as at vii. 7 Paul provides no object for the verb 'to covet'), **and any other commandment there be, are all summed up in this one saying: 'Thou shalt love thy neighbour as thyself'** (Lev. xix. 18). Paul quotes the LXX accurately. The meaning so far is clear: if you love your neighbour (Paul now uses this word because he is quoting; it must be assumed that he puts into it the meaning indicated by *v.* 8) you will treat him as the law requires – that is, you will not offend against him in respect of such matters as adultery, murder, theft, and coveting. That the law could be summed up in some such single precept was not unknown in Judaism. The same use of Lev. xix. 18 is found in Mark xii. 31 (and parallels). Paul gives no indication here that he was aware of Jesus' use of the same Old Testament passage. For the problem raised by his silence, see on xii. 14.

Love works no harm to the neighbour – does not (for example) 10
wish to murder him. This is of course an understatement (for a more
positive evaluation of love – which nevertheless still contains many
negatives – see 1 Cor. xiii); but it is regarded by Paul as the ground for
the claim of *v.* 8, for he continues, **That is why love is the complete
fulfilment of the law.** The meaning of 'complete fulfilment'
(πλήρωμα) is disputed, but it must be decided in the light of the use of
the cognate verb in *v.* 8. The man who loves has fulfilled the law, that
is, he has done what the law requires; the love, therefore, which he
exercises constitutes the fulfilment of the law's requirement. Thus
love is not the *completion* but the *performance* of the law. *V.* 9 shows
that by the law Paul means the Old Testament law in its preceptual
character. Love fulfils all negative and positive commandments
inclusively, from Lev. xix. 18 downwards. When Paul says this,
however, he is not instituting a new, though simplified, legalism. He
does not say that man is justified by fulfilling the law through love;
rather he is pointing out the ethical expression of the true meaning of
the law, which, when rightly understood, itself points to the way of
faith (see p. 56), which expresses itself in love (Gal. v. 6). The true
response to the law is faith (cf. p. 180); the true response to the law is
love. For Paul, both propositions are equally true, though they express
different aspects of truth. The same summary of the law appears in
Gal. v. 14; see also 1 Cor. ix. 21; Gal. vi. 2. It throws a clear light on
Paul's understanding of law. *Love* may cover abstention from
adultery, murder, and theft, but it cannot possibly be said to include
Sabbath observance, precepts concerning cleanness and uncleanness,
food laws, circumcision, and the like, except in so far as the Christian,
controlled by love, will always avoid giving unnecessary offence (xiv.
15; 1 Cor. viii. 11–13). These things therefore are not part of the
complete fulfilment of the law. The law understood in terms of love is
not a means of salvation, but does provide the ethical channel through
which the new life in Christ flows.

36 THE URGENCY OF THE TIME

CHAPTER xiii. 11–14

**(11) All these things you must do the more zealously because you
know the time in which we live. You know that it is already the
hour for you[1] to awake out of sleep, for salvation is nearer to us
now than when we first believed. (12) The night is advanced, the**

1 Instead of 'you', 'us' has very strong support (P[46] D G ω lat pesh), but is
probably due to assimilation to the first person plural in the next clause.

day is near; let us put off therefore the works of darkness, and let us put on the armour of light. (13) Let us, as if the day were already here, walk honourably, not in carousing and drunkenness, not in lasciviousness and uncleanness, not in strife and envy; (14) rather put on the Lord Jesus Christ, and take no thought in advance for the flesh, with a view to fulfilling its desires.

It was pointed out above (p. 214) that the whole exhortation of chs. xii, xiii is enclosed within an eschatological framework. In xii. 1 f. the reader is urged to dissociate himself from the present age; this requirement inevitably becomes more pressing when it is seen that the present age is hastening to its close, and that the Age to Come is near at hand. It is in this vein that this section of the epistle is concluded.

11 **All these things** (not only the command to love but the substance of chs. xii, xiii in general) **you must do the more zealously because you know the time in which we live.** 'The time' (καιρός) is a common eschatological term, fairly frequent in Paul's writings; for example, iii. 26; 1 Cor. iv. 5; vii. 29. The 'time in which we live' is that of the unique manifestation of God's righteousness preceding the judgement. It is further defined in the following words: **You know that it is already the hour for you to awake out of sleep.** Like 'time', 'hour' is an eschatological term, though it is not characteristic of Paul (e.g. 1 John ii. 18). 'Sleep' too is a metaphor which often occurs in eschatological admonitions (e.g. 1 Thess. v. 6–10). Men who live on the edge of the Age to Come cannot afford to relax their vigilance; **for salvation is nearer to us now than when we first believed.** The position of the pronoun in this sentence is such that it would be equally possible to translate (with AV), 'Now is our salvation nearer than . . .'; but Paul is not here thinking of salvation in a pietistic way as something that happens to *us* in *our* experience, but as a universal eschatological event. The lapse of time between the conversion of Paul and of his readers and the moment of writing is a significant proportion of the total interval between the resurrection of Jesus and his *parousia* at the last day. The consummation of God's final redemptive act is near.

12 This truth is next expressed in metaphor. **The night is advanced, the day is near.** That 'the day' is not simply the day of judgement (ii. 5) is shown by the corresponding 'night'. Paul means that this age has almost run its course, and that accordingly the Age to Come must very soon dawn. It is vitally important to draw the appropriate practical inference.

Let us put off therefore . . . and let us put on . . . According to Dr

E. G. Selwyn[1] these words introduce fresh sections in that common catechetical code which he believes to lie behind many of the New Testament epistles. For the former word see 1 Pet. ii. 1 f.; James i. 21; Col. iii. 8; Eph. iv. 22, 25; Heb. xii. 1; and for the latter (1 Pet. iv. 1); Col. iii. 10, 12; Eph. iv. 24; 1 Thess. v. 8; Gal. iii. 27. It is certain that the metaphors are widespread in early Christian literature, and it is quite possible that some standardization of catechumen instruction took place. Yet it must not be forgotten that the metaphor is a very simple one, which might easily have occurred independently to many different minds. In the present passage, for example, the reference to night and day could have suggested the metaphor of putting off night clothes and putting on day clothes.

They are not, however, clothes which are put on and put off. Paul's readers are urged to put off the **works of darkness** and to put on the **armour of light**: activities proper to the 'night, that is, to the old age before the coming of the Messiah, must be abandoned (cf. Col. iii. 5); for them, a new life of positive effort ('armour' includes offensive weapons) must be substituted. For the latter metaphor, compare 2 Cor. vi. 7; also 1 Thess. v. 8; Eph. vi. 13–18. When a man embarks upon the Christian life he enters a career of conflict.

The image of night and day has not been lost sight of ('armour of light'), and Paul returns to it. **Let us, as if the day were already here** 13 (it is implied that it is not yet here; cf. *v.* 12, the day is *near*), **walk honourably.** It would be equally possible to translate his words, Let us walk honourably as it is proper to walk in the day (which is in fact here). But the interpretation adopted in the translation is more appropriate to the context. Paul requires that Christians should live as if the Age to Come (this, rather than the day of judgement, is in mind) were actually here – as in some sense it is. For this sort of command, which is fundamental to Paul's conception of Christian ethics, compare vi. 11 f. 'Honourably' is very nearly, 'with nothing to be ashamed of'.

Negative examples follow. **Not in carousing and drunkenness** (cf. Gal. v. 21; 1 Pet. iv. 3): the nouns are difficult to distinguish. Paul perhaps uses them more or less as synonyms, reinforcing each other; the former, however, may suggest the revelling, the latter, the actual drunkenness which results from it. Both nouns are in the plural, suggesting frequent indulgence. **Not in lasciviousness** (the Greek word is used in a different sense at ix. 10) **and uncleanness** (again the two nouns are plural), **not in strife** (cf. i. 29; 1 Cor. i. 11; iii. 3; 2 Cor. xii. 20; Gal. v. 20; Phil. i. 15) **and envy** (cf. 1 Cor. iii. 3; 2 Cor. xii. 20; Gal. v. 20). The last pair evidently is a Pauline formula. All these

1 *The First Epistle of St Peter* (1946), pp. 393–400.

practices constitute a failure in love, which 'works no harm to the neighbour' (*v.* 10).

14 Instead of indulging in these immoral practices, **rather put on the Lord Jesus Christ.** Compare Gal. iii. 27, where Paul uses a past (aorist) tense; in baptism, Christians have already put on Christ, entering into him by incorporation into his crucifixion. But the relation thus sacramentally begun must be morally renewed (cf. vi. 11 f.). Those who have put on Christ in baptism must put on Christ by living in conformity with his mind (cf. Phil. ii. 5). This must be their sole object; it accordingly follows that they must **take no thought in advance for the flesh** (see pp. 128 f., 137) **with a view to fulfilling its desires** (see on vii. 7). In Paul's Greek, *desires* is accompanied by no possessive pronoun. The word can hardly stand alone in English, but it could be argued that a preferable supplement would be *your*, since *flesh* itself means something like *your desires*, your passion for self-fulfilment, whether this is thought of in physical or spiritual terms. *The flesh* is not something that I can detach from myself; it is myself, devoted to my own ends. In this passage Paul turns first to what are conventionally called carnal sins, but he moves on to *strife* and *envy*, which unfortunately are by no means incompatible with the practice of religion. *Putting on the Lord Jesus Christ* and *taking thought for the flesh* are opposites; the one means that life is ruled by Jesus Christ in his interests, the other that it is ruled by me in mine. Paul reminds his readers that they cannot serve God and mammon. The flesh will present its claims powerfully enough; there is no need to go half-way to meet it. That to which men should look forward and for which they should prepare is the Age to Come and the judgement; this they will do by cultivating love and expressing it in the ways indicated in chs. xii, xiii.

37 THE STRONG AND THE WEAK

CHAPTER xiv. 1–12

(1) **Welcome a man who is weak in faith, and do not take him in simply for discussions of his scruples. (2) One man has faith so strong that he can and does eat all things; but the weak man eats[1] vegetables only. (3) Let not the man who eats despise the man**

---

1 An important group of MSS (P[46] D* G lat) reads, 'But let the weak man eat...'. The text makes a statement; the variant gives a precept, which is in accord with *v.* 23. It is not impossible that the variant is original, but on the whole it seems more probable (especially in view of the construction in *v.* 2) that Paul is here stating the facts of the situation rather than recommending a course of action.

who does not eat, and let not the abstainer judge the man who does eat, for God has welcomed him. (4) Who are you to judge another man's servant? It is to his own master that he stands or falls; yes, and he shall stand, for his master is able to make him stand. (5) Again,[1] one man distinguishes day from day, while another counts all days alike. Let each one be fully convinced in his own mind. (6) He who is concerned about the day, is concerned to the Lord. And he who eats, eats to the Lord, for over his meal he gives thanks to God; and he who abstains, abstains to the Lord, and over his meal he gives thanks to God. (7) For none of us lives to himself and none of us dies to himself; (8) for if we live, we live to the Lord, and if we die, we die to the Lord. Whether then we live or die we are the Lord's. (9) For Christ died and came to life for this very purpose, namely, that he might reign as Lord over both the dead and the living. (10) Well then, you – why do you judge your brother? Or you – why do you despise your brother? For we shall all stand before God's judgement seat. (11) For it is written, 'As I live, saith the Lord, every knee shall bow to me, and every tongue shall render praise to God'. (12) Every one of us therefore shall give account of himself to God.[2]

In xi. 13–24, Paul urged Gentile Christians not to think too highly of themselves over against their Jewish brethren. In xii. 3, 16 f., he gave a more general warning to the same effect. In the long section xiv. 1–xv. 13 he returns to a similar theme. His reasons for doing so are disputed. The simplest explanation is that he had been informed of the existence in the Roman church of the two groups whom he describes as *the Strong* and *the Weak*, and sought to end, or at least mitigate, the division between them. It is objected to this view that Paul had not been in Rome and would not have known so much about the affairs of the church there. The objection has some weight, but not much. News of Christianity in Rome had spread (i. 8), and Paul was by no means without personal contacts with Rome; see Acts xviii. 2 and especially Rom. xvi. 3–16 (if it is correct to think that these verses were addressed to Rome; see pp. 257 f.). A second explanation is that Paul, well aware of the problems of the church in Corinth (1 Cor. viii–x), thought it likely that a similar situation might have arisen, or intended by prompt action to prevent such a situation from arising, in Rome. It is against this that there are differences between Romans and 1 Corinthians, and that Rom. xiv, xv give a very realistic picture. A third

1 Omitting 'for' (γάρ) with P⁴⁶ B D G ω pesh.
2 The words 'to God' are omitted by B G it, perhaps rightly. The short text is intelligible, but the tendency to add to it would be very strong. 'To God', if an addition to Paul's text, is undoubtedly correct interpretation.

explanation, which equally encounters the difficulty just mentioned, is that the picture of the Strong and the Weak is simply an imaginary illustration invented by Paul as a framework for the theological lesson he means to teach. Of these explanations the first is the best. Paul's knowledge of affairs in Rome was doubtless limited, but he probably knew a good deal more about them than we do. For the identification of the two groups see below.

1   **Welcome** (cf. *v.* 3) **a man who is weak in faith**: receive him into the Christian family. For 'weak' Christians, see xiv. 1–xv. 13 *passim*; also 1 Cor. viii. 7–11; ix. 22. Their 'weakness' is expressed in a number of abstentions which will be noted in detail below; it attests a failure to grasp the fundamental principle, which page after page of this epistle emphasizes, that men are justified and reconciled to God not by vegetarianism, sabbatarianism, or teetotalism, but by faith alone – or, better, by God's own free electing grace, faith being man's recognition that all is dependent not upon himself but God. So strong is this emphasis that it comes as a surprise to find that Paul recognizes that both strong and weak have a place in the Church, and that both can stand before God and be accepted by him. This has led some to the view that this cannot be a true description of the Weak; if it were, Paul 'would not have regarded them as genuine believers' (Cranfield, p. 691). To say this, however, is to fall into the condemnatory error that Paul finds in the Strong, who despise the Weak (*vv.* 3, 10) and, it seems, doubt whether they have any standing with God (*v.* 4). The Weak are *weak in faith*; they are weak, but they have faith; they have faith, but they do not draw from it all the inferences that they should draw. From the beginning the Church has had many such believers; their existence is reflected in, for example, the prohibition of meat not slaughtered in the Jewish manner (Acts xv. 29, things strangled, πνικτά). They do in fact trust Christ alone for salvation, but they do not understand that *alone* with full logical rigour; they must therefore not be despised, still less excluded from the Church, but lovingly instructed till they understand better. 'It is also his (Paul's) opinion that there is a faith which does not adequately fill its place' (Käsemann, 354, English translation, 367).

The remaining words of *v.* 1 are very difficult to translate. They might be literally rendered, 'not for disputes of doubts'. It is almost certainly wrong to take the genitive 'of doubts' as a genitive of definition, describing 'disputes' (AV, 'not to doubtful disputations'). The doubts are the doubts of the weak Christian, and Paul's advice to his readers is, **do not take him in simply for discussions of his scruples.** He is to be welcomed not as an opportunity for theological debate on the part of his superiors, but as one 'for whom Christ died' (1 Cor. viii. 11); that is, he must be accepted in love.

In the next verse, Paul set out, in their simplest form, the facts of the case. **One man has faith so strong that he can and does eat all** 2 **things;** that is, he is completely uninhibited by relics of a pagan or Jewish past, expressing itself in religious scrupulosities. Like Paul himself (who undoubtedly is one of the 'strong'), he knows that the 'kingdom of God is not eating and drinking' (v. 17). **But the weak man eats vegetables only;** that is, he believes that foods have a religious value, and that his relation with God demands that he avoid the use of meat. Who is this 'weak man'? Paul allows us to learn three things about him: (1) he eats vegetables and no meat (vv. 2, 21); (2) he regards some days as having special importance (vv. 5 f.); (3) he does not drink wine (vv. 17, 21). It is impossible to pick out from the many examples of religious scrupulosity to be found in antiquity any single group of persons corresponding exactly with those described here by Paul. In view of Paul's earlier warnings against mutual disparagement between Jews and Gentiles it is natural to think of the Weak as Jewish Christians who retained the food laws and calendar of Judaism. In its simple form this view will not stand. There is no Jewish law against eating meat and drinking wine. Both are indeed subject to the law of tithing, and certain kinds of meat were forbidden, and a method of slaughtering was laid down. Those who, as Christians, continued to observe Jewish practices would be obliged to eat vegetables only and to drink no wine if Jewish butchers and wine merchants refused to supply them. It is likely that many would so refuse; but if R. Penna[1] is correct in the figure of 20,000 Jews in Rome in the time of Nero the possibility of finding compliant – or even Christian – shopkeepers does not seem too remote. Moreover the abstainers seem to be acting on principle: 'I eat vegetables because I believe it to be right to do so', not 'I would gladly eat meat if only the Jewish shops would sell it to me'. Judaism is a more likely influence than the Pythagoreanism of, for example, Apollonius of Tyana, who avoided meat and wine.[2] The closest parallel, perhaps, is to be found in the heretics of Colossae. These men gave special veneration to certain days (Col. ii. 16), and practised various kinds of abstinence (Col. ii. 16, 21 f.). There are traces of both Judaism and Gnosticism in their practices and beliefs. It may be that some such fusion had occurred in Rome, though the 'weak' in Rome were much more Christian (and much less gnostic) than the heretics of Colossae. The possibility was mentioned above that Paul was speaking of the scrupulous in general, without reference to particular persons; it seems however more probable that he is addressing a real than a hypothetical situation. This is strongly suggested by direct speech addressed to the person concerned (vv. 4,10).

1 *NTS* 28 (1982), p. 328; his n. 53 on p. 341 mentions other estimates rising to as many as 60,000.
2 Philostratus, *Life of Apollonius*, i. 8.

3   There must be no ill-feeling between the two groups. **Let not the man who eats despise the man who does not eat.** This he may be tempted to do, for the strong inevitably tend to despise those who are weaker – in mind and conscience as in other matters – than themselves. He thinks them inferior Christians. **And let not the abstainer judge the man who does eat.** The peculiar danger of the weak is censoriousness; for the weak Christian is apt to suppose that his fellow Christian, who does something he (the weak man) regards as sinful, must be sinning against his conscience, although in fact his conscience is more enlightened, and does not condemn the course of action in question. He thinks him an undisciplined Christian. But the weak man, who abstains, must not judge his brother in this way, **for God has welcomed** (cf. *v.* 1) **him.** If God himself is willing to receive the meat-eater into his household, the weak Christian has no reason to take offence.

This verse is not only an exhortation to charity; it implies an acute analysis of the situation, in which it appears that both strong and weak are exposed to the same danger. The weak is exposed to the danger of externalizing God's righteousness, and supposing that his outward acts and abstentions *are* the righteousness of God, and that vegetarianism and the like constitute in themselves a sufficient standing for man before God. This is evidently false. But as soon as the strong despises the weak he falls into the same error, for he is treating his actions, or his 'faith' ('faith … to eat'! – *v.* 2), as a visible sign of his superiority. For this reason, neither is in a position to condemn the other.

4   Paul proceeds to develop his point in a different way. **Who are you to judge another man's servant?** It is the weak man who is addressed; see *v.* 3. That is, Paul is here taking the part of the strong Christian. **It is to his own master that he stands or falls** – his master, not his fellow Christian, determines the acceptability of his service. There is a strong case for taking the dative (τῷ κυρίῳ, *master*) as a dative of advantage: it is in his master's interests (not yours) that he stands. But the verse as a whole is about judging, and it seems better to take the master as the true judge of his servant's standing. **Yes, and he shall stand, for his master is able to make him stand.** God alone is the judge of his servants; and before his judgement the achievements of strong and weak alike are dissolved; but it is he also who establishes their works (Ps. xc. 17), whether the free action of the strong or the observances of the weak. These alike are incomplete and lack significance in themselves (cf. ii. 7); but God has the power to complete them and fill them with meaning.

Paul turns to another example of the different beliefs and practices
5 of weak and strong. **Again, one man distinguishes day from day, while another counts all days alike.** This verse is most easily

explained on the view that the weak, whether full Jews or not, keep the Sabbath. Compare Gal. iv. 10; Col. ii. 16. Whether this be true or not, we are confronted here with a significant difference in Christian practice. Paul does not pronounce upon it, but comments, **Let each one be fully convinced in his own mind.** See the note on iv. 21; compare Col. iv. 12. It is probable that 'own' (ἴδιος) has at least some of its proper force, though it is true that in Hellenistic Greek the word has sometimes an 'exhausted' sense. Each man should be convinced in his *own* mind, not affected by the contentions of others; and he should act in accordance with his own convictions. Only when he does so act is the statement of the next verse true.

He who is concerned about the day, is concerned to the Lord. 6 **And he who eats, eats to the Lord, for over his meal he gives thanks to God; and he who abstains, abstains to the Lord, and over his meal** (of vegetables) **he gives thanks to God.** The sabbatarian observes the seventh day rest not because he values the institution as an invention of his own, but because he believes that he is obeying a divine command: he keeps it with reference to the Lord who commanded it. Again, both the meat-eater and the vegetarian observe the (originally Jewish) custom of saying a blessing (that is, a thanksgiving to God) over their meals. Their meals, therefore, whatever they may consist of, are eaten with reference to the Lord; they are not secular functions. Here it appears that strong and weak, whom we have already seen (p. 238) to be exposed to the same danger, share equally in the same positive virtue. In what he does, each gives thanks to God, that is, each recognizes his lordship. We may contrast i. 21: the heathen 'did not glorify him as God or give thanks to him'; they did not recognize his lordship. Strong and weak are both servants, belonging to and dependent on the same Lord. The strong is not independent, and the weak is not abandoned to his own resources.

For none of us lives to himself and none of us dies to himself. 7 Paul does not mean (as is sometimes supposed) that our actions affect our fellow men, but that we live in relation to God. **For if we live, we** 8 **live to the Lord, and if we die, we die to the Lord. Whether then we live or die we are the Lord's.** Paul is speaking of Christians, and what he says is scarcely more than a definition. The faith and obedience of a Christian mean that he belongs not to himself but to God. Further, they are not confined to this life only. Having already 'risen with Christ' (Col. iii. 1), the Christian belongs to him even in death.

It might have been supposed that in *vv.* 7 f. Paul was speaking of a relation with God enjoyed by all men in virtue of their creation. That this is not so is shown by *v.* 9: **For Christ died and came to life for** 9 **this very purpose, namely, that he might reign as Lord over both the dead and the living.** The slave–lord relationship between the

Christian and Christ rests entirely upon the death and resurrection of Jesus, which led to his exaltation and heavenly reign. It has been suggested that the verse should be analysed into two parallel statements:

> Christ died that he might reign as Lord over the dead;
> Christ came to life that he might reign as Lord over the living.

This, however, is not probable (cf. iv. 25 and note); the death and resurrection together formed one complex event which ushered in the period of Christ's reign. It is, nevertheless, probable that Paul intended the rhetorical balance of the sentence: die – dead, come to life – living.

Paul returns to the main theme and addresses at once both the weak (who is prone to judge) and the strong (who is prone to despise).

10 **Well then** (in view of what has been said), **you – why do you judge your brother? Or you – why do you despise your brother?** Compare *vv.* 3 f. A further argument is now added: **For we shall all stand before** (not each other's but) **God's judgement seat.** In the end everyone must recognize that God, and not his own wisdom, or folly, or even conscience (1 Cor. iv. 4), is the arbiter. Freedom and scrupulosity alike (as human practices) fail to touch the cardinal point

11 of justification. This is reinforced by Old Testament references. **For it is written, 'As I live, saith the Lord** (cf. Isa. xlix. 18), **every knee shall bow to me, and every tongue shall render praise to God'** (cf.

12 Isa. xlv. 23). **Every one of us therefore shall give account of himself to God.** He is not accountable to his fellow-men, but he is accountable to God. This should lead him to avoid judging, and at the same time to examine the bases of his action. If he supposes that either his abstinence or his intelligent and well-instructed 'faith' will justify him, he would do well to think again, and to consider what it means to stand before God's judgement seat. Only God's creative verdict, heard in anticipation by humble and obedient faith, can justify the most religious or the most irreligious of men. The strong, then, is right; but if he boasts of his superiority he instantly becomes as wrong as the man he despises. The weak is mistaken, yet accepted; and he must not put himself in God's place, and judge the strong.

38 WALKING IN LOVE

CHAPTER xiv. 13–23

(13) Let us therefore no longer judge one another; but come rather to this decision, that you will not put a stumbling-block or

an offence in your brother's way. (14) I know, I am quite confident in the Lord Jesus, that nothing is unclean in itself; only to a man who reckons anything to be unclean, to him it is unclean. (15) This fact must govern our attitude. For if your brother is grieved on account of food which you eat, then you are no longer walking in love. Do not by your food destroy him for whom Christ died. (16) And do not let this good thing of yours become a source of reproach. (17) For the kingdom of God is not eating and drinking, but righteousness and peace and joy in the Holy Spirit. (18) For he who serves Christ in this way is pleasing to God and irreproachable with men. (19) Let us therefore ardently pursue the things that make for peace and the things that make for mutual building up. (20) Do not for the sake of food destroy the work of God. All things are clean, but they work harm to the man who eats them so as to cause offence. (21) It is well not to eat flesh nor to drink wine, nor to do any other thing by which your brother may be made to stumble. (22) Keep to yourself before God the faith which you have.[1] Blessed is he who does not waver in respect of what his conscience affirms; (23) but if the waverer eats, he is condemned, because what he does is not of faith; and everything that is not of faith is sin.[2]

The point of the previous paragraph is assumed and summarized: **Let 13 us therefore no longer** (the tense of the verb supports the view that Paul is addressing a real, not a hypothetical, situation) **judge one another.** Neither strong nor weak is in a position to adopt the superior attitude of the judge. Paul now presses on to a further point, using the word 'judge' (κρίνειν) in a verbal play impossible to reproduce in English. The word changes its sense (though it retains the fundamental meaning of 'come to a decision'), and also its tense, for whereas the reader has been told to stop judging, he is now urged to come, once for all, to a specific judgement. **Come rather to this decision, that you will not put a stumbling-block or an offence in your brother's way.** Paul has already laid it down (xiii. 8 ff.; xii. 9 f.) that the supreme command is that of love. This must therefore be applied to the present problem, and its application will mean that each man will seek not to express his own convictions but to serve the interests of his brother Christian. This he will do by taking care not to place in his way anything that might cause him to fall from his Christian faith and

---

1 The relative ('which' – ἥν) is omitted by D G ω lat pesh. This seems to be an attempt to ease a difficult construction. If the short reading is accepted, we may translate either 'Have you faith? Keep it to yourself before God' for 'You have faith. Keep it . . . ' The former alternative is preferable.
2 The textual problems of the last chapters of the epistle begin at this point. See Introduction, pp. 10–13.

practice. His actions must not be governed by self-interest. This principle Paul proceeds to apply.

14   **I know, I am quite confident in the Lord Jesus, that nothing is unclean in itself.** Paul underlines emphatically this deduction from his theological principles, indicating thereby that he is one of the 'strong'. When the whole of life lies equally under the judgement and under the grace of God it is idle to mark out certain areas as in a special sense 'unclean'. The word (κοινόν) means properly 'common'; hence 'profane', and, in the religious sense, 'unclean'. This derived use of the word is almost exclusively Jewish. Paul's attitude is to be found in the gospels (cf. Mark vii. 14–23), but it is incompatible with orthodox Judaism, even though Paul himself seems to have believed that he could at will revert, when occasion demanded it, to Jewish practice (1 Cor. ix. 19–23). 'Uncleanness' cannot affect those relationships (sin, acquittal, peace, and the like) which Paul grasped as central. This is his own view, and that of the strong; yet there is something to set over against it.

Only to a man who reckons anything to be unclean, to him it is unclean. Paul has stated his own view uncompromisingly; but he acknowledges at once that there are others who take a different view. Many a man can be found who regards a certain food as unclean; if he were to eat it, he would be defiled, not because the food is in itself unclean, or offensive to God, but because his action is an offence against his conscience, and sinful (*v.* 23). To him, 'it is unclean'; the language is not rigorously logical, but clear enough. The doubtful

15   eater cannot 'give God thanks' (*v.* 6); he is acting disobediently. **This fact must govern our attitude** (these words are an insertion, required to make sense of the 'for' which follows). **For if your brother is grieved on account of food which you eat** (these last three words also are an addition, which brings out the sense – the 'brother' is grieved not by food in general but by the food which his fellow Christian eats), **then you are no longer walking in love.** How is the 'brother' grieved? (i) The mere sight of a Christian doing what he (however wrongly) regards as sinful will give pain to his sensitive conscience. (ii) He may nevertheless be emboldened by his fellow's example to do that which he regards as sinful; but he will do it with a bad conscience, as a waverer, who is condemned by his doubts (*v.* 23). Thus the attitude of the strong Christian, unless carefully regulated, is almost certain to result in injury to the weak Christian, who is likely either to suffer pain or to fall into sin. To allow this to happen is not to walk in love; and it is more important to walk in love than to express one's Christian freedom at the table. Therefore, **Do not by your food destroy him for whom Christ died**, that is, your weak Christian brother. It is possible to do what is itself right in such a way, and in such circumstances, as to undo the effects of the death of Christ. The

same truth is now expressed more generally. **Do not let this good** 16
thing of yours become a source of reproach. 'This good thing of
yours' is probably 'your Christian freedom'. This in itself is good; but
wrongly used, used, that is, in defiance of love, it can serve only to
bring disgrace upon the Church.

To insist upon one's freedom without regard to the scruples of
others is not only to fail in the primary Christian virtue of love but to
misunderstand the real basis of the Christian faith. **For the kingdom** 17
of God is not eating and drinking, but righteousness and peace
and joy in the Holy Spirit. Faith is not 'faith to eat all things' (*v.* 2);
Christian privilege is not the privilege of being able to eat and drink
what one likes.

The phrase 'kingdom of God' is not frequent in Paul's writings: 1
Cor. iv. 20; vi. 9 f.; xv. 50; Col. iv. 11; 1 Thess. ii. 12; 2 Thess. i. 5;
compare Col. i. 13; 1 Cor. xv. 24; Eph. v. 5. It often refers to the future,
occasionally (as here) to the present. The infrequent usage is against
the view (Denney) that the phrase could here almost be translated
'the Christian religion'. (i) Reference to the kingdom emphasizes that
the life of faith, though it is truly a life of freedom, is nevertheless life
under the rule of God. Christian freedom is gained by presenting one's
members as slaves to God (vi. 13). (ii) It was recognized by at least
some Jews (e.g. in *Berakoth*, 17 a) that 'in the Age to Come there is
neither eating nor drinking . . . '. If this was true of the Age to Come,
conditions in the kingdom of God as anticipated in the present age
could not be radically different. It follows from both considerations
that to set too much store by the Christian's privilege of eating what
he likes without religious scruple, is to fall into error as serious as that
of reverting to Jewish food laws. Compare Gal. vi. 15, which also
throws light on the reference to the Holy Spirit, by whom the
anticipation of the kingdom of God in the present is effected (viii. 23).

Righteousness, peace, and joy might be described as the fruit of the
Spirit (Gal. v. 22). It is true that in Romans, and elsewhere in Paul's
writings, righteousness and peace usually describe an objective
relation with God; but in this verse joy is certainly subjective, and
probably determines the sense of the other two words. Righteousness
therefore will be righteous action (which, of course, is bound to spring
out of the objective relation of righteousness); peace will be a peaceful
state of mind (which again arises inevitably out of the relation of
peace with God).

The next verse follows immediately. **For he who serves Christ in** 18
this way (that is, by recognizing that food and drink are secondary
matters) **is pleasing to God** (cf. xii. 1 f.) **and irreproachable** (tried
and approved; cf. pp. 53, 97) **with men.** The translation is probable
but not quite certain. 'In this way' is literally *in this* (ἐν τούτῳ). *This*
may well be taken, as here, to refer to the whole of the preceding

verse, but it might be understood in relation to the immediate antecedent noun, Spirit (πνεύματι): He who in the Spirit serves Christ. 'Irreproachable with men', or *approved by men*, is not immediately clear; probably Paul is thinking on the same lines as in 1 Cor. x. 32 (Be men who lay no stumbling-block before Jews, or Greeks, or the Church of God); Gal. v. 23 (against such things there is no law). By such behaviour the whole Christian fellowship will be built up, and Christian life will not become a 'source of reproach' (*v.* 16).

19   **Let us therefore ardently pursue the things that make for peace and the things that make for mutual building up.** The Church is one body in Christ (xii. 5). It cannot make for the unity of this one body if the several members are more concerned to practise their private convictions than to live in love. It is better that the community as a whole should be at peace than that one group should get its own way. What all should seek is the peace of the community, and its edification. 'Edification' is for Paul not individualistic but corporate. The Church is God's building (cf. 1 Cor. iii. 9), and 'building up' means the building up of the Church. This observation determines

20   the sense of the next sentence. **Do not for the sake of food** (which you would like – and feel free – to eat) **destroy the work of God,** that is, not the individual Christian (as in *v.* 15 b), but the Church, the outcome of God's work in Jesus Christ. Inconsiderate behaviour may lead to the destruction of that which God himself has wrought.

Paul now returns to a point even further back in the argument; *v.* 20 b recalls *v.* 14. **All things are clean;** compare Mark vii. 19. **But they work harm to the man who eats them so as to cause offence.** This translation involves a certain amount of interpretation of Paul's Greek, which is elliptic and obscure. The first words are, literally, 'But evil to the man who . . .'. They may mean simply 'Evil *happens* to the man who . . .', but in the context it seems more probable that 'all things' continues to form (in thought, if not grammatically) the subject. 'All things are clean, but *they cause* evil to the man who . . .'. Alternatively, we may supply 'his eating' (ἐσθίειν): *His eating works harm to the man who* . . . (so Cranfield 724). The words, 'so as to cause offence', are literally 'through offence', 'through a stumbling-block'. The preposition (διά) is evidently used to describe 'attendant circumstances', but even so its bearing is not clear, for we cannot be certain who is the eater. *V.* 21 suggests that he is the strong Christian, who by his eating causes offence and lays a stumbling-block before his weaker brother, who may be tempted to do that of which his conscience disapproves (*v.* 23). It is not, however, impossible that the eater is the weak Christian who eats *because* he has been tripped up and made to stumble by the strong man's action, and thus suffers injury because he is acting against conscience. It may be, perhaps, that the vagueness and obscurity of Paul's sentence are due to the fact that he is thinking of both possibilities, and expresses himself so as to allow for both.

We do not know how well informed he was about the circumstances of the church in Rome. In any case, Paul proceeds at once to give specific advice to the strong. **It is well not to eat flesh nor to** 21 **drink wine** (this shows that the weak abstained from wine as well as meat), **nor to do any other thing by which your brother may be made to stumble.** It is far more important to preserve unharmed the conscience of your fellow-Christian and the unity of the Church than to exercise your undoubted right as an instructed Christian to eat flesh and to drink wine. This does not mean that all Christians should take vows of abstinence. The infinitives 'to eat' and 'to drink' are aorists, and the meaning seems to be that if on any particular occasion it seems likely that to eat flesh or to drink wine will cause a brother to stumble, it is right on that occasion to abstain (so BDR, § 338. 1.1). Eating and drinking are not wrong in themselves, and on other occasions the danger may not arise.

Keep to yourself before God the faith which you have. Do not 22 boast about the faith that gives you your freedom. For this use of *faith*, cf. *vv.* 1 f. True faith is an invisible relation between man and God, a confidence in God so complete that the man who has it knows that no religious scrupulosity can add to the security of his relation with God. But the moment 'faith' begins to parade itself as a visible thing which can be demonstrated by such acts as eating flesh and drinking wine, it ceases to be faith and becomes weakness. This is not to say that the position of the strong is wrong. **Blessed is he who does not waver in respect of what his conscience affirms.** This sentence cannot be translated with confidence. The subject is, literally, 'he who does not judge himself'; but this man clearly corresponds to the waverer of *v.* 23, and it seems well to bring out the correspondence which is suggested by the Greek forms (ὁ μὴ κρίνων ἑαυτόν – ὁ διακρινόμενος). 'Judge' is used in the sense of 'condemn'. The sphere in which judgement does or does not take place is 'what he tries and approves'; the sense of testing is represented in the translation by the introduction of the word conscience. Once this man's faith and reason have affirmed a course of action he does not waver: happy is he in that he does not.

There are others, however, who do waver. They are not fully convinced that as Christians they stand under grace and not under law. These men must be warned. **If the waverer eats, he is** 23 **condemned, because what he does is not of faith; and everything that is not of faith is sin.** If, for example, the waverer eats meat, it will not be because he has 'faith so strong that he can and does eat all things' (*v.* 2), but because he would like to do so; because he fears the scorn of his stronger brother; because it is inconvenient or irksome to observe the rules he believes to have divine authority; or for some such reason. To act on such terms is not to 'give God thanks' and recognize his lordship (*v.* 6), but rather to make one's own convenience or pleasure the standard of one's actions, and thus to fall back into the worst kind of idolatry, in which the idol is – self. To eat, therefore, *in these circumstances*, is sin. There is only one proper relation between God and man, that which is described on man's side as faith; every other relation is a false, negative relation – in fact, sin. It is this sin which the strong Christian may, by unguarded behaviour, trip his brother into committing; nevertheless, the weak Christian is responsible, and is condemned, for his own act.

39 UNITY IN LOVE
CHAPTER xv. 1–13

(1) We who are strong ought to bear the weaknesses of those who are not, and not to please ourselves. (2) Let each one of us please his neighbour with some good purpose, so as to effect building up. (3) For even Christ did not please himself; on the contrary, as it is written, 'The reproaches of those who reproached thee fell on me'. (4) (For all the things that were written beforehand in Scripture were written for our instruction, that we, through our endurance and through the exhortation that comes from Scripture, might have hope. (5) And may the God from whom all endurance and exhortation spring grant to you that you may have a common mind according to Christ Jesus, (6) that with one accord, with one mouth, you may glorify the God and Father of our Lord Jesus Christ.)

(7) So welcome one another, as Christ also welcomed you,[1] to the glory of God. (8) For I tell you that Christ has become[2] a servant of the 'circumcision', for the vindication of God's truth, so as to confirm the promises made to the fathers, (9) and that the Gentiles may glorify God for his mercy, as it is written, 'For this cause I will praise thee among the Gentiles, and I will sing praise

---

1 Instead of 'you', B D* sah read 'us'. There would be a natural inclination to change 'us' into 'you' in harmony with the second person plural of the verb 'welcome'; this observation is in favour of 'us'. But Paul had used the first person in *v.* 1, whence it might be introduced into the present verse by readers who failed to note that whereas in *v.* 1 Paul was addressing the strong, and counting himself with them, in this verse he was addressing the whole body. 'You' is the more probable reading.

2 Instead of 'has become' (γεγενῆσθαι), B C* D* read 'became' (γενέσθαι). The perfect implies that Christ continued to be what he became, the simple past tense not. The former is the more difficult, and more probable reading.

to thy name'; (10) and again he says, 'Rejoice, ye Gentiles, with
his people'; (11) and again, 'Praise the Lord, all ye Gentiles, and
let all the peoples praise him'. (12) And again, Isaiah says, 'There
shall be the root of Jesse, and he who rises up to rule the Gentiles;
in him shall the Gentiles hope'. (13) May the God who is thus the
ground of hope fill you with all joy and peace in your faith, that
you may abound in hope, in the power of the Holy Spirit.

In this paragraph, addressing primarily the strong (v. 1) but also
turning to the whole church (v. 7), Paul shows how the attitude of love
which he has advocated might work in practice, and also supplies a
further reason for adopting it.

We who are strong (Paul is one of the strong – none knows better 1
than he that man does not stand or fall by his abstinences) ought to
bear the weaknesses of those who are not. Their weaknesses are
their special practices, their abstinences from meat, wine, and the
like, erroneous in themselves and troublesome to their fellow
Christians. 'Bear' is in Greek (βαστάζειν) as ambiguous as it is in
English. Here it probably means 'endure' (as at Matt. xx. 12; Acts xv.
10), as the following clause suggests. It is less probable that it means
'carry' (as at Gal. vi. 2); though it is possible that Paul means to make
use of the ambiguity of the word and to play upon both meanings.
Strong Christians must endure the vagaries of their weak brethren,
and help them in their difficulties.

Further, we who are strong ought not to please ourselves. See the
note on viii. 8; compare Phil. ii. 4. We must not consult our own
interests but those of others; especially of those weaker than
ourselves. Paul continues: Let each one of us please his neighbour 2
with some good purpose (as vague in Greek as in English, but
probably explained by the following words), so as to effect building
up. For 'building up' see on xiv. 19.

Paul now produces a further argument for the course of action he
commends: he appeals to the example of Christ. For even Christ did 3
not please himself. The verb sums up the work and character of
Christ throughout his earthly life. Paul adduces none of the incidents
known to us in the gospel tradition (cf. p. 222); yet it must be admitted
that in one word he gives an admirable summary of the impression
conveyed by the gospels. Instead of appealing to narrative he appeals
to prophecy: on the contrary, as it is written, 'The reproaches of
those who reproached thee fell on me' (Ps. lxix. 9). The use of
Scripture at this point is significant. It means that the example of
Christ is more than an example; it belongs to the pattern of revelation.
To this point Paul returns in v. 7; for the present his quotation leads
him to a parenthesis on the use of Scripture.

For (the conjunction justifies the application of the passage just 4 quoted to the problem in hand) **all the things that were written beforehand in Scripture were written for our instruction;** compare 1 Cor. ix. 9 f. The special use of Scripture is to foster hope. It was written **that we, through our endurance** (cf. ii. 7; v. 3 f.) **and through the exhortation that comes from Scripture, might have hope.** This is not perfectly clear. The word translated 'exhortation' (παράκλησις) sometimes means 'comfort', but, followed as it is by a genitive, is most naturally taken as in the translation; but this does not explain why exhortation should be coupled with endurance as the ground of hope. We may conjecture that Paul's real meaning is: Scripture exhorts us to endure in hope, and gives us good ground for doing so. But it must be admitted that this is not what he says. It may be best to paraphrase his words thus: In a situation marked by reproaches (*v.* 3) we have hope (a) because we practise that endurance which looks to God for the meaning of its present lot, and (b) because Scripture, by foretelling our situation, encourages us to pass through it in hope.

5   Paul turns back to the main theme. **And may the God from whom all endurance and exhortation spring grant to you that you may have a common mind according to Christ Jesus** (cf. Phil. ii. 5),
6 **that, with one accord, with one mouth, you may glorify the God and Father of our Lord Jesus Christ.** It is possible, though incapable of proof, that Paul is drawing upon a liturgical doxology. In any case, the emphasis lies not upon the form of words used but upon the unanimity with which it is uttered.

Verses 5 and 6, with their summons to the united praise of God, suggest that Paul has now concluded his treatment of the problem of the weak and the strong; in *v.* 7 however he returns to his main theme, and gathers up what he has written since he began to deal with it in
7 xiv. 1 (cf. xiv. 3). **So welcome one another, as Christ also welcomed you, to the glory of God.** The last five words form an adverbial phrase (suggested perhaps by *v.* 6), but it is not evident to which verb they apply. On the whole it is more likely that they should be taken with 'welcomed'; this is suggested by *vv.* 8 f. But it is probably not wrong to take them with both verbs. Christ's act in welcoming men is directed to the glory of God; but so is the unity of Christian men in love. When the strong receive the weak, and the weak the strong, they are in the most significant way glorifying God.

A new thought is now introduced, but unfortunately the language is so obscure that it is difficult to be sure of its bearing on the argument.
8 **For** (evidently the new material is intended to add further justification for the precept 'Welcome one another') **I tell you that Christ has become a servant of the 'circumcision'.** In the present translation the use of inverted commas is intended to make it plain that *circumcision* is taken as a collective, equivalent to 'the Jews'. Christ

became (and – as the perfect tense shows – remains) a servant of the Jews, who, especially when described as the 'circumcision', may be regarded as the most awkward and irritating of scrupulous persons. He thus provides an example for all strong Christians (cf. *v.* 3). This seems to be the best interpretation. Other suggestions are (i) Christ became a minister of circumcision in that he carried out the promises implied in the covenant the seal of which was circumcision, and (ii) he has become a minister of circumcision even to Gentiles, because he has admitted them to all the privileges promised to the Jewish Church, of which circumcision is the symbol. Cranfield (p. 740) rightly describes these suggestions as 'decidedly forced'.

Why did Christ become a servant of the 'circumcision'? **For the vindication of God's truth, so as to confirm the promises made to the fathers, and that the Gentiles may glorify God for his mercy.** 9 The fathers of the Jewish race had been promised a Messiah, and if the Messiah had not been sent into the realm of circumcision God's truth, or faithfulness, would have been impugned. The construction of the sentence now becomes very difficult. There are two main possibilities. (i) The whole sentence is dependent on the 'I tell you' at the beginning of *v.* 8; the two main verbs (infinitives in Greek) are 'has become' and 'may glorify', 'so as to confirm' being parenthetical. In outline the sentence runs: I tell you that Christ has become ... (so as to confirm ...), and that the Gentiles are to glorify (*or*, that the Gentiles glorify) ... (ii) The governing sentence is 'Christ has become', and on this the two other verbs ('to confirm' and 'that they may glorify' – both infinitives in Greek) are dependent. In outline the sentence runs: Christ has become ... so as to confirm ... and that the Gentiles ... Each of these constructions is harsh because each involves a change of subject; but it seems evident from the connection of thought that the statement about Christ controls the sentence, and accordingly alternative (ii) should be chosen (as in the present translation). The coming of Christ may be viewed in two ways. On the one hand he came to vindicate God's faithfulness by fulfilling the promises which had been made within Judaism. On the other hand he came that the Gentiles might be included with Israel among the people of God. As the Jews glorify God for his faithfulness, so the Gentiles will glorify him for his mercy. There are longer discussions of this difficult construction in Cranfield (pp. 742–4) and in Wilckens (3, p. 106); both reject the way in which the sentence is taken here. Lietzmann's laconic note (p. 119: 'δοξάσαι Inf. abhängig von [infinitive dependent on] εἰς τό *v.* 8) seems, however, to make the essential points.

The inclusion of the Gentiles is not to be regarded as a happy afterthought; it was foretold in Scripture. This Paul proceeds once more (cf. ix. 25 f.; x. 19 f.) to document. **As it is written, 'For this**

cause I will praise thee among the Gentiles, and I will sing praise
to thy name'. The quotation is from Ps. xviii. 49 (=2 Sam. xxii. 50);
the point (as in the quotations that follow) lies in the reference to
Gentiles, and, secondarily, in the offering of praise for God's
10 faithfulness and mercy. **And again he says, 'Rejoice, ye Gentiles,**
11 **with his people'** (Deut. xxxii. 43); **and again, 'Praise the Lord, all**
12 **ye Gentiles, and let all the peoples praise him'** (Ps. cxvii. 1). **And
again, Isaiah says, 'There shall be the root of Jesse, and he who
rises up to rule the Gentiles; in him shall the Gentiles hope'** (Isa.
xi. 10; cf. xi. 1). In all these passages, Paul sees a reference to
'Gentiles'; in most, or all, of them, the original meaning was 'nations'.
Paul in general shows no interest in the Davidic descent of Jesus (see
on i. 3), and offers no exposition of it here.

The discussion of the relations between strong and weak in the
13 Church comes to an end with a brief prayer for the readers. **May the
God who is thus** (that is, in the light of the passages just quoted) **the
ground of hope fill you with all joy and peace in your faith, that
you may abound in hope, in the power of the Holy Spirit.** The true
content and goal of faith is not the right to eat and drink, but joy and
peace in the Holy Spirit (cf. xiv. 17). Hope also occupies a prominent
place in this prayer; compare *v.* 4. The quotations of *vv.* 9–12 have led
Paul back again to the great theme of the union of Jew and Gentile in
Christ, an event significant in itself, but still more significant in that its
completion marks the full end of God's purposes (xi. 12, 15). It seems
unlikely that the introduction of this theme is here merely ornamental
(Lietzmann). It may be that the division existing at Rome was simply
that between Jew and Gentile (see p. 237); or that Paul is arguing *a
majori ad minus* – if God can unite these he can unite anyone; or that *v.*
6 concludes the argument, and that *vv.* 7–13 are a summary which
looks back to chs. ix–xi as well as to ch. xiv.

40 PAUL'S PLANS AND GOD'S PURPOSE
CHAPTER xv. 14–33

**(14) But I am confident, my brethren, yes, I myself am confident
about you, that you yourselves are full of goodness, replete with
all knowledge, and able also to admonish one another. (15) But I
have written to you somewhat boldly, partly with the intention of
reminding you of what you already know, because of the grace
that was given me from God (16) that I might be a minister of
Christ Jesus to the Gentiles, acting as a priest for the Gospel of
God, in order that the offering of the Gentiles might be
acceptable, sanctified in the Holy Spirit. (17) Here then is the
glorying I have in Christ Jesus, in things relating to God; (18) for I**

will not dare to say anything of the things which Christ did not carry out through me for the obedience of the Gentiles – in word and deed, (19) in the power[1] of signs and portents, in the power of the Spirit; so that from Jerusalem and round about as far as Illyricum I have completed the Gospel of Christ,[2] (20) being in this way ambitious to preach the Gospel not where Christ had been named, lest I should build upon someone else's foundation. (21) I acted rather so as to fulfil the Scripture, 'They shall see, to whom it was not told about him; and they shall understand, who have not heard.'

(22) So these many times I have been hindered from coming to you; (23) but now, since I have no more scope in these parts, and for some[3] years have had a desire to come to you (24) when I am on my way to Spain . . . ; for I hope to see you on my way, and to be helped thither on my way by you, if I may first have my fill of your company – in part; (25) but now I am travelling to Jerusalem, engaged in ministering to the saints. (26) For Macedonia and Achaea have decided to make a contribution to the poor among the saints who are in Jerusalem. (27) They have decided, yes, and they are under obligation to them; for if they shared their spiritual things with the Gentiles, the Gentiles ought to minister to them in the things of flesh and blood too. (28) So when I have completed this matter, and sealed them this fruit, I shall be off to Spain, through you; (29) and I know that when I come to you I shall come to bring and to find a full measure of the blessing of Christ.

(30) I beg you, brethren, through our Lord Jesus Christ and through the love created by the Spirit, to join me in earnest prayers to God on my behalf, (31) that I may be delivered from the disobedient in Judaea, and that my ministry to Jerusalem[4] may prove acceptable to the saints, (32) that by the will of God I may come to you with joy, and that we may together find refreshment.[5] (33) The God of peace be with you all. Amen.[6]

---

1 P[46] D* G it have 'in his power', an unusual expression which may be original. *God's* power, expressed in signs and portents is, of course, intended.

2 The Western text (D G it) has: 'So that from Jerusalem as far as Illyricum and round about the Gospel has been completed'. This is evidently a weakening of Paul's words.

3 The majority of MSS. (including P[46] א A D G) have 'many years'. This is a more usual expression, and to be rejected.

4 B D* G have 'my gift (or, offering – δωροφορία) in Jerusalem'.

5 There is much textual confusion at this point. P[46] and B omit altogether 'and that we may together find refreshment'. This may be not unconnected with the fact that P[46] continues immediately with the Doxology (xvi. 25 ff.).

6 For the reading of P[46] at this point, and the problem of the text of the last chapters of the epistle, see Introduction, pp. 10–13.

The main theological argument of the epistle is at an end (though there are in this paragraph remarks which have important theological implications). Paul turns to consider his own plans. These were not merely personal, but bound up with the divine plan (cf. chs. ix–xi) for the short period before the *parousia*. He begins with a *captatio benevolentiae* (cf. i. 12). He has written strong words, and does not wish by tactlessness to ruin his relations with the church in Rome before setting foot in the city. Of course this does not mean that he is insincere in what he says.

14   **But I am confident, my brethren** (see on i. 13), yes, **I myself am confident about you, that you yourselves** (notwithstanding my rebukes and admonitions) **are full of goodness, replete with all knowledge, and able also to admonish one another.** These words do not suggest that the Roman church had been founded by an apostle.

15   Why then had Paul written? **I have written to you somewhat boldly, partly** (we do not learn the other part of Paul's intentions) **with the intention of reminding you of what you already know** (this is more than tact; the believer who has accepted the Gospel knows the essence of the truth, but he may – and generally does – need many reminders), **because of the grace that was given me from**

16 **God** (cf. i. 5; xii. 3, 6) **that I might be a minister of Christ Jesus to the Gentiles.** For the word 'minister' see on xiii. 6; in itself it means no more than 'public servant' in the most general sense, but here the context points to priestly service. Paul's activity is directed specifically to the Gentiles; compare xi. 13, and especially Gal. i. 16; ii. 9. Paul serves by **acting as a priest for the Gospel of God** (i. 1), **in order that the offering of the Gentiles might be acceptable, sanctified in the Holy Spirit.** Paul acts as a priest in presenting to God an offering which consists of ('of the Gentiles' is appositional) the Gentile Christians who have been converted in his missions. This living sacrifice (cf. xii. 1) is acceptable not in virtue of its own intrinsic merit, but because it has been set apart for divine use by the Holy Spirit, given to the converts in their conversion and baptism. It is noteworthy that it is at this point that Paul uses the language of priesthood to describe his office; noteworthy also that (by accident, as it were) a Trinitarian formulation is introduced (... of Christ Jesus ... of God ... in the Holy Spirit). It seems clear that a majority of the Roman Christians must have been Gentiles; cf. i. 13; xi. 13; and p. 6.

The authority of the epistle thus rests upon Paul's vocation to act as a special minister of Christ in relation to the Gentiles. This vocation, and its evident fulfilment in his activity hitherto, are the sole source of

17 his confidence. **Here then is the glorying** (v. 2) **I have in Christ Jesus, in things relating to God.** As a priest, he acts *coram Deo*. Things that were gain to him by human reckoning he had already

counted loss for Christ (Phil. iii. 7). **For I will not dare to say** 18
anything of the things which Christ did not carry out through me
for the obedience (i. 5) **of the Gentiles.** The sentence is confused
because Paul is trying to say two things at once. These are (i) I would
not dare to speak of this if it were not Christ's work (rather than
mine); (ii) I would not dare to speak of this if it were not Christ's work
through me (rather than anyone else). The conversion of the Gentiles
has been the work of Christ, through Paul. This double fact is that in
which he can glory. It implies that he himself as an apostle holds a
special place in the unfolding of the events of the last days (see on i. 1,
apostle).

The apostolic work is further described: **in word and deed, in the** 19
power of signs and portents, in the power of the Spirit. For the
work of the Spirit as the accompaniment of the apostolic preaching cf.
1 Cor. ii. 4; 1 Thess. i. 5. At 2 Cor. xii. 12 Paul refers to signs, portents,
and mighty works, not without a certain qualification (see *2
Corinthians*, 320–2); cf. also Gal. iii. 5. The Gospel is the power of God
working toward salvation (i. 16), and though salvation in its fullness
lies in the future its effects are felt in the present also. Thus **from
Jerusalem and round about** (*either* round about Jerusalem, *or* in
circuit from Jerusalem to Illyricum) **as far as Illyricum I have
completed the Gospel of Christ.** For Paul's preaching in Jerusalem
see Acts ix. 29. He had not been active in Judaea (Gal. i. 22); this
means that we must accept 'in circuit from Jerusalem to Illyricum'
(above). His missionary journeys had begun in Antioch and taken him
round the eastern end of the Mediterranean and through several of
the provinces of Asia Minor. Thence he had crossed the Aegean to
Macedonia, and visited Greece (Athens, Corinth). Acts gives no
account of work in Illyricum, though from Macedonia the *Via Egnatia*
struck across the Balkans to the eastern coast of the Adriatic, and it is
not impossible that Paul or his associates had made tentative
excursions in this direction as far as Illyricum. It is evident therefore
that when Paul says that in this region he has completed the Gospel of
Christ, he does not mean that he (or anyone else) has preached the
Gospel to every person in it, but that it has been covered in a
representative way. The Gospel has been heard; more could not be
expected before the *parousia*. Thus Paul is free, or, rather, is impelled
to break new ground in the fulfilment of the eschatological pro-
gramme entrusted to him as an apostle (*v.* 23). In doing so he would
only be continuing to follow the principle which had always guided his
activity: **Being in this way ambitious to preach the Gospel not** 20
where Christ had been named (the position of the negative invites
the supplement, 'but where he had never been heard of'), **lest I
should build upon someone else's foundation.** Paul's motive is not
simply to avoid possible rivalry (cf. Gal. ii. 9; 2 Cor. x. 13–18, with the

notes in *2 Corinthians* pp. 262–9) but to cover as wide an area as possible. The metaphor of building (cf. 1 Cor. iii. 10 ff.) is not chosen at random; the Church as a whole is the new temple, or new Jerusalem, of the last age. For his missionary method Paul is able to

21 cite scriptural support: **I acted rather so as to fulfil the Scripture, 'They shall see, to whom it was not told about him; and they shall understand, who have not heard'** (Isa. lii. 15).

These considerations have an evident bearing upon Paul's plan to visit Rome, for this church was not of his founding. It is possibly the delicacy of the situation that leads to the obscurity of Paul's words here,

22 and the actual breaking off of the sentence in *v.* 24 (cf. i. 11 f.). **So these many times I have been hindered from coming to you; but now,**

23 **since I have no more scope in these parts** (as is explained in *v.* 20),

24 **and for some years have had a desire to come to you** (cf. i. 13) **when I am on my way to Spain . . . .** The connection of the opening particle (διό) is not clear. The meaning suggested by the context is, 'I have been prevented by the fact that up to now I have been fully occupied in the East'; but 1 Thess. ii. 18 (where the same verb is used) suggests that a different kind of hindrance may be meant.

Since the eastern end of the Mediterranean had been dealt with and Paul had 'no more scope in these parts' there remained for missionary work the north coast of Africa (from Alexandria to the province of Africa), Gaul, and Spain. Strangely, Paul never alludes to African territory; but he expresses the intention of making a missionary journey to Spain (quite possibly intending to take Gaul (Narbonensis) on the way). His immediate task, however, was a visit to Jerusalem (*v.* 25), the outcome of which is told in Acts xxi–xxviii. Paul reached Rome, but as a prisoner. Was he ever able to carry out his plan of visiting Spain? There is no certain evidence. There is no further reference to Spain in the New Testament, and most later writers are evidently reduced to conjectures based on no more evidence than we ourselves possess. According to 1 Clement v. 7 Paul came to 'the limit of the west' (τὸ τέρμα τῆς δύσεως), but it is not certain that this is a reference to Spain. A release from prison, and a Spanish journey, are not impossible. More than this cannot be said with certainty.

The sentence breaks off, and Paul repeats himself in order to make the essential point clear: he wishes to visit Rome, but this visit will not contravene his principle of avoiding mission fields already worked, because he will take Rome on the way as he passes to fresh work. **For I hope to see you on my way, and to be helped thither** (to Spain) **on my way by you, if I may first have my fill of your company – in part;** for Paul will never really have his fill of Christian fellowship with the Roman Christians. In what way he hoped for help from them does not appear.

Before the journey to Spain intervenes a more immediate task. **But** **25** **now I am travelling to Jerusalem** (Acts xx. 3, 16, etc.), **engaged in ministering to the saints.** 'Ministering' (like 'ministry' in *v.* 31) is one of Paul's terms for his collection on behalf of the Jerusalem church. For the verb, see 2 Cor. viii. 19 f.; for the noun, *v.* 31; 1 Cor. xvi. 15; 2 Cor. (vi. 3); viii. 4; ix. 1, 12 f. (cf. Acts xi. 29; xii. 25). 'The saints' also has (in addition to its use as a term describing Christians in general – see i. 7) an almost technical sense. It denotes the Christians of Jerusalem here and at *vv.* 26, 31; 1 Cor. xvi. 1, 15; 2 Cor. viii. 4; ix. 1, 12. See below on 'the poor' (*v.* 26). Paul's collection occupied a good deal of his time and attention. It must have been a politic expedient, designed to foster unity between the Jewish and Gentile wings of the Church; but it was far more than this, for, as the context shows, it was intended to play a vital part among the events of the last days. See 1 Cor. xvi. 1–4; 2 Cor. viii; ix; also *1 Corinthians*, p. 23 and *2 Corinthians*, pp. 25–8, in addition to the notes on the passages mentioned.

Paul proceeds to give further details. **For Macedonia and Achaea** **26** **have decided to make a contribution** (literally, 'a fellowship', or 'a sharing' – another of Paul's quasi-technical terms: 2 Cor. viii. 4; ix. 13; cf. *v.* 27; Gal. vi. 6; Phil. iv. 15) **to the poor among the saints who are in Jerusalem.** Paul's use of 'poor' recalls the righteous and trustful poor of the Psalms (e.g. Ps. ix. 18); in Hebrew, *'ebyonim*. Whether the successors of the poor saints in Jerusalem are to be found among the Jewish Christians later called Ebionites cannot be discussed here. It must not be forgotten that Paul may use the word 'poor' in its literal sense. It was because these saints had little money that a collection was made for them. **They have decided, yes, and they are under** **27** **obligation to them** (cf. i. 14; viii. 12; also xiii. 8); **for if they** (the Jewish Christians) **shared their spiritual things** (not 'spiritual gifts', for these came direct from the Spirit; but the original tradition which, interpreted by the Spirit, was the basis of the Gospel) **with the Gentiles, the Gentiles** (the subject is not expressed, but there can be no doubt what should be supplied) **ought to minister to them in the things of flesh and blood** (the Greek mentions flesh only, but this is liable to misunderstanding) **too.** This is only fair. Paul develops the theme of fairness, equality (ἰσότης) in 2 Cor. viii. 13, 14.

Paul winds up this statement of his plans. **So when I have** **28** **completed this matter, and sealed them this fruit** (the metaphor is commercial, but Paul curiously omits to say that having sealed his produce he means also to deliver it), **I shall be off to Spain, through you** (*v.* 24); **and I know that when I come to you I shall** **29** **come to bring and to find a full measure of the blessing of Christ.** Literally rendered, the last words run, 'in the fullness of the blessing of Christ'. By this somewhat vague language Paul probably means to suggest that both sides, he and his hosts, will share in the blessing; compare i. 11 f. Acts xxviii. 14–31 says little about the fulfilment of this hope.

30   The execution of the plans will not be without risk. **I beg you, brethren, through our Lord Jesus Christ and through the love created by the Spirit** (literally, the love of the Spirit; the genitive cannot be objective, and the clue is given by v. 5), **to join me in earnest prayers to God** (another 'unintended' Trinitarian formulation; cf. *v.* 16) **on my behalf.** 'Earnest prayers' conceals a metaphor drawn from the games, of a kind of which Paul was evidently fond; compare Phil. i. 27; iv. 3; and especially Col. iv. 12. All should contend

31   strenuously in prayer like athletes in the games **that I may be delivered from the disobedient** (or, perhaps, unbelieving; cf. ii. 8; non-Christian Jews are meant) **in Judaea** (no doubt Paul had reason to fear what they might do), **and that my ministry** (cf. *v.* 25) **to Jerusalem may prove acceptable to the saints** (probably he had reason to regard this also as uncertain; his relations with the

32   Jerusalem church were not assured), **that by the will of God** (cf. i. 10) **I may come to you with joy, and that we may together find refreshment.** For the last clause compare 1 Cor. xvi. 18; 2 Cor. vii. 13; Philem. 7, 20; for Paul's hope for a shared benefit, cf. i. 12.

The present section of the epistle closes with a brief prayer,
33   probably already reflecting liturgical use: **The God of peace** (cf. xvi. 20; 2 Cor. xiii. 11; Phil. iv. 9; 1 Thess. v. 23; 2 Thess. iii. 16; also Test. Dan v. 2, but it does not appear to have been a regular Jewish expression) **be with you all. Amen.** For Paul's use of 'peace' see p. 1.

41 PERSONAL GREETINGS
CHAPTER xvi. 1–23

(1) I commend to you our sister Phoebe, who is a minister in the church in Cenchreae, (2) that you may receive her in the Lord in a way worthy of the saints, and help her in any matter in which she may have need of you; for she herself has been a protectress of many, and of me myself. (3) Greet Prisca and Aquila, my fellow-workers in Christ Jesus, (4) who risked their lives for mine, to whom not I only but also all the churches of the Gentiles are grateful. (5) And greet the church which meets in their house. Greet Epaenetus my beloved, who is the first-fruits of Asia unto Christ. (6) Greet Mary, who toiled much for your benefit. (7) Greet Andronicus and Junia, my kinsmen and my fellow prisoners, who are notable in the ranks of the apostles, and were Christians before me. (8) Greet Ampliatus my beloved in the Lord. (9) Greet Urbanus our fellow worker in Christ, and Stachys

my beloved. (10) Greet Apelles, that genuine Christian. Greet the slaves of the household of Aristobulus. (11) Greet Herodian my kinsman. Greet those slaves of the household of Narcissus who are in the Lord. (12) Greet Tryphaena and Tryphosa, who toil in the Lord. Greet Persis, my beloved, who toiled hard in the Lord. (13) Greet Rufus, that outstanding Christian, and his mother – who is also mine. (14) Greet Asyncritus, Phlegon, Hermes, Patrobas, Hermas, and the brethren who are with them. (15) Greet Philologus and Julia, Nereus and his sister, and Olympas, and all the saints who are with them. (16) Greet one another with a holy kiss. All the churches of Christ greet you.

(17) I beg you, brethren, to give attention to those who cause divisions and offences, contrary to the teaching you learned. Keep away from them. (18) For such men do not serve our Lord Christ but their own belly, and through their gentle and fair speech deceive the hearts of the innocent. (19) Avoid them, for the report of your obedience has reached all men. That is why I rejoice over you, and I wish you to be wise over what is good, uncontaminated with evil. (20) But the God of peace will soon crush Satan under your feet. The grace of our Lord Jesus Christ be with you.[1]

(21) Timothy my fellow-worker greets you, and so do Lucius and Jason and Sosipater my kinsmen. (22) I Tertius, who wrote the epistle in the Lord, greet you. (23) Gaius, who is my host, and the host of the whole church, greets you. Erastus the city treasurer greets you, and so does brother Quartus.

This paragraph consists mainly of personal greetings, together with a short section (*vv.* 17–20) of admonition and encouragement. For an account of the textual phenomena of the last chapter of the epistle, see Introduction, pp. 10–13. The view has often been maintained (on grounds partly textual) that xvi. 1–23 was not addressed to the church of Rome. It is said (a) that Paul is unlikely to have known so many members of the Roman church, which he had never visited; and (b) that some of the names mentioned point rather to Ephesus (which Paul knew well) than to Rome. Neither these nor the textual arguments are convincing. (a) In writing to a strange church Paul might very naturally include as many personal greetings as he could in order to establish as close contact as possible. (b) The possibility of movement on the part of members of the Pauline churches must be reckoned with. See below on Prisca and Aquila; for the migration from

---

1 The words 'The grace of our Lord Jesus be with you' are omitted here by the Western text (D G it), which has an almost identical formula in *v.* 24. The majority, including P⁴⁶ B ℵ, do not contain *v.* 24.

Asia Minor to Tusculum of a household of 500 persons (including slaves), who formed a 'house-church' of initiates of Dionysus, see Lietzmann, pp. 129 f. (c) Arguments based upon names are worth little in view of the fact that men of all races met in Rome. Literary and other evidence for the occurrence of the names in this chapter will be found in Lietzmann, Michel, and Cranfield.

The first two verses are devoted to Phoebe, a Christian travelling to
1 Rome (or Ephesus, if xvi. 1–23 be addressed there). **I commend to you our sister Phoebe, who is a minister in the church in Cenchreae** (the eastern port of Corinth). 'Commendatory letters' were well known in the ancient world, certainly to Paul himself (2 Cor. iii. 1 and *2 Corinthians,* p. 106). Phoebe is described as a 'sister', that is, a Christian. For the corresponding masculine title see on i. 13; the feminine appears at 1 Cor. vii. 15; ix. 5 (*not* Rom. xvi. 15). Phoebe is further described in this translation as a *minister,* but it is by no means clear exactly what sense should be attached to this word (in Greek, διάκονος, transliterated rather than translated as *deacon*). Phil. i. 1 suggests that it was already in Paul's time on the way to the technical sense that it has in 1 Tim. iii. 8, 12 (cf. Rom. xii. 7). 1 Tim. iii. 11 may refer to women deacons or to the wives of deacons; the former is slightly more probable (see *Pastoral Epistles,* pp. 61 f.), but certainty is not attainable. Pliny (*c.* AD 112) speaks of *ancillis quae ministrae dicebantur* (*Epistles* X. xcvi. 8), and deaconesses are mentioned in the *Apostolic Constitutions* (ii. 26, 57; iii. 7, 15). It seems that Phoebe is travelling to Rome on private, not church business; she was therefore not a full-time worker in the church at Cenchreae. In the New Testament period, however, the line between the 'part-time helper' and the minister set apart to the service of the Church was not as sharply drawn as it is today, and it may be that the question whether Phoebe was a minister or a valued church worker is wrongly put. It was more important to Paul that the various kinds of Christian service (such as acting as protectress, *v.* 2) should be performed than that certain official positions should be filled. Phoebe was not the only woman minister in the New Testament Church; cf. Prisca (*v.* 3; Acts xviii. 2 and elsewhere, where she is called Priscilla), Mary (*v.* 6), perhaps Chloe (1 Cor. i. 11), Euodia and Syntyche (Phil. iv. 2, 3), and others. This of course is primarily because, for Paul, every Christian was a minister of some sort; not a few women member-ministers stood out sufficiently to be named.

Whatever her precise status, Phoebe had as a Christian a claim upon the hospitality and help of the Roman church. Paul commends
2 her, **that you may receive her** (it would be possible to place a full stop after *v.* 1, and to begin *v.* 2, Receive her, taking ἵνα imperatively) **in the Lord in a way worthy of the saints, and help her in any matter in which she may have need of you.** To receive her 'in the

Lord' is to receive her as a Christian, and to receive her 'in a way worthy of the saints' is to do so as Christians who practise the law of love should – *Christiano more* (Bengel). Phoebe deserves such treatment, **for she herself has been a protectress of many, and of me myself.** The Greek noun here (προστάτις) is often equivalent to the Latin *patrona*, but Phoebe cannot have stood in this relation to Paul (since he was born free, Acts xxii. 28), and the word must therefore have the more general sense given in the translation.

Having transacted this business, Paul sends greetings to his friends. **Greet Prisca (another woman minister) and Aquila, my fellow-** 3 **workers in Christ Jesus, who risked their lives for mine, to whom** 4 **not I only but also all the churches of the Gentiles are grateful.** These two are no doubt the Aquila and Priscilla of Acts (ch. xviii. *passim*); compare 1 Cor. xvi. 19. They had been expelled from Rome (see Introduction, p. 5), made their way to Corinth, and thence to Ephesus. There is no reason why they should not have returned to Rome, especially if Romans was written after the death of Claudius (13 October 54). That 'all the churches' had reason to be grateful to them confirms that they had numerous contacts over a wide area. How, or on what occasion, they risked their lives on Paul's account, is completely unknown to us. Paul adds, **And greet the church which** 5 **meets in their house.** The first Christian meeting-places were no doubt the private houses of those Christians who were fortunate enough to have them. The early Church owed a considerable debt to Christians who were wealthy enough to possess houses large enough to accommodate a church meeting and were willing to use for Christian purposes the gifts that in the past had won them financial success.

Greet Epaenetus my beloved, who is the first-fruits of Asia unto Christ, that is, the first convert in Asia. Compare 1 Cor. xvi. 15.

Greet Mary, who toiled much for your benefit. For 'toiled' 6 compare *v.* 12. The present verse suggests the meaning, 'to take part in Christian work', and this is confirmed by Paul's usage in general, for example, 1 Cor. xv. 10.

Greet Andronicus and Junia (or *Junias*), **my kinsmen** (that is, 7 probably, fellow Jews; cf. *vv.* 11, 21 – it is a fair inference that others not so described may be Gentiles, though this does not apply to Prisca and Aquila, and perhaps not to Rufus) **and my fellow prisoners** (we do not know when they were imprisoned with Paul, but there is no reason why the word should be taken metaphorically), **who are notable in the ranks of the apostles** (a much more probable rendering than 'well known to the apostles'), **and were Christians before me.** The names Junia (a woman's name) and Junias (a man's name) are alternative renderings of a name which in Greek may be accented in two different ways; taken in one way ('Ιουνίαν) it is a

woman's name, in the other (Ἰουνιᾶν) it is a man's. It is most
improbable that Tertius (*v.* 22) used accents; they are seldom to be
found in the earliest MSS of the New Testament. The earliest readers of
the New Testament seem to have taken Andronicus and Junia to be
another husband and wife pair, like Aquila and Prisca (*v.* 3); see
Cranfield (pp. 788 f.) and Wilckens (3, pp. 135 f.). Certainty is
impossible, but it is an important fact that the male name Junias
seems to be without precedent in Greek use. The two, one probably a
woman, were apostles, and as Christians senior to Paul himself. For
Paul's use of the word *apostle* see on i. 1 and *Signs*, pp. 34–47. In the
New Testament the word is sometimes used of the twelve disciples
specially appointed by Jesus, but also in a wider sense, as here.

9   **Greet Urbanus our fellow worker** (cf. *vv.* 3, 21) **in Christ...**
10   **Greet Apelles, that genuine Christian.** The adjective is the opposite
of that used in i. 28; the pair are used, for example, of genuine and
11   counterfeit coins. **Greet Herodian my kinsman** (see on *v.*
12   7) ... **Greet Tryphaena and Tryphosa, who toil in the Lord.** 'To toil
in the Lord' means 'to work as a Christian', not necessarily but
13   probably 'to do Christian (that is, church) work'. See on *v.* 6. **Greet
Rufus, that outstanding Christian** (the adjective is literally 'elect',
which can be used of all Christians, as at viii. 33; there would be no
point, however, in using it in this sense here), **and his mother – who
is also mine.** A Rufus is mentioned in Mark xv. 21 as one of the sons of
Simon of Cyrene. It has often been remarked that he plays no part in
Mark's story and must have been named only for identification. This
means that he must have been known in the church (probably Rome)
for which the second gospel was written. For what it is worth, this
confirms the view that this chapter was addressed to Rome, not
Ephesus.

15   **Greet Philologus and Julia.** The same doubt must arise as at *v.* 7:
Is Paul speaking of Julias (a man) or of Julia (a woman)? In this verse
we have a reference to the sister of Nereus, and it is by no means
impossible that another woman is intended. **Greet also Nereus**
(possibly a name borne by a freedman of Nero's) **and his sister, and**
16   **Olympas, and all the saints who are with them. Greet one another
with a holy kiss.** Compare 1 Cor. xvi. 20; 2 Cor. xiii. 12; also I Thess. v.
26; 1 Pet. v. 14. Later (e.g. Justin, 1 *Apology*, 65) the kiss became a
part of the liturgy; it may be that this was so earlier, and that the
apostolic letters were read in the course of the Church's worship,
being taken at this point in it. See *1 Corinthians* 396–9; *2 Corinthians*
343.

All the churches of Christ (represented by Paul, who speaks from
the base of oriental Christianity to Rome, whence he himself means to
go further West) **greet you.** Paul refers to the whole Church, but does
so as the sum of a number of local churches.

Here the greetings break off, and we have four verses in quite different vein. It is not necessary to regard them as an interpolation; such parenthetical remarks are in Paul's style. They may reflect additional information brought to him before the letter was completed. The circumstances which evoked this vigorous admonition can only be conjectured.

I beg you, brethren, to give attention to (for the word cf. Phil. iii. 17, where it has the opposite motive) **those who cause divisions** (Gal. v. 20) **and offences** (as, e.g., at xiv. 13; possibly the division between weak and strong is still in mind; Paul writes as one who is not uninformed about the circumstances of the congregation he is addressing), **contrary to the teaching you learned** – the teaching of the all-sufficiency of faith and the all-importance of love. **Keep away from them.** Cf. 1 Cor. v. 11. Paul does not ask his readers to go out of the world but to exercise discipline within the community. **For such men do not serve our Lord Christ but their own belly** (cf. Phil. iii. 19; not by gluttony but by their preoccupation with food laws), **and through their gentle and fair speech deceive the hearts of the innocent. Avoid them** (a supplement to explain the 'for' (γάρ) which follows), **for the report of your obedience** (the Greek has 'for your obedience') **has reached all men.** The Christians of Rome must not spoil the report of them which is in general circulation. **That is why I rejoice over you** (because you are known to be obedient) **and I wish you to be wise over what is good** (that is, with a view to doing it), **uncontaminated with evil** (that is, so that you do not do it).

Paul concludes this parenthetical section with a renewed assertion of his confidence. **The God of peace** (xv. 33) **will soon crush Satan under your feet.** There may be an allusion here to Gen. iii. 15, though if so Paul must be referring to the Hebrew text, for the LXX translates differently. In any case, Paul is looking forward to the final defeat of the prince of evil, and believes that this defeat will take place soon (cf. xiii. 11).

Paul adds, **The grace of our Lord Jesus be with you.** He uses this or similar expressions at 1 Cor. xvi. 23; Gal. vi. 18; Phil. iv. 23; Col. iv. 18; 1 Thess. v. 28; 2 Thess. iii. 18. At 2 Cor. xiii. 14 it is expanded into a Trinitarian formula. Compare the opening greeting (i. 7).

The greetings, broken off in vv. 17–20, are now resumed, but the names now mentioned are those of Christians in Paul's company who send their salutations with his. **Timothy my fellow worker greets you, and so do Lucian and Jason and Sosipater my kinsmen** (for this word see on v. 7). For Timothy see especially Acts xvi. 1, etc.; and many Pauline epistles; for Jason, Acts xvii. 5–9; for Sosipater, Acts xx. 4 (Sopater). **I Tertius, who wrote the epistle in the Lord, greet you.** For Paul's custom of dictating his letters compare 1 Cor. xvi. 21; Gal. vi. 11; Col. iv. 18; 2 Thess. iii. 17; (Philem. 19). **Gaius** (cf. Acts xix. 29;

17

18

19

20

21

22

23

xx. 4; 1 Cor. i. 14; 3 John 1), **who is my host, and the host of the whole church** (which met in his house (cf. *v.* 5); or possibly Gaius entertained travelling Christians), **greets you. Erastus** (cf. Acts xix. 22; 2 Tim. iv. 20) **the city treasurer greets you, and so does brother Quartus.** Gaius and Erastus must have been among those well-to-do Christians who had their own important contribution to make to the Christian fellowship. See p. 259.

For *v.* 24, which is added in some MSS (The grace of our Lord Jesus Christ be with you all. Amen), see on *v.* 20, the proper place of these words.

42 THE DOXOLOGY
CHAPTER xvi. 25–7

(25) Now to him who is able to establish you, according to my Gospel and the preaching of Jesus Christ, according to the revelation of the mystery, which through eternal ages has been kept in silence (26) but has now been manifested, made known, according to the decree of the eternal God, through prophetic Scriptures, so as to produce the obedience of faith for all the Gentiles, (27) to the only wise God, through Jesus Christ, to whom[1] be glory for ever and ever.[2] Amen.

For the textual problems connected with this last paragraph of the epistle see Introduction, pp. 10–13. Apart from the textual evidence, its contents themselves raise doubts regarding the Pauline authorship. The language recalls that of the Pastoral Epistles, not least in its not very convincing imitation of Paul's style. The substance is not distinctively Pauline. For the whole, compare Eph. iii. 20 f.; 1 Tim. i. 17; Jude 24 f.

25   **Now to him who is able to establish you** (cf. i. 11), **according to my Gospel** (cf. ii. 16) **and the preaching of Jesus Christ** (elsewhere in Paul (1 Cor. i. 21; ii. 4; xv. 14; cf. 2 Tim. iv. 17; Titus i. 3) 'preaching' (κήρυγμα) never has a genitive of content, as here), **according to the revelation of the mystery** (1 Cor. ii. 7–10; Eph. iii. 3–6; 2 Tim. i. 10; Titus i. 2 f.), **which through eternal ages** (2 Tim. i. 9; Titus i. 2) **has been kept in silence** (Paul uses this word only in 1 Cor. xiv. 28, 30, 34 – of women and others keeping silence in church; but cf. Ignatius, *Ephesians*, xix. 1). The secret has now been revealed in the Gospel; but

---

1 'To whom' is omitted by B pesh. The result is to produce a straightforward ascription of praise to God, whereas the text translated is (like the translation) ungrammatical. The more difficult text should be accepted.
2 'And ever' (τῶν αἰώνων) is omitted by P⁴⁶ B C L – perhaps rightly.

this is expressed in a difficult sentence. Cranfield, pp. 811–13, rightly draws attention to a Greek connecting particle (τε) which introduces the clause that begins with a reference to the prophetic Scriptures, and was in ancient times found so difficult that most ancient versions and a few Greek MSS omitted it (see the apparatus of Tischendorf and von Soden). Very literally, the verse (with the inclusion of τε) could be rendered 'but now has been manifested and (τε) through prophetic Scriptures, by command of the eternal God, has been made known with a view to the obedience of faith, for (*or perhaps* to) all the Gentiles.' Not surprisingly Zahn (p. 585) describes this as 'stilistisch sehr hart'. It must nevertheless be accepted (or rephrased) as the sense of what is probably the best text we have: **but has now been 26 manifested, made known according to the decree** (cf. 1 Tim. i. 1; Titus i. 3 – 1 Cor. vii. 6; 2 Cor. viii. 8 are not parallel) **of the eternal God** (this expression does not occur elsewhere in the New Testament; cf. 1 Tim. i. 17), **through prophetic Scriptures, so as to produce the obedience of faith** (cf. i. 5) **for all the Gentiles.** The best one can make of this is that the prophetic Scriptures are the means by which the preaching of Jesus Christ (*v.* 25) is interpreted. This is indeed a Pauline thought, but the form of the sentence is such as to add weight to the hypothesis that an originally Marcionite proposition (see Introduction, pp. 11 f.) has been made orthodox by the insertion of a reference to the Old Testament. Marcion would have found no fault with ' . . . the mystery which through eternal ages has been kept in silence but has now been manifested, made known according to the decree of the eternal God.' The doxology is resumed: **To the only** (cf. 27 1 Tim. i. 17; Jude 25) **wise** (there is no parallel in the original text of 1 Tim. i. 17, and no other in the New Testament) **God, through Jesus Christ, to whom** (the doxology up to this point has prepared us for an ascription of glory to God the Father; the author now forgets the datives he has already set down, and ascribes glory to Christ) **be glory for ever and ever. Amen.**

The defective construction (it would be hard to pass over *Jesus Christ*, the natural antecedent, and make the relative refer to *God*) may serve to remind the reader that glory should be ascribed at once to God the Father, the Creator (i. 20), in whose unfathomable wisdom and mercy (xi. 33–6) the work of salvation was planned, and to Jesus Christ his Son, through whom and in whom redemption was effected (iii. 26; v. 8).

INDEX OF GREEK WORDS AND PHRASES
DISCUSSED

INDEX OF NAMES AND SUBJECTS

INDEX OF ANCIENT SOURCES